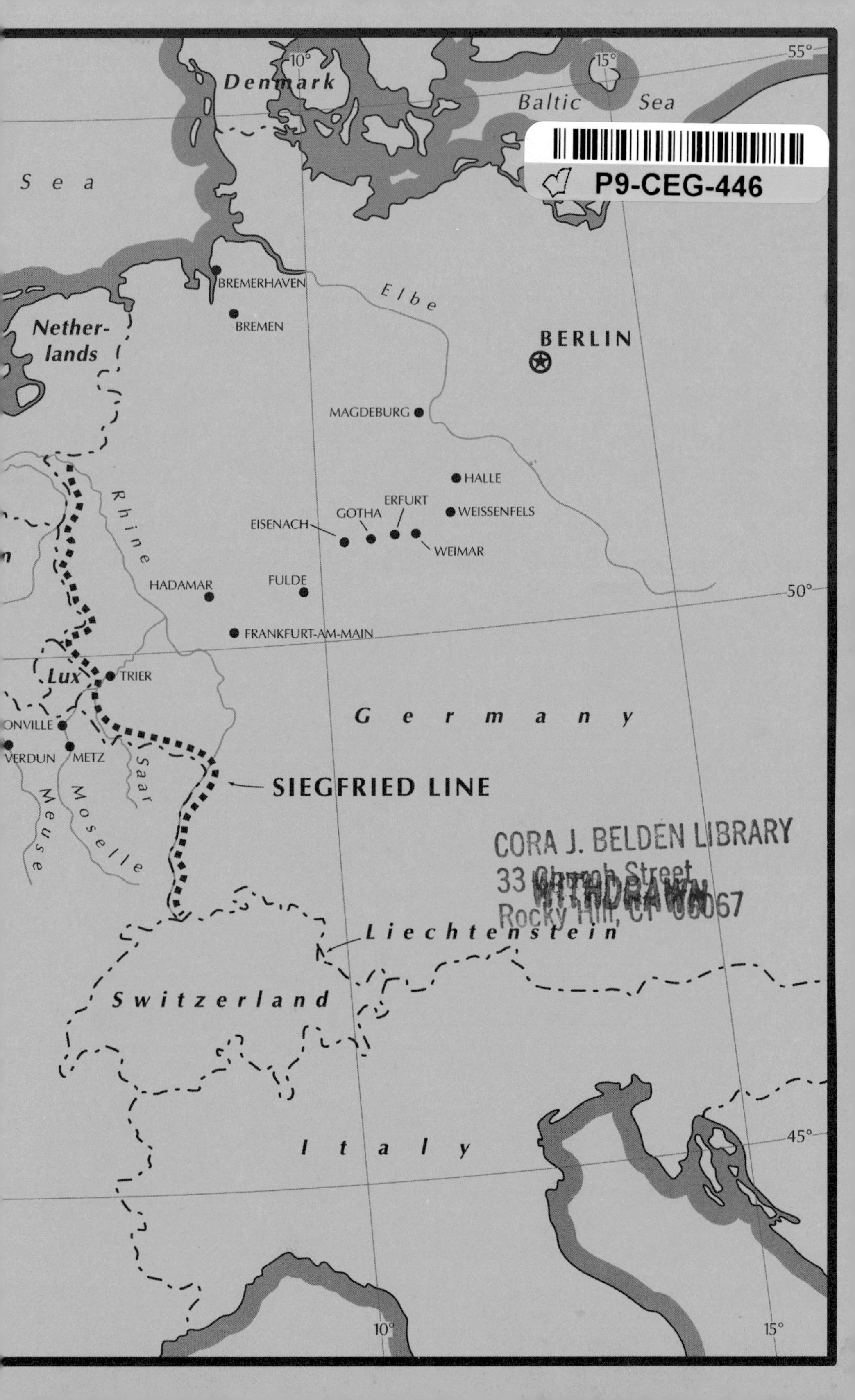
Denmark
Baltic Sea
Sea
Netherlands
BREMERHAVEN
BREMEN
Elbe
BERLIN
MAGDEBURG
HALLE
ERFURT
GOTHA
EISENACH
WEISSENFELS
WEIMAR
Rhine
HADAMAR
FULDE
FRANKFURT-AM-MAIN
Lux
TRIER
ONVILLE
VERDUN
METZ
Saar
Meuse
Moselle
Germany
SIEGFRIED LINE
Liechtenstein
Switzerland
Italy
10°
15°
55°
50°
45°

Unsung Valor

Unsung Valor

A GI's Story of World War II

A. Cleveland Harrison

University Press of Mississippi
Jackson

www.upress.state.ms.us

Manufactured in the United States of America

08 07 06 05 04 03 02 01 00 4 3 2 1

Library of Congress Cataloging-in-Publication Data

Harrison, A. Cleveland.
Unsung valor : a GI's story of World War II / A. Cleveland Harrison.
p. cm.
ISBN 1-57806-214-4
1. Harrison, Allie Cleveland. 2. World War, 1939–1945 Personal narratives, American. 3. United States. Army—Biography. 4. Soldiers—United States—Biography. I. Title.
D811.H342 2000
940.54'8173—dc21 99-38771
CIP

British Library Cataloging-in-Publication Data available

To my wartime comrades in
the Army Specialized Training Program and
Company B, 301st Infantry Regiment,
Ninety-fourth Infantry Division, and
the Political Division, U.S. Group Control Council,
who went, like me, when called,
serving dependably and loyally,
in the best ways they knew how,
regardless of their duties or fears.

All squalid, abject, and inglorious elements in a war should be remembered. The intimate mental history of any man who went to the War would make unheroic reading. I have half a mind to write my own.

Siegfried Sassoon, *Memoirs of a Fox-Hunting Man*

Contents

Preface

My service in the Army of the United States in World War II was brief but intense. Inside thirty months, I was a college student in the Army Specialized Training Program, an infantryman in a combat division overseas, a transient in the Army's medical and replacement pipelines, and a message center chief in a division of military government.

Not a volunteer but a reluctant draftee, I earned no high marks as an engineering student, won no special medal for valor as a rifleman, and was not promoted to the rank warranted by my position in military government. But my several different Army assignments, though not unique, may have been more diverse and incongruous than those of the average enlisted soldier.

Still, why bother to record the military experiences of an undistinguished GI more than half a century later? Chiefly, to help balance in some small way the weightier achievements of statesmen, generals, diplomats, and heroes by describing the ordinary work, rest, and combat of a naive soldier boy.

A Marine Corps veteran who fought in the Pacific, G. D. Lillibridge, sees war as "a country no traveler ever forgets," observing that "memories of war cling to the mind with astonishing tenacity . . . because the memories raise so many questions about oneself, particularly the unanswerable one: Why am I the one here to remember?" He suggests that the "ordeal of not forgetting may well be the only heroism of a survivor."

The British officer-poet Siegfried Sassoon opposed the glorification of the Great War of 1914–1918, and believed the "intimate history of any man who went to the War would make unheroic reading." Inspired by these two points of view, I can, as a survivor, recall my unforgotten, truly unheroic participation in World War II to convince my children, grandsons, and others that any reluctance to go to war doesn't diminish patriotism, nor deter serving honorably, even when one quite sensibly does not wish to join the madness.

My experiences in the Army long ago remain so deeply imprinted upon my mind and emotions that they doubtlessly shaped me in ways I haven't yet recognized. Remembering those thirty months, even now, provokes heartache, sometimes tears, and the sense that the events contain within them something that has never quite been revealed to me. To plumb my memories for their secrets, if any, I needed to put the happenings in a form more solid than my random mental ramblings.

But after the war, my marriage, children, academic career, and the pain of recalling combat and fallen comrades prevented me from writing. Only after retirement did I find the time and the desire to recall and set down my World War II experiences. Perhaps this memoir—I hope in the voice of the youth I was without too many ironic observations from the man I became—will help heal my invisible wounds. Maybe the small and fearful events I underwent as a teenage boy who didn't shave, drink, smoke, swear, or drive a car when sworn into the Army can convey once again for a new generation war's boredom, misery, fright, pain, and waste.

All the episodes occurred as I have described them, and the invented dialogues are faithful to the spirit of the occasions. In many instances, the names of persons have been changed to protect their privacy.

A few books helped me recall, with greater accuracy, the many details of Army training, combat, and military government. Louis E. Keefer's *Scholars in Foxholes* traces the aim, curricula, and end of the Army Specialized Training Program. *The History of the 94th Division in World War II,* edited by Lawrence G. Byrnes, verifies the chronology of my service in Company B of the 301st Infantry Regiment. Harold Zink's *American Military Government in Germany* and Franklin M. Davis Jr.'s *Come as a Conqueror: The United States Army's Occupation of Germany, 1945–1949,* confirm many of the official government matters. But the personal details of this memoir are drawn entirely from my memory of observations in garrison and field; any mistakes about dates, places, and persons are mine.

I owe my deepest gratitude to my parents who shaped the mind and spirit of the boy appearing in these reminiscences. They blessed my life immeasurably and forever—my mother, Floy Estelle Harrison (née Honea), through her deep Christian faith and devotion, and my father, Allie Harrison, through his love and lore of the outdoors.

I must acknowledge, also, my more recent debts to my family for their continuing devotion and support. My loving thanks to my son and daughter, Lee and Kathleen, who encouraged me to write these recollections, and to my sister-in-law Kathleen Gammill, whose unwavering interest has kept me from faltering along the way. My eternal love and appreciation go to my wife Marian (Tumpy) who shared the years described in this memoir mostly by mail and all the years since then by my side.

Introduction

I am staring at Paul Baumer, who is leaning against a parapet of sandbags at the front of a trench. Bright sunshine is drying up the surrounding sea of the battlefield's glutinous mud. This beautiful spring morning, like most days on the front line, is quiet; only the nights leap alive with patrols and the drumbeat of artillery.

How depleted Paul must be! Pained by the loss of his comrades and resigned to the war's horrors. After four years in the German trenches, he awaits still more fighting.

In the stillness and comforting silence of the early morning, Paul sees, at the cluttered edge of the dirty trench, a butterfly flitting from one empty tin can to another. He reaches tentatively across the top of the parapet to touch the butterfly's quivering colored wings, the fragile reminders of his peaceful childhood hobby.

But wait! Now a French sniper takes careful aim through a telescopic sight, before cracking the silence with a sharp, dry rifle shot. Paul's fingers tense, then relax; only his limp hand and arm betray that the sniper's bullet snuffed out his young life.

On the screen, the movie *All Quiet on the Western Front* fades in a montage of ghostly transparent images of Paul marching with his old comrades—all now dead—floating over and past the long rows of white crosses in a military cemetery.

The year was 1934. I was ten years old, sitting between buddies in a theater in Little Rock, Arkansas, trying to hide the tears I shed for the lost lives of the young boys on the screen and filled with hate for war, in or out of the movies. For the horrors of the Great War hadn't ended in my neighborhood on Wright Avenue, where three veterans relived the conflict through their injuries and memories and told me their personal stories, impressing images on my mind more terrifying than those on the screen.

One veteran and his wife rented space for their trailer home in the vacant lot next to my dad's grocery and market, where our family was living in the rear of the store during part of the Great Depression. For many months, the couple remained parked in the lot beside us, often inviting me to visit and share cookies and cocoa with them.

Their invitations and sweets were irresistible, even after the man's talks took a darker turn and he described fighting in the trenches in France. He showed me a pamphlet with photographs taken on the Western Front by the U.S. Army Signal Corps, featuring dead, wounded, and crippled men on battlefields, mutilated and decaying corpses in cemeteries, disfigured faces and bodies of survivors at hospitals, the rubble of village buildings, and the scarred French countryside. His other booklet *War Against War* was in German and had similar pictures. Stirred by the pacifist's stories and the photos, I cowered in the same scenes in my terrified dreams.

Awake, I observed the maimed body of another veteran of the Great War who came each month to sharpen utensils used in the meat market at my father's store. The veteran's arrival in his miniature green wagon, pulled by goats in a leather harness jingling with shiny brass bells, attracted all the neighborhood children living near the Park Street intersection. Only for me it wasn't the veteran's tiny wagon and his goats' decorated harness that enthralled but his injury and horrifying tales.

The cutler sitting in his little wagon's high driver's seat looked like a normal man at a distance. But when he lowered himself to the ground with his muscular arms, you saw he had no legs, only stumps protected by a padded apron of leather. On his hands, which had become his feet, he wore heavy leather mittens, and he lifted and pulled himself forward "walking" around the wagon to unload the grindstone to sharpen my father's knives, cleavers, and saws. How the legless veteran turned the whetstone I can't recall. Yet his stories of fighting in the trenches and being cut down by an artillery shell when attacking the Germans were branded upon my mind.

In what now seems an eerie coincidence, a female veteran of the Great War lived directly across the street from us. Mrs. Keith, the wife and mother in a printer's family, had served as a nurse in the American Medical Department in France and England. She too told stories of the war, while doing chores with her baby boy astride her hip, as I played inside the house with her other children on cold or rainy days. Upon my insistence, she even brought down from her attic and modeled the long black skirt, cape, and broad-brimmed hat of her nurse's dress uniform.

Mrs. Keith described the temporary field hospitals—in ruined churches, cellars, and caves—where she worked with the medical staff and patients as shells exploded around them night and day. Without intending to frighten me or being aware of doing so, she related stories of doctors and nurses standing through the night, knee-deep in mud, operating on the wounded and tending men whose lungs were poisoned by gas.

The stories of all three veterans hypnotized and terrified me, and yet I sought to read books and see movies about the Great War, with the perversity of a child pulling away the bloody bandage from his arm or leg to inspect a nasty gash. At East Side Junior High School, reading Erich Maria Remarque's novel *All Quiet on the Western Front,* I empathized more consciously than I had at the movie with the pain and disillusionment of the young German boys fighting and dying in combat. Their perils in the obscenities of battle were so real that I wondered if I could have withstood it, little suspecting that such an ordeal would face me in my lifetime. For I never under any circumstances aspired to be a soldier.

Then in September 1939, the same month I entered Little Rock Senior High School, the war erupted in Europe, and President Franklin D. Roosevelt responded to existing conflicts involving Germany,

Russia, and Japan by issuing a proclamation of national emergency. The newspapers and radios across the country exploded with stories about Hitler, the Nazis, and the persecution of Jews; and the newsreels accompanying every movie featured films of German attacks on Poland, France, and England. But at fifteen, I callously assumed such dire events occurring so far away wouldn't disturb my life and plans. Still, I strongly opposed the war in class discussions, leading my high school English teacher Miss Emma Scott to recommend the poetry and memoirs of World War I veterans—Siegfried Sassoon, Wilfred Owen, and Robert Graves—who opposed war's brutality and uselessness.

A year later, in October 1940, the U.S. Congress, shocked by the blitzkrieg of events in Europe, enacted our country's first peacetime military conscription in history. My twenty-nine-year-old brother was drafted and assigned to the Army Air Corps the next year. My family assumed the law required only one year of military service because Congress believed the whole insanity would soon end. At sixteen, I believed I didn't need to worry because five years stood between me and the draft.

Nevertheless, the signs of our country's mobilization had already appeared in and around Little Rock. Doc Cockrum, a roomer at our house, trained at nearby Camp Robinson before being commissioned a second lieutenant in the Army. He and his wife, Elsie, had been renting a room from us for more than three years when he volunteered to serve in the Philippine Islands. Elsie, remaining at our house, soon was joined by other soldiers' wives who rented rooms while their husbands were training at Camp Robinson.

In the summer of 1941, before Pearl Harbor, my teenage pals and I, sitting astride our bicycles on shady South Broadway, watched the passing of long convoys of Army trucks filled with soldiers, some Arkansas National Guardsmen called into federal service. We yelled and waved enthusiastically, and a few of the soldiers tossed us little silver tins stuffed with resinlike wads of dehydrated coffee. Where the soldiers were heading we didn't know. Nor did we foresee that the war was drawing closer to our country each day and that we, like the passing soldiers, would soon be in military service heading toward unknown destinations.

I was diverted from the war's imminence by my high school participation in music, theater, and student government. I sang first tenor in the a cappella choir, performed at assemblies, and represented my homeroom on the student council. In the spring of 1941, the students elected me president of the high school for 1941–42, the result of my popularity as an actor, singer, and impersonator. But the humbling truth and wisdom for me was a quotation I had memorized along with Bible verses for Sunday school and Royal Ambassadors at the Second Baptist Church: "Fame is a vapor, popularity an accident, riches take wings, those who cheer today will curse tomorrow, only one thing endures—character."

Though I didn't know it at the time, my role as presider over weekly upper-grade assemblies, pep rallies for football and basketball games, and other programs was preparing me for the future. My most serious act as student president came on Sunday, December 7, after hearing Robert Trout announce over the radio the Japanese attack on Pearl Harbor. Shortly after, Mr. John Larson, the school principal, phoned and asked me to organize the students collecting console radios to place on the high school stage so the whole student body could gather in the auditorium to listen to President Roosevelt's speech to the Joint Houses of Congress asking for a declaration of war against Japan. The declaration of war was almost unanimous, with only one opposing vote. Then, three days later, Germany declared war on the United States, ending our neutrality in Europe. Although our country was now engaged in war on two fronts, Congress did not change the upper and lower age limits of the draft. I still expected to go to college in the fall of 1942.

In early May, I gained a better understanding of the philosophical and physical battles going on in Europe while performing the role of an arrogant Nazi in our senior play, Clare Booth's *Margin for Error.* My classmate Gertrude Selz, a German Jew who had escaped from Berlin with her family, helped me develop an accent and speak the portions of dialogue that were in German. In our daily dialect sessions, the small, dark émigré, whose residency in Little Rock was sponsored by Jewish groups, described her family's experience under the Nazis and their harrowing flight from Germany.

In June, two months after Bataan fell to the Japanese, it was finally revealed that the American soldiers who surrendered in the Philippines were forced to make a seventy-five-mile "Death March" to prisoner-of-war (POW) cages in Luzon. This disclosure was not just another radio report about a remote event but a direct blow to my family. We were shocked to learn that our former roomer and friend Doc Cockrum had died on the march. His wife received a telegram from the War Department, followed later by a letter of condolence from the Army chief of staff, General George C. Marshall. Sharing Elsie's grief, I wished more than ever to stay out of military service.

Graduation from Little Rock Senior High School occurred on the hot, humid evening of May 29, 1942. Although I ranked twentieth scholastically in a class of 650, I didn't win a college scholarship. This unexpected and humbling slight made finding a higher-paying summer job to earn enough for college in the fall even more crucial.

Fortunately, an engineer who parked in the backyard of our rooming house, helped me land a job in the finance division at the district office of the U.S. Army Corps of Engineers. As an underclerk and everyone's gofer, I was chiefly responsible for compiling a cross-index of War Department circulars, bulletins, and Army regulations, a much needed document at the Little Rock office. Since I couldn't type, Mr. Pilcher, the division head, allowed me to handprint the index, a tedious piece of work that convinced me to enroll in typing class my first year in college. Compiling an index and taking typing courses would determine part of my future in the Army.

But my serious efforts to pay for college in the fall didn't stifle my theater interests that summer. I was one of three male civilians in the United Service Organization (USO) production of *The Royal Family.* Most men in the Victory Theater cast were noncommissioned officers (NCOs) at Camp Robinson, who as civilians acted professionally. In the juvenile lead, I wore handsome clothes and had few lines, but the play production offered an opportunity to learn more about theater and Army life and allay some of my anxieties.

In late July, my family was still worried about paying for college, when an unexpected visitor called one evening. Professor J. H. Atkinson, an Arkansas historian representing Little Rock Junior College brought word that the school's scholarship committee had awarded me the Lamar Porter Scholarship, their premier grant-in-aid, which would cover all my tuition, books, and fees for the next two years.

With this windfall and the draft three years away, my future appeared promising and uncomplicated despite the war raging in Europe and the Pacific.

Unsung Valor

Reluctant Draftee

Little Rock, Arkansas

September 1942–August 1943

In September 1942, nine months after Congress declared war on Japan and Germany, I was an eighteen-year-old freshman at Little Rock Junior College. Half the students enrolled were teenage boys nervously expecting the minimum draft age to be lowered and complaining about the possibility of fighting before being eligible to vote. But our peevish suspense was short-lived. In November, the war was going so badly for the Allies that Congress amended the Selective Service Act of 1940, lowering the draft age to eighteen to meet the military services' manpower needs.

This sudden turn of an expected event would abort college for me, betokening the dreadful possibility of serving in a combat unit. Was I, twenty-five years after the Great War, to repeat Paul Baumer's life in *All Quiet on the Western Front,* only on the American side? I deplored the prospect of learning to kill and facing death in combat.

Less than one month later, on a bleak mid-December morning, I reported to the Boyle Building on Capitol Avenue and Main Street and registered with Pulaski County Draft Board B. I passed a jittery month before receiving a penny postcard from the board notifying me of my first physical examination, calling it a mere preliminary for "disclosing only obvious physical defects," which would not determine my "acceptance or rejection by the armed forces." The exam, on the evening of January 19, 1943, at the Arkansas Medical School across from the City Park, was superficial as promised. Breathing, possessing the essential human parts, and showing no obvious defects, I passed!

Still this token look-see frightened my feisty mother into thinking the Army was calling me instantly. My brother had already served in the Army Air Force for a year, and Mother didn't intend to let them take her "little boy" if she could stop it. Hoping to forestall that possibility, she phoned her first cousin H. T. "Will" Terry who just happened to be the chairman of Draft Board B. He assured Mother that her Cleveland would be treated like all the other registrants of his age who were in college; I should complete the spring term before receiving my next notice. His statement of the board's fair policy was not the exemption Mother wanted and I secretly hoped for. "Uncle" Billy had listened sympathetically because his only son Seymour was an infantry lieutenant fighting in the Pacific. (Seymour would later be killed, on May 11, 1945, and awarded the Medal of Honor on Okinawa.)

My preliminary physical was behind me, but the hot breath of change was on my neck, so I threw myself frenetically into college and fraternity doings, trying to distract myself from my growing uncertainty and anxiety. But the war couldn't be held at arm's length, moving every day inexorably closer to all able-bodied eighteen-year-olds. My boyhood friends and classmates R. J. Prickett and George Calder, eager to strike immediate blows against our enemies, quit college at mid-term to volunteer for the Merchant Marines and the Navy. Although I didn't share their patriotic fervor and wish to fight, the contradiction left me ashamed. When the vice president of our freshmen class resigned to enlist, classmates chose me to fill the vacancy, assuming, I'm sure, that I wasn't likely to volunteer and leave the office open again.

I was in a constant tussle with my mixed emotions and conflicting anxieties. I loved my country and knew we had to fight, but I had never chosen to fight physically about anything. The United States couldn't avoid engaging Japan and Germany, but I was totally convinced that all wars are madness. Emotionally and intellectually, I knew I had to serve, but I was certain I wouldn't make a good soldier or sailor.

In February 1943, a War Department notice appeared on the dean's bulletin board announcing an Army-Navy preinduction qualifying exam for seventeen- and eighteen-year-old males to be given at the senior high school. The dean predicted the test would concentrate on math and science, and I assumed he was right. I believed I couldn't pass such a test because I had only courses in biology, college algebra, and plane and solid geometry in the college preparatory program. My talents and interests in language arts focused on speech, English literature, history, and dramatics.

But the real reason for skipping the test was my inexplicably contradictory and passive reaction to the draft. My close friends Boykin Pyles, Herbie Cunningham, and Ed Rowland, who early on accepted the inevitability of the draft, were aggressively planning for military service, assuming that they should pursue any chances they might have for preferential slots.

Boykin lured me to the exam, saying, "If you pass, it may keep you out of a combat unit. Besides it's a good way to get excused from classes for a day."

I took the prequalifying examination on April 2, 1943, when it was given nationwide, but my sparse scientific knowledge and poor math skills weren't tested. Instead, the questions related to opposites and similars, figures and verbal analogies, number series, and arithmetic. Even so, I finished the exam convinced of my failure.

I thought, "Maybe, if I don't pass the mental test, they won't draft me!"

Only God knows why I foolishly clung to such a silly hope. And I certainly could not claim to be a conscientious objector, either on religious grounds or as a pacifist, believing as I did that all wars are morally wrong *but* this one was justifiable. In the end, my conscience hurt for even considering I was above other boys my age and could avoid the draft to live a placid life removed from the fray engulfing our country and the world.

My attitude toward the physical exam was equally contrary: I didn't want to go, but I wanted to be physically qualified. I was so lean at five feet eleven inches and 135 pounds that friends teasingly called me "Muscles." I didn't go out for varsity sports in public school because I didn't think of myself as athletic. Yet I had only to recall how physically active I was in neighborhood softball and football and athletic games in the Boy Scouts to recognize the sources of my excellent coordination, strength, and endurance. Also, without a car to drive, I had continued roller-skating and bicycling long after many other adolescents quit, going from our home downtown to the distant residential areas of my friends, traveling hundreds of miles in and around Little Rock.

Embarrassment about my poor muscular definition and inability to gain weight resulted in a negative image about my whole physique. Feeling scrawny and convinced that other boys were nearer to being amateur versions of the bodybuilder Charles Atlas, I dreaded lining up naked at the physical exam. My father laughed, pooh-poohing my concern, but his insistence didn't relieve my adolescent anxiety.

In early May, a letter from the War Department that surely contained my score on the Army-Navy exam arrived. I put off opening it all day, not wanting to see the confirmation of my failure.

As it turned out, I had passed. I mused, "Maybe my preparation for military service isn't so bad after all. If I can't avoid the draft, maybe staying in military college will keep me out of combat."

The letter required that I choose either the Army's or the Navy's college program. I should have discussed the decision with my parents and friends, but I didn't. I had barely passed swimming tests in the Boy Scouts when advancing to the rank of Life Scout and assumed I would be safer on terra firma than on a ship at sea. For that reason, I chose the Army Specialized Training Program (ASTP). If I had based my decision on the uniform, the Navy would have won hands-down. Whether this sartorial criteria affected my friends who had already chosen the Navy I wasn't sure.

No further word came from either the draft board or the ASTP, which left me vacillating between thinking it was a good sign and thinking it was a bad one. Meanwhile, my pals received orders from the Navy to report to the University of Oklahoma at Norman at the end of the spring term. Their college assignments so near home made me regret choosing the Army. When I later learned that they remained in college until the war's end, I wasn't bitter about their good fortune, only disgusted with my poor judgment.

Unstrung by waiting, I spent more thought and time on theater and fraternity than on my course work, tending to all my class assignments lackadaisically. To my surprised relief at the end of term, my name appeared on the honor roll, reflecting badly on either classmates or professors, or both. The undeserved recognition curbed somewhat my sense of shame for less-than-serious academic efforts. Properly compunctious, I wrote to thank my scholarship donors for their support, and warned, without wholly believing, that I might be drafted before the second year of their award.

But my chief distraction from academics was the first and only serious romance of my life. For months, I'd been going steady with Marian Gammill, nicknamed "Tumpy" from childhood. We had been classmates since the tenth grade but never dated before enrolling at junior college. I had been infatuated with many girls, but I had never developed strong romantic notions toward anyone until I dated Tumpy.

In the throes of my first true love and under the literary influence of the Cavalier poets being studied in my English literature class, I dedicated a poem to my sweetheart in what I thought was the style of the seventeenth century:

If thou were but a fragile rose
I from a thorny bush had chose,
I'd press thy petal lips to mine
To taste their nectar—sweet, divine.
If thou were but a weeping willow,
Whose limp limbs sway in the swift billow,
I'd bury my face in thy leafy hair
To breathe thy dewy fragrance there.
Ah, but where's the need for fairy dreams

That clearly cannot be?
For all of Nature's gentle schemes
Are satisfied in thee!

Neither Tumpy nor I was probably emotionally mature enough to know, but we were convinced of the depth and eternity of our love. For me, at least, the thought of leaving and being separated, which recurred daily while awaiting the draft notice, was especially painful.

The draft board's universally familiar "greetings," threatening my future life, arrived in the mail the day after the United States celebrated on July 4 our national independence and right to personal liberty and freedom.

Two weeks later, at 7:30 A.M., on July 21, I joined a large group of potential inductees from Pulaski County at the front doors of the Boyle Building. The soldier in charge ordered the jabbering crowd to quiet down, arranged us in pairs, and led us along Capitol Avenue and down Broadway Boulevard to a sprawling one-story building at the corner of Eighth Street, apparently hastily pressed into service for Army physicals. The joke was having our human bodyworks examined in a building where mechanics repaired auto chassis before the dealership went bankrupt in the mid-1930s.

Gathered in a dusty room barren of everything including lockers for personal belongings, we stripped our clothes, stuffed them in brown paper grocery bags, and placed them on the dirty asphalt-tiled floor against a wall. Resplendent in tan, pink, and white birthday suits, we displayed a surprising variety of shapes, heights, and weights. I had to admit my dad had been right, after all. . . . Adonises or Atlases? Not one!

Robbed of our clothing and dignity and cautious not to be touched by anyone's naked front or rear, we joined the long lines coiling around the many temporary partitions separating the different examiners. With small cardboard name tags hanging from cords around our necks, we held our medical forms protectively in front of us like fig leaves. The meandering lines of recruits passed ever so slowly through the gauntlets of doctors who pounded, poked, and pummeled each of us in turn, measuring and recording our bodies' suitability for the Army's rigors.

The most memorable examiner, a wiry, gray-haired doctor checking our urogenital systems, cupped in his hand the scrotum of the man ahead of me and asked, "Have you been a good boy?"

What answer the urologist expected I'm not sure. My response to his question, like that of the other men within earshot, was an embarrassed silence.

Most doctors were less inquisitive, not appearing to care a whit about our personal habits, or even our physical conditions, as they insouciantly applied blood pressure cuffs, tongue depressors, and stethoscopes to different parts of our bodies before scribbling illegibly, as doctors always seem to do, on the forms we carried.

The large number of examinees and the deliberateness of the doctors slowed the exams, extending them into the afternoon, but I reached the final station shortly after one o'clock. Although I had regularly peeked at the doctors' notations on my chart, I still couldn't tell from the scrawls if I had passed. Yet watching the lines on both sides zipping toward the vigorous sound of pounding on a table ahead, I could predict the inevitable outcome.

A thin, bespectacled corporal sitting with several other noncoms behind the long table was at the head of my line. When I reached the frowning NCO, he studied my papers without looking up, then announced loudly enough for everyone to hear: "Allie C. Harrison, *under*weight . . . with *low* blood pressure!"

Then, looking into my eyes, he said, with too much pleasure, "Well, *Allie,* the Army will *add* the pounds and *raise* your pressure!" The grinning corporal lowered his rubber stamp resoundingly: "accepted!" I was classified A-1!

The loss of my civilian freedom and lifelong identity as "Cleveland" raised my blood pressure instantly and added a lead weight to my heart.

Donning my clothes was a relief even though the air in the building was hot and still. Guided to another room, unfurnished except for the large American flag splayed across one wall, we were forced to sit on our haunches on the floor or lean against the walls while waiting for the other draftees who had also passed the exams.

About three o'clock, an officer swaggered into the room and called us to attention, climaxing the day by ordering us to get on our feet, stand up straight, raise our right hands, and swear the Army's oath of allegiance after him: "I will bear true faith and allegiance to the United States of America; that I will serve them honestly and faithfully against all their enemies whomsoever; and that I will obey the orders of the President of the United States, and the orders of the officers appointed over me, according to the Rules and Articles of the Government of the Army, Navy, and Marine Corps of the United States." Taking the oath in chorus, perhaps before the classification stamp's red ink had dried on our medical forms, we slipped into the Army as quickly as our upraised hands dropped to our sides.

After delivering the instantaneous blow of our induction, the officer, perhaps attempting to cheer us, said, "You'll be on *inactive* reserve for the next three weeks to put your civilian business in order. You're to report to the Boyle Building on the morning of 11 August 1943 to begin your active duty." Then to encourage our compliance, he warned, "You're in the Army now," and cited Articles of War fifty-eight (desertion) and sixty-one (absence without leave).

I was a soldier officially, though not attitudinally, now dependent upon ASTP to keep me in college for the war's duration.

I had no job and wasn't going to summer school, so there was no serious personal business to attend to during the unexpected leave. My only task was advertising in the newspaper the balloon-tired, chrome-fendered Western Flyer bicycle I had lovingly tended since junior high school. The buyer paid the same price my parents had at the Western Auto store five years before for a Christmas gift.

I visited old haunts, saying farewell to my few as-yet-undrafted buddies (who kidded that ASTP stood for "All Set To Party"), dated

Tumpy every day I could, and reassured my tearful little mother, who spoke as if both my brother and I were already lost. Mother behaved as if her boys were as good as dead, as if she were sure the two silver stars on the white silken banner in the living room window signifying loved ones in uniform would soon be gold.

Unlike older married men sworn in at the same time, I had neither family nor employee obligations to fulfill. But I did share a regret similar to the one they must have felt leaving their wives; I realized more fully that, as much as I loved my parents, the most wrenching separation would be from Tumpy. With our secret plans to marry after I returned, each day we remained arm in arm as much as possible.

A week before I reported for active duty, Tumpy and I attended the biggest social event of the summer at junior college, the distribution of the annual *Trojan* yearbook. Girls and boys from the freshman and sophomore classes gathered in the gymnasium on a sultry, late July afternoon, without fans or air conditioning, to drink bottles of Coke cooled in washtubs of ice and sign the conventional clichés in each other's yearbooks—sweet, sentimental, or mocking. Although many boys were joining some branch of the armed services, the conversations and inscriptions hardly noted our leaving.

Only our teacher-chaperons seemed to focus on the possible finality of our goodbyes, pointedly wishing us safe returns in their farewells. Mrs. Edith Scopp, my typing teacher from New York State, whose husband was an officer at Camp Robinson, wrote next to her picture: "Cleveland, I've certainly enjoyed your characterizations—both in and out of class. Lots of luck in the Army." Neither she nor I knew how much her typing lessons would affect my life in the Army.

With the knowledge of so many leaving either for military service or other colleges, a palpable melancholy welled up in the swirl of gay laughter as we traded annuals and wrote in the margins beside our pictures. Parting from the safe havens of home and college brought an ache to my throat, and I could only guess at the source of the new emotions bubbling within me. I had never before said good-bye to others without knowing where they or I were going, without feeling that we'd surely meet again. Even the mature kids among us, of which I was not one, had remained relatively untouched by life's serious pains and losses, at least until the end of our freshman year in college that fateful summer of 1943. At the book signing, I recognized probably for the first time life's deepening sadness as one grows older.

Now, in my callow way, I was empathizing more consciously with the losses I heard about through the radio, newspapers, and newsreels. Before, I had been too protected and too insensitive to empathize with others' distress. The only deaths I knew about were those described by my parents when older relatives with whom I had no direct emotional ties passed away. But the possibility of dying in the war became more immediate and probable when young friends died—R. J. Prickett, on a merchant ship torpedoed in the Atlantic, and George Calder, aboard an aircraft carrier sunk in the Pacific.

Three weeks of inactive reserve slipped by too quickly. On the sweltering morning of August 11, I kissed my parents good-bye on the front porch, walked down the steps past the thorny black locust trees framing the yard and out the lopsided front gate at 322 Spring where our family had lived for the last ten years. At the corner of Center Street, I looked back and saw my tearful mother and stoical father still standing on the porch watching and waving. I dared not turn again to wave at them or I would cry too.

And yet . . . after months of not wanting to go, I walked away from home, down Fourth Street, so fast that my parents must have thought I was happy to get away. Only the sentimental tug of old familiar buildings slowed me. I passed Harley-Davidson's motorcycle shop across from Rebsamen Ford's garage for secondhand cars . . . turned at the corner onto Louisiana Street, where the Kansas City Steak House, Arkansas Power and Light, and the Union National Bank sat catty-cornered from each other . . . and hastened one block south to Capitol Avenue, where I skipped across the alley, beside Franke's Cafeteria, to the front of the Boyle Building. Only five minutes later, I was merely three and one-half blocks from home but already an incalculable distance away from family and civilian life.

Sleepy-eyed men and boys were standing in groups at the white ceramic-brick entry of the Boyle Building. Some stood together on the broad sidewalk, others sat on the curb or squatted by the front steps off to themselves. Groups of three or four together shouted at newcomers they knew as they arrived.

Clyde Brockett, Billy Sims, and Earl Nichols, standing near the alley at the fringe of the other draftees, greeted me. Their familiar faces made me feel more at ease. Pint-sized Earl, about as big as a grammar school boy, had been my friend since we first had music together in the seventh grade at East Side Junior High. In high school, he sang baritone and I tenor in glee clubs and choirs, and at college we both sang in the Delta Kappa fraternity quartet. Clyde and Billy were among my high school acquaintances and on the track and football teams. The four of us talked about what we'd done since graduation and, observing the new arrivals, noticed that older men showing up were much less convivial than those of us in our teens who had recently been in college.

While we waited at the corner of Capitol and Main, the early morning traffic built to a roar. An old, olive-drab Army bus lumbered up to the curb, and a sergeant jumped off, shouting for our attention as if we, not he, were late. He asked us to answer when he called our names and climb aboard the bus. For the first time, I heard guys answering a roll call with "yo" instead of "here" or "present." Everyone on the roster from Draft Board B answered, and the bus geared up and turned left onto Main.

As the creaky old bus ground four blocks north up Main Street, we slid the windows open to admit the early morning breeze. The bus pulling onto the Main Street Bridge passed the Ben McGee Hotel and crossed the Arkansas River. In North Little Rock, it turned down Broadway Boulevard to U.S. Highway 65 and slipped through tiny Levy before turning right onto the old Camp Pike Road that led to Camp Robinson. I had been to the camp once when Boy Scout Troop

40 attended a statewide Camporal there in 1937. As proud scouts, we had stood stiffly at attention in a straight soldierly line, dressed in our olive-drab uniforms and broad-brimmed campaign hats, as Governor Carl E. Bailey and his staff passed in review.

By the time the rumbling bus reached the old Camp Pike Road, our voices had revved up to a deafening din, trying to be heard over the vrooming motor and shifting gears. But once we were inside Camp Robinson's front gate, the talking dwindled until total silence prevailed. Beside the road, men and boys in stiff new uniforms who had taken their first steps into Army life spotted our bus and gleefully shouted, "Fresh meat!" and "You'll be saw-reee!" as we rolled slowly past them.

At the Reception Center, we all huddled beside the bus as if we didn't want to be separated and identified individually. We didn't break apart until a chiseled, loud-mouthed buck sergeant called our names off his list, and we lined up to submit to the first rites of passage into soldiery.

When we assembled in a large hall, a sergeant announced that we would stay at the Reception Center for ten days. During the first five, we would be outfitted with uniforms, equipment, and identity tags, given the Army General Classification Test (AGCT) and other examinations, and inoculated against various diseases. The last five days would be spent in another area learning the rudiments of close-order drill and military courtesy. The sergeant warned us to be prompt in meeting all formations and to use "Army time," which numbers the hours of the day separately, from one to twenty-four (0100 through 2400), to prevent errors of timing.

After dividing us into smaller groups, several sergeants led us clomping along wooden-plank sidewalks to long counters in a supply room, where we picked up sheets, pillows, pillowcases, and blankets for our beds. Piled up to our eyebrows with bedding, we thudded along warped planks behind the sergeant to a small pyramidal tent that barely had space for eight cots. The sergeant sent eight of us into the wood-framed home-away-from-home, which had wooden floors, waist-high plywood walls, and canvas side flaps and roof.

My mates in the tent's close confines—all strangers but one—turned out to be a friendly lot. Apparently, we'd been assigned alphabetically, for Bill Hulsey, whom I knew at high school, was the only other person in the original group whose last name began with an H. Jon Kennedy, on the cot next to mine, became my frequent companion at the Reception Center. Older by several years and married, he had been the political cartoonist for the *Arkansas Gazette,* Little Rock's oldest and best newspaper. Jon and I shared satiric attitudes toward the cadre and the Army's decivilianizing steps.

A tall but overweight staff sergeant, obviously living a soft life while hardening draftees at the Reception Center, stepped inside our tent door. Without any preface, he brusquely proclaimed, "Tench-hut! There's a right way, a wrong way, and the Army way! From now on, you're all going to do things the Army way."

He picked a cot to show us how to make a bed properly by Army standards. First, he squared the corners of the sheets and the single blanket at the foot of the cot, making what my mother called "hospital corners." At the head of the cot, he folded the blanket and top sheet back several inches making a collar. Finally, he insisted that the blanket had to be tight enough to bounce a quarter off its surface. Completing his demonstration "by the numbers"—a phrase soon to become our military mantra—the sergeant snapped his quarter like a tiddledywink, proving the blanket drumhead taut. After pausing to admire his Army-perfect handiwork, he ripped off the covers, tossed them on the cot, and ordered us to follow his example making our own. Struggling under his critical eye to square corners and bounce the quarter, we made and remade our beds several times before softening the sergeant's scowl.

When I went to the bathroom, or toilet, which the Army calls a "latrine," I realized how modest I felt in those circumstances. Standing at the door, I saw strips of commodes and lavatories facing each other in parallel lines like soldiers on parade, with only a narrow space between them. I imagined myself on a commode cheek by jowl with others, staring at the bare or partially covered butts of soldiers shaving or washing in front of me. Hoping to relieve myself in private, I crossed to the opposite side of the center partition and found an equally long rank of urinals. Standing beside the other guys was like being in the watery dance-revue chorus of Esther Williams's recent Hollywood musical *Bathing Beauty.*

To tend at least part of nature's calls, the best temporary strategy was to wait until taps and lights out. At the rooming house my mother had run since I was ten, family members shared a common bathroom with roomers—but always one at a time. Any embarrassment in the latrine faded quickly without my conscious effort, though. By the time I left the Reception Center, I had grown accustomed to the place, and after a few weeks of community ablutions, I hardly noticed or cared what happened around me.

The first morning of active duty completed, we marched to the mess hall for our premier trays of Army chow. A slogan on the wall at the head of the cafeteria line admonished, "TAKE ALL YOU CAN EAT, BUT EAT ALL YOU TAKE." The sign's good sense didn't strike anyone as crucial. But when Jon Kennedy, Bill Hulsey, and I finished our meals and joined the line to clean our trays at the garbage cans, a young second lieutenant confronted us. Smiling benignly, the baby-faced mess officer warned those who left food on their trays not to be wasteful. But unlike my mother when I didn't clean my plate at home, he did not mention the "starving Armenians."

Mess hall food didn't occupy my thoughts, so I don't recall the content or quality of meals at the Reception Center. Apparently what I chose to eat was never more than my capacity because the leavings on my tray drew no reprimands at Camp Robinson, or anywhere else. With my appetite, I would never achieve the status of chow hound.

After lunch, the sergeant marched us to another supply room to pick up our first issues of uniforms and accessories. We expected the supply sergeant and his assistants to toss items at us without caring whether they fit, as the scuttlebutt (a new word in my growing military vocabulary) had predicted. But to my relief, the crew measured us individually for our uniforms and shoes, revealing the unreliability of Army rumors.

Draped like mobile clothes racks—holding our olive-drab, wool dress uniform, khaki cotton uniform, green herringbone twill fatigues, tan canvas leggings, and two pairs of brown brogans—we straggled back to the tent. We changed into the stiff new fatigues and donned our fatigue caps, then packed our civilian clothes and shoes in boxes that the Army was mailing home for us. I told the sergeant my folks could pick mine up when they came out that evening, but he insisted that everyone follow the Army's standard operational procedure (SOP).

After supper, Mother and Dad visited for a couple of hours. My mother commented repeatedly on how good she thought the uniform looked. I told her I would willingly let her wear it, and I would go home with Dad. That brought Mom's tears and my regrets.

Without pajamas, I slept in my shorts and T-shirt, as I had at Scout camp. The strange noises others made that night would have disturbed me if I hadn't spent summers in the Silver Fox cabin at Camp Quapaw, the nearby Boy Scout camp on the Saline River in Benton County. I heard muffled sobs in the tent that first night at Camp Robinson, but, although I felt like it, I didn't cry. Still too close to home to feel totally separated from my family and sweetheart, my eyes were damp and the aching lump in my throat wouldn't go away.

After breakfast the next day, the sergeant marched us under the early morning August sun along steamy asphalt walkways to a long classroom building that had open windows but no circulating fans. We sat squeezed together on benches at ordinary mess tables to take a series of tests. The "big one," the Army General Classification Test, consisted of 150 multiple-choice questions that had to be answered inside forty minutes. The three types of questions measured math, verbal skills, and spatial (nonverbal) reasoning, purportedly to detect our usable intelligence or trainability.

That afternoon, we took several other examinations measuring hearing acuity, pitch recognition, spatial perception, manual dexterity, and personal aptitudes. The excessive heat, poor ventilation, bad lighting, and continuous testing, with only ten-minute breaks every hour, turned the morning and afternoon sessions into marathons of misery, which probably weakened everyone's performance. We knew the importance of test scores in determining our Army placement and wanted conditions that helped us do best, fearing lower scores might mark us "stupid" throughout our Army careers. Even though I didn't answer all the questions on the AGCT in the time allowed (we'd been advised to move to the next one if we didn't know an answer), my score was in Class I, the top 7 percent of those tested. Equally astonishing, my special strengths were in spatial perception, manual dexterity, and clerical aptitudes.

All candidates for the Army Specialized Training Program had to submit the War Department cards sent to members of the Army V-12 program. An officer said we were excluded from Officer Candidate School and Air Force pilot training, two programs with normally higher priorities in assignment. When asked to choose between engineering and foreign languages, I picked languages because they seemed likely to take longer to master and less likely to expose me to combat. I was ashamed to tell the officer my choice since I was trying to dodge combat, but he showed no sign of detecting my guilt.

On our third day at the Reception Center, medics immunized us against several kinds of disease, creating tensions of a different sort. In single file, we walked between teams of languid medical corpsmen who fired, like incautious dart players, syringes into our left and right arms simultaneously. When the hairy, strapping target ahead of me was pierced, he sank to the floor in a dead faint. Screwing up my courage, I relaxed the muscles in my scrawny arms and accepted malaria, typhoid, and tetanus shots without flinching, then stood steady as a post for the scratches of the smallpox vaccination. An hour later, with a runny nose and fever, I was less assured.

Fainting spells weren't confined to the infirmary; after the shots many draftees passed out during drills on the treeless dusty fields. The cadre, assisted by the former ROTC members among us, attempted to teach the fundamental positions and movements of close-order drill. Under a relentless August sun, inductees who didn't faint or fall ill in the rolling dust clouds stirred by our feet grew bellicose.

Arguments between members of separate platoons broke out during ten-minute breaks for no apparent reason. If the sergeants in charge stepped away from platoons for orders or drinks, a murmuring circle of boys might spontaneously form and erupt in belligerent shouting. From the edge of a crowd, I watched two boys wrangling, with their fists flying, as noisy bands of supporters egged them on. One aggressor was Tommy Burch, a high school acquaintance known for his bad temper and pugilism. Short and wiry, he swiftly pecked at his much larger opponent like a bantam cock, then abruptly bent over, gasping for breath. He had hyperventilated, and several of his seconds scurried about like startled barnyard fowl trying to find a paper sack to cover his face so Tommy could breathe enough carbon dioxide to recover. The brawl would have been good comedy if it hadn't been so unnecessary.

The fourth day, after all our shots, we received two rectangular, stainless steel identity markers, which the Army called "dog tags." Both hung from beaded metal chains around our necks. Engraved on the lines were first name, middle initial, and last name; below that, Army identification number, year of first tetanus shot, and blood type; then name and home address of next of kin:

Allie C. Harrison
38511794 T 43 B
Floy E. Harrison
322 Spring
Little Rock, Ark

I didn't submit to a GI haircut because I had adopted a crew cut after admiring Tim Holt's hair in the movie *Hitler's Children,* which Tumpy and I had seen that summer. The longer-locked inductees had to sit in a line of chairs surrounded by rugs of fallen hair as GI barbers, with manual clippers, sheared off all their sideburns and left the maximum length of hair on the crowns of their heads at one and one-half inches.

The only nonmilitary occasions at the Reception Center were visits by families and friends each night. Mother, Dad, and Tumpy drove over from Little Rock in either Dad's old two-door Chevrolet coupe or Tumpy's black Studebaker sedan, bringing homemade chocolate muffins, tuna fish or chicken sandwiches, cold bottled Cokes, and ice water. Serious Army rations were bounteous and nutritious but not as good as snacks. We stood beside the car eating and talking about the day's activities because the few benches in the reception area were occupied by family members who had come earlier.

After visiting a while with my parents, Tumpy and I strolled along the asphalt paths between the compound buildings. Hand in hand, we wandered in and out of the mottled spills of light from windows, meeting and passing other romantic couples who seemed as reluctant to part from each other as we.

At the end of five days, our group moved to Area B of the Reception Center to complete orientation activities—a blur of fumbling assaults on close-order drill and exercises in military courtesy, the proper form of saluting, and policing the grounds.

In close-order drills, sergeants sang out orders in what sounded like a foreign language: "*Paw-toon, tin-hut. Ford, harch! Hup, who, hree, foh! Toothuh reah, harch. Rye-flang, haw. Chir-up, hup, too. Leff-oh-bligh, haw. Dee-tail-l-l-haw!*"

We learned how to salute and who to salute. For our first attempts, we copied actors we'd seen in war movies, but our sappy efforts didn't meet the sergeant's standards. Our gestures were limp like those made by flippant actor-pilots in Air Force pictures. For me, the proper American salute with the right hand palm down and fingers extended and tightly closed didn't seem as theatrical as the British salute—palm out and fingertips pointing to the right eyebrow. The cadre struggled to make recruits extend the right arm straight from the shoulder and

hold it, until the salute was returned, before snapping the arm straight down beside the right seam of our trousers.

One day we listened to a reading of the Articles of War, the Army's criminal code. By the time the bored, monotonous sergeant finished the articles and penalties—for being absent without leave (AWOL), desertion, fraudulent enlistment, false muster, and provoking speeches and gestures—we felt almost willing to commit the crimes. But the lesson was clear: don't say anything about anybody or do anything to anyone, for you'll risk hard labor in the stockade, or a firing squad at sunrise, if you do!

Policing for trash, we formed long skirmish lines, spreading out across the drill field. We walked side by side among the tents of Area B with our heads down, searching for odds and ends of debris. Our chief targets were discarded cigarette butts that afterwards had to be "field stripped" by tearing the paper, rolling it into a ball, and scattering the tobacco and ashes on the ground.

On my nineteenth birthday, Tuesday, August 17, 1943, Mother brought my favorite homemade dark chocolate cake thickly covered in seven-minute white icing, and Dad gave me a new fountain pen, none too subtly encouraging me to write home often. Tumpy brought muffins and a sterling silver bracelet engraved on one side with "A. Cleveland Harrison" (which I preferred over "Allie," my dad's androgynous name). The inscriptions on the back of the bracelet were my Army serial number and "Tumpy's." Although she and I had vowed to marry each other after the war, we hadn't yet told either set of parents.

The day after my birthday, I came down with a bad cold, probably from exposure to many new viruses at the camp and too many sweets. Mother and Dad came as usual but didn't stay long because a few of my college friends were visiting.

At the end of ten days at Camp Robinson, the first sergeant issued twelve-hour passes, allowing us off base from Saturday noon to midnight. Excitedly, I rode a bus to Little Rock expecting to enjoy what would be my last date with Tumpy for a long time. I divided the hours equally between Tumpy and my parents, although I really wished to spend the whole time with her. I didn't know it would be my last visit with all my loved ones for several months.

Tumpy and I were both leaving Little Rock, me to God knows where and she to the University of Arkansas at Fayetteville. Saying goodbye, we promised to write often and to be true to each other, even though we agreed it was okay to date others, if we chose.

On August 21, the day after our farewells, a dozen of us were ordered to pack our new uniforms and equipment in our canvas duffel bags and assemble at 1500. The sergeant said we were going to Fort Benning, Georgia, for basic training. Our small group included only two others from Little Rock, my little friend Earl Nichols, who was joining the paratroops, and Norton Stubblefield, who was also in ASTP. My old high school friends and new pal, Jon Kennedy, were going elsewhere.

We boarded a military bus for the ride to Union Station, at the foot of Markham and Victory Streets in Little Rock, to wait for a Missouri-Pacific train to Fort Benning that evening.

I knew I'd soon find out at the Infantry School if I had what it takes to make a good soldier.

Basic Trainee

Fort Benning, Georgia

August 22–November 23, 1943

At Union Station, we peeled off the bus following the sergeant who escorted us from Camp Robinson and squeezed ourselves and our bulging duffel bags through the terminal's revolving doors. Inside the waiting room's echoing cavern, the NCO ordered us to sit on the long slick oak benches near the ticket windows while he dealt with the railroad agent. When he returned, the sergeant handed the thick brown envelope filled with our personnel records and travel vouchers to a slender young man whom I had not seen before he joined us on the bus.

The soldier's sudden responsibility for our group froze him as still and silent as a cataleptic. But after looking over the roster unceremoniously bestowed upon him by the departing sergeant, the spirit of the commissioned officer lurking inside his small frame took possession of him. Actually, he was handed the job because he was the only one going to Officer Candidate School (OCS) at Fort Benning.

Meticulously reading the roster in his loud Yankee dialect, he withheld comment until he called my name, "*Allie*? . . . C. Harrison! Don't tell me we've got a WAC!"

"Yo," I said, smiling. "That's me."

After giving me a condescending look and snicker, he finished the names on the list, making sure everyone under his command was "present and accounted for."

Later, when a few of us went for cold drinks and gum at the large kiosk at the center of the high-domed station, Earl Nichols and I met the other ASTPers from Arkansas—Ernest Enochs from Texarkana, Victor Papoulious from Hot Springs, Adam Robinson from Pine Bluff, and Fred Dobbs from Dumas. Everyone was restrained and quiet but Robinson, who, I would later realize, was his usual buoyant self.

When our train finally arrived, "OCS" led us down the steep metal stairs from the station platform high above the tracks. As we boarded a chair car, he let us know that if we intended to sleep on the overnight trip to Georgia, we would do it sitting up because the Army hadn't provided Pullman accommodations. He then pursued the conductor he saw hurrying through our car to ask about a berth for himself, apparently having money enough to pay if one were available. While they haggled, a young woman smartly dressed in a form-fitting black frock was passing down the aisle and stopped close enough to the men to eavesdrop.

The conductor impatiently rebuffed OCS: "I've already told you, young man, there ain't no berths, for any amount of ready money!"

The woman glided to the soldier's side and spoke to him quietly. OCS turned to her, listening intently while appraising her figure. She pulled a paper from her purse. When he tilted his head down to read it, she whispered in his ear. Both of them left the car, without OCS's looking at us or speaking, apparently headed to her Pullman car ahead.

At least that was Earl's speculation, that the woman was sharing her berth for the night with OCS. It was hard to believe that peripatetic prostitution had developed on trains. The couple's casual violation of what I had been taught at home and at church about sex out of wedlock took me by surprise.

Later, when the conductor dimmed the lights in the car for the night, Earl and I lay back with our heads against the duffel bag between us, discovering what it's like to sleep almost upright—a capability that would serve us well in the months ahead.

Our train arrived at the station in downtown Columbus, Georgia, around noon the next day, and OCS rejoined us, looking neither better nor worse than those who actually slept—sitting up. The train creaked slowly through a maze of tracks before stopping in a burst of steam beside a corrugated steel canopy that was set up next to the station for troop arrivals. Carrying our bags, we stepped off the relatively cool train into the enveloping humidity trapped under the shed's hot metal roof.

Army trucks and jeeps soon pulled up, and we fell prey to several sergeants who sorted us out for different units at Fort Benning. OCS, our overnight leader, rode off in a staff car with a commissioned officer, but we ASTP boys were the spoils of a wizened, leathery-faced sergeant who looked at us, individually and collectively, as if we smelled bad. A muscular paratrooper sergeant in stiffly starched khakis and shiny jump boots called Earl Nichols's name. As Earl bid a hasty goodbye, I felt sorry for my diminutive friend; he had no buddies accompanying him to the paratrooper school. At least I felt a little more confident with other ASTPers beside me. Sitting on the hard benches in the bed of an uncovered two-and-a-half-ton truck, we caught brief glances of downtown Columbus before heading up the broad avenue leading to the Infantry School at Fort Benning.

After passing through the high portal of the reservation's front gate, our truck wound along an asphalt road, narrowed by drifting sand, through deep piney woods until it passed a faded sign, "Harmony Church," and stopped. We unloaded next to a field of scorching sand visibly radiating heat waves and stood by our bags sweating profusely. The wizened sergeant coolly strolled to the company orderly room. He returned with a roster in his own sweet time and assigned platoons and barracks.

He corralled all the Arkansas boys in Barracks 8115. Like the other dilapidated one-story frame buildings in the Harmony Church area, it was built in the early 1930s to house young men in the Civilian Conservation Corps (CCC), a federal work project devised during the Depression under Roosevelt's New Deal. Inside the austere old barracks, most of the double-decker bunks lined up on opposite sides of a wide center aisle were already occupied by the trainees who arrived before us.

At retreat formation later that afternoon, Sergeant Griffin said our group from Camp Robinson had filled the complements of both the Second Company and the Sixth Basic Training Regiment. He whined through his nose in a thick rural dialect, "Now, we'll git busy teachin' yaw'll to be so-jers," grimacing as if he doubted it could ever be done. With our Army Specification Serial Number, ASN 521-Basic, we didn't need to be reminded that we were on the lowest rung of Army privates.

The sergeant's attitude toward all of us made me wonder how Norton Stubblefield from Little Rock, in another platoon at the opposite end of our barracks, would fare in basic training, especially if he acted as he usually had back home at junior college.

My new bunk mate, ruddy-cheeked Adam Robinson, the good-natured son of one of Pine Bluff's foremost families, referred in jest to their mortuary business as "Robinson and Son, Old Southern Planters." Robbie was shorter than me so I took the upper bunk because I could jump to the top more easily. Describing us in a letter to my folks as the Mutt and Jeff of Second Platoon, I kidded, "Adam and Allie, sons of Robin and Harri, undertaker and sales-maker." Not good rhymes but accurate.

During the first week, we became acquainted with all the commissioned officers conducting our training. Our company commander, Captain Welch, was a short, pleasantly studious-looking man who unexpectedly smiled a lot and spoke softly. The company's executive officer First Lieutenant York was unsmiling and snobbish but neat. York was so seldom in the field during our training that we never discovered his true nature. Both the captain and his "exec" were probably a little older than the four young second lieutenants leading the platoons—Galloway (our man), Gordon, Spencer, and Whiteside—all in their mid-to-late twenties and recent graduates of OCS. Lieutenant Galloway was a lean, tanned Texan, soft-spoken and low-key. All our officers spoke grammatically as if they were college men, and their dialects suggested they came from the Northeast, the South, and the Southwest.

Sixteen noncommissioned officers—diverse of age, size, shape, intelligence, and personality—formed the enlisted cadre. Staff Sergeant Griffin, our wiry and excessively profane first sergeant, was middle-aged and displayed few signs of a formal education. I reckoned he knew little more than what was learned advancing through the Regular Army ranks in his twenty years of service. He let us know he was proud to have landed in Sitka, Alaska, in 1942, and to have fought against the Japanese in retaking Kiska in August of that year.

Brunet, baby-faced Sergeant North was in charge of our platoon. He was rumored to have flunked out of OCS, but no one could guess why. Although he did seem bitter about something, he guided our platoon in a smilingly cynical manner, proving pleasant and smart about the ways of the Army. North's best quality was his patience even with the slow, inattentive, unruly trainees, of which there were many. It was also our good luck that he and Lieutenant Galloway were a harmonious team, looking out for our platoon's best interests fairly and reasonably while submitting to the same drudgery they imposed on us.

All the other fat, thin, tough, or lazy noncoms, circling and barking at us throughout the days and nights, were less helpful or memorable. I recall only the tall, burly, redheaded Corporal Holden, a barrel-chested fellow who had a sense of humor and was neatly uniformed always. I smiled and followed orders, paying close attention to those teaching infantry skills that had best be mastered to stay alive.

In the first weeks, Robbie and I discovered we spoke the same dialect, enjoyed the same events, and could look out for each other, solidifying our friendship. Our different backgrounds didn't detract from our common bonds—the same home state, a year of college, and girlfriends at the University of Arkansas whom we intended to marry when the war ended. His photo of Betty Fox and mine of Tumpy conspicuously decorated the top drawers in our footlockers.

Victor Papoulious from Hot Springs provided unintended comic relief in our platoon. Bunking next to us, our chubby neighbor appeared dazed—not seeing, hearing, or reacting to what was going on around him. But he got along!

Fred Dobbs joined our platoon too, but shared few of our adolescent frivolities and less of our laughter. He was short, overweight, and more mature, though not much older than the rest of us. He never added a wrinkle to our conversations, but he seemed unable to wear a garment without making it look as if it had never been ironed. His appearance matched his quiet, slow-moving, down-home behavior. Like a miniature Buddha, he walked as if contemplating each step before taking it. Apparently Fred's early experience as a reporter explained his being accepted soon after our arrival as a stringer by the staff of Fort Benning's post newspaper.

I sometimes kidded Fred to get a smile on his round, cherubic face, alluding to a syncopated phrase in an old song: "Hey, you old 'ding-dong daddy from Dumas,' let us see you strut your stuff!"

Fred never replied, only grinned sheepishly as if he had some secret or was indulging my childish efforts at fun.

Ernie Enochs, an Arkansan or Texan, depending upon which side of State Line Avenue he lived in Texarkana, was about my height and weight, with light brown hair, and tan, lightly freckled skin. His slightly sardonic smile and frequent laughs made him appear unflappable, but beneath his surface of composure was an edginess about so many authority figures surrounding us.

Most of the others in the Second Platoon were southerners as well. Since many had attended military schools before being drafted, they seemed right at home with the Army routine. Cecil Lanier, a minister's son, who had attended a southern military school, practiced on passes the well-developed taste for alcohol he cultivated there. Others in the platoon had gone to the Citadel, Virginia Military Institute, and Clemson and were familiar with military regulations and customs.

Billy Henry, a slender but muscular dynamo from North Carolina, had the best proportioned physique in our group. Agnew Andrews, a short, tightly muscled, kinky-haired blond from Georgia, loved all girls and assumed they were equally fascinated with him. He often spoke of "having his bell rung" in feminine conquest. Ward Claussen, the sweet-spirited son of a South Carolina baker, was taller than most of us, part of his height in his exceptionally long neck and high forehead. His regular buddy, Ned Williamson, just as tall but heavier than Ward, came from Waycross, Georgia, near the Okefenokee Swamp. As good-natured as a Newfoundland dog until his temper kicked in, Ned lacked the couth that the rest of us thought we possessed.

Several trainees outside our immediate circle soon caught everyone's attention. Private Manny Shapiro, a Jewish boy from Brooklyn, whose square head with thick black hair was much too big for his body, became our most infamous trainee. Always slyly smiling, he tried many subtle and obvious ways to avoid Army discipline and was rumored to have written his congressman about being mistreated.

Another odd but appealing trainee was a cocky boyish Scotsman who looked and sounded as if he could be a kilted MacIntosh from the old country but was in fact a Canadian named Smith or Smythe. A student at an American college, he registered for our draft. No doubt he could have filed for release and gotten out, but I assumed he had his own reasons for choosing the U.S. over the Canadian Army.

The nearest to an outsider in the company was a mature man everyone called "Pop." How an older Ph.D. wound up with us teenagers in ASTP was never clear to me. Even though he was likable, I'm sure the modest philosopher's presence was equally uncomfortable for him and the teenage majority, as well as the poorly educated cadre.

The variety of personalities, intellects, and senses of humor among ASTP trainees often rescued everyone, including the jaded cadre, from sheer boredom in the tedium of basic training. Our exuberance helped us survive an almost unchanging schedule in good spirits: rising in the early morning; washing up and shaving (whether we needed to or not) in a crowded latrine; eating in the often malodorous mess hall; sweeping and straightening up dusty barracks; marching to field problems we would repeat without closure; returning to the company area to wash up and stand in line for lunch; waiting outside the orderly room for mail call before marching to the field again; honoring the lowering of the flag at the retreat ceremony in late afternoon by standing at attention wherever we happened to be when the bugle call sounded; taking tepid or cold showers in the thronging latrine at the end of the evening and preparing for the nightly bed check; and finally falling into our bunks at 2230 to sleep, when the charge of quarters (CQ) turned off barracks' lights before a bugler played taps over the PA.

We memorized the Army's special vocabulary for the letters of the alphabet, intended to prevent misunderstandings when conveying messages over field radios, sound-powered phones, and other modes of communication. We used them impersonating soldiers in movies, spieling off silly phrases composed from "Able, Baker, Charlie, Dog, Easy, Fox, George, How, Item, Jig, King, Love, Mike, Now, Oboe, Peter, Queen, Roger, Sugar, Tare, Uncle, Victor, William, X-ray, Yoke, and Zebra."

In the first week, the supply sergeant issued each of us a canvas field pack (one-half of a canvas pup tent, with guide ropes and pegs, and a blanket) and a mess kit (with knife, fork, spoon, a metal canteen, and a cup). Attached to our webbed cartridge belt, we carried canvas covers for the canteen, an entrenching tool, and a scabbard for the bayonet. After we were outfitted by the supply sergeant, Sergeant North led us back to the barracks to teach us how to lay out the equipment.

Standing by our bunks, Robbie sarcastically observed, "Now we've got all it takes to set up housekeeping, Cleve. And we're not even engaged."

Sergeant North overheard and retorted, "Robinson, you've got a helluva lot to learn! There are proper ways to care for equipment, do housekeeping, and lay out for Saturday morning barracks inspections. And they have to be observed."

The sergeant then showed us how to roll a full field pack, including bedrolls, and how to display our clothes and equipment at the formal indoor Saturday morning inspections. No one had the nerve to ask North why all the items had to be laid out in such exact order on the tops of our beds, at such precise distances from each other, or why the clothing and equipment had to be arranged in our footlockers and on shelves and hangers in particular patterns.

Robbie whispered, "It just gives 'em a better chance to be chicken-shits when they want to be."

Training sessions on fine points of military courtesy and standard operational procedures were conducted like play rehearsals, so I felt right at home. The catechism of General Orders had to be memorized and recited verbatim when a cadre member demanded all the orders or only selected ones. We also practiced reporting to the commanding officer for orders or for pay—marching in; standing at attention; saluting the person pretending to be the officer in charge; giving our name, rank, and serial number; and ending with a graceful about-face to leave. We practiced the routine for guard duty after our rifles were issued. The cadre member directing the session—giving password, countersign, and dialogue—blocked out the actions for "Halt! Who goes there? Advance and be recognized."

Most of the daily exercises were conducted outdoors, forcing us to march everywhere on the reservation, often "on the double," an Army euphemism for running. It didn't take long to become a corn-and-bunion platoon, for we never rode to training sessions in a truck or any other vehicle. "Oh, my aching feet" preceded "my aching back" because we began hiking two weeks before we started carrying full field packs.

As we marched, counting cadence kept us in step and broke the monotony. Sergeant North taught us a special cadence count on our first hikes, chanting in time with our steps, "We had a good home, but we left," as our left foot touched the ground. Then the sergeant shouted, "You're right," as we set our right foot down. After that, he called out, "Cadence count," and we chanted again but in syncopation, "one, two (pause) three, four."

Musically, we aspired to fly "off into the wild blue yonder" with the Air Force, or "hit the dusty trails" riding caissons "over hill and over dale" with the Artillery. Robbie before long introduced his favorite song when we route marched:

Please play for me
That sweet melody
called Doodle Doo-Doo, Doodle Doo-Doo.
I like the rest
But what I like best
Is Doodle Doo-Doo, Doodle Doo-Doo.
Simplest thing
There's nothing much to it
Don't have to sing
Just Doodle Doo-Doo it.
I love it so
Wherever I go
I Doodle Doo Doodle Doo-Doo.

After exhausting the songs of service branches and college fraternities, the boys who had attended military schools led profane or parodied versions of rival school songs. Fellows from Clemson and the Citadel delighted in making fun of the other's school in songs filled with scatological details. One mild verse remains in my memory:

Far above Cayuga's waters,
Near the gates of hell,
Stands an old deserted outhouse,
Called the Citadel.

My devoted but less-than-strict Baptist upbringing winnowed the really obscene ones from my mind.

By the middle weeks of basic, several recruits had established bad reputations. Private Shapiro's sly efforts to avoid work didn't escape Sergeant Griffin's beady eyes, and he checked the Brooklynite's and other Jews' whereabouts too frequently, leading me to believe that the sergeant was anti-Semitic. At formations after breakfast, Shapiro's sergeant often reported him absent, prompting Griffin to send someone to search for him. The searcher nearly always found Shapiro in the latrine purportedly answering nature's call, posed like Rodin's *Thinker* on a commode, reading a copy of *PM,* a liberal New York newspaper he subscribed to. He also retired "to think" when we assembled to police the grounds.

If Shapiro's platoon sergeant reported, "All but one present or accounted for," Sergeant Griffin fell into a violent under-his-breath cursing jag before shouting, "Git that sonuvabitch offa thuh can and bring him hee-yuh!"

Laughter swept through our ranks even though we knew silence was the rule at attention. Our breach infuriated the sergeant into lashing out profanely at the rest of us. In time, Shapiro's sergeant fetched the rebel from the latrine before assembly. But by then, Shapiro must have developed the worst case of hemorrhoids in the Sixth Training Regiment.

After a few weeks, Norton Stubblefield made himself conspicuous as well. In high school and junior college in Little Rock, he had always talked too much, and now he seemed even more zealous to air his knowledge by critiquing everything we did in basic training. His superior attitude toward and constant correction of other recruits and the cadre led them at first to razz him. But by the middle weeks of basic, Norton's platoon members proved less tolerant than Little Rock acquaintances.

One night a ruckus started at the back of our barracks. Norton's squad had lost their patience and decided to teach him a lesson. Wrestling him to the floor, they stripped off his fatigues and carried him to the latrine where they gave him a hot shower, lathered his body, and shaved off all his body hair. Although platoon members claimed Norton had failed to bathe often enough, their real aim was to humiliate him. After that episode, I don't remember seeing or hearing him again in basic.

Opposite Norton in manner was Victor Panayiotis Papoulious, whose alliterative name tempted me to repeat it always in full. Because his bunk was next to ours, Victor's quiet, peculiar manners were especially obvious to Robbie and me, day and night. Others in our squad, including his bunk mate, paid little attention to Victor's smiling passivity, but his increasingly secretive behavior aroused our curiosity.

Unlike most platoon members who opened boxes from home in front of everyone, Victor disappeared and stashed his out of sight. When we entered the barracks after mail call, he carefully concealed what he had received by standing between us and the lifted lid of his foot locker. Odder still, we never saw his empty boxes again. How or when Victor opened them and consumed their contents we didn't know.

That is, until one night after lights-out. Robbie, heading for the latrine, heard paper rustling and saw a light near Victor's bunk. He shook me awake and pointed at the raincoat hanging from Victor's clothing bar and at the pool of light below that revealed his excessively hairy legs and bare feet. Lifting the raincoat, we found Victor standing underneath in his shorts and undershirt, his mouth crammed and his hands filled with Greek pastries. The slanted smile of his lips and sad expression in his deep-set eyes never changed, and he offered no excuse, only told us his parents sent pastries weekly from their delicatessen in Hot Springs. Robbie and I agreed not to tell the others on the condition that he share his goodies with us fellow Arkies.

Luckily, I drew some attention in a more positive way than Victor had. Fred Dobbs wrote a story for the Fort Benning newspaper about my comic impressions of Ronald Colman, Charles Laughton, Uncle Ezra, and others. His singling me out as an impersonator was embarrassing, however, because I knew I wasn't doing anything original. Like other impersonators of the time, I recited Colman's final speech as Sidney Carton in the movie *A Tale of Two Cities,* using his elegant, nasalized British accent. To parody Laughton as Captain Bligh in *Mutiny on the Bounty,* I pulled my stomach in, thrust my chest out, extended my lower lip, and spoke in a thick British dialect. Tying the impressions together, I used the pitch and country dialect of Uncle Ezra, the master of ceremonies for *The National Barn Dance,* a popular country radio show originating in Chicago.

A Special Services officer read Dobb's story and invited me to perform on the Fort Benning radio station. After my appearance, he asked me to serve as master of ceremonies and singer with a swing band made up of musicians in our basic training battalion. They played for dances at post exchanges on a few weekends, and I introduced numbers, did impressions, and sang "I Don't Want to Set the World on Fire," "I'm in the Mood for Love," and "That Old Feeling."

In our free time after lunch, Robbie and I hurried to a small post exchange down the street from the mess hall to satisfy our addictions to sweets and swing. Very few of us drank or smoked; if we had, beer wasn't available at our PX, probably because most of us were under twenty-one. (Other PXs at Benning served 3.2 percent beer every day except Sunday.) Instead, we sought Cokes, ice cream, candy bars, and big band music by Artie Shaw, Glenn Miller, and Harry James.

The farm boys among the enlisted cadre must have controlled the record selection because country songs blared incessantly from the jukebox. Under the colored lights, at noon or in the evening, either the phonograph needle was stuck or the cowboy song "San Antonio Rose," composed and sung by Bob Wills, was the most popular platter. On every visit to the dinky PX, I would hear the plaintive refrain, "Deep within my heart lies a melody, a song of old San Antone," before I finished my Coke and candy.

All of us were assigned to kitchen police (KP) at least once during basic to prepare vegetables for cooking, serve trays in the food line, and wash dishes and cookware afterwards. Fellows who broke an NCO's rule or talked back might be assigned to work KP more often. A chief drawback was having to get up before the rest of the company to help prepare and serve breakfast. After clearing up following breakfast one morning, I joined a crew of other KPs peeling Irish potatoes and stringing beans for lunch. When we finished those chores, the mess sergeant put me on a detail splitting what looked like yellowish-green gourds with ridged outer rinds.

After halving them and seeing the yellowish-orange flesh inside, I asked the cook, "Are we supposed to eat this strange vegetable, Sarge?"

"Where you from, son?"

"Arkansas."

"You're from the South? . . . and you don't know what *acorn* squash is? Well, you're gonna eat half'uh one for supper tonight and find out."

I was unlikely to satisfy his prediction even before cutting the squash in half, scraping out the seeds and fiber, and smearing the inside flesh with butter or margarine. After sprinkling the squash halves with brown sugar, I followed the cook's instructions by lining them up in rows on flat metal sheets for baking.

When I served them at supper, a few soldiers screwed up their faces, asking, "When did they start serving gourds?"

I didn't care for acorn squash or KP and hoped I wouldn't have to repeat either one.

The cadre encouraged the habit of regularly checking notices on the company bulletin board for the day's proper uniform and necessary equipment—whether we'd carry full packs, combat packs, or no packs. I tried to keep up because NCOs didn't mince words about their impatience with your ignorance or poor habits. Platoon members wearing the wrong uniform or carrying improper equipment also tested the patience of trainees who paid attention to daily notices. Only the witty sallies of trainees or cadre saved goof-offs from ridicule or minor punishment. The best plan was to read the bulletin board frequently and keep your mouth shut and eyes open.

The training routine during the simmering early weeks of basic was relentless. As indolent recruits, eager officers, and begrudging NCOs got acquainted, the cadre attempted drilling new habits and attitudes into us, and some submitted reluctantly.

Those of us without ROTC training learned from scratch the positions, movements, and commands of close-order drill. Beginning with the basic alignment of our feet in the more or less stationary positions—at attention, at parade rest, and at ease—we mastered left, right, and about-face turns. After we had stopped stepping on our own and our neighbors' feet, we learned to march in cadence. Eventu-

ally, the cadre taught us the more difficult unit actions of right and left flanking movements and oblique turns. Without any instruction at all, we soon learned to leave formations as quickly as possible when dismissed, to avoid being put on some special details.

In close-order drills, our individual peculiarities of carriage were exposed to a cadre eagerly seeking to eliminate our deformities even at the risk of losing our goodwill. An NCO might shout at someone whose bouncing walk kept his head and shoulders moving up and down: "You're not a damned bouncing ball, Mandel! Let that fat ass hold you down."

Or someone's awkward stride, extending his legs too far or too little, might elicit: "What have we got here, Finney, your version of Groucho Marx?"

"Smith, you're not dancing a mincing minuet. Stretch 'em out."

Or swaying hips, shifting the body weight too widely from side to side, elicited: "Well, lookee here! Mae West's visiting us. We don't need you to move like a damned pansy, Penrod."

The cadre's aim was to eliminate our faults of carriage so that individual strides merged in a uniform style marching in Army cadence at 120 steps per minute. Those who didn't meet the standard were verbally berated before being pulled out for individual drills with a cadre member or a recruit who had mastered the proper form.

Daily calisthenics were conducted in much the same way. An officer or NCO demonstrated the proper form for exercises before leading the side-straddle hops or push-ups while other cadre stood by correcting and stimulating our vigor and spirit by vocal and physical means. The smokers, drinkers, shirkers, rotund, and uncoordinated had a tough time meeting the cadre's expectations and suffered verbal abuse. I knew my left and right hands and was fairly coordinated, free of fat and nicotine, and inconspicuous, so they seldom singled me out for criticism or special exercises. The only name sometimes shouted in my direction was "Slim" or "Smiley."

Early fall weather at Fort Benning made training exercises steamy tortures even for boys from southern states. I expected sunny, humid summer weather in Georgia, but cloudless skies and breezeless days in autumn imposed the same unremitting heat after the late sundowns. Because daylight extended past 2030, we sometimes had exercises after dinner when we should have been free.

The sparse foliage of the tall pine trees sprouting from the rolling Georgia hills made little shade. Beneath their spindly limbs, we dug foxholes as deep as we were tall to meet the cadre's exacting measures. When our entrenching tools first sank into the sandy loam, we thought digging was a breeze, but firmer hard pan was only inches below and required muscle and sweat to dislodge. Sand merely camouflaged almost impenetrable clay. But we continued picking the sandiest loam to dig until Sergeant North warned that a tank would test our foxhole's stability by making a turn astraddle it. Although a tank never came, the threat of one made us seek the firmest ground.

The rains that didn't fall in late summer and that would also have been welcomed in September deluged Georgia in October. The cool downpours not only washed away the summer's dust but cleared Captain Welch's mental cobwebs as well. Like summer lightning, infantry field maneuvers struck, teaching us how swampy Georgia lowlands really are and how much redder clay becomes when marching, digging, crawling, and lying in rain from dawn to dusk. Even on dry days, the moisture from morning fogs and mists on tree limbs and foliage dripped down on us. Beneath the drooling trees, we slipped and sprawled, staining our uniforms, shoes, and canvas leggings indelibly red. Then, by early November, sleet slashed us, darkening many of the days, while white frosts brightened the few clear, dry ones.

Eventually, changes of routine promising to be no worse than the activity previously scheduled were welcome. Even demanding changes—a five-mile forced march or a full-scale Saturday inspection—were acceptable relief from the daily monotony and exhaustion of drills and field problems. I preferred *doing* over sitting and listening to an officer or NCO hold forth on military deportment, care of equipment, and proper field maneuvers under certain conditions.

Cleaning rifles or digging slit trenches beat sitting on bleachers trying to stay awake through an officer's speech.

During his lectures, Lieutenant Whiteside, without reference to anything but our slumping boredom, frequently startled us by abruptly shouting, "Are you *with* me?"

Or a more boring NCO, droning us into insensibility, might ape Whiteside and yell, "Everybody on your feet! NOW! For side-straddle hops!" And we struggled up, grumbling and half asleep because lectures often came after meals, only to wake up doing the exercises and sit down to be benumbed again.

During the middle weeks of basic, a major change of pace shifted the company's gears. The supply sergeant issued single-shot, .30 calibre Lee-Enfield rifles of World War I vintage, promising to replace them as soon as the latest Garand M-1 rifles were available. We were to use the temporary issue to learn the Manual of Arms and accustom ourselves to carrying a rifle at all times. Though we would never fire the old rifles, we regularly cleaned their barrels. In idle moments on march breaks or in the barracks, I enjoyed playing with the rifle's simple bolt action, taking aim with its old-fashioned sight and caressing its smooth, brown hardwood butt.

But the late-nineteenth-century rifles were truly toys compared to the Garand M-1s that arrived in the company area before lunch one day. Sergeant Griffin announced their delivery and ordered platoons to report one at a time to the supply room, as soon as we finished eating, to exchange our Enfields for M-1s. Squads waiting beside the supply room door as the sergeant opened each crate could see the rifles wrapped in sealed green plastic bags. When distributing them, the sergeant warned, "The Cosmoline on these weapons is an odorless preservative that protects 'em from rust while they're in storage." Then, smiling as though he had a secret, he added, "You have to clean it off real good before you use these rifles."

Back in the barracks, we discovered the reason for the supply sergeant's Mona Lisa smile. The petrolatum, or Cosmoline, had seeped into all the rifle's deepest nooks, crannies, and crevices. Sergeant

North, checking our cleaning methods, didn't suggest ways to remove it; he merely reminded us that we had to memorize our rifle's serial number and clean it thoroughly before rifle inspection the next morning. Like everyone else, I had expected the greasy stuff to come off easily but found holding the slick piece was awkward and chancy. The rifle barrel slipped against my forearm and chest, staining my fatigues.

Billy Henry, sweating from the effort along with everyone else, shouted, "Hell, nothing but hot water's going to take this greasy crap off!"

Spontaneously, a unanimous chorus of approval spread through the barracks, "That's it! Hot water! Wash 'em in the showers."

"That way, the stuff won't get all over us and our things."

Stripping our fatigues and hollering like Confederate rebels, we lifted our rifles over our heads and ran naked across the parade ground to the latrine. Except . . . the magic dissolution of grease under hot showers wasn't fulfilled; with so many washing at once, the water cooled too soon for thorough cleanup.

Nevertheless, at the next morning's inspection, we proudly presented what we thought were immaculate rifles. Lieutenant Galloway and Sergeant North examined each of our rifles separately and discovered traces of Cosmoline in places we hadn't seen or known existed. Deflated, we hurriedly tried to remove greasy specks before marching to a classroom for formal instruction in the rifle's parts and care.

The rifle instructor, introducing its technicalities, described the Garand M-1 as "a calibre-.30, gas-operated, semiautomatic weapon, with a 24-inch barrel, rifled with four grooves, fed by an eight-round clip, and weighing about nine and a half pounds."

Holding his rifle above his head, he declared, "A rifle is called a 'piece,' not a *gun,* which is only the proper name for a cannon."

By "field stripping," we broke our rifles down into their separate component parts, then learned to reassemble them in a limited time with and without blindfolds. The instructors warned us not to remove the spring in the firing pin because mishandling that powerful device could put out someone's eye. They also introduced methods of regular care and cleaning, using the tools enclosed in the rifle's hollow butt. A ramrod flagged at the end with flannel was the magic wand to propitiate Mars, the god of war, and weapon cleaning was a ritual as important to an infantryman's life as eating.

After this orientation, we learned to load and aim the rifle. In loading an M-1, controlling the bolt proved especially difficult. To close the breech, you held the bolt handle with the side of the little finger of the right hand while releasing the magazine-follower with the thumb of the same hand. This allowed the bolt to shoot forward to firing position, powered by a strong spring that could smash your thumb if you didn't get it out of the way quickly. A lot of our thumbs were sore until we mastered the knack.

We had daily "dry-run" sessions, adjusting to the Army's four firing positions—standing, kneeling, sitting, and prone—and mastering the use of the rifle's leather sling in firing. Like contortionists, we wrapped the slings around our forearms and elbows, bending our bodies into pretzels, to steady our aim in all the positions. Long before adjourning to a firing range, we had grown sore and impatient with practice and eager to pull the trigger of a loaded rifle.

But before taking us out to the range, the cadre tried to teach us by precept and example to handle the pieces safely. With M-1s finally in our hands, I worried about the dangers of loaded weapons, but I could have spared myself. The rifles were checked in at the supply room at the end of each day, and ammunition was issued only at the range or when we walked sentry on battalion guard duty. Fortunately, the M-1s, our permanent daytime appendages in basic, were empty; if they had been loaded someone would have been wounded or killed every day.

Along with riflemanship, we practiced using other explosive devices—mortar shells, hand and rifle grenades—as well as nonexplosive weapons like knives and bayonets for hand-to-hand combat. The cadre's teaching methods, before we performed, included lectures, films, demonstrations of the weapon's proper use, and hands-on experience under their supervision. We practiced without the weapons and then, ready or not, fired them or fought a partner with a knife and bayonet.

If these exercises didn't arouse our sense of mortality, other forms of basic training did. On our first trip to the grenade range as we were climbing up a steep hill, the two columns ahead separated. I thought nothing of it until I saw a soldier lying between our files, apparently without aid. Soldiers in both columns slowed down trying to see who it was.

An NCO standing beside the road impatiently shouted, "Pick it up! Keep moving! He's being taken care of."

The image of that stricken boy reappeared in my mind off and on all day. He was the same overweight recruit I met at the infirmary the only time I went on sick call.

At the range, we pulled pins from live grenades and tossed them from one trench to another, simulating an attack on a position. We aimed and threw toward trenches that were deep enough to contain the metal fragments from the explosions. For additional safety, NCOs taught us the proper throwing form, stressing that we face the enemy trench with our bodies at an angle to control the trajectory and avoid pitching a live grenade into the area occupied by waiting grenadiers. After the company spent half the morning throwing grenades, a GI carelessly or recklessly sailed one toward a group waiting their turn.

When someone screamed, "Live grenade!" everyone scrambled wildly like John Gilpin in the old English ballad, running in all directions at once, shouting curses and hurling themselves flat on the ground. Luckily, the fragments hit no one, but the dusty groundlings cut down the discombobulated pitcher of the errant grenade. Their least profane remark compared him to "Wrongway Corrigan," the 1930s aviator who aimed for California and landed in Ireland!

The potential for injury with bayonets affixed to our rifles may have been less because our opponents were stuffed canvas bags. Dummies, supported by wooden stanchions, set about ten feet apart, were hung at a man's height. Swinging loosely on pivots, the torsos were targets for our lunging attacks on the body's most vulnerable areas, which were marked with circles of red paint. First, you struck the dummy's chin with the rifle butt, then thrust the bayonet's tip into the body's soft spots. The instructor insisted that by avoiding bone and gristle, the blade would be easier to remove if you chose to strike again, or attack another enemy. The sickening thought of disemboweling a man made me doubt I could do it, even if my own defense required it.

Fighting with a knife or unattached bayonet in hand involved human rather than canvas-and-straw opponents, and the chance of personal injury was supposedly minimized by having sparring partners about our own size and weight. A special Fort Benning team demonstrated the holds, turns, and flips we were expected to master and repeat. I certainly hoped never to face such a situation in real life, for no matter how skillful I might be in exercises facing an equally awkward buddy, a real enemy would likely be someone larger and stronger who didn't follow a preset ballet of turns and holds. Sometimes even our friendly opponents were formidable.

To improve our level of physical fitness, we frequently ran obstacle courses to develop muscular strength, agility, and coordination. The course we ran most often was rough terrain about one hundred yards long and wide enough for a squad of twelve soldiers to run abreast at the same time. Various kinds of barriers set apart at irregular distances required us to climb cargo nets, jump hurdles of different heights, crawl through narrow culverts, hop through rope mazes suspended above the ground, and swing across water-filled ditches on a rope. Our rewards, when we succeeded, were blistered palms, overstretched hamstrings, scraped backs and knees, sore muscles, and muddy shoes and uniforms.

In addition, we had to crawl through "infiltration" courses, both day and night. Machine gunners fired live ammunition over our heads as we dragged our bodies around mud holes, hugging the ground and sliding under low barbed-wire latticeworks crisscrossing parts of the range. The cadre sadists planted nitro-starch charges beside the water holes and strung barbed wire about twelve to eighteen inches above the ground to make the course "realistic." The nitro-starch explosions nearly shattered our eardrums and tossed gobs of mud high in the air to plop down on us. No matter how slender our bodies or how close we pressed to the ground, the sharp wire barbs inevitably snagged uniforms or equipment, forcing us to extricate ourselves under the fusillade of bullets.

Our daily marches to these training grounds seemed to introduce us to every practice field, theater building, classroom, and bleacher at Fort Benning, but my guess is that all our exercises took place inside the boundaries used for infantry basic training. Several marches covered measured distances to determine how far we could travel on foot in a specified number of minutes and hours. Such forced marches tested not only a unit's speed but the individual endurance of each soldier. A few recruits always dropped out along the route from heat exhaustion, leg cramps, nausea, blisters, and feigned incapacity.

Those of us who didn't quit assumed the dropouts in other platoons were malingerers, especially if we weren't acquainted with them. But we unquestioningly sympathized with our own platoon mates. Following us always was the "meat wagon," or ambulance, which picked up and hauled the infirm back to Harmony Church and was always jeered by those continuing to march.

On our daily hikes, either routine or forced, to any area of Fort Benning, we seemed almost always to march along some stretch of Leonard Wood Road (named for the general), which seemed to meander and intersect every other road on the reservation. Approaching so many intersections kept platoon leaders dispatching road guards repeatedly. A bit of my verse derided the road:

For Wood, our company's disdain
prevails in sunshine and in rain.
How do we get from here to there?
Wood Road!
How do we march to anywhere?
Wood Road!
What leads us nearly to despair?
Double-U . . . Oh . . . Oh . . . Dee! Wood Road.

But Robbie didn't kid, he cursed its familiar contours on every march, especially in the latter weeks of basic, claiming to hate the road more than anyone while swearing against "toting a damned gun wherever we go on this godforsaken reservation."

As we marched one cold, rainy day near the end of basic, "picking them up and laying them down" along Wood Road, Robbie made a vow: "When this damned war ends, I'll buy a Cadillac and hire a chauffeur to drive me from one end of Wood Road to the other, so I can piss on every foot of it out the back door." He trumped the vow with his threat to lean an M-1 against his back porch steps in Pine Bluff so he could "urinate on the damned thing every morning until it vanishes in rust."

It was Wood Road that led us to the Second Company's two one-week bivouacs after the bitter cold of winter weather set in. Sergeant Griffin said the first camp-out was designed so that we "seety and call-idge baw-ees" could learn how to live outdoors and perform simple infantry field maneuvers; the second would let us "faw-err" mortars, machine guns, and rifle grenades. Both bivouacs, he said, would allow us more marksmanship practice "to larn to hit the side-uva barn" with the M-1.

The weather's freezing temperatures set the tone for everything we did. Staying warm outdoors in cotton fatigues required long underwear, heavy jackets, and gloves, though they restricted our movement. And for added warmth, we collected wood constantly for campfires and connected two pup tents so four of us could retain extra body heat inside one tent.

Robbie, Ward, Ned, and I joined our four shelter halves for combined body heat. Our raincoats spread out side by side insulated us from the cold, damp ground. On top of them, we laid two blankets and kept the other two for cover, overlapping them at our feet to retain as much heat as possible. With our feet at the center and our heads at the two ends of the tent, we had easy access and fresh air. But Ward's and Ned's legs were so long compared to Robbie's and mine that their feet practically reached to my calves and Robbie's knees. By wearing our knit caps to bed, we retained more of our own body heat. What we hadn't taken into account in the arrangement was our diet of beans and vegetables and the incidence of flatulence.

Every day the cooks brought a meal in insulated containers from the company mess hall at Harmony Church. Our other meals were C-rations from tin cans and K-rations from waxed containers. We heated our cold rations over the campfires we built to keep warm. We quickly learned the importance of saving toilet paper from K-rations and keeping a key to open C-ration cans. We filled our canteens with drinking water from the large canvas "Lister" water bags suspended under metal tripod hangers at opposite ends of the bivouac area. Even though the two bags contained sufficient fresh water for the whole company, the cooks distributed chemical tablets to purify any water we took from a stream, lake, or river. I had first used the Halizone tablets, which tasted like iodine, on Boy Scout camping trips.

Keeping my body clean on the bivouac proved difficult and uncomfortable. The most painful part of my personal toilet wasn't washing or shaving in the below-freezing temperatures but sitting on the narrow, horizontal rail of a tree trunk erected as a toilet seat on one side of a slit trench. Robbie named it the "TURDle-hurdle." Balancing on that contraption, seeking relief over a trench, demanded equipoise and assurance. Fortunately, a low canvas wall set up around the trench hid our awkward gymnastics.

On the first bivouac, we developed our skills in pioneering, infantry squad, and platoon tactics. In open countryside and thick woods, we practiced security, scouting, and patrolling. Using squads from the company, the cadre demonstrated formations for flanking attacks on enemy strongholds and proper firing positions for enfilade on an enemy battle line. At the end of the demonstrations, the cadre divided us into squads to practice the new tactics against another group. The blank ammunition handed out for the mock attack led the jokers among us to turn the exercise into a cowboy-and-Indian farce until the captain called it off.

Only one unpleasant episode occurred between us tent mates.

When we were free from duty on Sunday afternoon, Ward and Ned wrestled playfully while Robbie and I taunted them from the sidelines, joking about their abilities and strength. The big guys put up with our razzing until they good-naturedly turned on us in a free-for-all. But the roughhouse turned serious when someone wouldn't loosen his hurtful hold, and frenzied efforts to escape turned to anger. I don't recall who offended first, but a real fight broke out after Robbie squeezed Ned too hard in a scissors hold and wouldn't relent when Ned yelled "uncle." We quit fighting, split up, and sat apart in a long silence. But by nightfall, without apologies or recriminations, we were all friends again.

On the second bivouac two weeks later, we fired different weapons. This time we slept in canvas-roofed hutments, heated by pot-bellied stoves, and used enclosed latrines with steel commodes. In the unremitting cold, men occupying each little hutment and using indoor toilets were far more comfortable than with pup tents and outdoor slit trenches. We were also warmer out on the firing ranges because the cadre built fires in empty oil drums so we could warm our hands between rounds of firing—standing, sitting, and prone.

On the first day on the range, the instructors introduced us to firing range procedures and what the conventional "calls" meant. To preserve our safety, those on the firing line were required to fire more or less in lock step, after calls of "Ready on the right? Ready on the left? Ready on the firing line? Commence firing! Cease firing!"

The comic tradition at the firing range was to raise a large pair of women's bloomers, "Maggie's drawers," if a marksman missed the target entirely. Any woman who wore the garment flown that day must have been Amazonian in size. Maggie flashed the men on the firing line many times, but didn't violate her modesty for me. I scored expert with the M-1, the only weapon we fired in basic for an official rating. Aiming at the target, I thought of hitting not an enemy but a bull's-eye I had to hit in a game to please my dad. Hey, Dad, look at that score!

On another range, a sergeant introduced "bangalore torpedoes," which destroy wire entanglements standing between soldiers and their battle objectives. The torpedo is a length of ordinary galvanized pipe like that of household plumbing that contains a firing mechanism and enough explosives to cut through a tangle of barbed wire.

The sergeant warned, "After the torpedo explodes and breaches the wire, a few of you, up front, throw yourselves on the mangled strands, as stepping-stones for the others to cross over!"

Whoa! Along with all the groaning soldiers on the front row, I backtracked, leaving the next line of men exposed.

The sergeant slid the pipe under the twisted mass of barbed wire, and everyone dropped flat on the ground to avoid being hit by the metal fragments. The torpedo exploded with a loud thud, and a swirl of dust and gravel rose above the site. A few docile or brave boys, without direct orders, ran forward and hurled themselves across the mangled wire. The rest of us, relieved that we weren't lying there, bounced across their backs; I tried to be as light as a ballet dancer *en pointe.* Fortunately, the width of their prostrate bodies prevented the barbs from injuring our buddies just as an Indian fakir's feet are unhurt by a bed of close-set nails.

On the mortar and rifle-grenade range, our day began like all the others. The first half of the morning, the cadre demonstrated the firing of 60-mm and 81-mm mortars with us watching from a safe distance as rounds exploded within our sight. Afterwards, we each pulled the pin of a single 60-mm shell and dropped it down the tube so it could be noted in our records that we knew how to fire a mortar. The rest of the morning we learned how to attach rifle grenades to our M-1s and discharge them.

The freezing cold days in the wind out on the range whetted our appetites for steaming hot food. Ravenously hungry by noon, we formed lines without orders, our mess kits in hand, and greeted the kitchen trucks and cooks with happy shouts. After meat and vegetables, everyone wanted a sweet, even though we had already eaten several candy bars during the morning breaks. The dessert that day was a delicious rice pudding, which we quickly and totally wiped out by going back for seconds.

After cleaning our mess kits, many guys lay down to rest in the sunshine before the afternoon drills resumed. Sitting down and leaning against a tree, I saw a soldier vomiting at the edge of the woods and turned away to avoid the sickening sight so soon after lunch. But when our platoon was ordered to fall in a few minutes later, other men started throwing up. Two or three, including cadre members, fainted before our company could assemble.

Those of us standing in formation seemed okay and began marching to the next range. For ten minutes along the way, soldiers dropped out of ranks to stand, sit, or lie beside the road, dizzy and vomiting. We realized the situation was serious when ambulances, forcing our platoons to make way for them on the road, came to pick up sick company members.

Runners brought word to the platoon sergeants to march those of us still on our feet back to the bivouac area. Many who finished the march upright fell out and ran to the latrines as we reached the assembly ground. When the company was dismissed, I joined the race, for by then I suffered from nausea and griping diarrhea. Happily, my sickness ended quickly, but many soldiers were disabled by dehydration and hospitalized overnight.

Top brass arrived early the next morning to investigate the source of the food poisoning. The day's scheduled exercises were canceled, and the company confined to quarters for the morning to aid the official inquiry and our recovery. The officers and cooks decided that our dessert had been the cause of our illness. The cooks had prepared rice for the pudding the day before to save time and left it in a large metal container overnight. Milk and other ingredients were added the next morning, so it must have been bacteria in the rice that multiplied overnight in the warm kitchen tent. Although demand for rice pudding died, the requests for desserts never slacked off.

Several other basic training exercises—field patrols, guard duty, and infiltration courses—took place at night. Soldiers approaching enemies at night must recognize the nature and origins of sounds they hear to get their bearings. One evening, to help us learn to identify ordinary activities in the dark, the cadre seated us on bleachers in the woods. We listened to someone urinating against a tree and on a pile of leaves, tapping a spoon and fork against a metal mess kit, unscrewing a canteen cap and rattling its chain against the neck, and individuals and groups walking through leaves and brush. We shared a laugh when the NCO in charge asked who among the cadre was answering nature's call. Many trainees shouted in the safety of the dark, ridiculing the worst anatomies and personalities among the noncoms.

Our patrols across swampy scrubland on the darkest nights of the year were serious tests of our courage and woodsmanship. At least I don't recall patrolling under moonlight, beneath one of the gigantic harvest moons that beamed over Georgia. Our challenges were to read maps by flashlight in the pitch black and find our way through thick woods, avoiding brush and sinkholes in the sand and staying clear of rattlesnakes. Although many lost their way and were rescued, and others received medical attention after being slapped in the face by underbrush, no one was bitten by a snake.

Yet our fearful expectation on the infiltration courses, day or night, was snakes; and the talk afterwards included close calls, real or imagined. After all, crawling on our bellies under barbed wire, squirming around mud holes, and keeping our heads and buttocks below the machine-gun slugs cracking over our heads certainly reduced us to the same level as reptiles. The chances of facing one nose to fang were not improbable, and rumors about wounded, bitten, or dead victims on infiltration courses always included either venom or bullets. The possibility skewed us on the horns of a dilemma: whether to risk a rattlesnake bite or a machine-gun slug. I chose fang over lead but never had to decide while staring into a reptile's cold, beady eyes.

What I had always confronted in bad weather as a civilian was a higher than average susceptibility to common colds, particularly after getting wet from either rain or sweat. At home, I suffered extreme sinus and chest congestion with common colds so when rain drenched our outdoor exercises, I dreaded catching an upper respiratory infection. I didn't mind standing long hours outdoors on guard; I just feared rain when my turn came to guard the battalion gate.

Sure enough, rain was falling heavily on the night I followed the corporal of the guard to my post. From midnight to 0400, I walked sentry at the main gate in a succession of mists, sprinkles, droplets, and downpours before the relief squad and my replacement arrived late. But when I awoke the next morning, I discovered that being soaked from head to foot didn't always bring a cold, sniffle, or cough.

I suppose illness of any kind, considering our numbers and close confinement, was no greater than could be expected. We saw at sick call, at the first formation each morning, how many claimed to be ill. During the early weeks of basic, sick call triggered an exodus of many suffering bad colds, sprained ankles, and infected blisters, as well as a few malingerers. But by the middle weeks, the number going to the infirmary had dwindled. Either company members had grown stronger or immune to disease, or they developed a healthier sense of duty under the observation and opinion of others.

The only time I went to the battalion infirmary was for a bad cold. That's when I met the chubby young man who collapsed on the way to the grenade range before eventually dying from genetic heart disease. Although I was miserable enough to go on sick call, my cold wasn't serious, and the medical corpsman prescribed the Army's panacea, APC—containing aspirin, phenacetin, and caffeine—and sent me back to my platoon for duty.

The most serious infectious disease that struck our battalion during basic was spinal meningitis. The sick soldier was in another company, but Army physicians tried to halt the spread of the disease by administering medicine to the whole battalion. The news of meningitis hadn't reached us via the grapevine when at supper Sergeant Griffin ordered us to fill our canteens and assemble on the parade ground as soon as we finished. His orders took everyone by surprise, and we wondered what we'd done wrong or what new exercise he was putting us through.

When the whole company had formed, including Shapiro, the first sergeant ordered each of us to swallow the sulfanilamide tablets our platoon sergeants gave us and to drink a full canteen of water afterwards. As Sergeant North stood in front of each of us, making sure we swallowed the pills and drank all the water, a contest materialized to see who could drink their canteen of water faster than all the others. Except for the flurry of activity at the urinals that night, we heard no more about the disease; no one in our company contracted meningitis.

The first time Sergeant Griffin issued passes to Columbus on Saturday and Sunday, he warned us—after spouting profane expletives about the town, gamblers, and women—"Yawl stay 'way from Phenix City, Alabamie, 'cross the Chattahoochee."

The sergeant's beady eyes bored into us, "I'm tellin' yuh bay-bee boys, stay 'way frum see-un city. Thuh town's off limits to so-jers, 'cause it's dangerous. It's kur-rupt with gamblin,' likker, and whoors."

I thought, for a place that's off-limits, he sure seems to have a lot of firsthand information.

Our uniforms neat, our brass insignia polished bright with our Blitz Cloths, and our passes in order, Robbie, Ward, Ned, and I walked from Harmony Church to the main gate because city buses didn't drive onto the reservation. We stood in the aisle of the crowded bus traveling along the wide avenue that's now called Victory Drive. The bus drove past weedy fields on both sides before making a right turn on Broadway, a brick-surfaced street with an island in its center, to go downtown. Eager to see the Alabama sin town with the misspelled name, we stayed on until the bus reached the Fourteenth Street Bridge that spans the Chattahoochee and got off to gaze across at Sodom and Gomorrah on the other side.

Standing at the foot of the bridge marked by the Army's large off-limits sign, I couldn't understand why anyone would cross the river to the run-down buildings on the opposite bank. None of us was seriously interested or brave enough to visit Phenix City, but the sergeant had stirred our curiosity about the kinds of sex going on over there. After our long-distance view of the low-down town and sophomoric quips about shady ladies in seedy shanties, we turned our backs on Alabama's corruptions to pursue Georgia's innocent diversions.

Robbie suggested we needed a drink, and I thought about a tall ice cream soda. But he and the others meant hard liquor and led us to a small bar on Fifth Street where the bartender didn't ask for IDs. The only liquor I had ever tasted was the peach brandy my mother poured over fruitcakes and date loafs at Christmastime, but my friends knew about whiskey sours, scotch, and rye.

For my "cold beverage" (Dixie's euphemism for drinks with an alcoholic content), I chose a Tom Collins. It was the first and only mixed drink I could think of instantly, though William Powell introduced me in the *Thin Man* movies to martinis. The drink handed me was so lightly flavored with gin that the bartender must have merely passed the bottle over the glass. Expecting some sort of exhilaration from imbibing for the first time, I enjoyed the maraschino cherry and cooled off.

Our group, after scarfing so many Army vittles, was convinced we needed to find restaurants in Columbus that served good civilian food. We settled on the Chickasaw, a restaurant on Broadway, for fried chicken with all the southern fixings like biscuits and milk gravy. For steak and celebrities (after being told they often visited there), we went to Pat O'Brien's, where just by chance we saw Jane Russell, the movie actress whose bust became famous in *The Outlaw,* a boring movie produced by Howard Hughes. Miss Russell was there with her tall husband, Bob Waterfield, a professional football quarterback who resigned from the pros to go to Officer Candidate School.

When my buddies weren't satisfying their insatiable adolescent appetites for home cooking and soft drinks, we attended movies or bowled at an alley on the second floor of the YMCA building downtown. Noisy like the PlaMor Bowling Alley in Little Rock, the rolling balls and falling pins must have drowned out whatever went on down below. We also stopped a few times at the USO on Ninth Street, but the club was so crowded with other servicemen and eager, plain girls that we didn't go often. Robbie and I had our pictures made at Maurice Photo Service in our khaki summer uniforms and sent the sepia-colored portraits to our girlfriends and mothers.

Stopping at the soda fountain of a downtown drugstore one Saturday afternoon, we met a gaggle (or giggle) of pretty girls who asked us to go to church with them the next day. We accepted their tittering invitations and got passes for the next two Sundays to sit beside them at church, expecting to go to their homes for dinner afterwards. When the invitations weren't forthcoming, we abandoned our religious pursuits, at least at the Presbyterian church downtown.

About two weeks before basic training ended, those of us who chose a specialty other than engineering in ASTP were ordered to meet Army counselors. Sergeant Griffin called so few names that I was afraid it meant bad news, and in a way it was. According to my counselor, I wasn't eligible for languages because I wasn't twenty-two years old and proficient in at least one foreign language. The Army didn't tell me that requirement when I entered the program with the promise that my choice would be honored. Now I had to choose engineering or the infantry. But deciding didn't require pondering, although mathematics courses beyond arithmetic and algebra were major challenges for me. If I had known the number and difficulty of the math courses I would face, I doubt that I would have chosen engineering.

Our final physical exam in ASTP basic training required us to do thirty-three push-ups and eleven burpees (squat-jumps), run three hundred yards in forty-five seconds, carry a man piggyback seventy-five yards in seventeen seconds, and march four miles in fifty minutes. I wondered how my dad and brother Buster, both outdoorsmen, would have fared on such a test. They certainly wouldn't have expected their bookish actor son and brother to be able to keep up the pace. But I no longer fit their picture of me.

Although I had grown physically and mentally, I was relieved when basic infantry training ended. To mark our unit's success, or perhaps to record our youthful brown faces for posterity, the entire company of trainees, cadre, and officers lined up stairstep fashion on bleachers beside the barracks for Maurice Photo Service to take our photograph. The sepia prints delivered a few days later were thirty-two inches wide and nine inches high, their oversize dimensions symbolic to me of the longest, physically roughest thirteen weeks of my life. I had not been a standard setter or a goof-off but ranked somewhere in the middle for knowledge, skill, and physical stamina.

The officers and NCOs of Second Company organized a banquet for the mess hall, no doubt to celebrate their relief as much as our soldierly accomplishments. Sergeant North and Lieutenant Galloway, who had seen me perform on bivouacs and during ten-minute breaks, asked me to join a singer and an accordionist to entertain after the meal. If my platoon leaders had known I would satirize and do comic impressions that included them and other cadre members, they might not have invited me. But they did, without suggesting or restricting what I should do.

Using Robert W. Service's poem "The Shooting of Dan McGrew" as a framework, I interwove incidents, personalities, and Army procedures that had provoked either pain or laughter among us during our training. The opening lines were:

> *A bunch of the boys were whooping it up in a Company-B platoon.*
> *Captain Welch who commanded recruits was calling the Army tune.*
> *Back of his desk in the orderly room sat the dangerous sarge of the band.*
> *Watching our luck, running amuck, was the toughest cadre in the land.*

Standing on a mess table, I did my version of Shapiro's *Thinker* position reading *PM* in the latrine; our platoon's naked race to the showers bearing our greasy M-1s over our heads; and Lieutenant Whiteside's training refrain at lectures, asking the rhetorical question "Are you with me?"

In *A Tale of Two Pities* by Quarrels Pickens, Private Cigarette Carton, entering ASTP, declares, "It's a far, far better thing I do today than I have ever done before"; and later, heading to an ASTP unit at college, he says, "It's a far, far better place I go than I have ever been before." The company laughter and applause were so spontaneous that I added impersonations of Uncle Ezra at the *National Barn Dance* and the little girl's high-pitched radio appeal, "Mother, Mother, buy me a Salerno Butter Cookie," a now meaningless but in 1943 popular radio commercial of a Chicago cookie company.

A day or two later, with only its own members, our platoon celebrated at a more intimate farewell party. Gathered at the Cherokee Club, a private roadhouse just outside Columbus, entertainments were alcoholic for drinkers and gustatory for eaters. I personally celebrated having proved mentally and physically able to meet every test the cadre and training required, without complaining or whining the way many others had. Dad would be proud of me, and my older brother would be flabbergasted!

A few days after Thanksgiving, the two hundred men in Second Company were sent to colleges and universities in several states. Adam, Ned, Ward, Ernest, Agnew, and I were assigned to the University of Mississippi. I don't recall our Specification Serial Number (SSN) as students, or why so few went to the nearby state of Mississippi when so many others were sent farther afield.

It was already clear that the Army didn't explain the whys and wherefores of enlisted men's assignments.

University Student

Oxford, Mississippi

November 1943–February 1944

We left Columbus for Oxford, Mississippi, on an afternoon train, passing through Montgomery, Alabama, and getting off for a layover at Birmingham at twilight. We waited for our train connection to Memphis, Tennessee, sitting up on the station's mezzanine level, gazing through a broad window across the wide, busy railroad yard. Since the train for Memphis didn't depart until quite late, we scrambled for our supper, paying out of our own pockets.

When we arrived in Memphis around 0330, an NCO from the ASTP unit at the University of Mississippi met us and led us through the noisy throng filling the station. The crowd of civilians and military men was colorful; sailors in their blues with wide collars and bell-bottomed trousers, their white caps tilted rakishly over their foreheads; and the soldiers a mix of enlisted men in olive drab and officers in forest green and pink. The number of sailors at the station surprised me until someone reminded us of the naval training base at Memphis.

The train station bustled so much like midday that pushing through the crowd with our bags was difficult. Alongside the endless stream of travelers who struggled toward ticket windows and gates to different tracks were black porters in red caps and shoeshine boys in stocking caps and porkpie hats begging for business. Providing background to the spectacle was a small band of lively black musicians serenading the passengers with jazzy music. A few played homemade instruments; the most unusual was an upside-down washtub with a catgut string extending from the center of its bottom to the top end of a broom handle held upright on the tub's outer edge by the player. Balancing the handle and varying the tension of the string, he plucked the catgut with his fingers, making a deep hollow twang like a bass violin. The passersby, showing either sympathy or appreciation, tossed coins into a tin bucket on the floor beside the band.

Outside at the curb, we packed our duffel bags into the storage compartment of an old chartered bus. All the way along the bumpy highway to Oxford, most of us were weary enough to sleep.

Two hours later, we awoke when the bus stopped at a small station about the size of a taxi stand, near Oxford's silent, dimly lit square. Dragging our duffels off the bus, we fell in line to march in route-step to the campus, singing quietly along the narrow, empty streets of an obviously tiny town.

A boy from up North sneered sarcastically, in a dreadful imitation of a Southern accent, "We-all's going to the You-all-iversity of Mississippi."

A southern boy asked him, "Is you-all ready to be a Rebel? You-all is in the heart of the Confederacy now, boy, and that's the name of their football team."

Only a few blocks farther down the street, at the front of the campus, we crossed a bridge spanning railroad tracks below in a deep ravine. Looming ahead in the faint morning light were the high pediment and plain columns of an old building at the top of a circular drive, off the campus's central avenue. It was the Lyceum, which, we later learned, was where our mathematics classes met. Bearing to the right of its white columns, we followed the narrow road past a small chapel and an equally old but undistinguished three-story, red-brick classroom building with a tower, where our military science class later met.

Reaching the center of the campus, we faced a cluster of contemporary red-brick buildings, which included the student union, cafeteria, and several dormitories. The time was shortly before reveille, and our

ASTP guide left us standing in the street outside the dormitories, waiting for someone else to tell us what to do next.

Suddenly the dorm doors flew open, and the ASTPers in residence barged out, forming platoons in the street beside us. Altogether there were five hundred soldiers at Ole Miss. After a desultory roll call, the old first sergeant asked us to join the others at breakfast in the cafeteria across from the dorms. Inside the large dining room, we encountered not only soldiers but lots of girls and a few civilian boys. What a welcome change for breakfast in the Army!

After ogling and commenting about the pretty coeds throughout the meal, we reluctantly reassembled out front for our room assignments. First Sergeant Hunter, the white-haired retread who had greeted us, called our names and room numbers in a gentle southern drawl. I was placed with three other fellows in a suite—two bedrooms, a bath in between, and a central study area—on the ground floor of the dorm directly across from the cafeteria.

I knew Ernie Enochs at Fort Benning, but our other roommates were strangers: Bill Graham—medium in height, broad-shouldered, and older-looking—and Jack Davis, about my height and weight but more athletic in appearance. Bill turned out to be quiet and never bragged about his great physical strength, although he could do more consecutive pull-ups than anyone on campus. Both the fellows were southerners.

My old buddies—Robbie, Ward, and Ned—were bunking in different wings of the same dormitory and were separated from each other by our alphabetical assignments. Although my new roommates were bright, pleasant fellows, I would never develop the same close relationships with them that I had with my buddies from basic. Maybe the bonds in basic training were deeper because of our common helplessness in a new environment. Luckily, I shared courses, meals, breaks, and weekends at movies and dances with old friends.

When classes for our group didn't begin immediately, Robbie and I toured the campus. The dorms, cafeteria, and student union formed a small island at the heart of the campus, but the real center was a large, open field surrounded by our dorms on one side and, on the other, fraternity houses, where members held meetings and parties but did not reside. Only women lived in organized houses on Sorority Circle, a campus street in the direction of town. At the farthest end of the campus, away from town and our dorms, was the university infirmary. The U.S. Post Office in the student union assigned each of us a postal box like those of civilian students and faculty. Across the campus were signs featuring the blue and red school mascot—a short-bodied, big-headed, assertive-looking southern colonel who sported a droopy, white mustache and a wide-brimmed hat.

Since Ole Miss was much nearer to Little Rock, I hoped the shorter distance would make it possible to visit my folks. Visiting Tumpy, two hundred miles beyond Little Rock at Fayetteville, in the remote Boston Mountains, was highly improbable.

As Christmas week approached, everyone expected at least three-day passes, if not furloughs. We were told that no leaves would be granted, including those of us not yet taking courses. The university was required to complete a specific number of instruction days in the ASTP engineering curriculum.

What depressing news! But instead of bellyaching, I asked my parents and Tumpy to come see me during Christmas week. I knew Dad's B-Permit allowed more gasoline for his company car, and he had to apply to the rationing board right away. What excuse he'd use for the round-trip under the regulations I couldn't guess. I was aware, too, that Tumpy had to take finals before the holidays and how difficult it was getting to Little Rock from Fayetteville. She was dependent on the bus or train getting in or out of the Ozarks and would have to juggle her exams to fit their schedules.

Mother answered a few days later that all three were coming. Dad had been saving gasoline stamps for such an opportunity, and Tumpy would take tests early and ride the bus to Little Rock to join Mother and Dad.

I hurried to Oxford's only hotel, one block off the downtown square, to make reservations but found only one room available. I reserved it for Tumpy, not knowing where I'd find a place for Mom and Dad. Robbie reminded me that Sergeant Hunter, who'd been around Oxford for a long time, might help.

The next day, I told the grandfatherly sergeant about my parents and girlfriend coming and needing a room. He knew a landlady near the campus who might have an empty one at her house during the holiday break. I visited her that evening and found she had available a spacious, daintily decorated room on the second floor, with a big double bed. After seeing the room, I decided it would be better for Dad to stay with me at the hotel in the room with twin beds, and let Mother and Tumpy share the bigger, nicer room at the boardinghouse. That way, I wouldn't have to meet bed-check at the dorm, and we could all spend more time together.

Mother, Dad, and Tumpy, sitting side by side in the single seat of Dad's Chevrolet coupe, drove 139 miles of the narrow, potholed concrete highway from Little Rock to Memphis, and another 75 miles on the poorly maintained Mississippi highway to Oxford. At noon, on December 23, they drove up to the front of the student union where we had agreed to meet.

My mother noticed how much bigger I had grown and exclaimed, "Oh, dear, Allie, Tumpy, look at his swollen face! Bees must have stung him."

Squeezing into the crowded sample space behind the front seat, I shared a good laugh about Mother's naive remark, along with hugs and kisses.

I guided Dad to the rooming house near the edge of the campus, and we left Tumpy's and Mom's luggage before going to lunch at the Blue Plate Cafe. After lunch, Dad and I checked in at the hotel a block away, leaving his suitcase and my shaving kit.

On the two days of their visit, we did little sightseeing or anything that required driving the car because Dad had to save gasoline stamps for the trip back. Most of the time, we sat talking at the hotel and the rooming house. My folks worried about my brother in the Air Force in England. Mother found food rationing made planning meals difficult, and Dad claimed that metal shortages had all but stopped the manufacture of home appliances, which he sold. Tumpy described life at the University of Arkansas, with and without soldiers, after some ASTP and Air Corps men had been shipped out.

Mother clung to me so tightly that Tumpy and I had little time alone together, but after four months apart, we enjoyed just being in the same room. On a walk around town, Tumpy noticed that the Boston Store was on the northwest corner of the square like the one in Fayetteville. That similarity roused my equally irrelevant thought of how much I missed not being at the university with her. Later, strolling on campus, we stopped for Cokes at the student union, and she had a chance to meet girls and boys of my acquaintance. Tumpy enjoyed talking to fellows I had basic training with, and they met the girl whose big colored picture was in my footlocker at Fort Benning.

At the hotel that night, Dad and I talked before going to bed. He shared for the first time that his marriage to Mother and his crippled foot, injured as a timber cruiser, kept him from going to work on the Panama Canal in 1911 and from being drafted in 1917–18 during the Great War. His younger brothers, Fred and Charley, who both had served in the American Expeditionary Force overseas, roomed at my folks' home after their discharge, filled with disillusionment about serving in the Army and not finding civilian jobs after the war.

On Christmas Day, we gathered in Mother's and Tumpy's room to exchange our simple gifts, and later had dinner at the Colonial Inn Restaurant. That evening, after returning the folks to the rooming house, Tumpy and I had some time alone, walking on campus. We eventually became so cold that we sat in Dad's car outside the rooming house and talked for the longest time, not wanting to part.

Being with my folks and Tumpy again, I realized how much I missed them, but I also sensed that I had become emotionally accustomed to our separation. Nevertheless, watching them drive away on the cold quiet morning of the day after Christmas, I was filled with the same sadness and loneliness that first engulfed me saying goodbye to them at Camp Robinson in August.

When our group from Fort Benning arrived in Oxford, many men had already completed terms in ASTP and were near the end of a term. My group, in Phase-1 of basic engineering, all of whom had recently been students at other colleges, weren't surprised when we read the military schedule and found it heavier and more intense than at civilian colleges. Phase-1 courses included English, history, geography, mathematics, physics, and chemistry. Engineering drawing should have been included, but Ole Miss did not offer it in Phase-1.

The university squeezed two semesters of work that was ordinarily covered over nine months into one quarter of twelve weeks. To cover the material, the courses met every weekday, and difficult math courses met on Saturdays as well.

When classes began after the New Year, the qualities of our instructors proved as varied as those in civilian programs—good, bad, and indifferent.

College algebra, calculus, and trigonometry were taught by thin, middle-aged Miss Watson. Soldiers before us had nicknamed her "Miss Twitch" because her head jerked from side to side, especially when she was nervous or agitated. She suffered from the disease called Saint Vitus's Dance.

Our straight-backed chemistry professor, Dr. Green, was also small and thin, but unlike Miss Watson was intense and often intimidating. His behavior inspired many criticisms but no fond nickname. I'm sure he was a learned scientist and impatient with teaching basics to disinterested or disinclined pupils. But Dr. Green on the stage of the formal science amphitheater, faced by rows of tiered seats, struck poses between the laboratory table and blackboard like an actor insulated by the stage's "fourth wall."

Our other physical science instructor, portly, dawdling Mr. Slater pitched the principles of physics in such a low key that he might have been chatting with us boys over a cup of coffee at the cafeteria. Unlike Dr. Green, his classroom was an ordinary one that had a lab table and blackboard on the same level as the students. He roamed among our desks, facing us close up as he did his daily hands-on demonstrations of physics principles.

The other professors taught courses by a variety of methods in contrasting styles too. The course organized and presented most nearly like those at junior college was English for Engineers. Professor Kitchens, a pale, partially bald blond, delivered well-organized lectures and assignments in a soft, gently cultivated Mississippi accent.

His physical opposite was Coach Kayat. The hairy, dark-complexioned, muscular midwesterner supervised physical training for GIs and introduced us to a wide variety of sports. Kayat's course was the best planned and most skillfully conducted physical education I ever had at any school level. His aim and efficiency in classes put to shame a pleasant, white-haired older southern gentleman who taught a rambling geography-military history course. A traditional history professor in peacetime, he came out of retirement for military science and ASTP.

We rose at 0600 each morning, stood our first formation at 0615, ate breakfast at 0630, began classes at 0730 and continued until 1145, when we went to lunch in the cafeteria. After lunch, my group checked our mailboxes at the union and went to the soda fountain to sit with girls who ate their lunches there. At 1300, we resumed classes until 1730, when we dropped our books at the dorms before dinner at 1800. After that, we observed mandatory study hall in our rooms, or at the library, from 1900 to 2200. The CQ ordered lights out in dorms at 2230.

Our Saturday morning schedule extended from 0600 until 1145; after that we were free to do as we pleased on campus and in Oxford until Sunday at 1800. The cafeteria served weekend meals on the regular schedule. On Sunday morning, a nondenominational religious service was held in the university chapel for all students. Attendance for soldiers, of course, was optional, but my group often went to sit beside the girls who were required to be there and who were enamored of the young chaplain.

Most of the time, ASTPers were restricted to the precincts of the campus and Oxford. On weekends, our more adventurous classmates violated the rules by visiting nearby towns without passes, apparently with impunity. I asked myself, "Even if you don't get caught, what is there to do in the rural hamlets that is worth the risk?" Our freedom ended at supper, and we resumed our studies at 1900. Overall, the majority observed the rules without much complaint. I think we were lucky not to put up with the military rigmarole we heard about in other Army outfits.

Despite ASTP rules at Ole Miss, our opportunities for fun at a state university with a party-school reputation were numerous. Our biggest social break was the lack of civilian male competition for the attention of the attractive southern coeds who were as eager as GIs to date, formally and informally. We mingled with girls everywhere on campus except in classes, which were intended exclusively for us. At the student union, before and after classes, we sometimes ate ice cream or sandwiches with girls in the booths, or watched, flirted, and danced on the flagstone porch outside to the swing hits on the juke box like Harry James's "Cherry" and "Back Beat Boogie."

Those soldiers with serious romances had a chance to date at midweek during study hours at the university library. Libraries metaphorically represent the beating heart of intellectual life at a university, but an unusual ASTP procedure and the Ole Miss library's architecture made the edifice a center of emotional enterprises causing some real hearts to beat faster as well!

The ASTPers operated a clandestine dating system. If a soldier and girl were mutually attracted and agreed to meet at the library, the soldier asked the officer of the day (OD) for permission to do research at the library. If there weren't many requests on a particular evening, the OD granted the entire study period. But the library's limited capacity and number of requests sometimes forced the OD to limit the number of soldiers visiting at the same time. To allow more to do research on crowded nights, some were granted only half the study period.

GIs with library permits kept their dates in two ways. If they had half the period, they lowered themselves from a library window and sat with their dates on benches they had placed against the library's outside walls behind the tall hedges ringing the building. But if a soldier had the entire study period, he escaped through a window to take his girlfriend to the lone movie house downtown. This arrangement had succeeded long before our group arrived, with no interference from either the school or military authorities. But careless shenanigans by soldiers and dates behind the bushes at the library and their ostentatious necking at the movies were reported to Hunter.

One evening after the OD had granted all the library passes, the first sergeant waited until soldiers had sufficient time to reach either the library or the theater. The sergeant then sent the OD to the library to take the roll of soldiers who were there while he went to the theater. The OD discovered that almost all of those given three hours to study and half of those granted less time were not inside the library.

At the theater, the first sergeant persuaded a manager to stop the movie and turn on the house lights. The sudden overhead glare stirred howls of protest from an audience liberally polka-dotted with olive-drab uniforms. Quickly removing their arms from their dates' shoulders, GIs turned to shout impatiently at the projectionist. Instead, they faced Sergeant Hunter standing at the front rail of the balcony, which at that time in Oxford was reserved for black patrons. The GIs fell silent at his presence, and the sergeant quietly asked them to assemble in front of the theater. Groaning goodbyes, they abandoned their dates to file into the street.

Gentle as ever, the sergeant avoided further public embarrassment by marching the soldiers to the dormitories before dressing them down and imposing his penalties. He denied those at the theater any further library privileges for the rest of the term but was less severe with soldiers sitting outside the library. He had them move the benches from behind the hedges and told them they had lost their library privileges for a month. Innocent soldiers had to show proof of a real need to do research. The ODs began more frequent checks to be sure soldiers were where they belonged.

A major part of campus social life involved the sororities. I hadn't visited the Phi Mu house until after going stag to a weekend dance at the American Legion Hut. Agnew Andrews gave me a Coke laced with a shot of Four Roses. Finishing the drink in a slightly pixilated daze, I saw through the cigarette smoke swirling beneath the Hut's dim lighting an attractive girl with whom I felt compelled to dance. Considering my usual anxieties about dancing with anyone but Tumpy, the urge must have been alcohol-induced. Eloise proved so alluring that I invited her to Sunday dinner at the Colonial Inn, the town's white-pillared restaurant. Still later, at the Phi Mu date-call, Eloise's lingering kiss confirmed the wisdom of my invitation.

But late Sunday morning standing in the foyer of the Phi Mu house, I wondered if the girl coming down the stairs was the same one I twirled and kissed the night before. Eloise was identical, of course; only my less-spirited perception had changed. When we arrived at the Colonial Inn, Robbie was there and, to my great relief, joined us. Ironically, my hazy vision and judgment on Saturday night led to a well-fed trio and another new female friendship.

Eloise and her sorority sister, who was Agnew Andrews's girlfriend, introduced our group to other Phi Mus. Their hospitality at the house and on campus added spice and interest to our social life. One girl whose father owned a fishing cabin on Sardis Lake, eleven miles from Oxford, invited half a dozen soldiers and an equal number of Phi Mus to a Sunday outing and picnic.

Her GI boyfriend drove the old truck that belonged to her "day-uh-dee" (her slow accent stretched every vowel into an elongated diphthong). Our group stood in the open truck bed holding onto the railings as we drove out a dusty, deeply rutted road to the lakeside cabin. The truck had barely stopped before the romantic couples set off for the woods or lakeside. Before taking a walk, those of us without attachments explored the primitive shanty, which had no indoor plumbing and only a table and a few chairs, with layers of dust on everything. The cabin's only pleasure was the porch, a shady place out of the blazing Mississippi sun, where we ate cold chicken drumsticks from a basket and drank icy lemonades from a ceramic thermos jug.

I enjoyed being welcomed to the Phi Mu parlor, going stag at the American Legion Hut, and being a hanger-on with girls at the student union, but I had no romantic inclinations toward any Phi Mu. Even though Tumpy and I had agreed it was okay to date, I had no strong urge to do so. Tumpy and I had written letters to Colonel and Mrs. Gammill asking permission to be formally engaged, but neither of us had received replies from them.

On weekends, ASTPers explored the tiny village of Oxford, not yet famous as the hometown of novelist William Faulkner. Instead, Oxford's favorite son at the time was Stark Young, a theater and drama critic for the *New Republic* who had written the Civil War novel *So Red the Rose,* made into a movie of the same title in the mid-30s, starring Margaret Sullavan and Randolph Scott. Young's childhood home was turned into a museum, which became a favorite place to visit with dates on Sunday afternoons. The other well-known but "secret" place in town, which attracted the soldier and civilian tipplers in dry Lafayette County, was a hardware store selling bootleg whiskey. In Faulkner's 1929 novel *Sanctuary,* the central character, Popeye, bought "white lightning" there.

A blind idiot savant's visits to campus were fascinating diversions in the middle of the week. A black teenage boy led the large black man, Big Tombo, who always wore overalls and a railroad worker's high-crowned, striped denim cap. We assumed from the frequency of the visits and from Tombo's wide smiles and hearty laughter that he loved having us test his extraordinary calendrical skills. Encircled by GIs calling out dates and years, the savant straightaway named the days of the week on which they fell.

Someone would shout, "January 16, 1805."

And Tombo would say, "Wednesday."

Another voice would ask, "June 26, 1779?"

Before the questioner could take another breath, Tombo would answer, "Saturday."

Since none of us shared the savant's gift, we had to write down his answers to check almanacs and perpetual calendars for accuracy. He was always correct.

The countryside surrounding Oxford also became familiar to soldiers being punished for infractions of ASTP rules, as few as they were. Minor rule infractions like tardiness might result in marching for one or more hours around the rectangular field at the center of the campus. But committing a major infraction like failing to meet a formation could result in being driven several miles out a country road and left to walk back to the campus. Some soldiers just stuck out their thumbs and caught rides back with obliging farmers. But a quick reappearance gave them away, and Sergeant Hunter soon had someone drive out to be sure a culprit was progressing on foot.

Although I never took the forced nature-study walk, I did show proper respect to a campus post by saluting an oak stanchion for an hour one Saturday afternoon.

My former bunk mate, Robbie, and I spent time together every day at the cafeteria and student union, and on weekend jaunts. To give him a break, his mother invited me to join them for a weekend at the Hotel Peabody in Memphis. Word of our projected excursion to Memphis got around, and our close buddies applied for passes to join us. That suited Robbie and me because we were only having meals with his mother, whose real reason for going to Memphis was a shopping spree.

We rode the bus from Oxford to the Memphis station, where his mother picked us up in her car and drove us to the Peabody. We checked in at the long desk in the wide, high-ceilinged lobby, surrounded by massive square columns and glistening marble floors. It completely outshone the lobby at the Marion Hotel on Markham Street in Little Rock. Despite Mrs. Robinson's generosity and gracious manner, I felt uncomfortable in such a fancy setting and at formal meals in the Peabody's elegant restaurant. There were too many choices to make from the many items on the menu and among the flatware, hollowware, and china. Picking up the silver, I had to keep reminding myself to move from the outside to the inside. Still the food was delicious and attractive compared to the always plain meals served at the university cafeteria.

After dining with Robbie's mother, we joined Jim Werrell and Walter Siegenthaler, two of Robbie's roommates, and visited special places in Memphis like Beale Street, famous for W. C. Handy's blues composition of the same name. We also rode a bus to the Pink Palace, the former home of Clarence Saunders, founder of the Piggly Wiggly grocery stores and originator of the concept of chain stores. After Saunders went bankrupt, his home with the pink exterior became a museum.

That Saturday night, we went to the Plantation Roof on top of the hotel and sat around drinking Cokes flavored from a pint of Four Roses, which we paid a bellhop an extravagant price for. Without any dance partners, we drank, talked, and ogled the cute cigarette girl who was dressed in a skimpy, sateen romper suit and carried a cigarette tray. As she roamed among the tables, swinging her hips, she repeatedly asked, "Cigarettes, cigars, and *rubber* dollies?"—and she wasn't selling a child's plaything.

Later that night, Robbie invited our buddies, who had no room and little money, to share our room. Four of us sleeping in one double bed demanded a little ingenuity and flexibility, and we managed by putting the top mattress on the floor for them while Robbie and I slept on the covered inner springs. We cheated the Hotel Peabody out of rent and ourselves out of a good night's sleep.

That weekend, Robbie described his annoying suite mate from Boston, calling him a braggart. Claiming to be a hypnotist, Rodney offered to psychoanalyze everyone in their wing, but no one would agree to be his subject. So Robbie asked me to help play a trick on Rodney and pretend to fall under his hypnotic spell. I agreed, and Robbie set a date, time, and place.

Robbie told his best friends about our ruse, and they came, sitting on the upper and lower bunks on both sides of his room to watch. Rodney had me sit in a chair at the center of the room. He held up and slowly swung a shiny disk hanging from a cord in front of my eyes. In a quietly persuasive voice, he "hypnotized me." I sank into a deep trance, following the young Dr. Mesmer's instructions, to prove I was under his influence. He asked me to do as he said when he snapped his fingers once and to come out of the spell when he snapped them twice.

"Open your eyes," he commanded, snapping his fingers once. I opened my eyes.

I followed his orders precisely, until ordered to bark like a dog. I meowed like a cat.

Remaining cool, he ordered, "Walk around the room." I jumped up and stood on the chair.

After snapping his fingers under my nose, he demanded curtly, "Sit down!" Onlookers offered suggestions and critical comments about controlling me.

When he couldn't get me to sit down, Rodney shifted to questions. My answers were appropriate at first, but then evolved into bizarre responses. The laughter of the onlookers falling off bunks made me lose concentration. I laughed until tears filled my eyes.

My hypnotic trickery was a prelude to a conspiracy cooked up by the Phi Mu sisters and my buddies, who knew I was unofficially engaged and steered clear of involvements with the Phi Mus.

Formal invitations to "Ole Miss Soldier Students" announced a military ball to be held in the gym on Friday, February 25, at 8:30 P.M. The ROTC cotillion had been a tradition at Ole Miss and being selected queen was a coup for university women, especially among the sororities. A buxom, sophisticated Phi Mu, Hazel Walker, who stirred raucous comments by GIs and envy among less physically endowed women, was chosen queen of the cotillion.

The queen's choice of an escort was almost equal in importance among Phi Mus and the GIs. Guys in our dorm claimed they possessed the physical and social qualities to play the role. I assumed a former ROTC officer would be suitable because his military experience would let him observe the rituals with dash and flair—showing the proper courtesies escorting the queen under the honor guard's arch of sabers, and after the crowning dancing the honorific first waltz. None of my buddies, including those close to Phi Mus, had the credentials.

When the queen named "Cleveland Harrison" her escort, a progression of surprise, awe, and fear ran through me. Slowly falling apart in stunned anxiety, I repeated a litany of trepidations: "I hardly know her. I hardly know about military protocol. I hardly know how to dance."

When I threatened to resign, those who had secretly set up the stunt wouldn't let me. Instead, a good ballroom dancer taught me to waltz doing a turn in either direction. A former ROTC officer taught me to walk with a saber at my side without entangling my legs. Hazel's girlfriends furnished the name of the town's florist, the color of the queen's gown, and the type of flowers to buy for her corsage and wrist bouquet. And a girl whose family lived in Oxford volunteered to drive us to the gym.

The evening of the cotillion, I walked to the Phi Mu house for my date. I waited in the foyer holding a flower box in each hand, while on the second floor, the grinning faces of sorority sisters peered around door frames and through railings at me down below, smiling but trembling. Finally, the queen, surrounded by chattering Phi Mus, appeared at the top of the stairs and regally descended. I struggled awkwardly through the ritual of the corsage by trying to pin it on without sticking or touching her bounteous bust. On the drive to the gym, I was anesthetized by her perfume and my fear.

The formalities at the cotillion completed—our arrival, our march under the arch of swords, the crowning ceremony, and the first waltz—I felt comfortable with Hazel, who was unpretentious, full of laughs, and so popular with others that her dance card filled right away. After the ball was over, I escorted her to the house, thanked her for choosing me, and unwound on my way back to the dorm.

My roommates waiting up to hear what happened alone with such a "hot" number after the dance expected more than I had to tell. Disappointed, buddies put me down a bit by saying that when Hazel agreed to the plan she called me "sweet and cute." At least, she didn't say "harmless"! This was my biggest moment in society at Ole Miss.

The university gymnasium where the military ball was held was the center of physical education for both men and women. It housed Coach Kayat's office and the rooms and equipment for gymnastics and boxing. In fact, considering the number of ASTPers, offering sports that required individualized instruction surprised me. Coach or someone higher up apparently believed boxing and gymnastics would develop our agility and defensive ability in hand-to-hand combat, for boxing instruction emphasizes stance and footwork and introduces proper form for jabs and hooks. Our gymnastics training involved chin-ups on a horizontal bar, vaulting over a long horse, and tumbling and doing cartwheels on mats. Bill Graham, my roommate, was the school champion in chin-ups and push-ups. Both were difficult for me.

When training sessions in boxing ended, Coach Kayat organized an elimination contest to determine the best boxers in each weight class. He planned a night of championship bouts open to the university as a whole. In the eliminations, we picked our first opponents from classmates. While I was cautiously surveying likely guys in my weight class with whom I might survive three rounds, my roommate Jack Davis chose me. Taken unaware, I soon decided Jack was ideal: he was my height and weight and hadn't shown belligerence toward anyone.

In the first round, I learned that Jack was experienced, combative, and fast-moving. I was amateurishly hesitant, "riding a bicycle, mostly backwards," as my dad used to say of some boxers in the Gillette radio fights. In the next round, I was determined to be as aggressive as the second in my corner instructed. Advancing to the middle of the ring, I plowed straight toward Jack. Throwing out a solid right jab with proper footwork, I dropped my guard, exposing my jaw, which I thought was bone until Jack shattered it like glass. The blow's impact knocked me out but not down. A mindless automaton still flailing away, I absorbed one solid blow after another as Jack waltzed me around the ring. The merciful referee stepped between us; and although Jack had knocked me out, he declared I had lost by a TKO (technical knockout).

My early loss didn't shame but relieved me; I wouldn't have to fight again. A few days later, I watched the public bouts without any concern about my own skin. Jack met his pugilistic Waterloo in the tryouts, pitted against a chap who looked no more threatening than I but who wasn't the same pushover. At the championship bouts the next Saturday night, a host of cheering, jeering "losers" packed the gym to the rafters, enjoying their girlfriends' close hugs instead of shots to their mugs. Unlike the Gillette broadcasts of Friday night fights at home with my dad, I could see these.

The university stadium was the other site for physical education, plus football and track. Similar to stadiums on most college campuses in the 1930s and 1940s, it seated spectators on only one side of the field, in a roofless, rectangular concrete-and-steel stand of tiered rows. We never sat down in the stadium at Ole Miss. Coach used its hundreds of steps to build endurance by having us run to the top of each aisle and down the next until we had traversed the entire edifice, vertically and horizontally.

Following an exhausting stadium run, we gathered in the middle of the football field for a series of side-straddle hops, sit-ups, push-ups, squat jumps, and piggy-back runs. In the latter, one soldier carried another on his back from one end of the field to the other. Piggybacks separated men from boys; at least, the smaller guys seemed to stand farther away from larger ones when partners were chosen. Coach checked our individual progress, measuring improvement in each exercise weekly by counting the jumps, push-ups, and so forth that we performed within specific time limits. As a still-growing boy under this regimen, I gained weight, muscle, and strength.

Yet despite my improving physicality, I suffered a minor public illness. One morning shortly after breakfast, I felt sick to my stomach in chemistry class but not sick enough to risk making a spectacle by leaving the lecture hall. Because my seat was on an aisle, I could easily escape to the rest room if my nausea worsened.

I awoke without warning lying beside my seat, hearing Dr. Green's distinctively dry voice, "One of you will have to take Harrison to the infirmary, if he can walk."

From the sloping surface of the aisle, surrounded by a circle of crew-cut heads, I looked up into Green's wry face before I insisted on standing, even though still faint and more nauseated. An obliging classmate, probably eager to escape class, volunteered to accompany me to the infirmary at the far end of the campus.

Walking outside in the fresh air awakened me without relieving the roiling in my stomach. I had to stop twice to throw up. At the infirmary, the chief nurse disregarded the intensity of my distress and sent me to the end of the line of patients. In the waiting room mirror, my reflection was ghostly white. The doctor who finally heard my symptoms prescribed a tumbler full of castor oil and sent me to my dorm for the rest of the day. Drinking the viscous oil was almost more daunting than the griping in my stomach. Needless to say, I hurried back to my dorm room.

The doctor's loathsome prescription succeeded, and by day's end when my suite mates returned, I was ready to eat a light supper and tell my story. The comments that followed my recovery didn't end as quickly. My chemistry classmates, friends and strangers alike, kidded me for days, praising my physical collapse in the aisle and comparing me to Garbo in her last scene in *Camille.* They claimed it was a ruse to escape one of Dr. Green's more soporific lectures.

Dr. Green's sleep-inducing lectures were incongruously delivered at breakneck speed. He assumed, I guess, that all of us had sufficient background without extensive explanations to understand chemistry. For students like me, who had no high school chemistry and had difficulty remembering the table of chemical valences, Dr. Green rarely said enough. In the evening, my suite mates, who were prepared in chemistry, helped me straighten out my jumble of half-understood notes. In return, I helped with weekly essays in engineering English, suggesting topics and titles and reading proof.

Dr. Green's other shortcoming affected even the most knowledgeable and was the basis of my impersonation. Writing chemical formulas on the blackboard with his right hand, he removed them immediately with an eraser in his trailing left hand. Then he would turn to the class and ask, "Did you get that?"

Despite craning to see around Dr. Green's body as he wrote, we couldn't decipher the complete formulas. If the professor were willing to repeat when a student was brave enough to ask for the formula again, he rewrote it and wiped it away at the same speed.

Even had Dr. Green been patient and more informative, I was in jeopardy from the start in chemistry, and my comic impression of him in a talent show he attended didn't improve my chances.

The morning after, Dr. Green said, "I always thought Private Harrison one of my most attentive students. I assumed he was interested in chemistry, but I was mistaken. Last night, I realized the aim of his concentration. His impression of me at the blackboard made it clear. I'm glad to know how I look to him and the rest of you."

With that verbal stiletto, the professor eviscerated any gut of hope I had for his sympathetic aid in passing his course. With the probability of failing chemistry a reality, the possibility of being dismissed from ASTP occurred to me. Academic fear and the prospect of failure were ones I had never faced before.

At the same talent show, I did an impression of Miss Watson, who taught math to almost every civilian and military student on campus. A dear lady who had no sense of command in her classroom, she was sincerely concerned for her "soldier boys," all of whom she feared would be sent into combat if they failed their schoolwork. Her kindness and sentiment were hardly reciprocated by us callous boys. I wasn't innocent of mocking her, for I shook my head from side to side performing my impression of her for friends. But in the variety show, not wanting to offend her if she were present, I just repeated her favorite phrase when boys teased her in class.

One dramatic instance of teasing Miss Watson evolved from empty Coke bottles knocked over accidentally in her classroom. The floor at the back of her room was six to eight inches higher than the front and slanted down toward her desk beside the blackboard. A drink machine was in the hall outside her door, and we often brought Cokes into her classroom to drink while sitting around talking during the break. At first, everyone observed the rule posted by the machine—RETURN BOTTLES TO CASES—but at times someone forgot, set a bottle down beside his foot, and accidentally knocked it over. The bottle rolling down to the front of the room made an awful racket. These circumstances and the ten-minute break in the middle of a two-hour Saturday trig class set up the trick.

By agreement, we all kept our coke bottles in the room and set them beside our feet. When Miss Watson turned her back to write a problem on the board, a soldier down front raised his hand signaling "bombs away." The Coke bottles kicked over simultaneously and rolled with a hollow rumble on the wooden floor to Miss Watson's feet. The clatter and shrill laughter created pandemonium.

Miss Watson's back was to us, and her head shook uncontrollably. Without turning, she steadied herself, standing quite still until the last bottle rattled to a stop. A long silence was broken only by someone's soft snicker.

Miss Watson then faced us, the deep lines on her thin face more furrowed and her head shaking badly. She pleaded, "Now-uh, baw-ees, we have so-o much to do-o and so-o little time to-o do-o it in," elongating every vowel into a diphthong.

Several boys, down front, whispered, "We're sorry, Miss Watson."

Smiling, she forgave us all instantly, "Now-uh, baw-ees, let's get back to work." Embarrassed by her gentleness and our sense of guilt, we buckled down.

But all of us were not equally shamed. The very next day, when her back was turned, some Sad Sack tossed a piece of chalk at the board, and a few days later another removed the chalk box and hid it, forcing her to go to her office for more.

Censured by these painful moments, my impression at the variety show was strictly vocal. I said "so much to do and so little time to do it in," teasingly reproving the audience for laughing at something naughty that I had said or mimed. And her phrase, familiar to everyone, drew bigger laughs. I liked Miss Watson. She taught me enough about cosines, tangents, and retorts to pass her courses, miraculously, without a slide rule.

The talent show produced surprisingly contradictory results, for afterwards Dr. Green and Miss Watson treated me fairly though differently. My big success with the student audience caught the attention of the ASTP commandant, a colonel I had never seen or heard of in the months on campus. He called me to his office, complimented my performance, and asked me to head a campus committee for soldier entertainment. I realized after meeting him that he was the only commissioned officer I'd ever seen or spoken to on campus.

The colonel's proposal was not important though. In a matter of days, apparently without his or our knowledge, the ASTP program was slated to be abandoned across the country. General Dwight D. Eisenhower had requested 55,000 more men from the Joint Chiefs of Staff for the planned invasion of Europe. To supply them, the Army Chief of Staff, General George C. Marshall, who never supported the program, chose the corps of ASTP as the most quickly available, organized body of men in the Army. The general requested that the Secretary of War Henry M. Stimson shift 120,000 men from ASTP to the ground forces for combat training.

Official word of the ASTP closure reached Ole Miss the week before we were to take final exams for the quarter, on February 18. A message from the Army adjutant general was distributed to us: "The time has come now for the majority of you to be assigned to other active duty. To break the enemies' defenses and force their unconditional surrender, it is necessary to hit them with the full weight of America's manpower. Because of this imperative military necessity most of you will soon be ordered to field service before the completion of your normal course. . . . Most of you released from ASTP will be assigned to the Army Ground Forces for duty with divisions and other units." We didn't know where or what our new assignments would be, but I suspected the infantry.

Ironically, the end of the program cast as heavy a pall upon the faculty as on the soldiers; everyone felt sad and betrayed. As soldiers we faced tougher roles in the Army, but the faculty sensed our absence might eliminate their jobs. When we assembled for exams, our professors expressed their pleasure teaching us and regrets about our leaving.

I passed all my courses except chemistry, falling seven points short. Even so, by passing trigonometry, calculus, and physics—solid, difficult courses in which I had no previous preparation—I recovered my self-confidence as a student. But I assumed failing chemistry would end my ASTP career, regardless of the manpower shortage.

With final exams meaningless and ASTP ended, we turned in textbooks and packed our duffels, reluctant to rejoin the Army's hierarchy, hassles, and anxieties, once again facing the prospect of combat.

Rifleman-Clerk

Camp McCain, Mississippi

March–July 1944

Soldiers and coeds alike cried foul when General Marshall ended most of the Army Specialized Training Programs across the country. The GIs at Ole Miss had deep misgivings about being transferred into the Army Ground Forces, particularly to the infantry or artillery, and the coeds were dismayed about social prospects on campus without five hundred stalwart men in uniform. Most of us GIs at Ole Miss were being sent on February 26, 1944, to Camp McCain, just fifty miles south of Oxford on State Highway 7.

The weather on the bright, blustery Friday of our departure contrasted sharply with the mood of gloomy soldiers inside the Army bus vowing to return as soon as possible, and the sorrowful coeds alongside pledging to be faithful until they came back. Assuming my own ties at our brief but happy collegiate home had ended, and with Robert Frost "knowing how way leads on to way," I doubted I'd ever come back.

Sweating from our wool uniforms or our unknown prospects, we opened the windows on both sides of the bus, and the fellows with girlfriends hung their arms out to hold their sweethearts' hands for as long as they could. With so many outstretched arms, the bus must have looked like a giant centipede crawling away from the curb.

Many aching hearts rode one last time down Oxford's few narrow but now-so-familiar streets. Farther down the road, the quiet talk of seat mates slowly rose to a crescendo. And by the time Camp Mc-

Cain's front gate came into view, everyone was singing at the top of his lungs, straining "into the wild blue yonder" and galloping "over hill and over dale" as if Ole Miss had already been forgotten. Perhaps our boisterous talk and singing were really exuberant pretenses to calm the fears we felt about our new beginnings in an infantry division preparing for combat overseas.

The driver stopped at the main gate to ask the camp guard for instructions, giving us a chance to read the plaque that honored the camp's Mississippi namesake, Brigadier General Henry P. McCain (1861–1941), on the red-brick gatepost.

The reservation, which appeared to have no trees or bushes, was like a western town on a flat wasteland. We swiveled our necks to look at the gridwork of streets and the long lines of monotonous buildings covered in tar paper, battened down by narrow, vertical strips of wood two feet apart, as the bus crept slowly down a main avenue stirring dusty wisps of sandy topsoil at the blacktop's edges. The weathered one-story tar-papered barracks on both sides were connected to each other by gravel paths inside wooden two-by-four borders, bringing to mind Harmony Church at Fort Benning. The primitive barracks and their surroundings were inklings of the infantry's harsher prospects and gave me a sense of being in the real Army.

The bus stopped next to a movie theater, where we unloaded and stood beside our duffel bags like recruits again, silently awaiting orders. Finally, a thick-necked master sergeant, accompanied by several first sergeants, appeared. The bristly sergeant, his flinty eyes shining with disdain at us college boys, announced we were joining the 301st Infantry Regiment, then introduced the sergeants who would call the names of those joining their rifle companies. Company A's sergeant stepped forward and yelled a few names, including that of Ernie Enochs, and the men strolled off.

Next up, First Sergeant William M. Kelly of Company B called my name, along with others, and we followed him. While Company A's sergeant let men amble off in any way they chose, Sergeant Kelly ordered us to fall in, sling our duffels over our right shoulders, and march in cadence. I waved a cheery goodbye to Robbie, assuming I would see him again soon.

The First Battalion companies stood on rectangular plots set at right angles to the main regimental street. The company areas and streets were empty and quiet, for all the troops were on field exercises in the country. Company B's signboard, near a circle of whitewashed rocks in front of the Company Headquarters building, came into view. We crossed a plank bridge over a shallow ditch to stand around the flagpole at the center of the circle. Under the flapping American flag, Sergeant Kelly assigned us to the various platoons and barracks of Company B, First Battalion, the 301st Infantry Regiment of the Ninety-fourth Infantry Division.

My squad was in the Second Platoon, which lived in the second barracks from the main street. Stowing my stuff, I surveyed every part of a rough barracks full of bunks—unvarnished wooden floors, bare light bulbs suspended from long cords—and smelled the hot dusty air trapped under the low ceiling of the long hall. For the first time, my bunk was on the bottom, near one of the pot-bellied stoves in the center aisle. But with cold weather in Mississippi already past, my proximity to the stove would make little difference. As in basic training, I had a shelf on the wall behind my bunk, with a short bar under it for hanging my uniforms, and my locker was at the foot of my bunk next to the aisle. Although the barracks at McCain were of more recent vintage, they looked as old as our antique CCC barracks at Fort Benning.

The orderly room and company commander's office were in the front half of the headquarters building, and the dayroom and supply room were behind them. Although supply could be reached through a Dutch door from the orderly room, the dayroom's only entrance was from outside. The lounge was furnished with writing tables and chairs, and ping-pong and pool tables for our leisure. On one wall was an almost life-size poster of Betty Grable in a one-piece white bathing suit, gazing over her shoulder. No matter where you stood or sat in the room, she looked directly into your eyes. On other walls were charts showing the black silhouettes of American, German, and Japanese airplanes that we would learn to identify.

The company's assembly area was an open space between the headquarters building and the long latrine that faced the shallow porches and screened double doors of four barracks, whose axes were parallel with the regimental road. The mess hall at the back of the company area extended from one side of the plot to the other.

A tiny chapel stood catty-cornered across the street from the Company Headquarters. Despite the chapel's small capacity, it never filled on the Sundays when I attended. But the battalion PX, which was slightly larger and on the same side of the street, was packed, inside and out, every night except Sundays, when they didn't sell beer. That first Saturday night, I heard the 3.2-percent-beer celebrants at the PX from our dayroom and barracks. Snacks, candies, soft drinks, and cigarettes on Sundays never aroused such jubilation.

The Regimental Headquarters was nearer the camp's main gate and only a short distance from a large service club, which had a cafeteria, snack bar, telephone booths, poolroom, and a lounge-auditorium with a mezzanine level. The movie theater we stopped beside on our arrival was also close to the camp entrance.

Throughout my first weeks at Camp McCain, I explored places in and around the compact regimental and battalion areas. The only other setting for weekly military routines, besides nearby fields and firing ranges, was the Holly Springs National Forest.

On the first afternoon, the company returned from exercises just before retreat. Before Captain Herman Straub dismissed the men, he critiqued the day's problem. The captain was about five feet eight inches tall, with a thick neck, broad shoulders, and bulging, muscular thighs. The executive officer beside him, First Lieutenant Thomas Sundheimer, was taller by almost a head, slender, and well proportioned.

Most members of Second Platoon filing past us ASTPers on the barrack's shallow porch just nodded to us, curious. But Technical Sergeant Howard Muth, the tall brunet leader of my squad, welcomed those joining the platoon. And a slightly older blond, Sergeant Leeds, in the bunk next to me, offered to tell me what I wanted to know about the company. Though other platoon members were not nearly so cordial, none was unpleasant. Some were older and overweight, not nearly as physically fit as we were after basic training at Fort Benning and physical education classes at Ole Miss.

The next morning, a scuffle broke out behind me in the breakfast line.

"What tha' hell do ya think you're doin' . . . hittin' me in the back of the head? I oughta knock the bejeesus outuh ya, ya dingbat!"

I looked back and saw a soldier holding the side of his head, yelling into the oafish grin on the face of a thin, hairy little guy behind him.

The goofy little soldier's arms were held by a soldier who was pleading, "Come on, Landowski . . . forget it. Rufus couldn't help it. Somebody goosed him."

Landowski said, "I'll give the SOB more than a goose if he hits me again."

I learned to stay out of reach of Rufus Boates, a jolly illiterate from the Georgia backwoods who unconsciously said and did odd things. When Rufus was tickled or goosed, he lashed out involuntarily with his gangly legs and arms, striking indiscriminately anyone within range. Platoon mates, amused by his behavior, goosed him at mail call or in the chow line just to see his tornadic action and others' reactions.

In a few weeks, I found that most of the 187 men in Company B had joined when the Ninety-fourth was activated in late-1942 at Camp Phillips, Kansas. At mail call, the names were an international mix, not all Anglo-Saxon—Aliseo, Aronson, Borschnack, Capicotto, Hudzick, Hackmyer. Many were coal miners or their sons and farmer boys. Most were midwesterners from Illinois, Michigan, Missouri, Ohio, and Wisconsin, or northeasterners from New York, New Jersey, and Pennsylvania. Among the few southerners, I was the only "little boy from Little Rock" and the lone Arkansan in the company. Like the other ASTPers, my assignment was as a rifleman (SSN 745).

After bunking with the Second Platoon for a week, the profanity and bad manners of some members disappointed me, although most seemed respectable enough and of average intelligence. Perhaps comparing the old-timers with the young men from Ole Miss wasn't fair. Naturally their behavior and talk were different.

Only one subject seemed common to everyone. I learned in a few weeks more graphic details about sex, real and imagined, than I had in all my previous nineteen years. ASTPers, by contrast, seemed more romantic and less intent on making immediate physical conquests.

At our calisthenics session the next morning, Captain Straub kidded various men and groups during exercises. Though demanding, he had a good sense of humor. Only twenty-six years old, the captain came up through the ranks in the Michigan National Guard before being commissioned. But Lieutenant Sundheimer, his executive officer, was an OCS graduate, more aloof in manner and perhaps slightly older. At least, he seemed more intent on an officer's privileges than the captain, who had already learned our names and something personal about each of us. Being commanded by men with Teutonic forebears and names in a war against Germany seemed to me ironic.

The other commissioned leaders of the three rifle and one heavy weapons platoons were also in their twenties—Anthony Unrein, David Randolph, George Elder, and Sam Perkins. During March and April, I met only Lieutenant Randolph of the Second Platoon, so I didn't learn much about the other officers until I'd been around a while. Randolph, though outgoing and friendly, looked like a businessman in uniform, conveying little sense of command.

First Sergeant Kelly—neat, trim, and erect—personified command. About forty-five years old, five feet nine inches tall, and 145 lean pounds, he was really the professional Army veteran of the whole outfit, who had already served more than twenty years as a Regular. He boxed as a lightweight before the war while stationed in China and Hawaii. Immediately before joining the Ninety-fourth, his outfit was posted to Reykjavik, Iceland, where President Roosevelt sent the

Fifth Infantry Division of the Old Army in the fall of 1941 before the United States entered the war.

When Kelly knew me better, he nostalgically recalled his sexy girlfriend and steam baths in Iceland, without making clear whether they accompanied each other or were separate delights. Kelly, an impatient stickler for protocol, had smooth, pink skin that glowed dark red when someone broke his or the Army's regulations, which didn't always coincide. He frightened me at first, but I soon learned to respect and like him.

Kelly's good friend, in charge of company supplies, was Technical Sergeant Arthur Shocksnyder. From Michigan, like our captain, he looked about the same age as Kelly to my unpracticed eye, but was younger. Obviously an outdoorsman, his low-key manner was right for a companion of our volatile first sergeant. His laid-back attitude and calm assurance belied his nickname, Shock.

A trio of young NCOs managed the company's other administrative duties. I wouldn't cross paths with the company clerk, who was most important to the unit's operation, for several weeks. I watched the mail clerk Technician Fifth Class (T/5) Morris Berry quietly accepting with smiles the razzing that accompanied his daily distribution of letters and parcels. "Mo" didn't fit the stereotype of the flamboyant, loud-mouthed mail clerks so often featured in war movies. He appeared short, square, and heavier than he actually was under his loose-fitting fatigues.

T/5 Arthur Davenport, the third member of the triumvirate, who was restrained in manner like Morris, issued my equipment and new M-1 rifle. Tall, thin, and bespectacled, he resembled a high school English teacher and was the company's "armorer artificer." As Shock's assistant, he ordered, stocked, and issued supplies for the company before we went overseas. Yet I never saw Art repair, assemble, or test a firearm, which his title implied were his duties.

The NCO in charge of the Second Platoon was raw-boned Wilbert Herring, a good old country boy. I wouldn't learn the other side of Herring's personality until we went overseas. The other noncommissioned platoon leaders, whom I seldom encountered, were James Bradley, Robert Gokey, and Nelson Stephenson. The company's head cook was Louis Buschel, whose girth and weight suggested he enjoyed the pantry supplies and his own menus. The NCO I eventually knew best and spent the most time with was Anthony Palma, a buck sergeant in charge of the communications squad in the headquarters platoon. Tony was steady, compulsive, and theatrical.

Although ASTPers were shipped to the Ninety-fourth to bring the division complement to full strength, it was rumored we were sent to raise the division's average IQ enough for it to be sent overseas. Sergeant Leeds said that trained men had twice been stripped from the Ninety-fourth to go to combat divisions heading overseas. After we arrived, a third of our company was ASTPers, but we weren't likely to advance in rank and gain responsible positions because positions in the table of organization (TO), except for nonrated riflemen, were filled when we joined. With so little chance for advancement, it would have been easy to be despondent, but our busy new routine left little time to bemoan our fates.

March and April 1944 were unusually wet months in Mississippi, forcing the Ninety-fourth to conduct many field exercises in rainstorms. The Yalobusha River flooded an area of thirty-five miles around Grenada, a town seven miles north of Camp McCain, and engineering units of the division rescued many citizens from the surging waters. Although Company B was not involved in these rescues, we took the Expert Infantryman tests and maneuvered in rain and shine, across the wooded hills, deep ravines, and muddy trails of the nearby Holly Springs National Forest.

Our company's daily routine was far more physically strenuous than at Ole Miss. Each weekday morning at 0555, we rose at first call before reveille and stood roll-call formation at 0605 in the area between the barracks and latrine. After breakfast, we did housekeeping chores before marching to a nearby drill field for thirty minutes of calisthenics. We would then return to the barracks to change into the uniform and equipment of the day—usually fatigues and a combat pack containing a raincoat, canteen, and entrenching tool—and afterwards march to fields, woods, or ranges.

Older draftees and National Guardsmen already familiar with the various weapons infantrymen had to load, fire, and maintain, needed to practice their skills, but ASTPers had to learn many of them from scratch. To satisfy both groups, the rifle companies assembled at some kind of firing range almost every week. Good luck, excellent eyesight, and steady hands helped me with the weapons fired.

Scoring expert with a carbine and M-1 surprised me, but doing the same with the Browning Automatic Rifle (BAR) was unbelievable. That almost led to my becoming a permanent BAR team member in the Second Platoon, replacing a short soldier who purportedly couldn't carry the weapon without dragging its butt on the ground, particularly over rough terrain and rutted roads. Without further ado, Sergeant Kelly had me lugging that long, clumsy piece down country roads and through the woods. I was convinced my height was really more important than my score; whatever the reason for my assignment, my position on the team seemed settled, much to my regret.

Strangely enough, my stress about becoming an infantryman was relieved. Worry is concern about what *could* happen, and now my assignment to a combat outfit, which I had feared from childhood, was no longer a cause for worry. Ironically, as the long, arduous hours of infantry training narrowed my focus each day, there was less time to think about the future, for the war seem further away. At taps each night, I often fell asleep in the midst of my prayers, too tired to fret about anything.

In late April, while awaiting a turn at the firing range, I heard my name called over a bullhorn. Because individuals' names were rarely singled out, I feared I'd done something wrong. The officer in charge, after returning my salute, faced the T/5 beside him, saying, "This is Harrison" and walked away. The jeep driver had come to take me to Regimental Headquarters. On the way, I feared something had happened to either one of my parents or my brother in the Air Force in England.

The driver led me into an unpartitioned common room at Regimental where all the company clerks sat in rows of desks behind a hip-high rail on either side of a wide center aisle. The driver walked ahead of me to Corporal Howard Davis, who asked me to sit in the chair beside his desk. He said Kelly had chosen me to be assistant company clerk because I typed and was familiar with Army Regulations (ARs). The job involved typing company rosters, payrolls, and correspondence, and keeping enlisted men's records up to date.

Davis was a short, small-boned young man whose pale skin and thin blond hair made his age difficult to determine, but I guessed him to be only a year or two older than I was. He was about as nervous as anyone I'd ever met, but in view of the many details he handled, he was surprisingly soft-spoken and reticent when dealing with soldiers, even the testiest and densest ones. He probably knew more about each of their lives through daily access to personnel records than they could immediately recall themselves.

I was glad to have the job and even happier to contemplate avoiding field problems. Unfortunately, Kelly said my new duties didn't free me; I'd be carrying the BAR if I wasn't needed in the orderly room, or at Regimental. My military occupational specialty (MOS) would remain rifleman, not clerk (SSN 405).

On my first pass, I took the bus to Grenada just down the road from Camp McCain. Along with other ASTPers, I was eager to buy a new overseas cap, decorated with the light blue infantry piping along the edges of its folds and to pin on its front our blue-and-silver regimental crest, bearing the motto "From This Center Liberty Sprang." I also wanted to attach the two brass infantry badges, *US* and crossed rifles, to the lapels of my dress blouse and to sew the black-and-gray division patch on the right sleeve of my uniform. Even though I had been forced to join the "Queen of Battle," I was proud to wear the insignias of my new outfit.

While I was still in the Second Platoon my only assignment to KP gave me an opportunity to observe the patterns at the company mess hall, which fellows who served there regularly claimed were absolute. Anyone who offended the cooks in any way would at the end of the day clean the biggest, nastiest grease trap in the main sink. Others who goofed off in some fashion would scrub the baked-on residue from cooking pots. On the other hand, cans of fruit like plums, with insufficient volume to feed the whole company, were reserved as treats for KPs at breaks or after meals. Sunday-night supper was always cold cuts, braunsweiger and bologna (regularly compared in GI lingo to part of a donkey's anatomy), cheddar cheese, and rye and white bread, accompanied by tomatoes or potato salad.

By this time, Sergeant Palma had heard about my interest in theater and asked me to do impressions on a company show; otherwise, he said, he had only instrumentalists and singers. Tony, whose mother taught at the Goodman Art Institute in Chicago, had the dark complexion and volubility of a southern Italian, and theatrical instincts, which his mother had probably encouraged. We did the show after supper in the mess hall, and the officers joined the enlisted men. A Mexican American, Santo Aliseo, sang Latin songs; the favorite, "Besame Mucho," was requested every time he sang. Alan Kraft, an ASTPer, did a moving interpretation of "Love Letters in the Sand."

Some of my slightly risque jokes got big laughs and would be requested at later shows. Eventually, after telling them repeatedly, I protested, and Tony said, "They love the dialects and embroidering you do relating them." My dialects included cultivated English, Cockney, Irish, and Yiddish, the latter in the mode of Mr. Kitzel who appeared regularly on Jack Benny's radio show.

After my first performance, men from various platoons told me off-color stories, but I refused to use the risque material while performing at the service club. My impressions and patter wouldn't offend women or families visiting husbands, fathers, or brothers. Sometimes, emceeing with a band, I sang sentimental songs like "I'll Be Seeing You" or imitated the lead tenor of the Ink Spots, a popular group who sang

"If I Didn't Care." When I entertained I felt like an individual again instead of an olive-drab cog.

Not long after starting at Regimental, Company B practiced throwing live grenades on a range whose layout was similar to that in basic—a deep trench to throw from and a deeper trench to throw into. Grenadiers waited at a safe distance, angle, and direction away from the detonation pit. Sometimes a soldier would throw a grenade off course and it would fall among waiting soldiers. Albert Hendricks heard the shout "Live grenade!" and picked it up to throw away. Too much time elapsed after the pin was pulled, and the explosion tore off his hand and riddled him with fragments.

When word of the accident reached the orderly room, Kelly had a hard time telling the captain. Hendricks, an ASTPer at Benning and Ole Miss who was always positive and energetic in his attitude and action, received the Soldier's Medal for his heroic act. Apparently, he was discharged because I never saw him again.

Challenging times came to all of us on other firing ranges when we began the Expert Infantryman tests. The Ninety-fourth Division was the first organization in the U.S. Army to seek the newly created award, and we didn't know its purpose or what it would require of us. Near the end of March, in the first phase of Expert Infantryman tests, the company qualified by marching twenty-five miles in seven hours and nineteen minutes.

Before the marksmanship tests, a veteran combat soldier instructing us said combat troops had found firing M-1s from the hip, rather than the standard positions, was more efficient in battle. The instructor said, "Combat shows that the fire power of a squad, moving forward in attack, is more powerful than firing from stationary positions." In a field exercise practicing the new approach, we had clips of live ammunition, lined up ten abreast, and advanced toward the targets firing from the hip. Walking in an open field on the side of a hill, we emptied two eight-cartridge clips firing at plywood silhouettes of enemy soldiers, which popped up at scattered points along the horizon.

Following this exercise, the instructor introduced us to estimating distance and windage for long-range sniper fire, giving special attention to the "degrees of sight deflection necessary to compensate for wind displacement in aiming a rifle." I hit the target three hundred yards away, but I certainly had no ambition to be a sniper.

Sure enough, we fired from the hip in a crucial test for the Expert Infantryman Badge. With our rifles at hip level, we walked along a wooded path firing at targets snapping up ahead or to the sides of us—plywood silhouettes suddenly flashing into view, leaning around trees, rising from behind logs, or standing up in trenches. Targets also noisily snapped up behind us, and to hit them under time restraints, I alternately turned, twisted, and wheeled while walking briskly forward. Operators concealed near the targets scored any hits made, and I struck often enough to pass easily. Firing at targets remained only a game; I didn't think of shooting a living man, so no "enemy" was represented in the sloppily painted silhouettes challenging our marksmanship.

Although other Expert Infantryman tests were tactical in nature and judged on how well a platoon or squad performed, at least one other measured individual skills. They challenged us to "shoot an azimuth" in the dark with a compass to reach a specific numbered stake on the opposite side of a dense woods. (An azimuth is defined as a "horizontal direction expressed as the angular distance between the direction of a fixed point and the direction of the object," whatever that means.)

Referees placed numbered stakes on the far side of a woods and divided the platoon members into pairs. Each pair had a compass, flashlights, and a slip with the azimuth reading and the number of a stake (the fixed point). With the compass, we had to find our way (the direction of the object) to the stake on the opposite side of the woods (the angular distance) and come within a radius of five feet. In addition to the basic challenge, we had to read the compass under a raincoat with flashlights.

Helpless as a baby myself when it came to shooting an azimuth, I discovered my partner was an embryo! So he held the flashlight as I did the readings, and we both crashed about in the deep underbrush hoping to find our way out the other side, even if we missed our numbered stake. The modicum of information we shared about compasses and azimuths sustained our efforts, and Lady Luck guided us near enough to our numbered stick to pass. Many failed, though, and we didn't learn for a few weeks who would qualify overall for the Expert Infantryman Badge.

While we were taking the Infantryman tests, Lieutenants John Decker and Anthony Carbone joined the company as platoon leaders. The addition of these new officers and other quiet changes in the company taking place every day suggested that something important was afoot.

On April 24, Colonel Hagerty awarded Expert Infantryman's Badges to the 958 men in the 301st who had qualified. On May 9, 1944, General Order 236 awarded Expert Infantryman Badges to 35 officers, NCOs, and enlisted men of Company B who "successfully completed certain prescribed training and tests, conducted by boards of officers." I was proud to have succeeded.

Nearly a month later, on May 26, after the division was alerted to overseas duty and I was assistant company clerk, the Under-Secretary of War Robert P. Patterson visited Camp McCain to honor the Ninety-fourth as the first Expert Infantryman division in the U.S. Army. Celebrating the occasion, all three regiments of the division—the 301st (last to qualify), 302nd, and 376th—assembled on a hot morning, preparing to parade in full military regalia in the afternoon for General Malony, Secretary Patterson, and Major General Richard C. Moore, who represented the Office of the Combined Chiefs of Staff.

The scorching air, swirling with dust and flags, and the resounding drums and bugles lent real excitement to the occasion. A few soldiers standing at attention for such an extended period locked their knees, cutting off circulation, and fainted. When they sank into the dust beside you, it was difficult not to break ranks to help them. After the Under-Secretary's formal presentation awards to General Malony, all division units paraded past the official party assembled on the reviewing stand.

As if the parade were not sufficient recognition of the occasion, General Malony ordered a special nighttime military exercise on May 27. The First Battalion of the 301st took part in a regimental firing demonstration, staging a dawn attack by infantry troops supported by artillery. After the briefest reprieve, Sergeant Kelly had me rejoin the Second Platoon to carry a BAR on the sweltering afternoon that lapsed into a stormy night. I lugged the awkward, heavy weapon on a cross-country march we took along muddy, rutted back roads under torrential downpours and spectacular lightning that never let up. We saw the road only in electric flashes and heard each other only between thunder rolls.

Before dawn, the exercise ended without our having any sense of accomplishment. We marched to an assembly point and rode back to the company area. How the Under-Secretary watched military tactics in the rain on a moonless night was beyond me. The only pleasure I drew from the event was an additional five dollars a month added to my pay for qualifying for the Expert Infantryman Badge. After that night, although I was never totally free from infantry training, I spent less time on day-to-day exercises and went out on only longer field problems until we left Camp McCain.

Many Second Platoon members spent a lot of words guessing what our combat assignment would be before the War Department officially alerted our division, on May 5, 1944, to prepare for overseas duty. The preparations for overseas movement (POM) brought additional training rules that required a minimum of forty-eight hours of instruction per unit each week, quadrupling the paperwork at Regimental and Company Headquarters. Keeping each enlisted man's records up to date was so essential that Captain Straub assigned me assistant clerk permanently and transferred me to the headquarters platoon, removing me from the BAR team and KP duty.

I moved out of Second Platoon with few regrets, carrying my belongings to the headquarters barracks. For a change, my bunk was a single with no second tier overhead. Although the soldier on one side of me was very quiet, almost bashful the first few days, he gradually got beyond his laconic one-line answers to my questions. I wouldn't have guessed that Joe Boguski was from Plainfield, New Jersey, because his dialect didn't include the stereotypical "dese and dose." About my height, weight, and age, he was my close buddy within a few days.

Since the Ninety-fourth had been activated and in training so long, I asked Sergeant Kelly why the division hadn't already gone overseas. He explained that a hundred men from each battalion were transferred to the Eighth Infantry Division in November 1943 and weren't replaced until ASTPers filled their positions. The Ninety-fourth had always expected an overseas assignment but hadn't received one until we arrived.

Soon after the division alert, Tony organized another variety show, only this one was performed at the 301st Regimental Service Club. By a happy coincidence, Adam Robinson was there. We hadn't seen each other since joining different units, when Robbie went into a heavy-weapons platoon in the 301st. As we brought each other up to date, he let me know he was trying to transfer but promised to see me again now that we'd found each other. In the middle of July, Robbie sent a letter saying he was happily driving a jeep for a field artillery unit at Camp Bowie, Texas.

When I wasn't involved on weekends in shows or rehearsals, Boguski and I went to Grenada on Saturday afternoons and evenings. Although beef steaks were too costly in the little town, we ate dinner at a cafe on a corner of the main street where the meat was so good we didn't mind the expense. That's about all I ever spent money on anyway. After leisurely meals, we sometimes went to the USO for a soft drink and a game of checkers or dominoes. Young hostesses there served us coffee and iced tea, chatting politely as they drew out every vowel of their Mississippi dialects. On a few weekends, Joe and I stripped to our shorts and lay on a shelter-half between the barracks to get a tan, violating the division rule against sunbathing.

Meanwhile, Howard Davis patiently taught me the rudiments of company clerking, not only to replace him on his long-awaited furlough but to guarantee he wouldn't have to redo everything upon his return.

Working beside Howard placed me in contact with several NCOs who were "characters." Company A clerk Joe Hughey, who sat on Davis's right, was from Wichita, Kansas. Joe looked very much like Mick Jagger—thin and reptilian, with sunken cheeks and prominent lips and teeth. As we labored at our typewriters and files, his chain smoking wreathed us in dense clouds; clerks had ashtrays and could smoke as they wished without taking outdoor breaks.

Other than compulsive puffing, Joe's behavior seemed ordinary compared to one sergeant major. Broad-shouldered, muscular, and manly-looking, the sergeant had a badly pockmarked face, crowned with a thick, bristly crew cut. But his personality didn't match his tough physical appearance. He walked and talked in an effeminate manner yet dominated, roaming like a caged lion, rarely sitting, administering with his large, hairy fist in a suede glove. His efficiency insulated him from adverse comments.

The record I worked with was the most significant one for each soldier, DA Form 20—a white, pocket-size booklet containing the official details of a GI's military experience. The booklet had to be complete and accurate and listed birth date, birthplace, hometown, permanent address, names of parents or spouse, former civilian employment, AGCT score and ratings on other exams, Army schools attended and qualifying test scores, assignments, promotions, reductions, decorations, physical disabilities, and relevant personal facts or exceptions. Oddly, for an infantry outfit, the most frequent physical disability noted was *pes planus,* Latin for flat feet.

The DA Form 20 was kept in the soldier's 201 File (personnel file). Davis had screened the 201 Files, searching for a soldier in Company

B who typed and was familiar with Army Regulations before summoning me to Regimental Headquarters.

Keeping up-to-date entries in 167 Form 20s was an endless task under ordinary conditions, but our rapidly approaching overseas assignment made timely and complete entries more essential. I assumed that responsibility to free Davis to handle more pressing daily clerical assignments. Until I worked with Form 20s, I didn't know the Army accepted illiterate and non-English-speaking enlisted men; there were a few of each in Company B. Among the many foreign-born and first-generation Italians, Germans, and Poles in the regiment were even a few noncitizens. One soldier in our company changed his name from a Polish to an Anglo-Saxon one for easier pronunciation. Another received his citizenship papers just before he was transferred out.

Among the Army's clerical absurdities, which Howard explained, was adding three capital letters *N M I* between a soldier's first and last names if he had no middle name or initial. Another peculiar policy required special care preparing payroll rosters because erasures, strike-overs, and changes in ink color were not acceptable. In addition, perfectly spelled first names, middle initials, and last names had to be typed within designated spaces without touching the printed lines enclosing them.

As Howard's assistant, I stood beside him on the first payday after I became a clerk because when "the eagle flew" the company clerk sat next to the executive officer, supervising each soldier as he signed the payroll. The clerk ensured that each man signed his name precisely as it was spelled on the payroll sheet without touching the enclosing lines. Several illiterate soldiers in the company who could make only an *X* had to avoid touching the lines too. Any slip by a signatory meant redlining the name immediately and withholding the soldier's pay. The clerk submitted the offender's name on a supplementary payroll paid two weeks later.

Davis and Kelly said one of my duties overseas would be carrying documents such as insurance papers and allotment forms that required signatures to soldiers on the front lines. My regular duties, besides guarding the command post (CP) and being a runner for Straub and Kelly, would be operating a radio or switchboard, keeping in touch with platoons and observation posts (OPs), and laying communication lines in emergencies.

After becoming assistant company clerk, I was promoted to private first class (PFC), an attainment similar to advancing from a tenderfoot to a second-class Boy Scout, but I appreciated the extra five dollars a month in pay.

After I moved to Camp McCain, Tumpy's mother responded to my letter asking permission to be formally engaged to Tumpy. She wrote in behalf of herself and Tumpy's father, Colonel Lee C. Gammill, a property procurement officer in the Army Medical Corps, who was out of the country:

Your letter and one from Tumpy came in the same mail. Fortunately Mr. Gammill was in town and we could talk things over. As both of you seemed to have a sensible view of things, although very much in love, you have our consent to your engagement. This of course is with the understanding that there will be no sudden marriage due to overseas duty or separation.

I think you both very fine and good to want your parents' advice and consent. Your letter made us feel much closer to you. And I am sure now that Tump's Daddy knows why she thinks you so completely O.K.

After receiving Tumpy's parents' approval, I wrote Mom and Dad about our long-held secret commitment.

An interesting chore I handled as assistant company clerk was showing the Army's 16-mm black-and-white training films on military tactics and venereal disease. I picked up the film, projector, and screen at Regimental Headquarters and set them up in the mess hall. At the showing, the company sat on benches and tops of tables facing the screen, which was at the opposite end of the mess hall from the steam tables. All the films about warfare, including the series *Why We Fight*, produced by Hollywood director Frank Capra, combined instruction and propaganda. Sometimes, cartoons featuring the GI goof-off Private Snafu were included as they were with commercial Hollywood films at the post theaters.

Several times, I showed British military training films that were not only funny but crucially informative, for they treated serious topics—avoiding decapitation while riding in jeeps or steering clear of booby traps—in a mixture of wit and slapstick like black comedies. From beginning to end, the story and character values of British films held the attention of the usually bored soldiers, despite their prejudicial slurs about "Limeys." I recall a film about booby traps in which a British Tommy casually sat on a commode to answer nature's call, finished, pulled the chain of an overhead water tank, and was blown to bits. The compelling lesson: in even simple activities, a good soldier must remain alert to the violent potential of an absent enemy.

The "short-arm" examination came once a month, before or after the films about venereal disease. This demeaning exercise meant taking off all our clothing in the barracks, putting on raincoats, and crossing the company area in hot or cold weather to wait in line outside the dayroom before filing in to be examined for signs of VD. Each soldier stopped in front of a seated medical corpsman, facetiously called the "pecker checker," opened his raincoat, and displayed his genitals.

The black-and-white VD films shown aimed at not only discouraging promiscuous sex but teaching the proper use of condoms for safe sex and visits to prophylactic stations for those with little willpower. Usually, soldiers watching VD films found a lot to laugh at in the on-screen situation, bad acting, or embarrassing reminders of their own behavior. Whatever their reasons, laughter and obscene comments greeted all the films—before, during, and after.

One time I showed a film that stimulated a distinctly more serious response. When I snapped the projector on, the company cheered and applauded the Technicolor pictures flashing across the screen. But a few minutes into the film, the narrator's comments and the vividly colored images of syphilis and gonorrhea on the genitals of both men and women made clear the movie was different. Regimental had mistakenly given me a film meant for medical personnel.

The Technicolor sores and lesions on labia, vagina, and penis were stunning to see, and the physical deteriorations shown in the latter stages of the diseases were nauseating. Astonished reactions soon became sounds of disgust, with a few soldiers swearing half seriously to give up sex altogether. At the end of the thirty-minute film, the mess hall was silent; only the whir of film rewinding was heard as the men filed out. I decided the Army should stop kidding around with black-and-white fictional drama and show instead only nonfictional venereal infections in color.

Near the beginning of June, the 301st began a series of four-day field problems. For the first, they transported us in trucks to the Holly Springs National Forest at midafternoon, where we settled along the edge of a clearing in the woods to dig our foxholes. Digging under the large trees, we found the ground so hard and rocky that we shed our fatigue tops and undershirts to keep from sweating them through. The Ninety-fourth command didn't approve baring yourself from the waist up, risking a sunburn, but none of us was concerned because we were working in the shade.

When the sergeant came back and found us with our tops off, he gave us holy hell before ordering us to put them back on and finish our foxholes. At sunset, the temperature dropped while we were waiting for the cooks to bring our chow, chilling us in our wet fatigues. The mobile kitchen with our hot supper arrived after dark, and the cooks served us under the glare of lanterns and truck headlights, which hardly simulated combat conditions. After dark, I was expecting an uncomfortable night because we had carried only a raincoat and a single blanket in our combat packs. On guard, I played an Indian and wrapped my blanket around my shoulders.

To our relief, clear skies and bright sunshine waked and warmed us early the next morning before the cooks brought hot breakfast in insulated containers. But a careless KP doused both the steaming oatmeal and crisp pancakes with watery, artificially-flavored maple syrup. Then, after eating and dipping our mess gears in a GI-can full of scalding water, we readied ourselves for the day's combat exercise.

But the sergeant merely ordered us to fill the foxholes we had dug so laboriously the afternoon before and march to another position to dig another hole.

On the remaining days of the field problem, we set up other command posts, repeating the same procedure—dig a while, fill a while, move. No officer or NCO explained our overall military objective, a circumstance repeated on almost all our later field exercises. After the problem ended, we returned to camp, cleaned our rifles, and deposited them in racks at the supply room. I went to Regimental Headquarters to work on personnel files.

At first call, before reveille on the following Tuesday, June 6, the CQ replaced the usual obscenity "Drop your cocks and grab your socks!" with a shout, "The Allies have invaded Europe!"

Someone switched on a radio for the news: "Supreme Headquarters Allied Expeditionary Force has just announced that the invasion has begun."

No one cheered. We sat in silence on the edges of our bunks slipping into our socks and brogans and lacing up our leggings, without saying what we felt. I was relieved because I had feared the Ninety-fourth would reach Europe in time for us to be part of the inevitable invasion. Still, hearing the news of D-Day reminded me of our division's future: war was coming closer.

In spite of D-Day news, our company observed its usual daily routine. The only difference was listening to news of the invasion's progress on the radio every time we were in the barracks or dayroom.

We heard the general communique issued by the Supreme Headquarters of the Allied Expeditionary Forces (SHAEF): "Under the command of General Eisenhower, Allied naval forces, supported by strong air forces, began landing Allied armies this morning on the northern coast of France."

And later, we heard a recording of Eisenhower reading his own order of the day to the troops on transports before they attacked the beaches. We heard bits and pieces of radio reports, principally from Edward R. Murrow on CBS, and a few commentators on other networks, but I don't remember any reporter in the first waves of troops broadcasting from the beaches.

The third weekend in June, I wangled a three-day pass to spend a few hours at Little Rock. I'd be taking a chance with the military police (MPs) since my hometown was beyond the seventy-five-mile circumference officially permitted on short passes. On Friday, as soon after lunch as I could leave, I took a bus from the camp gate to Memphis, where Dad picked me up at the station at 2200 for the 140-mile drive home. On the way, I complained about a wart on the first joint of the middle finger of my left hand that had grown so large and painful it interfered with firing a rifle and typing. Dad offered his sympathy but didn't say much else. We reached Little Rock at 0230.

Before I got up the next morning, Dad had phoned several doctors trying to find one who would be in his office on Saturday. Only Dr. Rinehart, an X-ray specialist in the Donaghey Building, said he would remove the wart if I came to his office right away. His willingness to see me on Saturday morning was in the spirit of "anything for our boys in uniform" adopted by many civilians on the home front. Dr. Rinehart cut the large wart off with a scalpel and cauterized it with an electric needle, advising me to keep the wound covered until it healed.

Visiting Mother and Dad and eating my favorite dishes was great, but I missed seeing Tumpy, who couldn't skip classes. And Fayetteville was too far away for me to go there on a pass. In fact, the distance from Camp McCain to Little Rock forced me to leave early Sunday afternoon on a Rock Island train from the North Little Rock station, in time to catch a bus in Memphis that would get me back to camp before bed check. I had never been to the Rock Island Station, though my Uncle Roy Bunch worked as an engineer on the line. My folks drove me there, across from the Southern Cotton Seed and Oil Company, where the cottonseed processing always filled the air with an aroma like baked ham.

At reveille one Monday morning near the end of June, Sergeant Kelly ordered us to prepare all our uniforms and equipment for an inspection by company officers the next day. Such a checkup was a routine step in preparing for the division's shipment overseas. Officers would identify unserviceable garments and equipment—fatigues with holes, frayed web belts, or dented mess kits and canteens—which needed to be replaced. Kelly notified us of the inspection a full day ahead because dirty uniforms, even though they might be discarded, had to be washed before the inspection.

Kelly's orders led our company's prophets to predict we'd be leaving very soon for Fort Hamilton, New York. Really, the only sensible assumption was that the division was headed to Europe because Mississippi is too far from the Pacific Ocean to take us in that direction.

We washed dirty clothes throughout the remainder of that day and night whenever we had free time, bellyaching because Kelly ordered us "to shed everything that's not GI" (government issue). Within the week, I boxed and sent home the extra olive-drab shorts, T-shirts, socks, and dress shirts that my folks had given me over the eleven months I'd been in the Army. I hated losing an olive-green, single-piece jumpsuit that had been my costume in an acting game I sometimes played when off duty.

The jumpsuit, similar to a fatigue uniform authorized for officers only, made my serendipitously discovered game possible. Wearing the suit, I was returning to the company area from Regimental Headquarters one night when several passing soldiers saluted me. I returned the salutes, wondering why they'd taken me for an officer. Later my reflection in the latrine mirror explained it. In the dark, the epaulets on my shoulders resembled those on an officer's uniform, and the diagonal silver stripe across the blue regimental shield on my overseas cap looked like a metallic bar of rank. My uniform fooled other soldiers on other nights, inspiring me to wear the jumpsuit after dark to enjoy the power of an officer's image.

The company went on another four-day field problem at the end of June without any explanation of its objectives, so I assumed the activities were aimed at building our physical endurance. The full company, including the cooks and kitchen equipment, was transported by truck to a rather distant, wooded bivouac area where we set up a command post and defensive perimeter, and spent the night in pup tents. Because of the high temperature and humidity, company medics distributed salt tablets to help us avoid heat exhaustion.

The next day's exercises truly tested our physical and mental mettle. Over a period of twenty-two straight hours, our company marched forty-five miles, with only the usual ten-minute breaks every hour. The day-into-night march began under a scorching sun and extended into a moonless night, along the dusty back roads and trails of Holly Springs National Forest.

I actually fell asleep while walking. When the sergeant ordered us to fall out for a break, I responded automatically, dropping to the ground. The fall waked me as if I were coming out of a dream in the middle of the night. I wasn't sure where I was, where I'd been, or what I was doing; it was just as if I had been lying in a deep sleep.

The sergeant mumbled, "Fall out . . . Smoke 'em, if you've got 'em." While most guys lit up and smoked, I lay there wondering how long I had actually been asleep on my feet.

Our march continued, but I remained awake the rest of the night, in a kind of stupor, until the sun arose. Our exertions, the excessive humidity, and the salt tablets made some men sick to their stomachs. The ten-minute rest stops every fifty minutes, on such an extended march, didn't allow us sufficient time to recover. My stomach wasn't upset, but my feet and legs pained me the longer we marched.

In the dim light of dawn, we looked like a band of ghosts, for sweating constantly had crusted our green fatigues white with salt. At the end, we were allowed a mere two hours of sleep in a shady copse to recuperate from the ordeal. I thought my own extreme weariness came not only from the heat but from not having sufficient physical exercise because I was at Regimental Headquarters so much of the time. To acclimate to Mississippi heat, I needed to be outside with the company every day.

I felt so depleted that I wondered what I could do, without losing face, to avoid marching any farther. I decided to volunteer for KP, assuming if I could hitch a ride on a kitchen truck I'd soon be okay. I hesitated to ask at first, afraid of refusal. But after marching farther under the sun, I went to the mess sergeant, Lou, asking if I could do KP for the rest of the time we were in the field. He welcomed my help if Captain Straub okayed it. Full of apprehension, I approached the captain, who was easily convinced by my salty fatigues and bloodshot eyes.

After breakfast the next morning, I helped the cooks load the kitchen trucks that were parked in a grove on top of a steep hill. With everything in place, I climbed atop one of the large cast-iron field cookstoves. Because there was no road, the driver started down the hillside, underestimating the steepness of its grade. The truck teetered so precariously that the cooks walking beside it grabbed the railings to add their weight to level the vehicle. I inched across the stove tops to the high side too.

Staring down the hill, the irony struck me: I had volunteered for KP to escape the pain and exhaustion of marching, and the payoff might be injury or worse. I had never before fully appreciated our cooks' bodily bulk, but with their weight to balance the truck, the stoves and I survived to work another day. And did I slave! Cleaning vegetables, serving mess kits, washing pots and pans, and scrubbing stove tops, I was busy into the night, long after rifle platoons bedded down. I vowed not to risk my life or delay my rest by volunteering for KP on future field problems.

The night after we returned to camp, I was writing to Mom and Dad in the dayroom when the CQ told me I could take a long-distance call in the orderly room. My folks were on the line asking me to get another weekend pass. Dad had already applied and received stamps for extra gas to meet me at Memphis. Relieved that they had called long-distance with happy news and not an emergency, I promised I'd try, even though corps-area physical tests for our company began the next day and there seemed little chance of getting away.

But Mississippi's hot weather forced a change in Regimental orders. The extreme daytime heat had convinced the commander that exercises should be scheduled for early morning hours to prevent heat exhaustion. So at 0300, we hiked four miles in fifty minutes and followed that by doing the proper number of push-ups and burpees to pass the tests. After that, we ran 100 yards to pick up another soldier and carried him piggy-back fifty yards.

Despite the early hour and high humidity, our entire company did well. When we returned to the company area, the captain announced our showing was so good that he was approving three-day passes for half the company on each of the next two weekends. By that time, I had a letter from Mom telling me Tumpy would be coming to Little Rock, if my pass were approved. Sergeant Kelly promised me one the next weekend, and I phoned the folks the good news.

From the time I first joined the Army, I had burned with a young man's need to please and to be liked by everyone. My sentiments and patriotism made me want to be a good soldier, and I had no urge to complain out loud about other people or the Army's hardships. But that didn't mean that I didn't have opinions about the routines and behavior of others in the company. Four months in two different platoons as a rifleman and assistant clerk had acquainted me with almost every man.

One older fellow in Second Platoon told me more about himself than I wanted to know. Thirty-year-old Jim Moran was overweight and often stayed on base on weekends drinking Cuba Libres, a mix of rum and Coke. While I was in the platoon, Jim made me his unwilling confidant. Maybe he needed a new ear to bend because other platoon members had stopped listening to his drunken, maudlin stories. If he saw me in the barracks or dayroom reading or writing a letter, he sat down to describe his marital problems. If I couldn't think of an excuse to escape, he told me gross details about his wife dating other men back home and his retaliation through sexual forays in Holly Springs when he had the money to go. Why did he pick a virgin with an adolescent moral code as his confessor? To me, good and bad, right and wrong were clearly delineated. I must have covered my disgust and disapproval pretty well because he persistently unloaded on me.

Private Alberto Anastasia, an Italian American from Brooklyn, spoke only broken English. Sometimes, when Anastasia was lonesome for his family, he took off for home without permission or pleaded for and won a hardship furlough to tend to what he insisted were family difficulties. It was my impression that no one really cared if Anastasia were absent, but regulations required Kelly to have him picked up if he hadn't returned when his furlough ended.

Kelly usually sent either Sergeant Muth of Second Platoon or Palma from Headquarters on temporary duty (TDY) to bring Anastasia back. Palma said Anastasia would greet him from a seat on his front porch in Brooklyn and invite him to share family meals as if Palma were paying a social visit, for he had no sense of doing anything wrong. No one felt that Anastasia had committed a serious criminal act by not coming back; he simply didn't know enough English to understand how to observe Army regulations, so, unlike other AWOLs, he wasn't handcuffed.

Several men in the company were in the Regular Army. The Regulars were professionals and in the U.S. Army (USA), while draftees were in the Army of the U.S. (AUS). The distinction made little difference in how men were treated, although Kelly was especially impatient when Regulars fouled up or failed to follow the Army's standard operational procedures.

The behavior of two Regulars in our company was extremely "irregular." Lemuel Slate, a stubby, rotund PFC, was our bugler, even though a modern infantry company rarely needs such services because recorded bugle calls of reveille, retreat, and taps were played over the battalion PA system. Nevertheless, Slate's carrying an olive-drab plastic bugle illustrated how a few Old Army traditions persisted. Slate's uselessness as a bugler wasn't his fault, but his clever strategies for dodging other duties were. A chronic complainer, he made sarcastic remarks about those who worked their details without complaint. Smirking and sardonic, Slate was the most feckless and annoying person in headquarters platoon.

Slate's opposite in manner and style was another Regular, Ray J. LaFrenier, who pronounced his name, "Ray-Jay Lah-fren-ee-ay," putting equal emphasis on each syllable. A curly-haired brunet from the Louisiana bayous, at times too silly for a grown man, he was good-natured and friendly with everyone. When off-duty, his tousled hair matched his rumpled clothing—ragged denim or khaki cut-off shorts and a dress shirt without the collar and sleeves, his style before later generations of college students adopted it. Ray J. often suffered company punishment for some minor misdeed, by being limited to the company area or given extra menial duty. He had spent ten years in the Army as a private, playing the fool to avoid serious responsibility.

Sergeant Bill Leeds, a volunteer from Indiana, joined the Ninety-fourth at Camp Phillips. A good-looking married man, he was thoroughly professional, keeping himself, his uniform, and his equipment immaculate. As a squad sergeant in Second Platoon, he was smarter, more mature, and more ambitious than many outranking him. I thought he had only one minor eccentricity: parting his hair in the middle, 1920s style.

Entries in Leed's Form 20 showed that he had attended special schools and excelled in technical areas. As the company safety officer, he instructed us in how to protect ourselves in poison-gas attacks. The platoons, one at a time, entered a barracks with sealed windows and doors to smell samples of poison gas. Leeds demonstrated how to put on our masks, ensure a tight seal around the sides of our heads, and clear the fog inside the goggles. Then we donned our masks for brief periods of exposure to the different poison gasses.

Leed's bunk mate, Private Hines, was a different sort. With so many talkative members in Second Platoon, the small, extremely quiet Hines was easy to miss. Unlike the others, he never used ribald language or told nasty stories, which were common practices in the barracks. Frequently, his eyes appeared on the verge of tears and his hands were held in position to pray. I hadn't noticed his religiosity or his habit of thumbing a Holy Bible until the division was warned about going overseas.

Hines grew obsessive about his Bible reading after that, praying silently on his knees beside his bunk at night. After I left Second Platoon, as our overseas departure neared, Hines withdrew from others as his barracks mates drew nearer to each other. His behavior was distracting. Most of us didn't want to fight and prayed nightly for our future safety, but we tried not to show our fear and kept our thoughts to ourselves.

During our preparations for overseas movement, the more obvious illiterates, ne'er-do-wells, eight balls, and sad sacks were quietly transferred out of the division. After Davis and I completed their transfer orders, they just disappeared. Until they began leaving the company, I never thought about having to depend on them in combat. I don't think we could have trusted our lives to any of them.

On the positive side, POM brought furloughs for all company members. My ten-day furlough made it possible to see my parents and my sweetheart, separately and together. I spent two full days with Mom and Dad before taking a bus to Fayetteville to visit Tumpy. Mother prepared my favorite dishes and introduced me to the new roomers. Dad and I talked about Army life, speculating on where our division was likely to be sent. He kept comparing my infantry experience with my brother's in the Air Force in England. My parents were worried about his safety because he was overseas and a ground crewman in a troop carrier squadron in the Eighth Air Force. I didn't tell them that as an infantryman in combat I would be in more danger every hour.

After two days at home, my folks and I had little to talk about, and the awkward silences became more frequent. Even so, Mom seemed restive when I left the house to visit my old friends who were still at home. Since she stayed beside me almost continuously, I was not only excited but relieved to set out on a bus for Fayetteville.

The longer part of the trip on the crowded coach was uneventful. I was the only soldier aboard, and the other passengers asked where I was from, what military outfit I was in, and what the blue-and-silver Expert Infantryman's Badge on my chest represented. But once their curiosity was satisfied, they eagerly told stories about their relatives in the services.

At Mulberry, a small town two-thirds of the way to Fayetteville, a stringy-haired mountain woman boarded the bus with a dirty toddler. She sat on the bench behind the driver, and her little girl squatted in front of her in the aisle, getting her hands and dress dirtier. When the girl tired of scrounging on the floor and staring at passengers at the front, she stumbled up the aisle, keeping her balance by putting her hands on the knees and thighs of people beside the aisle.

When she laid her grimy hands on the knee of my only clean dress uniform for the two-day visit with Tumpy, I pulled my leg back, grabbing her hands and saying, "Don't put your dirty hands on my clean uniform. Go on back to your mother!"

Although her mother heard me, she didn't retrieve her daughter. Instead she told the passengers in the seat facing her how mean I was to her little girl. Perhaps I did speak too gruffly because the passengers near the mother seemed to take her side. No one spoke to me again.

After the little girl stared up at me and wandered away, I thought the episode was over. But the mother kept mumbling about what I said and did until we stopped at the Busy Bee Cafe at Alma. As the bus braked to a stop, the woman grabbed the girl, got off first, and complained to the proprietor of the station. As I went into the toilet, she was telling him I'd picked on her daughter. When I came out, she was talking to the customers. My uniform and our quick departure may have prevented trouble.

Tumpy was staying that summer with sorority sisters at the Pi Beta

Phi Annex. Although she had promised to find a room for me at Fayetteville, she hadn't written where I'd be sleeping. Fortunately, she told Glynn Roberts, a Delta Kappa brother, about my visit, and he arranged a room in the middle of the campus at the home of the dean of Engineering, where he rented. Glynn had been deferred for a disability and was enrolled in engineering. The window of my room next to his on the second floor overlooked the roof of the front porch and Maple Street. I joined Glynn for breakfast at the Dickson Street boardinghouse, where he had a meal ticket.

Without a car, Tumpy and I walked downtown from the campus to visit stores on the streets encircling the post office, which was in the center of the Fayetteville square. For lunch, we ate the blue-plate special at the Dutch Mill Cafe, just off the square. Afterwards, we strolled back up the hill on Dickson Street to lie in the sun on the lawn of the campus in front of Old Main. We talked until suppertime, when Tumpy ate with the Pi Phis and I joined Glynn at the boardinghouse. That evening, we sat very close on the steps of the agriculture building, visiting until it was time to return to the Pi Phi annex for date call.

The next day, Tumpy skipped classes to guide me around campus, introducing me to sorority sisters and friends attending summer school. Seeing where she lived and met her classes on the sprawling campus would help me picture her after we parted. Both of us, after our long separation and brief visits in Oxford and Little Rock, cherished being completely alone and were reluctant to say good night outside the annex when date call came.

My happy visit in Fayetteville ended too soon, but Tumpy lengthened our time together by riding to Little Rock to spend Sunday. We went to the Second Baptist Church with Mother, and she introduced us to her friends and the new pastor before taking us home for a fried chicken dinner. I saw Tumpy off at the bus station that afternoon, wondering whether I would ever see her again.

On July 23, a few days after I got back to Camp McCain, the units of the Ninety-fourth were ordered to Camp Shanks, New Jersey, our port of embarkation. Our new mailing address was Co. B, 301st Inf. APO 94, c/o Postmaster, New York, N.Y. Its ambiguity, I supposed, concealed our destination in Europe. We were on our way at last, yet too soon for me.

Army Transient

The *Queen Elizabeth* and Wiltshire, England

July 25–September 3, 1944

For five days, troop trains pulled out of Camp McCain on the way to New York State. Company B departed on a train pulled by a coal-burning locomotive in the late afternoon of the second day. We were crammed into the stiff, hard, upright bench seats of ancient chair cars, probably abandoned before the war began. Surrounded by our bulging duffels stuffed into the overhead storage racks and between the seats, we hardly had room to lie down or stretch out.

The train had no air conditioning, so we pulled up the windows for fresh air, only to catch coal cinders in our eyes and feel the sting of sulfuric smoke in our noses! We kept the windows open anyway. During the days and nights of our confinement, there was little to do other than lie in our seats or on the floor, lolling and napping, playing cards and gambling, reading and rumor mongering, arguing and complaining. Throughout the journey, some platoon members lay like lizards on rocks in the sun while others leaped around like Mexican jumping beans.

I preferred to study the landscapes of states that I had previously known only as colored shapes and names on maps in geography classes, as I had traveled outside Arkansas very few times. The only states I had seen firsthand were crossed on a family trip to Denver, Colorado, when I was five years old. Now, sitting next to a window most of the time, I watched the countryside as the troop train crossed portions of Tennessee, Kentucky, Virginia, Maryland, Pennsylvania, and New Jersey.

Although the states had beautiful fields, woods, and hills, sights along the route were often marred by unpainted farmhouses, their yards and fields overgrown with weeds and filled with piles of trash and rusty farm machines. Even the railroad right-of-way was littered with debris beside and between the cross ties and tracks along the gravel bed.

The ugliest landscapes were in the outskirts of the larger cities, where factory stacks spewed black smoke over the partially ruined shacks scattered in weed-covered fields and smoldering garbage dumps were heaped high. Parked on many railroad sidings inside the sooty mazes of larger rail yards were dilapidated freight cars. But shiny Cadillacs stood beside several poorly tended shacks in Pennsylvania and New Jersey. And steaming between Washington and Philadelphia, the close proximity of northeastern cities to each other surprised me.

Along our route to the Northeast, the train made long and short stops at major cities in stations and on sidings. In the larger stations, some guys invariably got off to buy cigarettes, candy, or newspapers, despite being ordered not to leave the train. When we waited on sidings in the early mornings so our troop train fit into the regular schedules of civilian trains, I saw black and white female railroad cleanup crews carrying away trash and lugging wash buckets and brooms between the parked coaches and sleeping cars. I hadn't known that women had worked on railroad crews since the United States entered the war. It hadn't been considered "woman's work" before the war.

Company B arrived at Camp Shanks, on July 26, two days after leaving Mississippi, but five days elapsed before all the division's units reached the camp. The final preparations for our departure began the next day, moving at breakneck speed. We had little free time between receiving additional inoculations, listening to more lectures, and grudgingly laying out uniforms and equipment several times a day for inspections, but boredom came easy because we were just waiting to get on a ship.

The Army's serious concern about poison-gas attacks by the Germans became clear when they saddled us with the least appealing piece of equipment ever issued in the infantry. Besides a gas mask, the quartermaster supply thrust upon each of us a suit of stiff, chemically-impregnated fatigues to protect us, which lent a repulsively sour smell to all the garments in our duffel bags. But the best new equipment had no scent and more practical value—an aluminum field stove for each squad leader to brew coffee and prepare meals. Its cylindrical storage canister also served as a cooking pot.

The most incongruous pieces of equipment issued were for recreation. A few men in each platoon received various types of athletic equipment—softballs, bats, basketballs, footballs, and rubber horseshoes with stakes. Strangely, with our prospective combat role, no one else thought their distribution odd.

I alone in our company was given a record player and a dozen recordings. The Victory-Discs were collections produced by the War Department for the exclusive use of the armed services. The recordings in volume one, which I received, featured Benny Goodman's orchestra. My preference would have been Glenn Miller, whose music scored movies like *Orchestra Wives* and *Sun Valley Serenade,* which Tumpy and I saw together before I was drafted.

Shortly before sailing, our squad visited New York City on twelve-hour passes. Boguski, to my disappointment, headed home to Plainfield to see his parents one last time before going overseas. But my other pals and I crossed the Hudson River on the ferry and stood on the windy deck all the way from the Jersey shore watching New York's skyline growing taller as we drew closer. I had always wanted to visit New York City because I believed Broadway and show business were my future. Sightseeing a few hours before sailing to fight in Europe was hardly what I had in mind.

Each guy in our group had different places in the big city he wanted to see so we agreed at the start to head to Forty-second Street and Times Square. On the way, we muddled through the caverns of tall buildings like typical small-town tourists, looking up, stretching our necks, our mouths agape. After roaming up and down streets without finding the special places we had heard about, we decided to ride up 102 stories on the elevator to the top of the Empire State Building, where we could check for our points of interest from the observation platform. Up there, we located the Chrysler Building, Rockefeller Center, and Radio City Music Hall easily, but back on the ground we couldn't keep our directions straight. A policeman helped but warned us to stay away from Central Park "because it's a dangerous place for soldiers."

After more aimless strolling, gawking at the displays in the windows of famous department stores, we found 99 Park Avenue, where theater tickets were on sale at bargain rates to GIs. But we had stumbled on the booth so late that no tickets were available for shows any of us wanted to see. Swallowing our disappointment, with no idea about where to go next, we walked until after dark.

Hungry, thirsty, and arguing, we stopped at a short-order cafe that was nearly empty and could have been the model for Edward Hopper's painting *Nighthawks,* stark and dark, inside and out. We ate New York hot dogs, the house specialty, and drank milk out of cardboard containers shaped like inverted cones, which I had seen for the first time at the Camp Shanks PX. Milk out of something other than glass didn't taste any different, but the hot dog wasn't as juicy as the footlong dogs at Sammy's Drive-in at the end of South Main in Little Rock.

Our appetites and thirsts quenched, we resumed our endless tour on foot, eventually bumping face-to-facade into a massive stone building, which I recognized from memories of photos as Grand Central Station. Standing inside the cavernous marble hall for about fifteen minutes, we surveyed milling passengers and listened to the echoing roar of "the crossroads of America," a phrase used by an announcer on a popular weekly radio serial.

Following that discovery, we also serendipitously found Radio City Music Hall and bought tickets at reduced prices to sit through the second half of *Hats Off to Ice,* starring Sonja Henie. The tiny blonde skater seldom appeared in the lavish but mildly entertaining extravaganza. Yet her disappointing performance in the Ice Capades was not as regrettable as missing a performance of *Oklahoma,* the biggest musical comedy hit in Broadway history.

Back at Camp Shanks, our division was restricted to company areas beginning on August 3. The next evening, only two days after we visited New York City, the first units of the Ninety-fourth began loading on trains for transport to a Hudson River pier, where we would board the *Queen Elizabeth,* a British luxury liner purportedly converted to a troopship before carrying a single civilian passenger.

For the trip to the pier, our units were among the first to board the commuter chair cars the second day, and we sat wedged in our seats, engulfed in our own sweaty odors because the coach had sealed windows. Our wool uniforms might be suitable for England's cooler temperatures but proved hot and itchy in August in New York, especially after carrying duffel bags, rifles, steel helmets, and athletic equipment under a blazing sun to the train. We smothered in the stifling air because our orders forbade leaving our seats and repeated delays kept the train from getting under way. As our train dawdled in the hot sun, excitement about sailing on the fastest passenger liner in the world slowly waned.

Finally at the pier, the huge gray ship cast a gigantic black shadow across the wharf where it was berthed. Weighed down by our equipment, we lined up in single file approaching the bottom of a steep gangway suspended from a loading port in the ship's side. As we inched toward the bottom of the steep incline, the transportation corpsmen, identified by red and gold arm bands, checked our names off rosters, and Red Cross women handed out coffee, doughnuts, and cloth ditty bags filled with toiletries and cartons of cigarettes. Though I had never smoked, I accepted a carton of Chesterfields, which my father, who preferred Camels, called "lady's cigarettes" because they were too mild for his taste. Ladened like pack mules on mountain trails, we struggled up the narrow gangplank to the loading port and followed guides along narrow companionways to a stateroom just above the waterline.

Our tiny cabin would comfortably accommodate two tourists in twin beds on a leisure cruise in peacetime, but now fifteen soldiers were to sleep in racks of five bunks each stacked against three walls. Slipping into my shallow middle bunk, I felt encased like an Egyptian mummy and ready to smother. Besides the narrow space of each bunk, the other areas in the cabin were a shallow space at the entryway, the bathroom, and the center of the room filled by our pile of packs. The cabin's restrictions were grudgingly accepted, and then Palma revealed we'd be sharing with fifteen other soldiers each day, twelve hours below and twelve hours above deck.

The bedlam of thousands of soldiers didn't subside a bit all night long, nor the next morning before we sailed. At 0730, on August 6, with half the division below deck, the ship weighed anchor, and pudgy, grunting tugboats guided her down the Hudson River. When the ship reached the open water of the Atlantic, the whole division was on deck observing the big city's receding skyline and the military fighter planes whizzing overhead, our aerial escort throughout the first full day at sea. Our ship's single defense against air attacks were anti-aircraft guns manned by the 301st Field Artillery. And the ship's only protections from a submarine's torpedoes were superior speed and zigzagging tactics every two to four minutes.

In the first hours, Boguski and I roamed through the crowds on the upper decks, weaving between bulkheads and rails. At the fantail, the exhilarating whoosh and turmoil of water in the ship's wake were exciting to hear and see. Gazing at the broad empty expanses of water on all sides made our liner only an infinitesimal dot upon the ocean, and Joe and I seemed microscopic specks upon that dot—not very important in the overall scheme of things.

As we sailed farther out to sea, the colors of the ocean's surface were startling to me, changing from brilliant green near the shore to aquamarine farther out, to white-capped, black waves when totally beyond the sight of land.

"Wowee, Joe, just look at the changing colors!"

Boguski laughed. "Haven't you seen the ocean before, Cleve?"

"Never. Only fresh water. The most water I've ever seen? The Mississippi River at Memphis and Lake Catherine at Hot Springs in Arkansas."

Although brisk, cool winds whipped us on deck, relieving the summer heat, the stagnant air down below in narrow companionways and cramped quarters remained stifling and rank. We were three full days at sea before relief came when the ship sailed into the cooler latitudes of the North Atlantic.

For anyone susceptible to sea sickness, which I thought I might be, the beautiful weather and calm seas were fortunate. But we'd been assured that if rough weather hit us the ship's gyroscope would maintain an even keel in stormy waters. Sailing in fair weather, I was never queasy at any time, perceiving no roll, side-to-side motion, or surge. The few alterations in the ship's pattern of movement came one night when the *Elizabeth* was near a brilliantly lighted hospital ship and altered course to escape being a target silhouetted against its lights. On two other nights, abrupt shifts in speed and zigzagging hurled some men from their bunks. The unexplained tactics reminded us of our peril. Usually, we felt only the reassuring vibrations of the ship's mighty engines.

Out to sea, the Ninety-fourth commenced a daily schedule that was to be observed by all enlisted personnel. Whether officers followed the same rules, I don't know, because we never saw them again after boarding the ship, until we encamped in England.

Sergeant Palma told us that only two meals per day would be served to enlisted men. There were at least eighteen thousand on board, and the mess hall, or galley, could hold only three thousand at one sitting. Each of us had a mess card for admission to one of the six meal shifts.

Near the end of one shift, an announcement on the PA warned the next group to take their places: "Number three mess cards, form your lines."

At my first meal the line was a block long. I certainly didn't want to sail from New York to the British Isles camping in the food line, so I decided to eat some meals and ignore others. But many bored or hungry soldiers never missed a shift in the ship's galley, no matter how long they had to stand in line, and then bitched about the quality of food after every meal.

"Where the hell did these Limeys learn to cook? Boiling clothes doing laundry?"

"What is 'bully' about beef?"

"The bull is having to eat this crap."

The British cooks prepared "bully beef," or corned beef, in a variety of ways for every meal. At breakfast, it appeared beside hard-boiled eggs and toast. At the second meal, boiled cabbage, potatoes, or brussels sprouts, which were new to me, joined the beef. Complaints about the food were universal, but I liked bully beef, whatever it accompanied.

Although waiting in long lines subdued my always meager appetite, standing smack up against sweaty strangers at a crowded table in a noisy, malodorous mess hall was more discouraging. After a meal, it was repugnant to stand pelvis to buttocks in another line waiting to clean my mess kit in a steamy, noisome wash room filled with overflowing garbage cans. So I usually settled each day on either breakfast or dinner. Between meals, I began smoking the Chesterfields the Red Cross gave me, even though I knew my mother would have been disappointed.

Although beginning to smoke regularly, I didn't copy the soldiers who survived almost exclusively on nicotine, candy, and booze. Many guys had stuffed illicit bottles of whiskey and gin into their duffel bags. Those men with ready cash bought sweets and other snack foods at a confectionery located forward on one of the upper decks. It was open a few hours each day and allowed a limited number of purchases by each customer to prevent hoarding or black marketing by GI operators like our company bugler Lemuel Slate.

Two other shipboard formalities were daily boat drills and nightly blackouts. The boat drills had to be observed by everyone, including the American nurses and pilots returning to England after furloughs in the States.

At 1100 each morning, alarm bells on bulkheads clanged. A stentorian voice on the PA ordered, "man your stations!"

Soldiers like lines of worker ants scurried from staterooms into companionways, racing to their assigned stations above decks and donning canvas life jackets, which we had been ordered to wear or carry at all times. Attached to the preservers were tiny, battery-operated, red signal-lights that were intended to help rescuers locate us in the waves. Did the Royal Navy honestly assume we could survive floating in the frigid waters of the North Atlantic if a torpedo didn't kill us?

My emergency station was beside a forward hatchway on the port side of the upper boat deck, far better than being wedged into the hundreds on the foredeck.

The other daily shipboard routine came near sunset each day when the British PA voice ordered, "the blackout will begin!"

All portholes, their window glass already painted black, were closed and securely fastened, the gangway doors covered with black curtains, and smoking on the open decks forbidden. Although smokers didn't ignore the rule, they adjusted to it by lighting up inside companionways and holding the cigarettes cupped inside their fists when on deck.

Another shipboard rule forbade throwing waste of any kind overboard. Although warned that floating debris might help German submarines spot, tail, and torpedo the ship, many soldiers didn't take the warning seriously. At least that was true where condoms in the little muslin ditty bags were concerned. Pranksters filled the condoms with as much water as they would hold to toss them like medicine balls at each other, or drop them as bombs onto decks below, or into the sea.

Proving that "boys will be boys," especially in sexual matters, some soldiers inflated rubbers to their normal dimensions to hold against their crotches, pretending they were phalluses. Or they released inflated rubbers in the breeze, intending that they be seen by nurses on the decks below. What that sexual gesture would accomplish was beyond my understanding. Gusty winds almost always carried the condoms beyond the decks into the ocean. The trail of latex in our wake failed to capture the attention of either the nurses or, fortunately, German subs.

To help 18,000 soldiers fill five days on board ship in a more profitable way, the Army stocked our rooms with hundreds of paperbacks, from the Armed Services Library, with well-known titles and authors. From the pile of books in our cabin, I chose Wallace Stegner's *Big Rock Candy Mountain* and a collection of O. Henry's short stories. When conversation, strolling the decks, and observing the behavior of others palled, I read. And when I tired of that, I did a lot of thinking. Though I wanted to reach England quickly, dreading even the slightest possibility of a watery grave, I fantasized about our voyage lasting until the war's end.

As I contemplated the best and worst of future possibilities, my buddies heard about tryouts for a variety show in the ship's theater on the main deck. Even though Palma and Boguski insisted on my auditioning, I wasn't eager to go. We reached the theater by climbing the ship's grand staircase, a curving masterpiece of marble that was as crowded and busy as an oriental bazaar. Going up the wide, deep steps, we squeezed past soldiers selling pens, knives, watches, and cigarette lighters, and stepped around and through circles of gamblers shooting dice and playing poker. At the theater, we shoved through a crush of soldiers to reach the only seats available in the back row.

I knew after watching the lineup of instrumentalists, singers, dancers, and impersonators that my talent and skill didn't match the others', despite my pals' insistence. Joe told me, "You're as good as those guys," but I wanted to be better. I was convinced the men in Company B enjoyed my stories and impressions in the same way a family laughs at its own inside jokes. So I didn't audition. An Italian American, whose singing received an ovation, may have been Anthony Benedetto, known after the war as Tony Bennett. At least, he had a similarly raspy tenor voice, tight, curly black hair, olive skin, and prominent Roman nose. Although I enjoyed the auditions, I didn't struggle through the mob the next day to see the performance.

Our first night on the *Queen Elizabeth,* I was too uncomfortable to sleep. Lying on my shelf of a bunk was medieval torture in a spikeless iron maiden. With the tips of my toes and nose nearly pressing the canvas bunk above me, there wasn't space enough to turn on my side. So when I went to the toilet and found the bathtub empty, I decided to spend the night in it. The tub was fairly comfortable even though it was too short to stretch out fully. Luckily, very few used the bathroom that first night, and it insulated me from the sounds in the crowded, poorly ventilated stateroom.

The second night, I planned on sleeping in the tub again, but another squad occupied the cabin and used the toilet more frequently, which forced me to move into the companionway. Out there, the noisy flow of traffic until long after midnight drove me up on deck, where I slept soundly in an out-of-the-way corner against a bulkhead until awakened by the sun. The same spot beckoned the third night, and I found the deck moon-drenched, cold, and breezy; we had sailed into the more northerly latitudes. Our last night at sea, the deck was so cold that I slept below in a corner of a noisy corridor.

On the morning of August 11, 1944, five days after leaving the United States, I heard that the coastline of Ireland was off the port side of the ship. When so many of us gathered at the rails to stare at the intensely green island and watch British combat planes on their routine patrols over the North Channel, it's a wonder the ship didn't list to the left. Instead the *Queen*'s mighty majesty swung due north toward Scotland, eventually sailing up the Firth of Clyde to Greenock near Glasgow, anchoring in the afternoon at midstream because the port's wharfing facilities couldn't handle her tonnage. Boguski and I stood on deck gazing at the miniature red-roofed cottages that looked like toy houses in a Christmas scene, scattered across cultivated, green-and-tan Scots fields divided by hedgerows and resembling multicolored checkerboards.

That night the British cooks served us our last hot meal on the ship and gave out K rations to sustain us on the train the next day. After eating, we sat around in the stateroom wondering how long we'd stay in the UK before getting an assignment on the Continent. Although our final destination remained a mystery, I slept soundly below deck, assuming we were safe from submarines or an attack of any kind. I didn't know until the next day that Greenock had been bombed severely early in the war.

The division debarked from the ship on the morning of August 12. As we stood waiting near a loading port, two MPs escorted a man wearing a straitjacket to the exit ahead of us. I thought the prisoner resembled Hines, the Bible-thumber in the Second Platoon. I asked others near me, and they thought he looked like Hines too. I never saw the little fellow again in England or on the Continent; perhaps he had finally broken down from fright.

We left the *Queen Elizabeth* through ports in the hull at the deck level of the tenders that carried us to the pier.

On Princess Pier, the transportation corps divided us into groups for entraining. We loaded into quaint, compartmentalized English railway coaches like those in old English movies. The corps effort to load as many men as possible into each compartment proved much easier than on American coaches. In the States, we stood in long lines at doors at both ends of the carriage and squeezed along crowded center aisles to reach our seats. But in Scotland, we stepped directly from the platform through separate doors into a compartment, which ordinarily seated six or eight, to sit down at once. It was crowded yet more comfortable than the coach from Shanks to the New York pier. And our wool uniforms were just right for the damp breeziness of Scotland's cool summer.

But the passenger coach's easy, modern access contrasted with what some guys called "the medieval window arrangement" in our compartment door. To open or close a window, you pulled on a leather strap attached to the center at the bottom of its frame, and secured the window at different heights by fitting one of the several strap holes, about four inches apart, over the brass peg at the bottom of the door frame. Our company "mechanics" declared the mechanism primitive, but it seemed practical.

I let the window down all the way to enjoy the cool Scots wind while watching the trimly meticulous passing scene. No papers, bottles, and cans littered the tracks, and no trash piles and abandoned equipment dotted the fields of Scotland as they had in the Southeast and Northeast in the States. To prevent such a mess, older Scotsmen, who waved as we passed, were patrolling the tracks collecting debris, and the fields appeared to have been swept with brooms by the farmers.

We traveled south over rolling green hills and beside rivers the widths of American creeks, past scattered copses of trees, before crossing the border into England.

Hospitality at the British railway stations was greater than in the States, where civilians, other than railroad crews, ignored troop trains; when we stopped at stations in the UK, passengers greeted us. Groups of English ladies in dark green uniforms served us hot drinks and food. The English ladies handed out pastry-covered meat pies with hot tea, which was less appealing to American taste than iced tea and often refused. The American Red Cross workers offered only doughnuts and hot coffee. I liked English meat pies, but others, after biting into them, waited until the train left the station to toss them out the window.

We traveled through Scotland and England without knowing where we were going because company officers and NCOs hadn't named our final destination. In fact, no officers were on our coach, and the NCOs weren't any better informed than us. Nor did we know what towns and villages we were passing through; the British had removed the names of railway stations for security, in case of German invasion, or sabotage. Our only information about our route came from the railway workers or women servers at stops. Although the absence of station signs prevented tracing our precise route, the most direct line south from Glasgow down the west side of England would be through Carlisle, Preston, Crew, Birmingham, Gloucester, Bristol, and Bath.

Elements of our regiment were dispersed in Wiltshire in southern England, and all units of the Ninety-fourth were quartered inside an irregular triangle in the northwest sector of the Salisbury Plain. The triangle's points were at Devizes, Melksham, and Trowbridge, where the 301st Regimental Headquarters was located. Division Command was farther north, outside the triangle, at Greenway Manor House in Chippenham.

Trucked from Bath to our camp, Company B was the only unit from the Ninety-fourth stationed at Erlestoke, a small village composed of a few thatch-roofed cottages, a Norman church, and a combination post office and bakery. These tiny buildings sat on both sides of a narrow road connecting several other villages of similar size that also provided housing for companies of the 301st.

Near Erlestoke's center, the low rock walls on both sides of the tarmac road forced vehicles to slow down at a sharp curve before they reached the military camp's front gate, set back about twenty yards from the main road. The camp, formerly occupied by British troops, had several one-story cinder-block barracks, a small headquarters building, and a large mess hall for enlisted personnel. Our barracks was shaped like a giant H, with two vertical strokes or wings for sleeping quarters, and two horizontal crossbars instead of one for offices and the toilet-shower room. The officers' billet was in sight in an old manor house on a hill.

The wings of the barracks were divided into cubicles of different sizes. Mine was a small office converted into a sleeping unit, with two wooden bunk beds, one above the other. As assistant company clerk, I had the cubicle to myself, with space enough for equipment and records. The mattresses, called "palliasses" by the British, were soiled bed-length muslin slips stuffed with so little straw they didn't cushion us from the hard wooden bunk bottoms. I slept on both rough palliasses in the lower bunk and stored the recordings and record player in the top one. The only other furnishing in the room was a small shelf attached to one wall.

The company training program that commenced the next morning seemed aimed at keeping men busy and in good physical shape, nothing more. Although our headquarters platoon didn't go on the field problems, we spent considerable time marching along Wiltshire lanes and roads in the unpredictable English weather. We soon realized that golden sunshine and cloudless skies at 0800 could be the prelude to low, black, scudding clouds and heavy rain by 1100. For protection, we always draped folded raincoats over the back of the web belts at our waists.

One formal training session that included our platoon was led by a British lieutenant who had escaped from a German prisoner-of-war camp. He informed us of the proper response if taken prisoner: "Answer any and all questions with name, rank, and serial number *only,* as prescribed under international rules of war, established by the Geneva Convention." The officer encouraged us to escape from prison as soon as feasible, reinforcing points with stories about the various clever means British soldiers and officers used to escape from deep inside Germany.

The simplest, cleverest escape plan was that of two POWs who stole brushes and buckets of white wash and painted a line down the center of a camp road through the main gate past the guards to the outside. We listened to the dapper raconteur's yarns sitting on bare ground on the high slope of a hillside next to Erlestoke's water-treatment plant. His stories of exciting escapes, embellished with his English wit, distracted me from the bare, wet ground beneath us and the breathy fog condensing in the cold air in front of my face.

One breezy overcast day, Kelly asked if I'd like to see Trowbridge, not because he intended a treat (although Thursday, August 17, 1944, was my twentieth birthday), but because he knew I hadn't been to any other towns. He asked T/5 Bradberry, Straub's driver, to take me to Regimental Headquarters with some papers.

Kelly showed Bradberry a map of Trowbridge, but the driver insisted, "I don't need no help, Sarge. I've been to Regimental before."

In response to Brad's claim, Kelly showed me the map, for he knew the smart-aleck driver often pretended to know something when he didn't.

Outside the orderly room, Bradberry tried to prove to "one of them ASTP guys" how smart he was without college and how neat and well-equipped his vehicle was. He cared for his jeep as if it were a limousine, or a thoroughbred horse. Strutting around, he pointed out the wire-cutting pole, recently welded upright at the center of the front bumper, which was used to prevent a driver and his passenger from being decapitated if an enemy had strung piano wire at head height across a road. He also suggested it was his idea to install additional racks for jerry cans, the rectangular five-gallon containers for extra gasoline, if fuel wasn't easily available in combat.

Suddenly motioning me into the jeep, Bradberry in one move leaped into the driver's seat and hit the accelerator. I was hardly seated before we rounded the narrow, walled curve at Erlestoke and had to grab the windshield and seat frame to hang on. As we careened onto the main highway to Trowbridge, I yelled, "Get in the left lane!" which he did, but still I had to beg repeatedly, "Slow down!" He knew I couldn't drive and enjoyed airing me out, careering on curves all the way to Wiltshire's county seat.

At Trowbridge, bustling civilian and military motor and foot traffic filled the streets, and Bradberry let me know that he had personal errands to take care of before going to Regimental. After several stops, he had lost the way. Puzzled trying to keep to the left on the narrow streets and at corners and roundabouts, Bradberry wouldn't admit his confusion, and he wouldn't listen to the directions Kelly gave me. Finally I persuaded him to ask an English traffic policeman.

The policeman ended his clear directions with the typical English bobby's refrain, "Right over the hill and bear to your left; you cawn't miss it."

We eventually found Regimental, and I delivered Kelly's papers.

Bradberry drove us back to camp with his usual jerky, squealing abandon.

On Sunday mornings, I attended worship services. Afterwards, with little else to do, I lay around in the barracks talking with my mates and writing letters home while listening to the V-Disc recordings of Benny Goodman and his orchestra—swing hits like "Sing, Sing, Sing," "One O'clock Jump," and "King Porter Stomp." I played them so often they soon became background for whatever else I was doing.

Getting a pass to nearby towns, as far as I knew, wasn't possible for enlisted men. It would have been great fun to have a Sunday pass to Trowbridge or Bath because the civilian amusements would fill the long daylight hours of a late-summer English afternoon. But talking, reading, and smoking helped fill my time, and combining empty hours with free Chesterfields confirmed my habit. A week after we settled at Erlestoke, I puffed away during breaks like the veteran smokers; and since nearly everyone smoked, my habit evolved unnoticed.

I knew I was hooked when I voluntarily bartered my beautiful fountain pen from Dad for an English-made cigarette lighter. I was attracted by a tacky silver-alloy lighter that had a tiny metal arm that had to be lifted to uncover the wick before striking the flint and a transparent container filled with pale lavender English lighter fluid. I had it only one day before realizing that it wasn't practical and that I should have traded for a stainless steel Zippo lighter like that carried by most smokers.

Shortly before shipping to the Continent—tired of talking, reading, listening, and writing on Sunday afternoons—Agnew Andrews, Joe Boguski, and I set out walking on the road that passed the front gate of the camp. We didn't intend to go all the way to Devizes, only take our time observing the countryside that we had marched or double-timed past every day without seeing.

The road was almost empty of traffic, so we strolled down its middle, past the cottage yards overflowing with colorful flowers; it was like walking a wide path through an enormous garden. And gazing at the broad range of harvest colors in the cultivated fields of the farms, I realized that Wiltshire was a rich agricultural county. Following the gradual undulations of the road over the low hills, under a clear blue sky, we passed at one point beneath a green canopy of trees about twenty-five yards long. Farther on, we stopped to study a huge calcium rock bulging out of the radiantly green turf as free of color as the proverbial white cliffs at Dover.

Distracted by many other natural surprises along the way, the sunlight under British Double Daylight Savings Time fooled us. We weren't aware of how late it was, or how far we'd walked until wandering into the sparse outskirts of the city. Already in Devizes, we walked past many fine old houses the rest of the way to the town center, where we stood in the fading light on the raised cobblestone curbing in the middle of the deserted market square, surveying the fronts of the quaint old buildings. Only the distinctive sign of the ancient Bear Hotel remains in my mind's eye.

So at sundown, with no flashlights and no memory of several crossroads we had passed, we turned back toward Erlestoke. The farther we walked, the darker the clear sky became. Dogs that had not heeded us in daylight now tore out of their yards snarling at our heels. Scrambling to escape, our feet sank in the mud and water of the ditches on both sides of the narrow road. At the highway's edge, which had been safe as a sidewalk in the afternoon, we now dodged passing cars, our only warnings their dark moving shadows and tiny slitted headlights. In the rapidly falling evening temperature without our jackets, we were soon chilled. Shivering and nearly blind, we stumbled along the faintly discernible road's edge in the darkness.

After a time, we heard loud voices and the struggling motor of an English lorry at a distance. As the truck rumbled toward us, the voices grew more distinct, singing "Bless 'Em All." Though it was too dark to be seen, we yelled and waved frantically at the truck until a lone voice shouted "Stop!" at the driver, who passed us before coming to a squealing halt.

We caught up, and an English voice asked, "Where ya' blokes 'eaded?"

Frantic for a ride, together we shouted, "Erlestoke."

Then the whole truckload exclaimed, "You're Yanks!" and "Jump on, mates."

So we joined a swaying band of English soldiers in the crowded truck bed and learned to sing all the verses of the raucous pub song, "Roll me over, lay me down, and do it again." When the truck slowed and stopped, we discovered the lorry driver had been guided by his own mysterious radar and braked at our camp gate.

At breakfast the next morning, describing how we walked to Devizes and back in one afternoon and evening, we found few at our table who believed us.

The company cooks had resumed preparing our meals after we settled at Erlestoke. They gave us a standard American breakfast with some wartime variations that the English probably devised: eggs, not fresh but powdered; fried Spam, not bacon; huge slices of toast, not biscuits; and mounds of marmalade instead of apple butter. Most of the meal's ingredients our Army supplied, but the marmalade, no doubt shipped from Scotland, was the thick, bitter, orange mix that the British prefer over sweet.

But marmalade in our mess hall had more than the average Scottish bite. The honey bees of Wiltshire were out in force in August, hovering over wildflowers and swirling around our heads, their numbers making them especially pesky when we ate or drank. The mess hall—food inside and garbage outside—magnetized the insects, which entered through its torn window screens. At every meal, bees landed and stuck in the marmalade pots in the middle of the tables. A bee, looking very much like a piece of orange rind, sitting inconspicuously atop a mound of marmalade on toast, sometimes ended in someone's mouth. Having one's tongue stung while enveloped by other buzzing critters hampers one's taster and appetite.

As we marked time in the Wiltshire countryside awaiting our division's combat assignment, the conditions on the Continent were changing radically. The American breakthrough at Saint Lo, July 18, 1944, freed the Allies from a stalemate, and they set off in hot pursuit of three German field armies retreating to the east across France.

In the west, Lieutenant General George Patton's Third Army, teamed with the First Army, launched a campaign against the coastal cities of Brest, Cherbourg, Nantes, Bordeaux, Lorient, and Saint Nazaire. The Allies were seeking ports on the Atlantic for military supplies. The first American assault against Brest by VIII Army Corps would last for two months, until September 18, when the city was finally captured after Americans suffered daunting losses in lives, time, and matériel.

While most Allied forces followed the German withdrawals toward their homeland, moving eastward, the Third Army tanks swept westward through Normandy against light resistance, seizing in rapid succession the towns of Contances, Granville, Avranches, and Pontorson to open the way into Brittany. When they cornered German troops in Lorient and Saint Nazaire, SHAEF feared a repetition of the costly losses at Brest and ordered the Third Army not to attack but to contain the troops.

SHAEF assumed the British capture of Antwerp, Belgium, at about the same time would furnish the necessary port for Allied supplies and that containment of the Germans would suffice. Their decision brought the Ninety-fourth Division into the planning of Lieutenant General William Simpson, commander of VIII Corps of the Third Army, who ordered the Ninety-fourth to replace the Sixth Armored Division at Lorient.

On August 30, Ninth Army, Eighth Corps, alerted the Ninety-fourth of an imminent move to France and ordered line companies to have each man prepare a full field pack and turn in the recreation equipment issued in the States. The Corps' second signal the next day warned Company B to prepare to move on six hours' notice after 0001, September 3. To our relief, the second signal ordered us to turn in the stinking, chemically-treated fatigues for gas attacks.

Stripped of our excess equipment, we still carried many items in our uniform pockets and packs: shelter halves, bed rolls, raincoats, extra K rations, mess gear, water purifying tablets, and toilet articles. Attached to the web belts at our waists were entrenching tools (spades with folding blades), first aid packets, and canteens. Now, for gas attacks, we had only masks in shoulder bags, which would soon become receptacles for any loose articles but the masks.

Though our physical loads were lighter, somehow my spirits weren't uplifted.

Switchboard Operator

Lorient, France

September 3–December 29, 1944

Foot soldiers of the 301st, under Lieutenant Colonel Hardin, were the first units to depart for the port of Southampton on September 3 in preparation for crossing the English Channel to France.

When orders for Company B came down from division headquarters that same night, rumors circulated that certain company officers were not in their quarters and had to be sought elsewhere. Purportedly, they were found partying with nurses at a nearby military hospital, one of them caught on a gurney with a nurse in flagrante delicto (a phrase I didn't yet know)! Company B didn't leave for Bath on trucks until the late afternoon of September 4.

The British railway cars we boarded at Bath looked on the outside more like American coaches, only half their length. Inside, the coach was not divided into small compartments like the ones we rode from Scotland; the seating was in units—a bench seat facing another across a table—down both sides of the center aisle.

Trying to reach our seats in the small car, we found our packs and all the pieces of equipment hanging from the cartridge belts around our waists made the free-for-all down the aisle a tight squeeze. We stashed our packs in the overhead racks and laid our rifles on the floor at our feet. With window blinds closed for security at night, many laid their heads on their arms to sleep while others played cards on the table tops.

The train carried us to the Southern Railway docks at Southampton. From there we marched a short distance to a vast spread of corrugated metal sheds near the pier and (in a practice that must surely have begun in the seventeenth century) stacked our rifles in pyramids, muzzles up and butts down, something I hadn't seen since basic training. Using our sixty-pound packs as backrests on the deck of the pier, most of us sacked out while waiting to board the ship. But unexplained delays kept us lying under the sheds—snoozing, smoking, talking, and cutting up—much longer than expected. We were observing the Army convention of "hurry up and wait."

In the late afternoon of September 5, units of the 301st boarded two small English ships, the *Crossbow* and the *Neutralia,* to cross the Channel. The name of the latter ship, which Company B boarded, struck me as ironic, considering our destination was combat. The Allies may have been winning the ground war on the Continent, but that didn't mean that narrow body of water separating England from France was neutral. Looking at the water, I thought, German submarines could be lying in wait below the surface. The possibility of an enemy torpedo striking our ship reminded me how much closer we were getting to the Germans.

While the ship slowly sailed out of the harbor, I stood on deck until ordered to go below, surveying the dark, moonlit waters, even though I knew subs would be out of sight underneath. Later, down in the ship's hold, the routine of eating, talking, and napping blotted out the dangerous possibilities as we crossed without incident. Nerves made it hard to wait for the smoking lamp to be lit to satisfy my new "nic fits."

At noon the next day, after a restless night below, we shouldered our packs and struggled up the dark passageways to cross out into blinding light and fresh winds on the deck. After all the overcast, rainy days in Wiltshire, we dropped anchor in brilliant sunshine off Utah Beach. Surveying the bloody battlefield of D-Day, we were overcome by a kind of electric silence . . . seeing in every direction refuse from that fateful landing. Thrusting out of the water at bizarre angles were portions of ships' bows, funnels, and masts, and sterns of destroyed landing craft. Farther out to sea behind our ship smaller boats were plying among the landing crafts, freighters, and tankers that were waiting to move closer to the shore to unload.

After crossing the deck to the rail, I looked down at the tiny LC/VP (landing craft, vehicle-personnel) lying alongside. Palma called it a "Higgins boat" and said it would take us ashore. The ship was rolling gently as I hoisted myself over the rail to climb down the cargo net suspended over its side. Because we'd practiced descents only on dry land with a net hanging against a stationary wall, without wind, waves, or tides, going down tested afresh everyone's nerves and hand grips.

Screwing up my courage tight as my helmet chin strap, I gripped the net, staring straight ahead at the ship's hull rather than down at the deck of the Higgins boat. I clung like a woodpecker on a tree trunk while those underneath me descended to the bobbing minuscule deck below—all of us carefully trying not to step on the hands of those beneath. We cautiously released our grips to grasp the next line down, feeling the centrifugal tug of our packs, rifles, canteens, bayonets, and entrenching tools.

With our whole platoon aboard the Higgins, the Navy coxswain gunned the motor, and the craft surged through three hundred yards of choppy water from the ship to Utah Beach. As we smashed through the waves, a shadow suddenly fell across us; a dark gray barrage balloon above, tugging and bobbing in the wind, was tethered by steel cables to a ship. Blimps discouraged or disabled low-flying enemy planes.

The coxswain didn't nose the prow of the Higgins near enough for us to step directly on shore but dropped the steel ramp a dozen yards out. As we stepped into the swirling water, the ramp rocked up and down, threatening to strike the backs of our legs if we didn't leap out far enough from its edge. With our rifles at port position against our chests, in surf up to our knees, we sludged through bits of military flotsam and jetsam partially submerged in the sand and water along the shore.

Soldiers, unit signs, machines, and stockpiles of supplies, surrounded by clusters of GI workers, were scattered in every direction across the beach. High up at the crest of the dunes stood German pillboxes and gun emplacements, their camouflage paint blistered and peeling off their thick, shell-pocked concrete walls. Protruding from their dark apertures, the slender barrels of silent cannons seemed menacingly aimed at us.

But on September 6, 1944, exactly ninety-four days after D-Day, the Ninety-fourth Division landed on Utah Beach opposed by only wind, water, and sand.

Our company followed the columns of men ahead of us through a sandy swale to the main road above the beach. On both sides of us were barbed-wire entanglements with German signs decorated with skulls and crossbones bearing the words *Achtung Minen.* But American engineers had encircled them and other areas with warning tape, posting reassuring signs in English, "Mines Cleared to Shoulder."

Above the beach, we marched between rows of shattered buildings along a road pitted with shallow, muddy craters. On each side of the road, in deep ditches, writhened tangles of telephone wires stretched out of sight ahead of us. The road led to the outskirts of a village where the 301st Regimental command post was temporarily set up.

Company B spent their first afternoon and night in France on a barren hillside off the main road, one-half mile southwest of Saint-Marie-du-Mont. Our campsite had no grassy turf but deep, rich, black soil, almost like a field prepared for planting. Boguski and I pitched our tent on the soft ground without ditching around the base to carry off rain water because the sky had been clear throughout the day, only high, thin clouds appearing in the late afternoon.

After eating K rations for supper, Joe and I wandered around the camp. Across the road from our tent were large piles of shell casings and empty cordite containers left by an American artillery outfit. The signs of earlier skirmishes were everywhere, and we heard a few rifle shots without knowing how far—or near—the actual front was nor where we would be going the next day. When it was too dark to see well, Joe and I returned to our tent to talk and smoke before crawling into our sleeping bags for the night.

When I went to the latrine several hours later, a light drizzle was falling. I trusted it wouldn't rain enough to run under our tent, so I didn't wake Joe to warn him.

About sunrise another strong urge to go to the slit-trench latrine struck me. Walking through the thick low-hanging mist hovering over our field, I knew how fortunate we were it hadn't rained, but how unlucky I was to have the "GIs" for the first time since leaving Ole Miss. After breakfast, my bowels griped more and nausea hit me, so I made another trip to the latrine before seeking help from Murray, one of our company medics.

Murray told me about others with the same complaint who had already visited him, and he dispensed his favorite panacea for cases of diarrhea in the field—charcoal tablets and bismuth powders. Chewing and swallowing the large, black, activated-charcoal pills wasn't too difficult, but choking down the white bismuth was like swallowing a dose of talcum powder. Murray also advised me to sit near the tailgate of the truck!

By the time transport arrived, my worst symptoms had subsided. The sun slowly burned off the morning mist and warmed us as the truck column plowed down the narrow, dusty roads. Although the fierce battles in this part of France had been over for a month and conditions were more nearly normal, some French farmers and villagers still greeted our convoy with cheers and offers of wine, *Calvados,* and apple *cidre,* as if we were their recent rescuers.

Seeing small American flags flying at a few houses, we joked about the owners alternating them with German flags depending upon who was winning at the moment. A few little French boys along the roadsides, displaying an aggressive streak they couldn't have safely revealed to German soldiers, pounded us and our trucks with tiny, hard, tasteless apples. But most young girls and older women waved enthusiastically, smiling at the randy remarks GIs shouted at them.

Across the countryside, fields lay gouged from explosions, and tank tracks and foxholes dug by American and German infantrymen scalloped the hedgerows. The fields and roadsides were littered with wrecked, burnt-out tanks, trucks, and jeeps from both sides.

The villages we passed through had been decimated by artillery barrages of allies and enemies alike. On streets through Contances, Granville, Avranches, and Pontorson our trucks drove over crushed masonry and broken glass, past collapsed buildings and shell-torn cottages. The extent of destruction in Norman towns made me wonder how any inhabitants had survived. When we took a rest stop in a shattered town, finding a private place among the ruins to answer nature's call was difficult because the few inhabitants were as inquisitive about us as we were about them. Fortunately, Medic Murray's odd prescription of charcoal and bismuth had worked.

In the late afternoon of our second day in northern France, our convoy pulled off the road to spend the night in a field near Rennes where company cooks had set up a field kitchen and mess tent. Happy to get off the trucks, we pitched our pup tents before having our first hot meal in three days. We relaxed, relishing the fresh, cooked food and quiet bivouac, not knowing that September 8 would be our last retreat from combat conditions for months. Joe and I lay in our sleeping bags on a grassy plot under the stars with no premonition about the days ahead.

The next morning, our convoy turned the elbow at Rennes, driving west at a much slower rate, from the middle of the eastern border of the Normandy peninsula toward the Atlantic coast. The Ninety-fourth command informed us that we would relieve the Sixth Armored Division of the Third Army, which was holding twenty-one thousand German troops penned at Lorient, one of Germany's main submarine bases on France's west coast.

We entered Brittany driving into the confinement of hedgerows, consisting of hedges, banks, and sunken roads. The huge earthen walls of thickly woven tree and brush roots bordering all the fields usually have only one entry, and roads between hedgerows are sometimes covered by thick arbors of chestnut and oak tree foliage. The embankments, high and low, surrounding irregularly shaped fields and orchards, at odd angles to each other, are excellent concealment for infantry but major obstacles for motorized troops.

Besides cultivated fields, orchards, and hedgerows, Brittany's terrain is heavily forested mountains reaching almost down to the seacoast. The front line at Lorient would lie along the numerous hills and ridges between these mountains.

At midafternoon, the convoy halted for no apparent reason, leaving all the motors idling. Our truck wasn't near the front of the column, so we couldn't see what stopped us; then the trucks began moving again, only more slowly. But a certain quiet settled upon everything, subduing motors, orders, and conversations, revealing our awareness of being in the combat zone. Word filtered back that veteran soldiers of the Sixth Armored Division in the lead vehicles were guiding our battalion to the front.

When our trucks pulled off the road into a clearing, they circled like wagon trains in Indian attacks to wait in the gradually fading sunlight for further orders. A Sixth Armored guide carrying a field radio emerged from the woods and greeted Captain Straub and Sergeant Kelly. He talked in whispers to the officers and NCOs while listening to his radio for orders from his forward contact. Our platoons were joining the Sixth Armored crews now manning the positions that Company B was taking over.

Suddenly, small arms fire broke out in the woods beyond our clearing, the quiet shattered by the sharp, staccato exchange of shots. But no one in our truck flinched, or jumped out and ran, even though the shots were the first we heard in combat. The fire fight allowed us an initial comparison of the rapid fire of an M-1 rifle against the blurp-blurp of a German MP-40 machine pistol.

As time passed without our moving, Captain Straub, impatient with the wait, decided to reconnoiter company positions himself. Despite the Sixth Armored guide's cautioning about the front's fluidity, he set out with his driver Corporal Bradberry to follow the map of our sector he'd just received.

When they ventured beyond American lines in the jeep, coming under German fire, Brad braked abruptly and flooded the motor in his frantic effort to back up and turn around. While he struggled to get the motor to turn over, the captain fired in the general direction of an enemy he couldn't see. After scuttling back to our lines and rejoining our platoon, the men were still visibly shaken. But by the next day, Bradberry, bursting with his usual bravado, recounted, with or without an invitation, how he and the captain were the first in the company to face the Germans.

To our relief, the guide's field radio finally buzzed with the static of a metallic voice rasping the message, which the guide relayed to Kelly. The first sergeant ordered us to dismount the truck and follow him and the guide.

In single file, we climbed over high, wide hedgerows crossing the soggy fields in between them until all groups had dropped off, leaving only our communications squad. The guide walking ahead kept hedgerows between us and the enemy until he spotted a church steeple off to our left. Because the steeple, several hundred yards away, was a perfect lookout for an artillery observer, I hoped it wasn't behind German lines. Walking toward it, the guide eventually turned through a gap in a hedgerow into an orchard.

Sergeant Palma ordered our squad to dig in. He, Kelly, and the Sixth Armored guide were going to walk along the company's front line locating platoon positions so Palma could make map overlays for the captain and platoon leaders.

Our squad was spending the first night in combat under short, gnarled apple trees surrounded by hedgerows. Trying to dig our foxholes, we found the ground so hard-packed with small rocks and roots that it was impossible to reach any depth. Discouraged, we quit trying to scoop our shallow trenches deeper, I guess not yet convinced that any location in combat is one of mortal danger. Then the dark and the temperature both fell, adding more chills to any fears we may have felt.

Even though our holes under the apple trees weren't deep enough to protect us from bullets or shrapnel, we were sufficiently savvy, without orders from an officer or noncom, to start an all-night rotation of sentries. We also lowered our voices and took special care lighting cigarettes.

On guard first, I watched the cool moonrise flood the orchard bright as day and chose to stand hidden in the shadow of the foliage of a large tree.

If, by chance, a German observer in the church steeple had called down artillery on the orchard, the shallow depressions under the disfigured trees would have been our tombs among the fallen fruit. We should have added crossed fingers, legs, and eyes to our prayers to God that night because our ignorance required every possible protection, superstitious and spiritual. Any hole was deep enough for a grave.

No one volunteered to say so the next day, but I doubt if anyone in our squad slept soundly that first night, even with the front line of our sector fully manned by the battle-experienced Sixth Armored and Company B.

We were roused the next morning by a flurry of scattered rifle shots in the direction of the front line, though some distance from us. Kelly and Palma, who had been away all night, returned soon after sunrise and rounded up our squad from the orchard's four corners. We set out in single file behind the sergeants for the B Company command post. Kelly and Palma, knowing those parts of the trail possibly under German observation, checked the less-concealed areas through binoculars before leading us across them. The sergeants also took advantage of the still-green, fully-leafed trees and tall hedges for cover, allowing us to walk upright most of the time.

Nearing our command post, we saw what we thought were black cowpats in the fields and joked about the lowly creatures defecating from fright. But up close, we found the cowpats concave, not convex; they were holes from artillery explosions, filled with dark amber water.

We were fooled once more when we climbed over a hedgerow at the bottom of a hillside to cross a field carpeted with deep, vivid green grass.It looked like solid ground but was so soaked from frequent rains that our feet sank about three inches into the turf, the muddy water oozing up over our brogans. The French troops who joined us later called such soggy fields *prairies marecageuses.*

More waist-high hedgerows to our far right lay between us and the corner of a smaller field where Captain Straub had set up the company command post. Above our CP, at the crest of a wooded hillside, a platoon had dug in behind a hedgerow on one side of an apple orchard. The company's other rifle platoons spread out in an uneven line to their left and right along the same ridge. That was our company's actual front.

Kelly ordered the communications squad to dig in or find holes left by the Sixth Armored in the area around the CP. A few men claimed more conventional foxholes some distance away, but I wasn't so lucky. Left with no choice, I stored my pack near the CP in a shallow, rectangular-shaped dugout, three feet deep and the length of my body. Covered with a sheet of corrugated, galvanized steel and six inches of dirt on top, I figured the trench wouldn't protect me from a direct hit but would stop shrapnel.

Near the CP, off to our left on a rise at the far side of another field, I saw two camouflaged Sixth Armored vehicles parked against a thick wall of tall trees. For the next day and night, the crews of the medium tank and armored car were never in sight. I wondered if those veterans were inside their buttoned-up vehicles or lying alongside our troops on the front line.

The Sixth Armored withdrew September 9, the second day after we arrived, leaving the Ninety-fourth the sole division holding German troops inside Lorient.

The night after the Sixth departed was the noisiest, without an actual attack, that I can recall at Lorient. The sounds in the orchards of small, hard apples falling from trees precipitated the ruckus. Although fruit fell to the ground throughout the quiet afternoon, the sounds weren't as noticeable as they were at night. In darkness, even with the hum and mumbling normally present along a battle front, apple thuds and rustling leaves suggested threats to soldiers facing an enemy for the first time.

All afternoon, the rifle platoons were calm. A few sergeants, though, possibly anticipating their men's fears that night, crawled along the line warning them to fire in the dark only if there was sufficient reason. But that night, falling apples pulled everyone over the edge, and rifle fire broke out. A few times, as tensions wound tighter, a single shot roused a dozen more. One frantic soldier sure Germans were advancing across the orchard toward him, fired a Very pistol and watched the ghostly white parachute-flare drift down, revealing only the misshapen forms of the apple trees.

When the firing continued, Straub, at the CP, insisted impatiently that the shots revealed we were untried troops and that the Germans would give us a hard time. Actually, no one needed to fire a round for the Germans to know they faced new, inexperienced opponents. A while later, when more shots rang out, the exasperated captain sent me for Palma and ordered him to warn squad leaders to control their men.

The captain was forced to send me on foot because company communications with platoons had not been set up. Our recent arrival, lack of equipment, and the fluidity of the front had prevented installing and routing telephone lines through a switchboard. The situation left me on guard and a runner most of the night, so I got very little sleep.

Our first lesson in combat taught us that the likeliest times for enemy attacks are sunrise and sunset. All company members had a standing order to remain awake and alert at those hours. Throughout the first weeks, we observed the order without pressure from officers or NCOs. But as we became familiar with our surroundings and inured to the static position, fewer men focused intently on the alerts. The lax attitude persisted until German attacks at twilight and dawn convinced us of the need for special caution.

On September 10, our third day at the front, the German troops in Lorient launched their first attack against the division. When a heavy artillery barrage fell on one company of the First Battalion, we heard the whomp-whomp of the German 88-mm Flak 42 guns for the first time, their firing and the shell's detonation seeming almost simultaneous. We'd been told in the States that Germany's 88-mm antiaircraft gun, which had been converted to ground combat, was their best cannon in range, accuracy, and penetrating power. Hearing and seeing it in action, we were convinced.

Although Company B wasn't attacked, we won honors that day as the first unit of the Ninety-fourth Division to capture German soldiers. I missed seeing the prisoners because Captain Straub, in his excitement over their capture by one of his platoons, hurried to where the Germans had been caught and personally escorted them for interrogation directly to Regimental Headquarters rather than to our CP. Aside from Company B's "triumph," our first week outside Lorient was uneventful.

The full responsibility for containing the Germans at Lorient passed from the Sixth Armored to the Ninety-fourth at noon on September 12. Colonel Roy Hagerty, commander of the 301st, had established the Regimental Headquarters at the town of Kervaise. He commanded a sector bounded by two rivers, the Blavet on the east and the Leita on the west. Between these rivers, the 301st's front line extended parallel to and south of Quimper, Redene, Pont Scorff, Hennebont, and Nostang. Along this line, our First Battalion, under Lieutenant Colonel George F. Miller, was responsible for the Hennebont sector.

With all units in place, the division settled down on the permanently static front to learn the art and ennui of stalemate.

The pattern of our lives on the line took shape slowly. Following division orders, the company regularly sent out patrols to reconnoiter areas in front of our sector. We stood alert for attacks at sunrise and sunset each day. With our rifles constantly at hand, under regimental orders we wore our steel helmets everywhere but in our sleeping bags.

Our practical combat lessons included learning to distinguish incoming from outgoing "mail" (artillery), to judge from the sound how close artillery and mortar shells were likely to fall, to identify threatening from harmless sounds at night, and to refrain from firing our rifles needlessly. At mealtimes, in the early morning and late afternoon, we left the line a few at a time to go back to less exposed places to eat the hot meals brought up by the cooks.

Without chairs, benches, or stools, we had to find ways to sit that would keep our butts off the cold or muddy ground. Consequently, even though ordered to wear our steel helmets at all times, we sat on them at meals, with only our helmet liners on. When shaving and washing up, we used our helmets as basins or buckets. We later discovered while traveling in boxcars that our helmets could serve as toilet bowls too.

Without any furniture to sit on and with boxes in short supply, we often did what mountain people in the Ozarks call "hunkering," squatting with our weight balanced on one or both hips. I created a comic routine about the different types and uses of hunkering, demonstrating the double and single hunkers and several variations of these simple positions such as rhythmic, alternating, and creeping. My light weight, agility, and strength made hunkering for long periods easy for me, but many found the position hurt their leg muscles or made it difficult to keep their balance.

The regimental order to remain clean shaven named beards without referring to mustaches so I assumed hair on my upper lip was acceptable. But the possibility of growing a mustache wouldn't have occurred to me if a shadow of whiskers hadn't shown on my upper lip in the dim, distorted reflection of my GI steel mirror. For several days, I didn't shave, waiting to see how much darker my beard would grow. Then I shaped the faint darkness into a mustache similar to ones on dashing Hollywood actors like Ronald Colman, Clark Gable, and Errol Flynn.

Captain Straub, who called me to carry a message, did a double-take before asking, "What's that on your upper lip, Harrison?"

I asserted proudly, "A mustache, sir."

He snapped, "Shave the damned thing off. It makes you look like hell!"

I said "Yes, sir!" smiling to hide my deflation.

I took exception to his order, but I knew the right answer of the three acceptable ones: "yes, sir," "no, sir," and "no excuse, sir."

After delivering the message, I checked in my mirror. The captain was right! My mouth wasn't smiling anymore; it seemed molded in a sneer, the bane of a mustache over a short upper lip.

On September 16, our First Battalion was relieved by elements of the 302nd Infantry Regiment, and B Company withdrew to reserve for the first time. Only one day later, the Germans, perhaps sensing the change in units, attempted to infiltrate the OPs and lines manned by the untried men in our old sector of the front.

The reserve area was several miles behind the front, supposedly beyond the range of German artillery. The paved road we took to the reserve area was cracking off at its edges and large potholes had formed on its surface. Under the division's heavy truck traffic, the road was collapsing, and only a few weeks later the surface was fractured and muddy, no better than unpaved ones.

At a break on our march to the reserve area, we stopped across the road from the olive-green tents of the battalion medical aid station where the operating theater, with a large red cross on its roof, had been dug into an embankment for protection. A large number of medics, officers, and men were roaming around the compound.

As we lay there beside the road smoking and watching the activity around the aid station, another outfit marched past, going in the opposite direction. For the first time since leaving Ole Miss, I saw Victor Papoulious from Hot Springs, Arkansas; he was walking along the road in that same dreamy way of his. I hollered at him several times before catching his attention. Although he nodded and smiled in my direction, I don't believe he recognized me after I shouted who I was.

At first, we didn't know that going into reserve simply meant moving from one field surrounded by hedgerows to another field of the same description, only farther behind the front line. The reserve area had obviously been occupied by another company because dugouts of all sizes were gouged in the surface of the field and the sides of the hedgerows.

The field was between the macadam road and a muddy trail leading to a farmhouse. Between us and the farmhouse trail stood a grove of large trees, with exceptionally heavy foliage. The importance of the grove to the farmer was dramatically revealed the first day. A few men in our platoon felled trees for dugout roofs and supports, and the landowner, protesting loudly in French, descended upon our headquarters. Since Kelly spoke no French and the farmer no English, the first sergeant sent me to find Stewart Kranz in Second Platoon to come interpret.

The farmer claimed the trees in the grove were a species of wood he used to make sabots, or wooden shoes, for his family to wear while farming. Kelly apologized diplomatically, promising to put the grove off-limits but not ruling it out as a latrine site.

Shortly after the farmer's complaint, Joe suggested the old man might sell us fresh eggs. Franz coached us in asking for "*des oeufs.*" Boguski and I, rehearsing "dayz-oof," walked up the muddy lane to the farmer's stone house. In front of the house we faced a doughnut-shaped pile of steaming manure, its center half-filled with the foul smelling liquid leaching from the compost. Seeing the "honey pot," the gooey fields, and dirty stables we understood why the farmer and his family wore wooden shoes.

We found the old Frenchman tending a sagging workhorse in his stable. After he understood what we wanted, he searched for eggs in the straw nests in the barn. He refused our offers of the paper invasion script issued to all American troops, indicating instead that he wanted one cigarette for each egg. Joe and I were lucky to trade with him first because soldiers after us paid him a higher price in "coffin nails."

Shock used the high, wide hedgerow next to the farmer's special grove as the backing for the supply tent. He attached a canopy to the front and hung two Coleman gasoline lanterns underneath for light at night when he and Kelly played cards, checkers, and dominoes. Shock insisted that our distance from the front and the lack of German air surveillance made lanterns, masked by a canvas canopy and blinds, safe.

One rainy night, standing guard under the edge of the canopy, I watched Shock brew coffee without a percolator. After filling the metal canister of a squad stove with water, he filled it with enough ground coffee to brew several canteen cups full and set the container over the burner. When the water and ground coffee in the pot reached a rolling boil, he removed it from heat and broke an egg, shell and all, into the pot. When I looked stunned, he said an egg, like cold water, forces grounds to the bottom, and you don't have to reheat and take away the coffee's fresh flavor. Before I smoked, I had no interest in coffee, but I discovered cigarettes tasted best with hot java.

Yet with or without coffee, I became a chain smoker in two months' time, and even though I didn't like some of smoking's effects, I continued. More alarming than the ugly taste in my mouth was the brownish yellow stain on the skin of the index and middle fingers of my right hand. Trying to wean myself, I was influenced by Private Tetzloff, a silent man with bisonlike shoulders in the Second Platoon, who had a pipe permanently wedged in his mouth. So I asked my father to send a pipe and smoking tobacco as soon as possible, hoping I might stop any further staining of my hands.

On our first reserve, Joe and I erected, for the first and last time at Lorient, a pup tent for sleeping. The tent was some distance from whatever safety our holes provided, but we slept in it without thinking of enemy artillery, as if we were on a field trip back in the States. It hadn't yet been forced into our hard noggins that combat's not a game where you can holler "king's x" like a child until you're ready to resume the game.

The tent didn't keep us safe from the weather when we failed to ditch around it. One night, in the midst of a heavy rainstorm, water flowed under its sides, wetting our sleeping bags. Then, standing up trying to avoid the puddles beneath us, our backs scraped against the canvas halves, causing them to drip like sieves.

I recall few other activities that first time in reserve; only two events remain in my mind. As soon as we were settled, a small, dark-haired fellow in our headquarters platoon, Harry Nunn, I think, set an ammunition box on end for a chair, pulled a surprising number of barber's tools out of his pack, and sold crew cuts for a small fee. No one's hair had been cut for weeks, so Harry had many customers, including me.

The other episode took place in the dark hours of an early morning while we were asleep. The sharp crack of a rifle shot spurred Joe and me to our feet, rifles in hand, expecting an attack. But no other firing followed the single shot, and no enemy came. What we heard but couldn't see was occurring on the opposite side of the hedgerow where another platoon bivouacked in the field next to ours. Even after we crawled back inside our sleeping bags, the confusion continued behind our tent.

At breakfast, we heard that a soldier "accidentally" shot himself in the foot, and the company medics carried him to the battalion aid station down the road. Shooting oneself in the foot or hand was a risk some soldiers were willing to take to escape combat, but those injuring themselves probably were court-martialed.

Even in reserve, we continued to be alert at sundown and sunrise. For me, the evening watch was a time for contemplation and prayer. Despite the potential for attack at that hour, I looked forward to the silence and absence of activity. In clear, dry weather, I could lie against the bank of a hedgerow and watch the sinking sun turn tree branches into delicate black filigrees against the pastel apricot light on clouds in the blue sky. I also used the time to read in the New Testament (King James version) that was given to all Protestant inductees at the reception center at Camp Robinson.

The arrival of our first mail overseas brought a surprise for me. Weeks before leaving the States, I wrote Dad how much I needed a pocketknife on field problems. The Army issued knives to paratroopers or other special units but not to ordinary infantrymen. Our bayonets didn't serve to slice cheese or spread pork from K rations on crackers. I had forgotten about asking him, and now he had sent a knife and note in a box of socks and hard candies from Mother. Dad had told his fellow hunter and customer John Mathis, owner of a furniture store on Seventh Street in Little Rock, about my need, and Mr. Mathis found one for me. The special camper's knife, the equivalent of a super Swiss Army knife, had three blades of different sizes, a spoon, fork, and screwdriver, all of which folded neatly into or beside its three-and-one-half-inch handle.

Only six quiet days passed in reserve before First Battalion returned to a new position in the Hennebont sector. Because many other companies were in the regiment, we hadn't expected to go back so quickly. Later, we learned it resulted from the extension of our division's overall containment mission to include the port and submarine pens at Saint-Nazaire.

We also didn't foresee, on September 22, that units of the 301st would remain on the front line for the next sixty-five consecutive days.

In Company B's new position, the headquarters platoon bivouacked near an old manor house on a large country estate. The rundown house and its outbuildings sat in the midst of extensive wooded grounds. Among the buildings was the largest dove cote I ever saw. It was empty, so I guess the birds had already been eaten. Despite being near the front, the owner of the manor, an upper-class Frenchwoman, still lived in the house, along with one female servant. Lean and in her fifties, the gray-haired grande dame acted as though there were no war taking place nearby.

Soldiers constantly walked and drove along the gravel road running in front of her house and past our CP, but the woman acknowledged only officers. I don't know how she identified them, because some officers removed their insignia to avoid being targets for snipers. But in a mysterious way, much like a bird-dog sensing quail, the Frenchwoman could detect commissioned officers instantly. While our CP was near, the grande dame entertained Company B officers and Colonel Hagerty, among others.

Our underground CP was left by men of the 302nd, whom we replaced. They had constructed the room totally below ground level using the prefabricated walls of a German building and a flat roof of logs covered with two feet of dirt and sod. Although we weren't threatened by German planes, the CP was undetectable from the air.

A set of earthen steps led down to the room's single entrance, a door frame covered by a blanket. Duckboards over the dirt floor kept our feet off the cold, damp ground and made cleaning the room easier. The captain divided the CP into two areas with a screen of blankets about two thirds the height of the room. On the side farthest from the entry were cots for Straub, Sundheimer, and Kelly, and on the entry side were the sergeant's desk and records and the company switchboard.

We rigged the switchboard from military and civilian telephones scavenged from the Germans, who had scavenged from the French, and combined all the equipment with our sound-powered field phones. The drops on the face of the switchboard identified each position on the front line, and plugs on lines connected all platoons to the CP and to each other. The telephone operator had a headset, mouthpiece, and earphones, freeing his hands to write and insert the plugs.

Although I spent part of every day and night at the switchboard, the captain didn't allow members of the communication squad to sleep in the underground room. We bunked in dugouts adjacent to the CP. I shared a shallow dugout, about four feet deep and six feet square, with several others. Its extremely low roof, which was part of a wall left over from the CP room, made ventilation so poor that no more than two of us could sleep in the hole at one time. By alternating our duties on the switchboard, running errands, and standing guard, we shared easily enough.

Captain Straub set up our first CP at Lorient out in the open, immediately behind the front line, but at each succeeding sector, he moved it farther back. Though the later locations were better protected, members of the communications squad were almost cut off from their friends in the rifle platoons. It's true we weren't as distant as the company clerk and mail clerk, who stayed back at Regimental Headquarters, but most of our contact with buddies was via telephone. When I met a rifleman while checking the wire to a platoon position, or carrying insurance or allotment papers sent up for signature, men seemed glad enough to see me. But I didn't want to be considered privileged for staying behind the front and not going on patrol.

On October 8, 1944, the Ninety-fourth joined the Twelfth Army Group, under General Omar Bradley, and the division reserve area was moved to the vicinity of Nozay. Corps and Army Group changes meant little to us enlisted men because they rarely changed our company's daily routine or rations.

The American Forces Network broadcast the World Series, and men behind the front lines gathered around vehicles that had radios to listen to the games. Although the Cardinals and Browns, both representing the city of Saint Louis, competed for the baseball championship, the loyal GI fans of each team argued loudly over insignificant points. Their enthusiastic support was surprising because most of the professional baseball stars were now in the armed forces. The jeep and command car drivers turned up the volume of their radios to allow groups of men to hear, far and near, including the Germans, who could have blasted us with artillery; it was a relief when the Cardinals defeated the Browns, four games to two.

The pipe and tobacco I requested from my father finally arrived. Dad enclosed special instructions on how to break in a pipe and avoid a raw tongue. Although I followed his advice to the letter, by the end of a week my tongue was irritated and the tip was sore. At the end of another week, after trying to keep tobacco alight in the bowl by puffing incessantly and relighting every few minutes, I surrendered to cigarettes again. I hadn't the heart to tell Dad my failure.

By the time we took our second front-line position, the mission of the Ninety-fourth had expanded again, not only to contain the German forces in Lorient and Saint-Nazaire but to assume responsibility for the troops of the Free French of the Interior (FFI), a large organization embracing all the partisan underground groups that formed in France during the German Occupation. The Ninety-fourth Division was responsible for coordinating the several FFI units serving alongside our companies and supplying them with food, ammunition, and eventually uniforms.

One company of the FFI joined Company B to fight, as they called the Germans, "*Les Boches.*" One evening when I went on duty at the CP, a young French lieutenant was speaking in English to Captain Straub and Sundheimer, who both left soon after. The slender blond's uniform looked as if he had stepped out of an operetta: polished boots; cream-colored, whipcord jodhpurs, with leather patches inside the knees; a blue military jacket with brass buttons; and a black beret, with an insignia pinned on its crown.

After our officers departed, he walked over to me and sat in the chair next to the switchboard. He introduced himself as Pierre-Claude Leglise, asking, in a British accent, "Where are you from in the United States?"

After I told him, he asked, "How were you employed?"

When I said I was a college student, he remarked that some soldiers in "*neuf-quartre*" (Ninety-fourth) didn't appear very cultivated or well educated. The officer's speech, manners, and obvious cultivation suggested to me that he was an aristocrat, which may also have accounted for one so young commanding a company of soldiers.

He said he was a Parisian studying medicine at the University of Bordeaux before joining the Maquis, or Resistance. According to him, the Germans decreed, in 1943, a compulsory labor draft for work in Germany, which made thousands of young Frenchmen like himself "take to the bush," which, he said, is what *maquis* means in French. Then he explained how the different resistance groups had maintained, even after the invasion, their separate identity within the Forces Francaises de l'Interieur.

According to the young captain, Brittany was the oldest, strongest center of resistance in France, for the Brittany farmers and persons in the Maquis had fervently opposed the German Occupation. Soon after D-Day the *maquisards* sabotaged railroads, fought pitched battles with German troops, and liberated whole towns, including nearby Quimper. Because of their activities, Patton's Third Army met little opposition in Brittany until units reached Brest, Lorient, and Saint-Nazaire.

Sharing personal opinions about our countries, the German occupation, and the European war in general, we talked all the time I was on duty. Before leaving, he gave me his personal calling card and invited me to visit him if I ever reached Paris after the war. He wrote his permanent home address and telephone number on the back of his card—98 rue du le Passionniere, Paris (X'), Tel TRU.-54.17.

Shortly after Lieutenant Leglise left, I went to my dugout to sleep and had barely settled in when bursts of rifle fire and shouting broke out along the front line. Leaping up to rush outside, I hit my head a resounding blow on the low ceiling of my new hole. It really shook me up and delayed my reaching the CP, where my replacement, who had rung up a platoon on the front line, had been told that the FFI were "having breakfast and cleaning their rifles." For breakfast, they drank a shot of Calvados, the strong Brittany brandy, to clear their throats; and they fired several rounds of ammunition to clear their rifles. By the time every Frenchman joined in, the ruckus at the front sounded as if a major attack were under way.

A few days later, Lieutenant Leglise returned with two other FFI officers to discuss with Captain Straub rations and ammunition for his unit. After their meeting, Leglise showed an interest in my olive-drab wool-knit "jeep" cap; he wanted the visor and ear covers for cold weather, and asked if I would exchange it for his Basque beret. I jumped at the chance, even though he wasn't willing to include the medallion pinned on its front. I figured if Colonel Hagerty wore a beret, I could too.

Not long afterwards, an ASTP friend of mine in the Second Platoon made a foolish mistake while on patrol. The chief activity of all rifle platoons was day and night reconnaissance patrols, and Stewart

Kranz, our French interpreter, went on patrol, checking for Boche in and around a cottage in an unoccupied area in front of our sector.

When the patrol found no German soldiers occupying the cottage, Stewart and another soldier went inside to explore its rooms. They found among the household items German military equipment; the most appealing piece was a leather case, possibly containing binoculars. Stewart picked the case up, and it exploded, blowing off part of his hand and blinding him in one eye. The patrol hurried back to our lines, and a company medic called the CP to send for a vehicle to evacuate Stewart.

Kranz was lying on a litter across the hood of the aid-station jeep when it passed our CP. The captain and I were waiting beside the road, and Straub stopped the jeep to check on Kranz. Since I didn't know what else to do, I laid my hand on my friend's shoulder while they talked. As the jeep drove away, the captain said it wasn't likely Kranz would come back and that he was going to miss him, especially his help translating. It puzzled me that someone smart like Kranz, who heard the mandatory lectures and saw British movies about booby traps, had made such a foolish mistake.

Shortly after Kranz was wounded, our company withdrew again to reserve for a brief time. I have no memory of the precise location, only details of a movie shown outdoors. Although the weather had been alternating between sultry heat and damp cold, the night they showed the movie was almost balmy. The screen was set up on one side of a narrow clearing in a woods, and we sat on the opposite side of the open space, leaning our backs against trees, to watch the western *Tall in the Saddle,* starring John Wayne and a boyish brunette, Ella Raines. My memory of the occasion persists, I'm sure, because it was outdoors and the only movie I saw for six months.

Our holding "action" around Lorient had become so routine for us and the Germans that the lone enemy plane that flew over nightly wasn't fired at. It appeared at the same time each evening; its pilot joshingly called "Bed-check Charley." Kelly claimed the plane probably carried newspapers and mail from Germany. If that were true, why was a plane "bringing aid and comfort to the enemy" not considered hostile and shot down?

The company and a spell of cold weather settled in at our new position simultaneously. For the first time, Straub didn't place our CP in dense woods, perhaps because the leaves that earlier furnished camouflage had fallen.

Kelly, Palma, Boguski, and I moved into a ramshackle stone farmhouse on the edge of a large pasture, which spread out on each side and to the rear to deep woods. We were a bit complacent about enemy artillery and didn't bother to dig foxholes near the house. The impenetrable appearance of the cottage's stone walls and slate roof may have influenced our carelessness.

The farmhouse wasn't occupied when we arrived; I don't remember whether the old farmer moved out voluntarily or was forced out. Although the farmer no longer lived in the cottage, he continued using his barn for pressing apples for *cidre* and milking his only cow, which grazed in the pasture all day and slowly wended to the barn in the morning and afternoon. Sometimes artillery rounds fell nearby as the farmer collected apples in the orchards, but he carried on without flinching. Under fire, the old man's deliberate pace and dour face suggested he was either brave or stupid.

Early one morning, Boguski and I were walking back to the cottage from a slit trench in the woods when we saw the farmer and two other elderly Frenchmen enter the barn. At that same instant, an 88-mm shell exploded over the field, and we ran toward the barn, which was closer than the house, to get behind its walls and under its roof. But once inside, we realized the thatched roof wouldn't protect us from rain.

The old farmers paid no attention to us or the explosions, talking laconically while turning a gigantic screw that was mashing a pile of apples on the bed of straw used to filter the juice. Shell bursts were advancing toward the barn, which convinced me it might be safer under the press. When I crawled up beside the juice bucket, the old farmers who had been watching me spit out a flurry of French that ended in laughter and slaps on their knees. The shelling stopped before reaching the barn; the only wounds Joe and I suffered were to our prides.

The farmer's cottage was smaller than his barn; it was a single open room with a fireplace at one end for heating and cooking. Two plank criblike beds, each a little wider than an Army bunk, stood against opposite walls. The only other furnishings in the room—a table, two chairs, and several low stools—served soldiers well enough but hardly seemed adequate for a farmer's family.

The cottage and property had no toilet of any kind that I detected, so I assume the family members answered nature's call the same way other Brittany men and women did. Frenchmen urinating against walls out in the open I expected, but women doing the same surprised me. I was astonished the first time I saw a stocky, ruddy-faced farm woman come out a cottage door, raise her skirts above her naked buttocks and chapped thighs, and squat down beside the front wall of a house to relieve herself. My presence didn't faze her.

The farmer's cow had remained on his property despite the firefights before we came, but empty chicken coops suggested the fowl had run away or been stolen. A few days after we moved in, a scrawny chicken came back and pecked around the yard for grain. Even though travel had probably toughened it, Kelly decided to cook the pullet to have a break from K rations. The sergeant hung a pot of water over the fire to boil, tied the chicken's feet, and chopped off its head. While Joe and I watched and dodged its bloody, headless body thrashing about on the barn floor, Kelly brought the pot of boiling water outside to dip the chicken and loosen its feathers for plucking. After refilling the pot, he deposited the thin, bare carcass and hung it over the fire.

The chicken simmered, and Kelly checked it all afternoon for tenderness. It was a tough old bird.

Exasperated, Kelly pulled a bottle of Calvados out of his musette bag, poured it into the pot, swearing, "By God, that'll tenderize the son of a bitch 'til I can chew it." Kelly's persistence and the alcohol didn't succeed, but we wanted a bite anyway.

The sergeant's experience with the chicken helped me realize how lucky I was to think about the next meal only when chow arrived. The kitchens were a long distance from the front, but the cooks, when possible, served at least one hot meal a day from insulated containers. Even so, many soldiers bitched about meals that I liked—creamed chipped beef on toast (the infamous "shit on a shingle"), and Spam, in whatever way the cooks camouflaged it.

Often, though, circumstances left us totally dependent on the packaged rations—K, C, and Ten-in-one. I liked portions of the K rations, produced by the Wrigley Company of Chicago, which were convenient, nutritious, and easy-to-prepare single meals. Their wax-covered cardboard container, the size and shape of a Cracker Jack box, held hard biscuits, canned meat or cheese, cubes of sugar, four cigarettes (brands like Old Gold, Twenty Grand, and Fleetwood), matches, chewing gum, and a metal key for opening cans. I was fond of cheddar cheese and ham, and warm pork spread lightly sprinkled with bouillon powder.

The breakfast had a fruit bar—a mix of dried figs, prunes, apples, and apricots—soluble coffee, and sheets of toilet tissue; and the dinner had flavored or plain dextrose tablets, plus a packet of lime or lemonade powder. Some guys hated the four-ounce chocolate bar that was enriched with sugar, oat flower, vanillin, and vitamins, but the chocolate D-bar was my dessert. C rations had pork and beans, and a mix of potatoes and beef in hash that I favored, seasoned with bouillon powder.

Ten-in-one rations would feed a squad. The dried beef and rice, to which you added water and heat, was always appealing, especially after long bouts of K and C rations. Accompanying ten-in-ones were olive-drab cans captioned "Butter" and "Jelly." The former, intensely yellow and thick as crankcase grease, and the latter, with an artificial and unidentifiable fruit flavor, still struck me as special when spread on biscuits.

One afternoon, Sergeant Palma asked me to accompany him in locating an OP in the Gacilly sector in an abandoned village on a hilltop between us and Lorient. The captain needed to know the precise disposition of OPs, platoons, automatic rifles, machine guns, and mortars, and Palma checked locations regularly, making up-to-date transparencies of them. The overlays were used on maps to pinpoint quadrants exactly when requesting artillery fire. Since we had recently moved into the Gacilly sector, Palma wasn't sure where Sergeant Herring had set up his OP.

We didn't leave the CP until 1500 because Palma wanted the fading light at sundown to help conceal us if the village was under observation. He also chose a roundabout path, part of it in front of our lines, not only to cover our approach but to inspect a large German gun emplacement he'd been told about.

We located the old emplacement about halfway to the village, its huge naval cannon still aimed seaward. In the hillside behind the gun was a deep, concrete tunnel that housed the crew's quarters and ammunition storage space. After examining the cannon, we trained our flashlights into the dark tunnel without entering more than a few feet and decided not to go farther into the corridor for fear of booby traps. Besides, the daylight behind the steep hill we had to ascend to the village was fading into shadow.

Climbing the path, Palma warned we had to avoid streets as much as possible by walking behind and through houses. The first house in the outskirts had a gaping hole in its back wall, and we climbed through it into a bedroom. The large bed was neatly made, its linens untouched except for sprinkles of plaster on the bedspread. However, the rest of the room was in total disarray, broken furniture and clothing scattered across the floor.

Walking through the rest of the rooms, we came to a closed door, which Palma kicked open. The dining room was totally undisturbed; finding a family gathered around the dining table, ready to eat the fly-covered food in the serving dishes and drink the wine from the filled glasses, wouldn't have been surprising. The scene looked as if the family, interrupted just as they sat down to eat, went out to check something and never returned.

We left the eerie room and walked out the front door heading for an alley between two houses on the opposite side of the street. Almost instantly, an 88-mm round whammed behind the house we'd just left. Palma, without saying anything to me, broke into a run, and I followed. His path was erratic, through houses and across streets and sometimes doubling back because artillery rounds were slamming closer.

Scurrying like rats in the maze of narrow alleys and streets, we dashed to where Palma thought the OP was located, dodging fragments of steel and masonry, expecting the next round to hit us. I was as breathless from fear as from running when shouts above and behind made us stop at the corner of a building to see where the voice came from. Herring waved from a second-story window across the street, and we ducked into the door below the window, relieved to have found him.

The sergeant greeted us as if we had dropped in for tea following an afternoon stroll. His casual manner didn't surprise me, though, because once we landed on the Continent, he was a daredevil who welcomed hazardous or unusual duty. Earlier, he had set up an outpost in a house still occupied by a Frenchwoman and after a few days developed a sexual relationship with her. I talked to him once on the phone, and he said he was in bed with the woman, naked. "Warmer that way," he chuckled.

We stayed at the OP until long after dark, sharing Herring's rations. Before we headed back to our lines, Palma called the switchboard operator to warn him when and where we'd be returning. Hoping the sergeant would take a more direct and protected route back, I vowed if we got back safely, I would never volunteer or agree to go on patrol again if I could avoid it, even with someone I trusted as much as Palma.

By late October, the weather was freezing and the landscape sere. The canopy of trees and bushes that had concealed us in September had browned, shriveled, and fallen. Beneath the bare trees in the orchards, rotting apples fermented in swirls of bees and flies, and the turf in the fields, still water-soaked from the frequent rains, had turned pale tan. Temperatures dipped earlier in the afternoon and dropped much lower at night. We seldom removed our combat jackets anymore, and wool shirts and pants, after running or digging, were no longer hot and itchy. Lying snugly in my sleeping bag at night and in the early morning, I relished the crisp, fresh air.

About this time, rocket launchers joined the 301st Artillery. The missiles were meant to harass the enemy, and the launcher's mobility and ease—quickly setting up, firing, and leaving a launch site—were advantages over more static artillery. Our first warning about the new weapon was an order for all companies to take cover when rockets were launched over their sectors and to remain concealed until firing ended.

A launcher had ten banks of eight rocket tubes each with electric detonators, which were mounted on the bed of a two-and-a-half-ton truck. The crew of the mobile launcher drove to a suitable site and laid metal covers on the ground behind the truck to prevent the dust stirred by the back blast from revealing their position to German observers. When the rockets were fired near sundown, we heard their metallic whomps upon ignition, followed by screaming whooshes in flight. The crew retrieved the back plates and drove away as quickly as possible to avoid the quick retaliation of 88s.

After the first rockets were launched over us, we needed no further reminders to stay under cover. Malfunctions caused misguided missiles to fall on our own lines and troops. One soldier eating dinner with a small group died when a rocket fell short and metal shards pierced his helmet, killing him and wounding the others. Despite their uncertain trajectories, rocket firings continued, adding novelty and danger to our sunset alerts by threatening Americans as well as Germans.

During the severely cold weather, one of my canine teeth ached, and I asked a company medic for something to ease the pain. For immediate relief, the medic soaked a small ball of cotton in oil of cloves and pressed it into the cavity. For the ache and pain, he gave me aspirin, but relief was only temporary. Kelly suggested I go to a dentist at the regimental aid station near Pont Scorff. The day I took off was cold, windy, and rainy, wholly unsuitable for riding in an open jeep. Even though I had my raincoat on over my combat jacket and had wrapped a wool scarf across my mouth, the icy wind in my face made the tooth ache violently.

Conditions at regimental aid didn't look promising either, for the dentist's chair was outside the clinic's tent, perhaps to allow the dentist more light on such a dark day. While I sat in the chair enveloped in a breezy mist, the dentist operated a treadle-driven drill with his foot to excavate the decay and fill the cavity. Despite the primitive setting and rudimentary tools, the young dentist accomplished the repair quickly and painlessly. Novocaine kept the drill from hurting, and the mist made it memorable.

Not long after, comfort reached my feet too. Kelly received word that sixty pairs of combat boots were coming to replace leggings. I'd always hated lacing canvas leggings and keeping them clean, and asked the sergeant for a pair of boots. He frowned at me and said, "I can't let you have boots until platoon leaders decide who needs them on the front." But the day the boots were delivered, he pointed at the pile, saying, "Harrison, pick a pair that fits you before I send them up on the line."

For some inexplicable reason, the regiment commander again shifted Company B's position. Instead of the usual jerry-built accommodations for our CP, we inherited a large concrete bunker built by the Germans on the military crest of a hill. Its only drawback was caused by the frequent rains—dripping walls and a cold, dank interior. The bunker had enough space for our whole platoon, but the captain claimed it for himself, his exec, and the first sergeant.

Kelly told us to find or dig holes; that didn't bother me, so long as I was near enough to reach the bunker quickly in artillery barrages.

Charles Schuette (Shootie), who had recently transferred from a rifle platoon, joined me in a dugout in the side of a hedgerow near the bunker. He was a replacement Kelly wanted me to befriend.

The first concentrated attack against the First Battalion came on October 20. Noisy and exciting, the German foray met with little success, and the front remained quiet for another week. Then the Germans launched a heavy barrage, beginning at 0725, on October 28.

Shootie and I had finished breakfast and were reading letters that came with the chow. I was outside the hole, sitting with my back against an oil drum that supported one corner of the wooden door that was the roof over the hole's entry. Shootie was farther back inside the hole, leaning against the dirt wall of the entry. An 88 shell whomped, bursting slightly above our hedgerow. I looked up from my letter as a second round whammed directly overhead, spraying red-and-white-hot shrapnel. The pieces whizzing past my head pierced the oil drum behind me. The hot shards tore through the side of the oil drum and rattled down inside it as I threw myself farther under the door and crawled into the deep recess beside Shootie. Artillery raked our company's line, round after round, until at least twenty-five air- and point-detonating bursts had saturated the area.

During the barrage, Shootie and I lay with our rifles at the ready, listening to the explosions and expecting Germans to charge when the guns quit. Finally, the barrage ended; we sprang from the hole and threw ourselves against the bank, prepared to fire at the enemy coming up the hillside. But no one advanced from the woods and crossed the field at the bottom of the hill. The Germans had merely diverted our company while attacking another sector and didn't harm anyone in our outfit.

Captain Straub, for his own reasons, decided that our communications squad should perform more than their regular duties of guarding the CP and operating the switchboard. Apparently, he believed that we needed to be "blooded" for combat for our own protection and warned us he would be sending us out on patrol.

Soon after, Palma gathered our squad to patrol in the woods in front of our CP where riflemen reportedly heard noises and spotted gleams of light at night. To reach the woods from the CP, we descended thirty-five yards down a hillside and crossed another hundred yards over an open field. Because we didn't know whether the hillside and field were under German observation, we slid down on our butts in chest-high grass and then ran, one at a time across the field, about fifteen seconds apart.

In the woods, we spread out, walking slowly through the thick underbrush and trees until we came upon a narrow, unpaved road leading through more woods, farther away from our lines. We walked in single file down the road, and scouts ahead came upon a narrow footpath off to our left. Palma decided that we were far enough away from our front line to stop; he didn't believe platoons could see lights through trees this far away.

With us searching the woods on all sides, a squad member saw a building at the distant end of a narrow lane. We approached it in a skirmish line, ready to attack from all sides if the house were occupied. After closing on the small shack, we found it empty, but there were signs in the yard indicating German patrols had been there eating and defecating. Scattered about the small yard were partially burned logs and ashes and tin cans with German labels. The human excrement was beside the house's foundations.

Shootie asked, "With woods all around, why in hell did they crap by the house?" Later, we learned that Germans had used such a calling card in other wars.

Our patrol milled about carelessly and loudly, cutting up while checking for other signs of the enemy until Palma called a halt to it. With my natural anxiety, I felt watched, though we had found no one there.

As we left the site, most squad members slung their rifles over their shoulders and strolled back toward the road as if we were on a picnic in a Stateside park. I felt like yelling at the guys, telling them how stupid it was to horse around beyond our line. Instead, I walked backwards at the rear of the patrol, my rifle in port position ready to fire.

The others kidded me, and Palma put them on alert too, going back to our lines.

Tense on my only combat patrol, I was more stressed out guarding the outpost in front of the CP, which our squad manned in pairs twenty-four hours a day. The land in front of the CP bunker gradually sloped down to a narrow promontory about thirty yards away, where an outpost sat on the forward edge of the hill. The position, camouflaged by high grass and low-hanging tree limbs, had a narrow opening in the grass through which the occupants could see to the left and right, down to and across an open field at the bottom of the hill.

I volunteered to guard the position with someone other than Shootie, for I had learned that his poor hearing accounted for his transfer into our squad. I knew I was expendable manning an OP, but I wanted to improve the odds by having a partner with senses as acute as mine. I had misgivings about sharing with my new buddy.

At sunset, we crept through the underbrush to relieve the fellows on duty. We were going to watch all night, changing places every two hours and warning the company about enemy activity by phone or, if taken by surprise, by rifle fire.

Until midnight, we sat side by side; then Shootie crawled into the rear of our grass nest to nap. Soon after, he was breathing deeply, sleeping like a baby. In an hour, my back was aching from sitting bent over, peering through the slot in the grass overhang, so I lay down on my side. I couldn't see very well in that position, and the longer I watched the drowsier I became. To avoid dozing off, I crawled outside.

The brilliant moonlight had turned the entire landscape silver. Glistening trees and chest-high grass on the hillside stood out in sharp relief against the black woods. The night, still and silent, had no movement or sound of any kind.

About an hour later, I was leaning against a tree in its dark shadow, when I saw shiny blades of tall grass slowly parting and a lone black figure rising. Bending forward at the waist, as if listening, the figure paused warily before moving toward our lines. My chest muscles were so tense I could hardly draw a full breath. I released my rifle's safety.

The approaching figure stopped and looked in my direction as if he saw me. But then he turned and signaled behind him.

Nearly a dozen black figures rose in quick succession from the silvery grass.

Not knowing what to do, I crouched lower, crossing in the shadows toward the OP, whispering desperately, "Shootie!"

When he didn't answer, I knew he was too deaf to hear me. I wanted to tell him to call the CP while I kept my eyes on the figures.

They were coming nearer. The leader reached a point close enough to hear me without seeing me in the shadows.

"Halt!" I growled.

The lead figure jerked to a stop, and the rest sank into the tall grass. I heard the password; it was Lieutenant Decker's distinctive voice.

After my countersign, the patrol glided past the OP. Why hadn't we been told a patrol would return our way?

At 0200, I waked Shootie and fell into my own deep sleep. Someone's failure to notify us about the patrol was lightly excused the next day as an oversight.

Shootie and I heard about men bathing regularly at a German bathhouse that had running water and a half dozen showers. It was found in no-man's-land, several hundred yards in front of our company sector, by men in one of the rifle platoons. According to platoon members, there were no signs of recent use by the Germans.

I was reluctant to venture that far beyond our lines until Shootie persuaded me to accompany him one raw, overcast afternoon. We rolled clean underwear, socks, and soap in towels and walked behind the frontline positions until we reached the platoon nearest the bathhouse. Fellows there guided us to a well-worn trail, which we followed through the woods to a field, where we saw the isolated bathhouse on the far side. Circling the edge of the woods, we reached the bathhouse without walking far in the open.

There were no signs or sounds of other GIs when we entered the door in the windowless wall of the frame building. The interior was concrete stucco from the floor up to the high, narrow windows on two sides. Against the wall farthest from the showers were low benches. The concrete floor slanted down to a central drain.

Showering in an isolated German bathhouse beyond our front lines was creepy. But we leaned our rifles against a wall and removed our uniforms. Naked and helpless as babies, we stepped beneath the shower heads, stuck our fingers through the ends of the long chains hanging down from them, and pulled. The icy spray struck like sharp pins and took our breath away; laughing and gulping for air, we rubbed our chests and legs to increase our circulation before soaping up.

We lathered all over, including our hair, making lots of suds. After so many weeks living in dirt, sharing ours and others' body odors, we relished all the free-flowing water and the fresh scent of the soap. Rinsing the suds out of our hair, I felt Shootie's hand on my arm. I opened my blurry eyes and saw two dark figures with rifles standing in the door.

The GIs, seeing our startled, wide-eyed stares, laughed and asked, "Who'd you guys think we were?"

We took our showers just in time. Three days later, just before the First Battalion moved to the Saint Severin sector, Company B retired to reserve again, bivouacking in the same field where we first stayed. The architectural efforts by outfits occupying the field since our initial visit were impressive. The slew of dugouts, following no standard Army forms, were extraordinary in their sizes and shapes. Some holes, extending in every direction underground in the hedgerows, had space enough for bed-shelves on three sides. In addition, many had stone fireplaces, inside or out, or stoves molded from tin cans of different sizes. A few shacks had been constructed from boxes, or "liberated" doors and window frames, showing their occupants' lack of concern about German artillery.

Joe and I had gained enough experience by this time not to sleep in our pup tent. Instead, we claimed an old foxhole in the shadow of the French farmer's special grove of trees, an ideal location near the hedgerow at the edge of the field and close to the latrine. But we enlarged and improved the hole, making it comfortable for two by expanding its width to seven feet and digging five feet deep. We didn't dig deep enough, though, for the roof to be sufficiently high for us to stand up. We scavenged longer logs from collapsed dugouts for the roof, without cutting trees, which were still off-limits.

Inside the hole, we laid our bedrolls on opposite sides, leaving an open space in the middle. To light the interior, we scraped out recesses in the walls over the heads of our bedrolls and lined them with reflectors fashioned from opened and flattened C-ration cans. The lamps were also C-ration cans filled with wax melted off K-ration boxes and had floating wicks. We were more comfortable and safer than the first time in reserve.

When we finished our dugout, Joe and I were so sweaty and smeared with dirt that we asked Kelly how soon an engineering outfit would bring the shower unit and clean uniforms. When he said there were no such plans, we decided to bathe outdoors on the cold, windy November day. Low clouds were threatening rain as we heated water in a large tin can borrowed from Shock. Standing naked, covered in goose bumps, we poured an even share of hot water into our helmets for lathering up and saved the remainder for rinsing off. Our bodies and underwear were clean, but we had to put our dirty uniforms back on. Still, our hasty washups in the brisk air left us feeling lighter, warmer, and more invigorated.

When Palma and I decided to produce the variety show we wrote at the front, squad members constructed an elevated stage platform with ammunition crates in a field next to our bivouac area. For a curtain to mask performers, they hung two shelter halves on a wire strung between two poles at the front of the stage.

For my part of the show, I repeated favorite jokes, sang an original song about our NCOs, and did an impression of Colonel Hagerty, costumed like the regimental commander. For that, I borrowed an officer's jacket and shoulder harness from Lieutenant Sundheimer.

And, since the colonel affected one, I wore the Basque beret that Pierre-Claude Leglise had traded for my wool-knit cap.

Until a few minutes before the performance started, we didn't know that Straub had invited Colonel Hagerty. Learning the colonel was coming, I wanted to drop my impression of him, but Palma protested, insisting that we do what had been rehearsed. He didn't believe Hagerty would be offended, and I hoped that was true because I exaggerated the colonel's physical and vocal behavior.

The colonel and his entourage swept in just before the curtain parted, led by the beaming Captain Straub, who was so proud that B Company was doing something special. Enlisted men sat on the ground near the stage, and our officers and visitors stood behind them. Tony was emcee and pulled the curtain, singers performed without accompaniment, and I told jokes before talk-singing the verses I had composed:

We crossed the Channel to France's battered shore;
Hit Utah Beach on D-plus ninety-four.
By foot and truck, through dust and muck,
To Brittany we went,
To hide like moles in dirty holes
At Saint-Nazaire and Lorient.

We've got Germans in a pocket by the sea.
We've got Germans? Who's a captive—they or we?
We hold them in, they keep us out.
You wonder who's in charge?
That's quite a doubt to think about,
A question for my sarge.

I've got sergeants; I have them every day.
I've got sergeants who have to have their say.
They rave and shout and cuss me out,
Then blame it on the brass.
I've got some gripes against these stripes
Who sit upon their . . . my pass.

I've got Kelly, the top kick of the crew.
I've got Kelly and Kelly's got the brew.
He loves to lay in old Plouay,

WAR DEPARTMENT
LITTLE ROCK ENGINEER DISTRICT
LITTLE ROCK, ARKANSAS

Name Allie C. Harrison
Designation Under Clerk
Race White Age 17
Height 5'11" Weight 137
Eyes Blue Hair Black

JUN 3 '42

Allie C. Harrison
Signature

Authentication
1267 Chief Adm. Assistant

Right Thumb Print

Top left and right: Senior class graduation photographs of Marian Blair Gammill (Tumpy) and me, May 1942, Little Rock Senior High School. Bottom left: My identification card when employed at the U.S. District Engineer's office on Broadway Boulevard in Little Rock, Arkansas, summer 1942. Bottom right: A photo made for Tumpy and my folks, by Maurice Photo Service in Columbus, Georgia, while I was in basic training at Fort Benning, Georgia, September 1943.

Top: Farewell visit with Dad (and Mom, who took the photo) in Little Rock in July, before shipping overseas to Europe with the Ninety-fourth Division in August 1944. Bottom: Company clerks and their assistants at Camp McCain, Mississippi, summer 1944: Corporals Joe Hughey of Company A and Howard Davis of Company B, kneeling, and their assistants. The tar-papered barracks and unpaved streets were characteristic of the camp.

Top: A fond farewell to ward nurse, Lieutenant Betty L. Copeland, and a medical orderly, in the office of Surgical Ward #3, 112th General Hospital, near Newton Abbot, Devonshire, England, April 1945. Bottom left: Me, Christy Vasile, and Frank Rotondo, in the idyllic setting of the *Stadtwald*, Hoescht, suburb of Frankfurt am Main, Germany, June 1945. Policies of nonfraternization and carrying weapons were still in effect. Bottom right: Private Frohlic and me swinging along a path in the park in Hoescht.

Top: A "formal" pose of softball buddies, with German *Jugend* of the neighborhood: Corporal Vasile (State Department driver) kneeling, three boys, and "Mother" Leshak (another Group CC mate) kneeling, and Spiegel, me, and Blumenthal (our resident baseball expert) standing. Bottom: Three Army comrades: me, Mitchum, and Rotondo in August 1945, all wearing our service ribbons and combat infantryman badges.

Top: Political Division, U.S. Group CC enlisted staff beside Ambassador Murphy's car, next to the *porte cochere* of OMGUS Headquarters. Bottom: The Misses Louise Byrnes and Anna Mary Gring, State Department message center clerks and girlfriends of Rotondo and me in Berlin 1945.

Top: In rehearsal, impersonating Don Jose Vallejo, a character in the comedy *Cradle Snatchers*, the first production of the American Little Theater of Berlin. The cast included Army officers and enlisted men, and WAC officers and enlisted women. Chet Elliott, OSS clerk and friend, is at far right. Bottom: A drink with friends at Club 48, for enlisted personnel in Berlin, Germany, winter 1945.

Top: Patch of the Ninety-fourth Infantry Division. Center: Patch of the Army Specialized Training Program. Bottom: Patch of the United States Group Control Council (Office of Military Government, United States Zone).

Top: Portrait made by Liselotte Winterstein in Berlin, 1945. Bottom: Me at Auburn University, 1991.

And if you'll take a peep,
Though he's reclined, I think you'll find
He isn't getting sleep.

I've got Palma, the communications man.
I've got Palma and Palma's got the plan.
These days he plays with overlays,
But if you'll check his maps,
Though they're refined, the plots you'll find
Are where he takes his naps.

After several verses about other NCOs, I left the stage and changed into my costume. Without an introduction, I strutted back on the jerry-built stage as the colonel, making a regimental commander's speech, using well-known Hagerty phrases.

Risky as it was, the crowd was silent. A few snickered before laughing out loud as I walked, gestured, and spoke. Hagerty smiled before he finally chuckled. And the officers, checking the colonel's reaction first, laughed too. It was jolly good fun, as the British say, kidding a field-grade commander in front of company-grade officers . . . and lowly GIs!

While our company was in reserve, other units of the regiment adjusted the front lines around Lorient. We returned to a new sector and found no ready-made dugouts and bunkers. Their absence stimulated our captain's imagination as if he were a newlywed home builder. He wanted another underground CP similar to the one we inherited from the 302nd on the grande dame's estate. He chose a site in a thick grove of small trees beside a major intersection of two paved roads. The roads had obviously been thoroughfares in peacetime because the shattered remnants of steel and concrete utility poles sprouted along their shoulders. The captain insisted that a CP at an intersection allowed easy access to platoons and Battalion Headquarters.

Kelly organized our platoon into two construction crews—a group to dig the hole and another to dismantle and transport a prefabricated room that the captain found on a hillside near the front. For the room (ten by fifteen feet, with eight-foot-high walls) to be assembled in the hole, the excavation had to be larger than its dimensions. With only standard picks, shovels, and wooden sleds, it was soon clear that the diggers needed larger tools and equipment. Otherwise, the dig would be too strenuous, even for the strongest men, and would take more than a day. Straub and Sundheimer, to encourage the digging crew, stripped off their shirts and helped.

The excavation took a day and a half. As the hole neared completion, Kelly assigned me to the moving crew that had already been taking the building apart and numbering its pieces for reassembly. When I reached the site in the truck, the building was completely down and most of its parts ready for loading. The crew worked fast dismantling and marking the building's parts because the site was within range of German observation.

A few crew members thought they had seen reflections off field glasses and were convinced the Germans had spotted the site. No one had to persuade us to load as quickly as possible, but Kelly prodded a smaller soldier who was having trouble lifting one end of a wall.

Straining under the wall's weight, the soldier protested, "Sarge, my name's Simpson, not Samson!"

As our loaded truck pulled away, the first 88-round fell just short of where we'd been. Then a round fell ahead of the truck, and another one fell short, as we raced away. Three rounds followed, whomping like giant footfalls behind us. If the Germans didn't see our crew, they may have heard the trucks on the road and fired a presighted ladder for anyone traveling there.

Back at the CP, our crew assembled the floor and walls in the hole as diggers felled trees to support the wide roof. With the beams and ceiling in place, everybody tossed and spread excavated dirt on the roof and dug stairwells to doors at opposite ends of the room for easy access. Like the other CPs, it was off-limits except for official business, and only Straub, Sundheimer, and the first sergeant could sleep there.

The weather steadily worsened in November. As temperatures fell, so did heavy rains, filling the craters in fields and leaking into dugouts that weren't covered or ditched properly. I had grown used to rains, mists, and fogs, even before the cold set in, but my feet and hands were never dry or warm once winter really set in. My socks seemed to stay wet all the time, forcing me to change them frequently to keep my feet dry and warm. But the overcast and humidity made drying socks so difficult that after washing them, I sandwiched pairs between my undershirt and uniform for body heat to dry them.

After the temperature began dropping below freezing every night, I fell into the throes of my first head cold in France and was looking forward to our next reserve because I thought staying indoors would give my clogged-up nose and croupy cough a chance to clear up. Luckily, only two weeks after assembling the underground room, Company B went into reserve again. It was the briefest time we had spent in one position since our first week in Brittany.

When the caravan of trucks arrived to transport us, I knew we were traveling a greater distance than usual from the front. They drove us to a former French or German army training center, many miles from Lorient. At the entrance, I saw lines of pyramidal tents to our right, a headquarters hut and mess hall straight ahead, and an outdoor amphitheater to our left. There were several small athletic or drill fields just beyond the tents. We unloaded and carried our gear along narrow, fine-gravel paths to the square tent we'd been assigned and found a pot-bellied stove at its center, a coal fire already burning, and our beds, which were cots, set against the four walls.

Shortly after settling in our tent, orders came to empty our uniform pockets of all personal belongings and report to the long tents at the edge of the nearest drill field. Inside the first tent, we took off our filthy uniforms and underwear and threw them on the rising pile of dirty ODs. Steam escaped around the flaps of the next tent where we had hot shower baths with lots of soap. The engineering outfit that furnished the baths handed out thick, warm towels and clean underwear and gave us new uniforms to replace our old ones. The steam and hot water opened my stopped-up sinuses, and a clean uniform and warm body made me feel better than I had for days.

But after supper, as the hour grew late, the bad cold gripped my miserable nose and chest again, and the endless talk and cigarette smoke of my tent mates kept me awake. When everyone fell asleep, my own coughing and nose blowing disturbed me.

The temperature dropped far below freezing that night. Although it didn't snow, a heavy frost covered the roofs of tents and buildings the next morning, and in the soft light a thin layer of ice glistened on the surfaces of drill fields. Even the moisture harbored in the loose gravel of the paths had frozen overnight. Although hot breakfast in the warm mess hall helped me breathe again, walking back to the tent in the icy air left my nose and chest raw.

The most hurtful necessity with my cold was doing calisthenics on the frozen playing fields under the lowering clouds that blocked the sun. After our exercises, the sergeants organized touch football games between squads. Running, passing, and blocking in the frigid air—wearing boots, combat jackets, and helmet liners—was torture for me. My healthy companions, away from the pressure and boredom of the front line, played with abandon.

When it was learned that a few men in each platoon would be given passes to a nearby town each day, everyone champed at the bit to go right away. My tent mates, scheduled to go to town together on the same day, tried to persuade me to join them. I begged off because I felt so bad. But when the OD waked everyone at 0430, Boguski and Shootie convinced me I'd feel better going rather than lying in the tent all day.

I shivered constantly in the cold, windy bed of the truck on our way to the medium-size town, which was probably Quimper. Jumping off the truck, someone saw a sign on the other side of the square, "Cafe Louis." We hurried across the cobblestones and piled into the small bistro to be greeted by a rotund, mustachioed Frenchman who acted as if rowdy customers after sunrise were an ordinary part of his day.

My older, experienced companions, disregarding the early hour, ordered liquor instead of food from the waiter who turned out to be Louis himself. Trying to perk me up, they treated me to a boilermaker, a drink I had never heard of, which turned out to be two—a shot of whiskey with a beer chaser. For an hour or so, we sat around drinking and talking until everyone had enough of both. With two boilermakers under my belt, I didn't feel the symptoms of the cold or much else.

The small town offered no entertainments, so we roamed the narrow streets, sightseeing. The younger guys, following the example of the older men, flirted with the women staring at us from their windows, sweeping the street in front of their houses, or washing their front steps. To us, their appearance or age didn't matter as long as they smiled and laughed at our foolishness. Perhaps the absence of young Frenchmen explained the women's friendly susceptibility to our outrageous manners.

My cold pills forced me to find a toilet, and I finally made an old Frenchman understand what I was looking for. He led me inside a building to a doorless booth in one corner of a large, empty room. The toilet was only a hole in the cement floor, with a large white footprint painted on each side to guide the user's position. There was no toilet paper, so to my good fortune, I still observed the Boy Scout slogan, "Be Prepared" and had paper squares from K rations in my combat jacket.

By noon, everyone was sober and hungry. Although we'd been ordered not to buy food from the French because it was in such short supply for civilians, we found a cafe and ordered sandwiches. No one spoke French, so I mimed making and eating a sandwich and then pointed to each of us.

The cafe owner nodded enthusiastically, "Ah, oui!" and disappeared into his kitchen at the back.

He returned with long loaves of bread and split them lengthwise. Dipping a full ladle from a mixture in the pot on his grill, he spread it across the bottom half of the bread, covered it with the top half, and sliced the loaf in two. Though we took a chance, not knowing the spread's ingredients, the sandwiches were savory. Those without "invasion francs" paid with cigarettes and dollar bills, which the owner accepted with even more enthusiasm than he had our orders.

After lunch, we resumed our aimless walking until we came upon a two-story house on a side street with a sign in English warning "Off Limits to Military Personnel." Women of different ages were hanging out the upstairs windows and over the front balcony rail. So anxious to be noticed and wearing such flimsy garments outdoors in frigid weather, they had to be prostitutes.

The rest of our group crossed to the house, but I sat down on the curb on the opposite side of the street. Our gang, emboldened by their number, shouted sexual proposals at the women in English and a few French phrases, chiefly "Voulez-vous coucher avec moi?"

The women, cackling with shrill laughter, made unintelligible comments and reached out to them with beckoning arms, shouting, "Oui, oui!"

A teenage girl among them signaled for me to cross the street. I waved back, shaking my head and ducking down. As the other prostitutes began throwing kisses at me, the youngest one left the window and reappeared downstairs at the front door in a filmy dress that revealed the rigid nipples of her breasts and her dark pubic hair. My buddies, hollering and whistling at the sight, urged me to accept her invitation. Blushing hot as they tried dragging me toward the house, I pulled back. Although they teased me and flirted outrageously with the women, only two older men appeared tempted to enter the house.

Before nightfall, we made our way to the town square where the truck was waiting to take us back to camp. Riding in the cold wind without feeling chills, I realized I hadn't been aware of my bad cold all afternoon, for my sinuses were open and my sore throat gone. That night, surrounded by talk and smoke, I slept without waking.

What cured my cold? Was it almost over when I went to town? Or did the boilermakers change my body chemistry, relieving the symptoms? Maybe walking in the fresh air and relaxing helped. Anyway, the day's excursion gave me long-term immunity, for I didn't suffer another cold for months.

When we first arrived at the camp, Palma began organizing a show, probably inspired by the amphitheater, which had a roofed stage and rows of wooden benches out front. Tony asked me to do something, but I didn't want to repeat myself, so we wrote a skit that included a female character for me to impersonate, singing, with guitar accompaniment, "I Can't Give You Anything But Love." A Jewish fellow from New York, who hung around rehearsals, taught me a parody of "The Face on the Barroom Floor," which I recited with a Yiddish accent. I don't remember the audience's response to the show, but I still remember the words to the parody of a poem I have never read.

In early December, the 301st Regiment and Company B transferred to another sector. By this time, our lines were so extended and thinly manned that small patrols delivered ammunition, food, and mail to areas that might be under German observation. I joined one such patrol taking allotment papers for a GI's signature after his wife had their baby. We walked some distance in shallow trenches to reach the out-of-the-way positions by midafternoon. The patrol, carrying C and K rations in boxes and hot food in thermos containers, also had letters and packages for mail call. We ran across the open spaces and crouched low going through the trenches. The possibility of being seen created tension, but the welcomes GIs gave us at OPs made up for the strain.

In the new sector, our command post was on the side of a mountain, just above a flat, triangular field. Below the CP, on the far side of the field, was the main road, which ran alongside a creek. There was a narrow wooden bridge leading to a small supply and parking area on our side of the creek. Tall, thick, brown grass and nut-bearing trees covered the mountainside and surrounded the field. The front itself was some distance away on the other side of the mountain at our rear. We reached the front by climbing the mountain, crossing open fields, and walking through thick woods to the different platoon positions.

For sleeping quarters, Straub and Sundheimer had a little clapboard hut, its back dug into the mountainside and furnished with two cots, a table, and two chairs. My own place, about fifteen yards away, was an enclosed chicken coop, large enough, after the chicken roosts had been ripped out, for only one human occupant.

Winter's deepening gloom and the monotonous days of early December drummed on while the routine of the headquarters platoon hardly changed. There was little to do during the day other than listen to the gabble of men over the switchboard lines. The rest of the time, I read paperbacks that I exchanged with others. Or shot the breeze with Boguski and Schuette while cleaning our rifles or washing our socks and underwear in the little stream below the CP. The gurgling of that little rivulet of water, day and night, made it difficult to hear suspicious sounds in the dark.

Standing guard at night, I found ways to distract myself. One mind game was estimating the passage of time by learning to count seconds at a rate that coincided with my watch's sweep hand. I assumed that by counting a precise minute I would develop an intuitive but exact sense of one minute's time, which I could eventually expand to quarter hours and half hours. The effort was about as empty of sense as the look in a cow's eyes when chewing her cud.

Checking my count against my watch at night would have been simple if its face had been luminous. But I had to light the numbers and hands by chain smoking. I lit a cigarette just before going on guard and kept it burning, using the glowing tip to read the watch face. I concealed the tip by cupping it inside the palm of my hand. Since I seldom took a drag, a cigarette burned for about ten minutes before it had to be replaced. With no distractions, I estimated even quarter hours fairly accurately, gaining distraction and nicotine-stained hands from the exercise.

I wrote letters to my folks and to Tumpy at least once a week, even though censorship by Lieutenant Sundheimer kept me from including information about the front or even personal feelings. Mother kept pressing in her letters for Christmas gift suggestions because the post office had warned how long it would take for boxes to reach us overseas. I told her that the most useful present would be a wool turtleneck sweater, which would keep my neck warm without my adding a scarf to an already multilayered uniform. Mother hired a lady in her Friendly Matrons Sunday school class to knit it.

One day, climbing the hillside behind the CP on my way to the front line, I saw, a few feet off the trail, a glint of shiny metal under a pile of leaves. Cautiously brushing the brown, wet leaves aside with a stick, I found partially exposed in a hole cans of food. None of the cans had been opened, and the labels were in French. I assumed the Maquis had once hidden on the hillside and stashed the food there. Although the cans weren't rusty, none of us was brave enough to sample their contents.

The narrow stream below the CP wound through a thick stand of trees on its way to the larger creek that ran along the edge of the road. Scattered below the huge trees were nuts, about the size of a large buckeye souvenir I had at home. I gathered a few to take to Kelly and find out what they were. He could hardly believe that I'd never seen or eaten chestnuts. To mend my ignorance, he told me he would roast them if I gathered a helmet full while he rigged a grill from a tall tin can and built a fire in it. I wasn't the only one in our squad to taste his first roasted chestnuts.

Each night Straub and Sundheimer shared another kind of treat. At sundown, during the company alert, they sat on the porch of their small cottage gazing across the field and stream below, sipping cocktails concocted from a mix of canned grapefruit juice and Cointreau, and enjoying the quietest of all the CP positions we'd had at Lorient.

It was quiet, that is, until the afternoon Kelly and I were talking with drivers whose jeeps were parked on the creek bank by the edge of the road. Suddenly, an 88-shell exploded over us, blowing the camouflage net off the stock of boxed supplies stacked by the road. Arching up into the air, like a fish net being spread at sea, it settled in a tree top. Paralyzed, Kelly and I watched it floating down into the tree limbs as other rounds burst over us in quick succession.

I ran to the nearest jeep to crawl under it, even though we'd been warned against using vehicles for cover. Flat on the ground, trying to get under the jeep, I couldn't move forward. Straining, able to get only my head and one shoulder underneath it, I realized my rifle was upright and flipped it to horizontal to slip under easily.

Kelly shouted, "You dumb son of bitch, get out from under that jeep!" He was standing precisely where we were when the shelling began, laughing.

The firing stopped as suddenly as it came. Neither men nor jeeps were hit, but we lost our complacent assumption that Germans didn't know the location of the inconspicuous road beside our CP.

"The CP was a chosen target, not an accidental one," in the opinion of fellows who posed as our enlisted "S-2 intelligence" officers: "Somebody told 'em where we are."

The chief suspect was the farmer whose house was across the road from the CP. "Don't he pass every day? In that two-wheeled tumbrel, loaded with God knows what? Maybe he told the Germans."

When we first arrived in this position, the farmer, trying to pass in his cart, had been held at rifle point by a sentry, though the road passed through his fields on his own land. When the guard rammed his bayonet into the pile of hay in his cart, the farmer had the right to protest but didn't. Others thought the guard's zealous caution was comic, but it wasn't, for he was making sure the stranger hadn't concealed something. Of course, the guard found no dangerous contraband or spy hidden under the hayload.

The farm family's attendance at church every Sunday helped us keep the days of the week straight. We knew the man and his wife and children were heading for church when they dressed in their formal costumes. The man and son wore black suits and round-brimmed, black felt hats with ribbons streaming down the back. His wife and daughter had on long black skirts and blouses, and high lace bonnets, with starched wings projecting from their crowns.

Throughout early December, with no official word to the contrary, we assumed our division would remain at Lorient until the war's end.

We didn't know that our commander, General Malony, continuously sought a more active combat assignment for the Ninety-fourth. It's not likely that his troops were as eager as the general; probably most of them would have chosen to remain in Brittany rather than attack inside Germany. But we had no professional ambitions and no vote. Although General Malony would get his wish, it would not be as soon or precisely as he expected. His requests had less to do with our leaving Brittany than did a series of unconnected events.

On December 5, 1944, General Omar Bradley notified Malony that the Eleventh Armored Division would relieve the Ninety-fourth by December 29. While division headquarters was preparing for the move, the Germans launched on December 16 a major counterattack along a forty-mile front in the Ardennes against a thin line of American soldiers resting and looking forward to Christmas. SHAEF assumed the attack would signal German troops at Lorient and Saint-Nazaire to break out of Brittany and ordered the Ninety-fourth to intensify security, but the Germans made no attempt to escape.

The smashing assault in the Ardennes forced SHAEF to alter plans. On December 18, they rescinded the orders for the Eleventh to replace the Ninety-fourth, sending the armored division directly from ports to the Western front. General Malony and the Ninety-fourth once again awaited a new assignment.

The stories I was reading in *Stars and Stripes* about the battle in the Ardennes left me relieved that we weren't involved. General Eisenhower's Order of the Day to Allied troops, printed in *Stars and Stripes* on December 22, included his interpretation of the situation: "The enemy is making his supreme effort to break out of the desperate plight into which you forced him by your brilliant victories of the summer and the fall. He is fighting savagely to take back all that you have won and is using every treacherous trick to deceive and kill you."

Ike claimed the German attack created an opportunity for the Allies: "By rushing out from his fixed defenses, the enemy may give us the chance to turn his great gamble into his worst defeat."

I hoped that American troops, without the Ninety-fourth, squeezed the life out of the German salient, which was sixty miles wide and forty miles deep. Our static confrontation with the enemy at Lorient and Saint-Nazaire had been marked by only useless forays on both sides. Although our company's moves at Lorient were boring and slightly hazardous, we were safer holding Germans in two remote French ports rather than attacking their homeland. Other platoon members may have been as reluctant to leave Brittany as I, but not even my closest pals shared that sentiment. We grumbled while keeping our innermost thoughts and fears to ourselves.

We'd been expecting to leave Lorient for nearly a month, yet we were surprised by the swift stroke of our departure when it came. SHAEF unexpectedly changed plans again, on Christmas Eve, when a German U-boat in the English Channel torpedoed the Belgian ship, SS *Leopoldville,* which was carrying units of the Sixty-sixth Infantry Division. Hundreds of their officers and men died in the channel's frigid waters. Other troops of the Sixty-sixth, on the SS *Cheshire,* were so emotionally shaken and their combat strength so drastically reduced that General Bradley ordered the Ninety-fourth to replace them in the Ardennes.

Combat Rifleman

Wehingen and Orscholz, Germany

December 29, 1944–January 20, 1945

On the dark, frigid morning of December 29, the Ninety-fourth Division set out for Germany to fight on the "real" front. Company B marched route-step to a forest of evergreens some distance behind the front lines to wait for trucks to pick us up for the first leg of the division's trek across France. Gathering far too close together inside the woods, we didn't observe basic infantry training that prescribed spreading out in most circumstances for safety. Instead, we lay under the pines in beds of needles side by side, talking and laughing loudly, snacking on K rations, and relaxing with cigarettes.

When the usual deuce-and-a-half trucks arrived, our driver told us we were going to Rennes. Sergeant Palma said we'd bivouac there until boarding a train to Reims in eastern France, where all units of the Ninety-fourth Division were to rendezvous. According to Palma, our division's new mission was to help straighten out the bulge that the Germans had punched in American lines in the Ardennes.

When we arrived on the outskirts of Rennes, light snow showers were drifting down. We marched under the weight of our heavy field packs along slick cobbled streets to an open field that appeared to be a public park, where Kelly ordered us to pitch our pup tents. The snow fell more intensely as Joe and I claimed a space on the city common to unpack, set up our tent, and build a fire. For once, we were far enough from any front not to dig in. The pup tents of the company sprang up from the surface of the white-blanketed field like olive-colored mushrooms. We were soon enveloped in smoke floating from campfires and the savory aromas of heated rations and coffee. We didn't know or care that our encampment in the park would last two days, while we waited for a train to take us to Germany.

Snow fell throughout the day and night, whitening everything and muffling the sounds of scores of men camping out in the severe cold, killing time. On the morning of the day of our departure, a thick mist hung over the white hillocks of our canvas tents, their walls sagging inward beneath the snow's icy weight. With our faces chapped and our hands and feet stiff from the freezing temperature and wet snow, preparing breakfast, striking tents, and packing our gear were painful and difficult.

But marching to a railroad siding, we warmed up quickly enough. There a small locomotive stood, steam poring from its engine, tailed by a line of tiny boxcars, each bearing on its side: "Hommes-40/Chevaux-8" (forty men and eight horses). Watching platoon members ahead struggling to board a boxcar weighed down by packs and equipment, I thought of old veterans in Little Rock who rode on 40-and-8s, only twenty-five years before, idealistically assuming they were fighting "the war to end all wars."

As I clambered aboard, hampered by my stiff wool overcoat, thick rubber galoshes, rifle, and full field pack, Joe's hearty, playful shove from behind helped me reach the boxcar's door. Luckily, a wide metal bar below the door, about halfway from the ground, shortened the stretch up. Once inside the sliding door, the only "comforts" were a few intact bales of hay and a shallow layer of loose straw across the floor.

I didn't count how many occupied our car, but there were certainly more *hommes* than the stated capacity, which the French estimated when men, as well as horses, were considerably smaller. Many soldiers, struggling for places in the melee, tried to settle near their best buddies, but my only aim was finding a warm spot for what I knew would be a long, cold trip. I moved to a place near the forward end of the car, assuming it would be warmer away from the side doors. But even before the train got under way, the frigid air leaked through the spaces around the closed door and blew through the narrow, high windows at the ends of the car. In transit, moving or standing still, the cracks in the car's scarred, broken floorboards and walls admitted drafts.

Up ahead, the little French steam engine shrieked, warning of our departure, before it jerked the long line of ancient boxcars to a start. By the time the train gained enough speed to set our car swaying, men broke out packs of cigarettes, commenced card games, and started arguing about their space.

So many men and their bulky equipment packed inside hardly left enough room for anyone to stretch out comfortably. The only direction to move was *up,* either by standing or simply straightening your back. When I shifted my arms or legs, or tried to face a different direction, I instantly touched someone's pack, back, arm, or leg. Even after being shaken down like crackers in a box by the swaying, bumping train and by individuals shifting, any effort to change positions forced others nearby to adjust.

From Rennes, the train first steamed east through the towns of Laval and Le Mans. Unlike in Scotland and England, our route in France was obvious because the station names hadn't been removed. Some of them were familiar from history lessons and plays I had read, but others I had never seen or heard before: Juvisy, Verneuil, Sézanne, Sommesous. Even the recognizable names would hardly fit my lips and tongue for what I knew were improper French pronunciations.

Nearing the outskirts of Chartres late in the day, I braved whipping, wet wind at the narrow window in a fruitless effort to see the famous cathedral's steeple in the waning light. After dark, the train bore north through Dreux before heading toward Versailles and Paris, cities the train bypassed in the night, as we tried to sleep.

The train's speed wasn't steady, nor did it move forward for very long at one time. Our frequent stops occurred for no apparent reason, most often stalling the train in a godforsaken countryside. At the first stops, we assumed there were mechanical failures, or tracks under repair. The stops struck a metaphor in my mind of the match between the train's slow movements and my reluctance about the journey to Germany. Considering our stops and slow progress that first afternoon and night, the locomotive might just as well have parked the train on a siding until the crew was ready to advance steadily. Surely, the crew's effort to locate passable tracks to Reims partially explained our train's erratic route across France.

The passing French landscape, seen through the car's window or door, was marked by many scars of old battles and Allied air raids. The train slowly wended through the yards at Meaux on its way to Château-Thierry, both names resonating in my mind from stories of the Great War. Adding to my loneliness was the eerie shriek of our little French locomotive, passing the empty platforms of desolate stations and snaking through railroad yards of twisted rails and gantries. I realized from the sights what the French people lost besides their freedom during the German occupation.

One long concrete station platform, parallel with the tracks and isolated from any town, must surely have been a tourist stop in peacetime because we were now near many famous battlegrounds of World War I. The train turned north again, heading to French towns whose names were a bit easier to pronounce, since I had heard them spoken—Soissons, Meaux, Château-Thierry, Dormans, and Épernay. Impersonating a Gallic train conductor, I called out the names in my best fake French accent, and wasn't corrected because no one in my platoon spoke French, or knew any more about European history than I.

During the short daylight hours, the train seldom stopped. But when it did, we got off to stretch our legs and relieve ourselves, for there were no toilet facilities in the box cars. We didn't stray far, though, because the train often began moving again without warning. At night, the inexplicable halts resumed, the train advancing several hundred yards, stopping, and then backing as far as it had gone forward like cheerleaders doing the "locomotive" yell at a football game.

If the train stopped for any length of time at night, the company runners walked up and down between cars whispering messages through doors to platoon sergeants, who started "pass-it-on" round-robins with the rest of us. Most of the time, they warned about loud talk, light, and noise, convincing us we were nearing a front and would soon be getting off.

At the end of each stop, our Toonerville-Trolley locomotive steamily snorted up ahead and wailed mournfully, before wheezily tugging the line of clanking cars behind it, jerking our own into motion. The train gathered speed, and I relaxed, believing we were at last on our way; then the train slowly ground to another stop. As we waited expectantly for orders, more whispered, useless messages filtered through our car. Thus, moving . . . stopping . . . backing . . . inching forward, our train trundled farther east through frigid nights and days toward the western front!

The men in our car were quiet, not noisy and argumentative as they had been on the train from Camp McCain to Camp Shanks in the States. And the farther we traveled, nearing Germany, the less anyone talked—a pattern prevailing all the time I was in the Army, when men were uncertain about what lay ahead.

Late one afternoon when the train stopped, a runner warned Kelly that we were nearing Reims, the division's rendevouz point. That was encouraging because we expected to get off the train there. It's hard to explain how confined you feel stuffed inside a boxcar with little light to read by and little view to look at. But our hopes were dashed! We rode past Reims to Épernay and on from there to Châlons-sur-Marne, before unloading and stretching in relief, on the assumption we'd reached our final destination, that we wouldn't have to ride farther. But Sergeant Kelly quickly dispelled our happy expectations by leading us to a line of trucks that he said were taking us to Verdun.

After we rode a few miles in the open truck bed, shivering in the piercing wind, Lemuel Slate, our redundant bugler, cursed and whined about not having a canvas cover to ward off the cold.

The first sergeant growled, "Pipe down, Slate! That makes it a helluva lot easier to get your fat butt off, if we're attacked."

With the temperature falling, the wind was an icy blade, cutting right through our heavy wool overcoats, uniforms, and long underwear. Even wedged side by side, our combined body heat didn't reach our hands and feet, which felt like blocks of ice. But locked into our positions on the hard, cold benches, leaning on our rifles, held upright between our knees, no one else bitched. At least, they didn't do it out loud.

Rocking with the motion of the truck, the wind and truck gears whining in my ears, I sensed the imminence of combat as never before. Sweet images of home bore in: Tumpy's face in the window of the bus leaving Little Rock . . . Mom in her apron hovering over the kitchen stove . . . Dad in the backyard feeding Old Joe, his bird dog.

The convoy reached Verdun after dark, and thereafter our truck, its headlights only tiny cat's-eye slits, blindly followed the trucks ahead. Looking over the row of helmets across from me, and out the rear of the truck, I barely discerned, in the faint light of the snow-covered countryside, only indistinct forms. But nearing the ancient city of Metz, a lone tree came into view; it stood against the thin line of the barely visible horizon, like a sentinel, guarding the fallen remains of a woods. The tree's splintered top, stripped bare of limbs and foliage, stirred an anxious feeling in my empty stomach about what we faced.

Our caravan, traveling down narrow cobblestone streets in Metz and smaller towns, squeezed between buildings, showing feeble seams of light around their doors and windows. Yet all the streets were empty, our convoy's deep rumble violating the silence of sleeping towns that Allied fighting had already passed. Before falling into an exhausted sleep, I imagined using the only German sentence I remembered from my senior play, *Margin for Error,* "Warum offnen sie die ture nicht schnellen?" (Why didn't you open the door sooner?) Maybe I would find an occasion to use it.

Our truck stopped violently, jerking everyone off balance, against each other. Angered by the jarring, someone yelled, "What the hell's going on up there?"

Another, like a kid, asked, "Are we there yet? Where are we?"

The driver shouted from his cab widow, "Still in France, just beyond Thionville."

The truck, its motor idling, paused at the edge of a steep embankment above a river that the driver said was the Moselle. Standing up on the bench, looking over the cab at the trucks and river below, I saw a long pontoon bridge afloat on dark water alongside the partially destroyed piers of an original stone structure. On the horizon, miles away, momentary flashes and low rumbles from artillery disturbed some part of the front, like heat lightning and distant thunderstorms troubling a summer night.

The line of trucks ahead revved their motors, grinding slowly down the steep incline of the riverbank to the bridge. We followed, easing cautiously onto the undulating metal tracks of the treadway bridge. Once on the other side, our convoy pressed on without the routine ten-minute breaks. Unexpected stops allowed a few of us at a time to jump off and relieve ourselves.

The shimmers of light across the horizon and distant rumbling drew nearer, but the urgent push of the convoy faltered, eventually slowing to a halt. Out of the darkness, an officer on foot materialized beside our truck, warning in whispers about the nearness of the front and the need to be absolutely silent and not use lights of any kind. Just as quickly and mysteriously, he dissolved in the blackness.

Shortly after, our convoy moved once more, chugging into the darkness ever more reluctantly, toward the irregularly glimmering horizon. I was nodding in sleep when the truck stopped and the motor was turned off. Our journey at an end, from France's Atlantic coast to Germany's western border, Kelly ordered us off the trucks.

In the frigid predawn of January 5, 1945, we slid off onto a street in an as yet unnamed, snow-covered German village. Palma ordered the communications squad to take shelter inside the dark houses on both sides of the narrow, icy street. Four of us, stiff from the cold and struggling with packs, eased off the truck, mutely and blindly staggering through the nearest doorway. Inside the house's small, pitch-black rooms, we fumbled around until we found a bed. Joe and I pulled the mattress onto the floor for ourselves, and the other two guys flopped down on the bed's bare springs. Our only covers, as we fell to sleep, were our overcoats.

The squealing brakes of a truck, in front of the house, waked us at dawn. Disoriented in the dark bedroom, we collected our gear and felt our way out to the street, where the cooks had a steaming GI garbage can full of coffee. Huddling around the can for its warmth, we joined the rest of the platoon drinking and smoking, while the cooks set up a serving line for hot breakfast.

As we ate, Kelly let us know that we were in the village of Wehingen, just south of the larger town of Ober Tunsdorf, at the southeastern tip of the Bulge. Our whole regiment was about ten miles south of the ancient city of Trier, in an area called the Saar-Moselle Triangle.

The Ninety-fourth Division was relieving the 358th Infantry Regiment of the Ninetieth Division, which was part of Patton's Third Army, Twentieth Corps, commanded by Major General Walton Walker. The Twentieth Corps was holding the southern flank of Patton's line, and our division's position was near a transition to the main defenses of the Siegfried Line, which the brass called "the Siegfried Switch." This fortified defense zone—a line of fieldworks, antitank barriers, pill boxes, and bunkers—was an east-west extension to Germany's main fortifications, which lay beyond the Saar River.

After we finished breakfast, Kelly ordered us to find permanent places to stay, and Palma chose the village cobbler's home and shop for the communications squad. It had been such a long time since any of us had stayed in a real house that we were eager to explore its indoor comforts. In our phrase book, the cobbler was a "Schuster."

The cobbler's was a compact stone house on three levels. The lower one was partially below ground, much like a walkout basement in the States; at the front end, the cobbler stored his winter food supply, and at the back was a stable for his animals, all of them gone. A narrow hall separated a tiny bedroom on the lower level from the stable's manure-covered dirt floor and straw-filled troughs. Outside the back door, a two-seated privy was in an alcove facing the shallow backyard, and open to the sky.

At the end of the basement nearest the street, we found two large barrels, one standing upright, filled with sauerkraut, and the other, on its side, with a spigot at one end. Someone turned the faucet, and a liquid clear as water flowed out. We consulted a squad member known for his alcoholic tastes and capacity, who drank some of the liquid from his cupped hands, pronouncing, with great enthusiasm, that we'd liberated a supply of white wine, which he called "Moselle." Reassured by our mate's survival and joy, we all filled our canteen cups and sipped wine, as we explored the rest of the rooms, poking through drawers and fingering the objects on shelves.

On the second level of the house were a small kitchen, dining room, and the shoemaker's shop, which was filled with tools and half-finished boots and shoes. From the second-floor hall, I climbed up a rough ladder to the attic and found potatoes, turnips, and apples stored on the deep bed of straw covering the rafters.

The happiest discoveries were on the third level—two bedrooms, each with wide double beds, armoires, and dressers. I was eager to sink into a soft, warm bed for the first time in months, but a dozen soldiers occupying one house with two beds made such a treat seem unlikely.

After settling at the cobbler's, Joe and I explored Wehingen. Our house, and two or three others, stood at the eastern edge of the village. Beyond us was an untrammeled white landscape of undulating farmland that gradually rose to meet the stone-gray skyline. Individual trees in the fields, like black-ink doodles on white paper, stood at irregular distances from each other, until thickening into a dense grove just below the ridge line. The two fences snaking up the hillside, their posts like black exclamation points, traced the path of the narrow road under the snow, which crossed the fields in the direction of our enemies. My loneliness facing the vista made me realize how alone we are in combat, even surrounded by close buddies like Joe.

A week after settling in Wehingen, a soldier with a camera asked a group of us in headquarters platoon to pose for a picture in front of the house across from the cobbler's. Most of us gathered together happily, jokingly assuming our tough combat soldier poses, but two fellows refused to join us. Asked why they objected to being in the photo, they didn't answer at first. Eventually, though, they admitted their superstition that having their picture taken would bring bad luck. Their fear, which none of us laughed at, reminded me of the aboriginals who refuse to be photographed because it would rob them of their life spirit.

Throughout our thirteen days in Wehingen, between January 6 and 19, the sun didn't fully break through the clouds a single day. Its muted light, diffused through the low-hanging snow clouds, shortened the days and lengthened the nights. Every other day, the gray clouds swelled bigger, sprinkling pristine snow on old layers, gradually rounding the edges and corners of all the buildings' walls, roofs, and steps.

After one heavy snowfall, the evergreens bent in half from the burden of snow. Gazing out the cobbler's back window, I realized the trees looked as I felt, under the weight of my anxiety. But the heaps of fresh snow also brought a happier thought to mind, one of my mother's wintertime recipes when I was a kid. I found a deep kettle in the kitchen and filled it with clean snow, stirring in powdered milk and two lemonade packets from K rations to make ice cream. Shootie and Boguski tasted the mixture and decided to make a batch for themselves. Other guys added cocoa powder to the snow, a delicious use for parts of our daily rations that some guys usually threw away.

We also devised a way for everyone in our squad to sleep in the two beds, by sharing each bed several at one time. As many as four could sleep together, if they were the right size. On many occasions, three smaller guys and I shared sack time, lying on our sides like spoons, all faced in the same direction to allow enough room.

I had noticed before, in such close quarters, a strong gamey smell about my buddies, like my father exuded when he returned from hunting squirrels and quail. I'm sure I shared the same aroma. And now that we stayed indoors much of the time, sleeping spooned up close on the feather beds, the smell was more pronounced. Everyone needed a good bath and clean uniform.

We couldn't have new uniforms, but we had goose-down mattresses and fluffy pillows for our comfort, and a chance to bathe in comfort, which I looked forward to. We had the same accoutrements as we'd had outdoors—a bar of soap, hot water in a steel helmet, and a makeshift washcloth. The important differences were warmth and privacy.

Stripping off my uniform, I saw my naked image in the dresser mirror for the first time since we left Camp McCain. I appeared farcical, a minstrel-boy in reverse; after all the months outdoors, my torso was ivory white, but my face and hands were a deep reddish brown. No Narcissus, I still couldn't resist staring at the differences the Army had wrought in my physical development and proportions: I was taller, heavier, broader of shoulder, with better defined muscularity in my biceps, chest, and stomach. Finally, I looked like a soldier who could fight, though I still didn't want to.

My squad's wait at the cobbler's gave everyone a chance to scrub himself and his equipment, and allowed the best rest we'd had in months. Facing the prospect of more active combat encouraged cleaning our rifles regularly and thoroughly, even though they hadn't been fired.

Hearing artillery and small-arms fire at a distance aroused our concern and curiosity about the location and strength of the German troops in our sector. Other regiments of the Ninety-fourth had been thrown into action the instant they arrived at the Siegfried Switch, but most members of Company B had a quieter time.

While we were waiting for a combat assignment, a transient chaplain conducted a Protestant service in the small Catholic church at the Y-junction in the middle of the village. A few guys and I walked down the main street of Wehingen to the church, seeing, for the first time, thick mounds of snow covering the bodies of dead German soldiers. Lying under the piles of snow, their frozen bodies were recognizable only when a port-colored or blackened hand or foot protruded through the white surface.

The church's outside walls were chipped from small-arms fire, and large chunks had been dislodged in several places. But inside, the pale-pink walls of the sanctuary bore no marks signifying the church had been in the midst of a battle. Its quietness and the familiar sight of a crucifix over the altar soothed my spirits, even before the brief service. The chaplain prayed before and after his Bible readings and gave a short sermon. Our small group sang a hymn, slightly off key, without accompaniment. The chaplain's spoken prayers, after months of my silent ones, were comforting. Maybe I believed God's representative was more apt to be heard seeking our protection.

Before the division suddenly pulled up stakes at Lorient, Christmas had passed almost unobserved, especially for those of us who didn't receive our holiday packages. But part of the holiday mailbags caught up with us in Wehingen. Among the boxes and letters for me was the olive-drab wool turtleneck sweater that Mother paid a woman in her Bible class to knit. After trying it on, I clambered upstairs to see myself in the dresser mirror. The sweater's snug warmth around my neck and over my chest was better than the soft date-nut loaf, hard candy, and sweet sentiments in the cards.

The day after we arrived in Wehingen, division headquarters warned that German soldiers, disguised in American uniforms, might be lurking behind our lines, and that heavy German armor had been heard crossing the Saar River in our vicinity. We were to make no exceptions with passwords when on guard and demand absolute identification from any soldier, whatever his rank, if he were a stranger. As an added precaution, headquarters often changed passwords during the day, keeping everyone on edge.

Shortly after these warnings, I was standing guard one night inside the recess at the front door of the cobbler's. At what had to be the darkest hour after midnight, I heard the soft crunches of footfalls coming down the road from the village outskirts, and leaned around the edge of the entry to peek down what I hoped was an empty street.

I strained to see what was coming around the slight curve in the road, but the shadows of houses across the way made seeing clearly impossible. Meanwhile, the soft squeaks in the snow continued advancing toward me.

Reluctant to stick my head around the door's edge again, I called out, "Halt! Who goes there?" hoping I could stop whoever it was.

No one uttered the password, and the footfalls came closer and were more distinct. With my heart pounding and blood surging in my head, I believed I just hadn't been heard. Challenging again, in a lower pitch but louder than I intended, I still heard no reply. Muscles in my chest and stomach tightened until I could barely breathe. Releasing the rifle's safety, I plunged into the street ready to fire.

A dark figure was in the shadows; a large man, his head down, lumbering in a crouch toward me. My finger tightened on the trigger, ready to squeeze off a round, when the silhouette turned into . . . a milk cow! My sigh of relief stopped the cow dead in her tracks, and she lifted her head. Bossy and my overwrought imagination revealed how afraid I was.

Off guard, I told the fellows who were still awake everything but the extent of my fear. After the farcical standoff with the cow, I wondered why I was so reluctant to pull the trigger, when I didn't know who was coming toward me on the street? After all, I might have been facing a disguised German, my life at stake. I still didn't know if I could fire point-blank at an enemy I could actually see.

To break the monotony of eating K rations at the cobbler's, we raided his attic, adding his fruit and vegetables to our meals. But, after some fellows fantasized about steaks, two farm boys set out to round up the cow that was still roaming Wehingen.

The cowpokes cornered, lassoed, and led her to a barn across the street from us, to shoot her. Other city boys and I, unfamiliar with livestock, gathered at the barn to watch the slaughter and dressing. The subzero temperatures were right for the ritual; my dad insisted cows and hogs had to be butchered on the coldest day of the winter. Back home I always enjoyed the sausage, souse, hams, and steaks that our relatives, who lived on farms, brought us after the coldest spell of the winter.

But a few guys didn't want the cow killed. I saw no reason for it either, especially if fresh beef didn't taste good, for I had always heard that beef needed to be aged to improve its flavor. Still, I didn't comprehend, either, why the dissenters minded killing the cow if someone else were going to eat it. To protest against killing a dumb beast while preparing to shoot human beings was a rich irony.

The farm boys allowed the cow no reprieve; they suspended her by the hindquarters in the barn, shot her in the head with a .45 automatic, and cut her throat to draw off all the blood before butchering. The cowboys shared their fresh kill with the whole platoon, including the protesters. My only bite of the fresh beef steak confirmed that it really did need to be aged for the flavor to be appealing. Nevertheless, many ate the rich steaks, which, after our usual bland diet, gave them bouts of diarrhea.

Two Company B patrols were sent out to reconnoiter the German positions that stood between the 301st and the town of Orscholz. The volunteers on the first patrol were Sergeant Walter Ascey and PFCs John Ankenbrandt and Calvin Lippel, all three of whom I knew at Fort Benning and Ole Miss. As buddies, they always seemed like a shark and two pilot fish. On January 16, they went out seeking information for our company and regiment in preparation for an attack on Orscholz a day or two later. The trio reconnoitered in the Forest of Saarburg, a heavily wooded area west and southwest of Orscholz, which was the only covered approach to the village from our positions. When they came upon an enemy pill box, they attacked it and were pinned down by a machine gun. Ascey, covered by the others' rifle fire, crawled close enough to toss grenades into the pill box, but in doing so stepped on a "Bouncing Betty" and was killed. Ankenbrandt and Lippel were wounded and captured shortly after.

A second small group, with the same mission—determine what German forces stand between us and Orscholz—slipped into the Saarburg forest and was never heard from again. These two futile efforts ended the First Battalion's actual on-site reconnaissance; thereafter, staff planning was based on map intelligence only. Thus, we had no firsthand knowledge of the terrain, fortifications, and German troops in the sector, and our battalion faced a fate similar to that of the lost patrols.

Although no one in headquarters platoon went on patrol, after we settled at Wehingen, the long wait in the village stirred up anxieties and fears. Without knowing division battle plans, we were uneasy, moody, and ready for something to happen.

On the night of January 18, Sergeant Palma gathered all members of our platoon at the house next door to the cobbler's, where most of headquarters was housed, to inform us of our company's first major engagement with the Germans. Neither company officers nor First Sergeant Kelly joined us. Palma had us train our flashlights on a map of the territory around the Siegfried Switch, while he described the First Battalion's mission and plan of attack.

We learned that Orscholz, perched atop a hill four hundred feet high, with fields sloping below it to the south, was the eastern anchor of the Siegfried Switch. Our major attack on the village would commence before dawn on January 20. When Palma announced that Company B was to be the leading unit or "point" in the attack, I paid even closer attention. Company A would be attacking on our right, and Company C would be held in reserve. Yet, as I listened to Palma, the prospect of fighting the Germans seemed unreal, much as if I were an actor hearing the director's instructions about how to play an upcoming scene.

Palma, Straub, Sundheimer, an intelligence and reconnaissance (I&R) platoon, and First Platoon of Company D (a forward observer and six 81-mm mortars) would be leading the attack. Our point group would pass through the Forest of Saarburg and reach the east-west Oberleuken-Orscholz highway, where we would turn east to strike the village. Our communications squad was to follow the main group into town center, cutting down any targets of opportunity. The only major physical obstacle in the assault on the town would be an antitank ditch. The company's march to the line of departure (LD) was set to start at 0001, on January 20, 1945, and H-hour, for the attack to begin, was 0600, after the 301st Artillery laid down a barrage.

This information hardly seemed adequate, especially with our lives at stake, even though I always knew that fighting in combat would be strictly improvisational. We were told little about our individual roles, platoon tactics, or what to do if the attack failed. For some reason, maybe my preoccupation about having to fight, I didn't ask what to do if the attack failed. I assumed our officers had been filled in better than the riflemen and that I would know what to do when the time came.

A few in our squad were primarily porters; some would haul folding ladders to cross the antitank ditch, and others, including Art Davenport (the artificer) and me, would carry fifty pounds of machine gun and rifle ammunition apiece. Joe Boguski, my buddy, was accompanying Sergeant Palma and Captain Straub in the group at the head of our company.

The next day, we had two chores facing us that helped take my mind off how poorly prepared our company was for the attack. The extra equipment that couldn't be carried with us—sleeping bags, blankets, and overcoats—was bundled inside our shelter halves, and our more personal effects—division patches, pipes, rings, and letters—were put in cotton ditty bags for safekeeping, because if taken prisoner such letters and unit insignia revealed too much about the division. Our belongings were to be guarded at the rear by PFC Frederick Nagel and another man, who were apparently held out of the attack because of some illness or personal problem.

Our second chore, which took more time, was an even better diversion. We had to make snowsuits to camouflage our OD uniforms because the quartermaster hadn't supplied them. We looked for any usable white fabrics in houses around the village. Like the rest of my squad, I first ransacked the drawers of the wardrobes and dressers in the bedrooms at the cobbler's, looking for sheets and pillowcases.

Luckily, in the dining room, I found a large, white linen tablecloth that had a broad lace border. I hated destroying such a beautiful piece of linen by removing the lace and cutting a hole in the center for my head. But after making the hole, and draping the cloth over my shoulders, it was obvious that keeping the lace would be more concealing, for it hung below my knees, even with the pack board on my back. To cover my helmet, I cut the end off a large pillowcase and tucked the loose ends between the liner and helmet to secure it.

Making and modeling the snowsuits distracted most of us, as we enjoyed trying on outlandish items just for the laughs. One short boy pulled a pair of women's large bloomers over his pants and used a huge pillowcase, in which he cut armholes, for a tunic, covering him from the waist up. But the bloomers and pillowcase were too tight for him to move easily, so he had to exchange them for looser pieces.

Our sartorial diversions ended in the late afternoon, transforming us from comic characters to pensive mutes. Shock issued the packboards and canisters of ammunition to us mules who were carrying the extra supplies; he distributed fragmentation grenades and bandoliers of M-1 clips to the whole platoon.

At suppertime, platoon members sat apart, sinking into our thoughts while eating K rations, our last meal before the attack. I climbed the stairs to a bedroom to be by myself and say my prayers. I don't recall anything different about them, only that I asked, as usual, for God's protection and that His will be done. After filling our canteens and double-checking our equipment, most of us tried to sleep. But napping, waking, and checking the time replaced resting during the apprehensive wait.

One minute after midnight, on January 20, 1945, Palma finally ordered us to fall out. Donning our sweaters, combat jackets, bandoliers, packboards, and our homemade snowsuits, we checked our rifles and ammunition, as a final precaution. Reluctantly filing out of the warm house onto the snow-covered street, we fell into formation for the four- or five-mile march through Ober Tunsdorf to the Forest of Saarburg. We were scheduled to cross the line of departure, Merl Branch, a small stream on the outskirts of Orscholz, when our artillery barrage lifted at 0600.

Until we assembled outside, I didn't know how heavily the snow was falling. Blinding clouds of huge white flakes made it hard to see more than six feet ahead. As we marched in the enveloping cloud, the snow piled up on the road bed, almost obliterating it. My initial sense of being too cold was short-lived. I soon sweated so profusely, trudging through the deepening snow carrying the heavy ammunition, that I tried to vent my body heat by unbuttoning the top of my combat jacket. But the snow cape covering everything made it impossible, and my wet long underwear gradually soaked my uniform too.

After slogging in the white downpour for what seemed like hours, we were engulfed by the black firs of the Forest of Saarburg, which was supposed to hide our approach to Orscholz. The blackness that enveloped us in the closely packed evergreen trees hid even the soldiers nearest us. So to keep from losing touch with each other, we grasped the uniform or equipment of the soldier ahead. But hanging on this way, in a long single file winding among the trees, was tenuous at best. The line jerked to stops and starts so often that I was convinced that whoever was leading us didn't know the way or had lost it. Our single file wove many loops, doubling back on itself like a silent conga line. Our meander was puzzling and discouraging, especially when it seemed we were going in the direction we had just come from. With every muscle clenching and the pit of my stomach sinking, I wanted to reach Merl Branch, wherever it was, and begin the attack.

We cleared the dark woods abruptly, coming out into the faint morning light, to face a barely discernible gravel road under the snow. Our single file slowly unraveled from the woods, the head of our line far down the road, stretched out several hundred yards ahead. Those in the lead were turning right where our road intersected what I figured must be the Oberleuken-Orscholz road. As we neared the intersection, by starts and stops, a series of 88 shells suddenly exploded over our heads, and our line broke apart, dropping on both sides of the road.

Lying in a deep snowbank, my stomach and bowels queasy and roiling, I couldn't draw a deep enough breath. Yesterday's waiting had been unreal, but this was real enough!

Squinting at my watch, in the dim light, I saw the scheduled time for our jump-off had already passed. We were lying still beside the road, at least two hundred yards from the LD, under a shower of glowing hot shrapnel from 88-mm rounds. I was terrified, feeling, for the first time, the blood coursing through my arteries.

Then shrill voices, approaching from our rear, pierced the din. Looking up from my snowbank, I saw Lieutenant Colonel Miller, our battalion commander, and an aide hurrying past toward the intersection, talking animatedly in high-pitched voices. With no orders to move forward, we lay flinching under artillery blasts for a quarter hour, until the two officers rushed back in greater haste. Day dawned almost imperceptibly through low-hanging snow clouds, and men ahead got on their feet again. I followed.

Those in the lead were turning right at the intersection, presumably onto the Oberleuken highway, heading straight into Orscholz. To the left of the road, rising almost vertically, was a steep, heavily wooded slope, and on the road's right lay a snow-covered, relatively level field. Farther to my right, beyond the field, I could barely see, through a thick veil of snowflakes, the inverted cones of concrete dragon's teeth protruding above the snow, against a background of thick evergreens.

Company A, passing among the concrete projections at the edge of the field, trying to reach the Orscholz road, encountered and set off mines, accidentally warning the Germans of our approach. But the lead elements of Company B had reached a clearing a few hundred yards south of Orscholz without being detected by the Germans. Apparently, the point of our attack had avoided the field, and the head of our column reached the road successfully by going in single file. Only those of us at the rear of the column bogged down under fire.

The German artillery intensified, as we neared the intersection, screeching ever closer over our heads. The Germans struck us so suddenly, before we attacked, that we were bewildered. Why hadn't our own artillery fired before our assault, as it was supposed to? I wanted our guns to return fire but none did. Now bullets from the hillside buzzed around us thick as gnats, the tiny spit-spits near my feet sprouting sprays of snow vapor. Crouching lower, I hurried ahead, scanning the heavy trees on the hillside, trying to spot the invisible snipers.

Even though entering the intersection of the Oberleuken Highway made us easy targets for snipers, fellows continued crossing that way into the line of fire. It was foolish, so I veered to my right into the open field and threw myself on the ground. As I went down, I saw a short bridge in the direction of Orscholz, about a hundred yards beyond the intersection, but no signs of the creek, only a low bank of snow piled up beside the bridge. If I could reach the bridge, I'd crawl under it. But before I got back on my feet, bullets cracked past my head, convincing me to stay where I was.

The Germans overlooked the clearing from pill boxes on the hillside, connected by communication trenches. They were spraying a continuous, withering cross fire upon us. As I hugged the ground, mortars and artillery commenced plowing across the field too, showering their deadly bursts. Under the curtain of shrapnel, soldiers to the left and right of me fell dead or wounded, attempting to cross the field to the woods on the hillside. Lying in the snow, like a wingless fly about to be swatted on a white table cloth, I pressed my face down into the snow, trying not to watch my comrades falling and writhing in the Germans' preset killing zone.

I wanted to burrow my whole body under the snow, but my training emphasized not being a stationary target. Taking my bearings from the bridge again, I ran toward the long shadowy indentation in the snow that I assumed marked the path of Merl Creek's banks and would offer protection. Art Davenport, dashing in the same direction, unexpectedly darted between me and the bridge, and vanished—without a sound. Gone, quickly and mysteriously, like the disappearing assistant in a magic act.

I didn't think when I ran upright toward where he disappeared. But before reaching it, I saw a black hole in the snow. Fearing the surface around it might break, I dropped to the ground.

Inching on my belly toward the edge of the hole, I shouted, "Art!"

When he didn't answer, I hung my head down inside the opening. It was black as pitch underneath. The jagged layer of ice still intact on the opposite edge of the hole was about four inches thick, so deeply covered in snow that light wouldn't penetrate.

Mortar rounds and whining bullets kept striking nearer me, so I couldn't stay beside the hole much longer. Hollering down it again, "Davenport! For God's sake, where are you?" I heard only the echo of my own voice.

Unsure whether Art died before falling through the ice or was lying down there unconscious, I didn't know what to do. I couldn't do anything! I thought of dropping into the hole myself. But the deep, black cavity beneath the snow threatened as much as the unseen snipers on the hill.

I scrambled for the bridge again, toward another shadow in the snow beside it. Once there, I saw it had been a mirage and turned to my right, facing open, flat ground that offered no cover. I scrambled on my belly in that direction anyway, as fast and far as I could, keeping my butt and head down, praying the smoke, snow, and mist would keep snipers from singling me out.

As I was crawling, I felt the packboard straps cutting deeply into my shoulders; the extra ammunition no longer seemed to matter. To shed the pack, though, I had to take off my snow cape. I tugged repeatedly and finally tore the tablecloth enough to remove it. Struggling to unhitch the packboard straps, I turned over on my back to release the pressure to slip out, expecting the snipers to shoot me. But they didn't. Maybe rolling around straining against the cape and harness made me look as if I were wounded and in the throes of pain.

In the midst of catching my breath and deciding what to do next, a machine gun stuttered behind me, its bullets whining over my head, very near the ground. After the gun's first sweep, it stopped, and I raised my head slightly, looking back to see where it was. I couldn't spot the machine gunner; I figured the Germans were in a concealed nest beside the intersection when we passed, and waited until the advanced guard and most of the company passed their position before firing. As I crawled farther away from it, the machine gun resumed, its slugs hitting in the snow on all sides of me, slamming into men caught running farther into the field. I lay very still.

After the machine gun quit, I crawled forward again, still believing there had to be a depression in the ground to crawl into or an obstacle to hide behind. Moving as little as possible, I scanned the field until I was convinced that another dark spot in the snow was deep enough for cover. I dashed for it.

At that same instant, Murray, with large red crosses emblazoned on his armband and helmet, lunged toward the shallow depression too. I was closer and fell into it, face down, ahead of the medic. Looking back over my shoulder as Murray reached me, I saw him straighten up, with a surprised look on his face. Blood spread across his jacket, like the diffusion of a drop of red ink on a blotter, before he crumpled on top of me.

He fell flat across my back, grunting loudly, the breath knocked out of him when he landed. Murray was so heavy I could hardly move or breathe, so I pushed up against him, trying to ease the pressure. He winced and moaned; my slightest move caused him to groan like a wounded animal.

"Murray, please tell me what can I do? I want to help you!"

He didn't answer, only exhaled quivering sighs several times. Lying beneath him, afraid even my breathing hurt him, I felt his warm blood seep though my uniform and spread across my back.

Murray sighed more deeply, slumping down heavier still. Suffocating under his weight, I stretched my arms and legs trying to shift his body a little. When he didn't moan, I pushed hard enough to get up on my hands and knees, and Murray tilted off me, rolling onto his back beside the hole. I quickly pulled his arm toward me, yanked off his glove, and felt for his pulse. Pressing my fingers harder and harder into his wrist, I detected no heartbeat.

Murray's body now lay between me and the snipers on the hillside. If I stayed where I was, his body would shield me. I was convinced that Murray would have saved my life, any way he could, if he hadn't been killed, so I dug deeper into the snow behind him, believing it wouldn't dishonor him to hide there.

After Murray's death, I wasn't aware of time passing. The German mortar blasts, rifle fire, machine guns, and artillery kept crashing about me, filling the air with slugs and shrapnel, as I lay angrily questioning why other units in our battalion didn't help us. Losing touch with us was unbelievable. Where was Company A? Why hadn't our own mortars and artillery struck the hillside where the snipers were concealed?

Gazing at the bodies encircling me, I couldn't tell who was alive and who was dead. None of them had moved or changed position for such a long time.

After a while, I heard voices through the din and saw six or eight soldiers creeping toward the woods at the far edge of the field, crawling into the snow-encrusted undergrowth that lay between us and the trees bordering the edge of the field. I thought maybe they had found a way out, when explosions in the bushes were followed by shrill cries for help.

"Oh, God, my arms!"

"Help me! Oh, Lord, please help me!"

"They've shot out my eyes! I can't see!"

"My legs! Somebody help me stop the bleeding!"

I didn't recognize any of the terror-stricken voices. Why had they crawled into the bushes without thinking of antipersonnel mines under the snow and ice? More explosions and cries of anguish from the bushes made me wonder how many GIs would continue making the same mistake. Unable to help them, I could still see in my mind's eye the legless veteran who used to sharpen my father's butcher-shop tools, and I lay in combat praying for young fellows who were hit like the veteran.

The mortar shells began dropping in the field again, and, thankful for Murray's body, I pushed tighter against his stiff side, wanting to curl up in a little ball under my helmet to escape the shrapnel. One mortar shell hit directly in front of me, making a hole in the snow not more than two feet from my face but no explosion.

Marveling at that escape, I heard the muzzle blast and shriek of an 88 just before the shell burst, sending glowing shrapnel down toward me, one piece ripping through my field jacket's left sleeve, scraping across the flat surface of my arm above my elbow. When I later saw the scar, I realized the searing shrapnel cut and cauterized the wound in the same instant. Lines from the Psalms welled up, reassuringly:

> *You will not fear the terror of the night,*
> *nor the arrow that flies by day,*
> *nor the pestilence that stalks in darkness,*
> *nor destruction that wastes at noonday.*
> *A thousand may fall at your side,*
> *ten thousand at your right hand;*
> *but it will not come near you.*

What was holding up the attack? From the very first shot, all was confusion, and no one took charge. In our officers' planning, no one had anticipated that Captain Straub and his group would become separated from the rest of us, leaving no way to contact us at the rear. Leaderless, with no NCO or officer in sight, frustrated and thrashing about on the ground, we couldn't see the Germans who fired at us, couldn't escape from the field, couldn't help the fellows who were wounded and dying.

The only command I heard, after the snipers and artillery zeroed in on us, was an anonymous voice shouting, "Keep your asses down and protect yourselves!"

The roar of the battle subsided at intervals, for a few seconds at a time, much like unexpected silences in animated conversations. Those soldiers apparently unhurt, whom I couldn't see, cursed and prayed out loud. The wounded pleaded for help; the dying moaned and sobbed. One man wept, calling out to his buddies who'd been wounded or killed by the mines. Another soldier was bitching about not being able to get at the German machine gun at our rear. I kept wondering what had happened up ahead to Straub and Palma and the riflemen, like Schuette and Joe.

We'd all been such easy targets for the snipers on the hillside. So many of us were wounded or dead or dying that my perception was distorted by the sights I'd seen. I expected to be hit any second. But praying to God to keep me safe, if it was His will, I never thought I'd be killed or taken prisoner.

More sporadic sniper, artillery, and mortar fire filled the hours. Through it all, I lay beside Murray's body without being hit. Nobody else stirred. I didn't know if they were dead or playing possum like me. After I decided I was the only one alive, a man without a helmet suddenly stood up beside the Orscholz road and staggered toward me, as if he wanted to tell me something.

I screamed, "You crazy fool! Stay down!"

But he kept coming . . . close enough to see he was T/5 Carmel Phelan, a new guy who joined us just before we sailed overseas. After a few more steps, he slowly sank down, facing me, with his eyes open wide. I couldn't tell if he'd been hit. He hunched over slightly at his waist, his head hanging forward, with his chin resting on his chest. Phelan looked as if he were studying something lying in the snow, several feet in front of him.

I called out, "Phelan, lie down! Crawl over this way!" He didn't move or answer. Then the color in his face began changing, chameleon-like, from chapped pink to pale green, then light yellow, and finally to the shade of old ivory piano keys.

As the afternoon waned, the subzero temperature dropped even lower. For the first time that day, I was shivering from the cold and fear. Since the 88s first burst over us at dawn, I hadn't felt chilled, thirsty, or hungry, although I had nothing to drink or eat. I hadn't needed to empty my bladder either.

The snow beneath me melted, even though the temperature was below zero all day; then it froze again, sticking my uniform to its surface. The toes of my wet boots were sunk in shallow cups of ice, and my feet were stiff and frostbitten inside. Assuming the snipers couldn't see me, I pulled hard enough on my legs to free my numb feet, and massaged my aching thighs through my pants, trying to restore the circulation.

Daylight faded. No artillery or mortar shells had fallen for a long time, and the small-arms fire was now at a distance and sporadic. In the foggy mist that settled over the field, the only light visible was reflected from the snow's surface. The silence at twilight seemed as menacing as the day's ambush. I held my watch close to my eyes; it was 1630. We'd been trapped in the field outside Orscholz for ten hours.

God blessed me all day, protecting me from the hidden riflemen on the hillside and the shells falling on the field. Maybe the riflemen thought me dead, an unfit target. Maybe Murray's blood all over my back fooled them, or the uncommonly dark day had concealed me. There was no logical explanation for my escape.

Those of us who were unhurt, whose voices I had heard during the day, crawled into a circle, with our heads together. I recognized only George Holbrook from our company; the others were strangers, probably from Company A. Fifteen had survived without serious wounds. No one had any idea of how to get around the minefield that lay between us and the safety of the woods. As we whispered to each other, distant voices and clinking metal broke the silence. We could only assume the Germans were checking for Americans who were still alive and taking them as prisoners.

Finally, George Holbrook, an unusually quiet ASTPer from Ohio, spoke up: "I think I can get through the mines. I watched the guys hit today. I think I know a way."

He spoke so positively that nobody asked, "If there's a safe route, why didn't anybody find it?" Eight of us chose to follow George, and not one raised a question. Maybe seven of us were stunned into a state of lethargy, and George was the only one with his wits about him. What the other six survivors decided to do I don't know.

There had been no firing for such a long time that we thought it safe to stand up and move about. My joints were so stiff that I had difficulty keeping my balance. I wondered about my mental balance too, when George led our group back toward the German machine-gun nest at the road intersection and I followed. We crouched so low going toward the intersection that we looked like a chorus of Groucho Marxes. If Germans saw us moving in the dark, they must have mistaken us for their own comrades, checking the wounded or taking prisoners.

Suddenly, directly ahead of us, loomed the silhouette of a tank; we stopped in our tracks. Was it American or German? Probably German, because it could have easily moved in during the day's uproar; besides, Company B had no armored support in the attack. Without attempting to find out whose it was, we quickly backed away from the vehicle, following George, who led us back in the direction of the dragon's teeth and bushes where so many had been wounded and killed.

Out of earshot of the tank, George warned us to stay three or four feet apart in the minefield and to step precisely inside the footprints of the man ahead to avoid the S-mines, Bouncing Bettys, and the maze of trip wires attached to booby traps. The mines were out of sight, but trip wires interlacing the underbrush glinted in the snow. To walk, we had to place our feet inside the narrow, irregularly shaped interstices made by the wires. The slightest contact with a wire could trigger explosive charges.

In the dim light, George picked a haphazard path through the low bushes and wires, stopping after each move to look ahead and choose his next step, almost by intuition, since there was so little to guide him. We followed, not making crucial choices, only stepping inside the footprints ahead. Our tight, narrow focus made going tediously slow and tense, inching forward, balancing on one leg while lifting the other, then lowering our foot into the just-vacated impression ahead. I pushed out of my mind the possibility of Germans firing again. Minutes seemed hours.

We were almost through the minefield when, lifting one of my stiffly frozen feet, I immediately sensed my lack of balance. Powerlessly, I watched my boot, as if it were someone else's, grazing a wire. The split-second contact instantly triggered a mine that sprang into the air and exploded. The muffled explosion struck a dazzling light-burst inside my head—multicolored, geometric patterns of sparkling stars radiating from silver, pink, and blue lines. I later recalled their resemblance to Aztec Indian designs or the colored figures in cartoon balloons over Jiggs's head when he was struck by Maggie's rolling pin in the Sunday funnies.

Trying not to fall and detonate other mines, I thrust my rifle to the ground to stay upright, as my body geared down into slow motion. The rifle butt, by miracle, missed all the other wires and mines. Everyone froze in place after the mine's stunning impact. No one knew who tripped it, except me. The fellows in front and behind me had caught shrapnel in their legs, and another was struck a glancing blow on the side of his head. They all claimed their wounds were slight but me. My left hand was hanging limply from my heavily bleeding wrist, and sharp pains were radiating through the calf of my right leg. The wetness behind my knees suggested I'd been hit in both legs.

George turned back and asked, "What'll we do now?"

I knew he meant me, and I insisted, "Keep on going. I can still walk."

After that, we picked our way ever more cautiously and slowly, for at least another hour, before reaching the woods, where we expected to encounter troops from the 301st. No one was there.

Going far enough into the woods not to be seen or heard by the Germans in the field, we checked our wounds again. My companions weren't bleeding, and their injuries didn't hinder them, but mine were throbbing and draining my energy. Buddies who removed the glove from my left hand and pushed up the sleeve of my jacket found thick blood oozing around the several large pieces of shrapnel stuck in my wrist. Considering my condition, the subzero temperature, and the uncertainty of finding our lines, they decided not to bandage the wounds. Instead they tied a tourniquet around my upper left arm and fed me sulfanilamide tablets. When a buddy removed the cap from my canteen to let me drink as much water as I could with the sulfa, nothing flowed out; the water was frozen. The others had drunk theirs during the day, so I ate handsful of snow for liquid enough to swallow the pills.

All of us felt safer in the woods, even though we were lost. We had no more sense of our location or compass directions than we had the night before, meandering in these same woods. The dense trees and snow-laden bushes looked the same no matter which way we faced. We found no fire lanes or trails and struggled through drifts and undergrowth, sinking in the snow up to our knees and hips, while stumbling over the uneven ground beneath. The snow, in drifts three or four feet high, was much deeper than it had been in the windswept minefield. Walking taxed everyone else but exhausted me.

The severe cold that stopped my wounds from bleeding also stiffened my knees. My right leg slowly drew up toward the back of my thigh, making it impossible to keep my balance and walk. My left hand and wrist were numb and useless; I couldn't use my rifle as a walking stick any longer, so I threw the piece away. A buddy pulled my right arm over his shoulders, wrapping his arm about my waist to help me keep up.

Trekking in the woods, in what may have been circles, we heard voices at a distance. Excited enough to shout in their direction, we hesitated to make a sound or go toward them, for fear we'd encounter a German patrol. We tried to identify whether their speech was English, but their voices were too far away for recognition. The group sounded as if they were moving, so we circled away from them.

Around midnight, we again heard voices and saw movement among the trees on the other side of a clearing. But as weary and eager as we were to get to our lines, we held back until someone could positively identify whether the soldiers' helmets were shaped like ours or German coal scuttles. Circling the edge of the woods to get nearer, without letting them see us, we waited until a soldier was within earshot before hailing him.

The man dropped to the ground, demanding the password, but since we didn't know what it was, we could only insist that we were from Company B of the 301st. The soldiers would have none of that and asked us about sports, movies, and music, things only Americans would know, obviously as afraid of us as we were of them.

Someone suggested that one of us, without his weapon, should cross the clearing to meet face to face. George Holbrook relinquished his rifle, walked across the clearing, and disappeared into the woods. A few minutes later, he signaled the rest of us to join him. A few soldiers, seeing me being supported, ran to help carry me.

Our withdrawal, through the minefield and woods, from the outskirts of Orscholz to the 301st regimental lines, had taken eight and a half hours.

New buddies from Company C of the 301st carried me and guided our group to the aid station manned by Company A of the 319th Medical Battalion, where medics logged me in "injured, litter bound, and wounded in action," at 0110, January 21, 1945.

Seeing Murray's dried blood on my combat jacket, the medics thought I'd been hit in the back. After I convinced them otherwise, they examined my actual wounds in a casual manner, without removing any part of my uniform, before giving me a shot of morphine. One medical corpsman handed me sulfa tablets and a full canteen of water, and another lit a cigarette and put it between my lips. The medics did nothing to treat my wounds, but that was all right with me.

I lay under a blanket on a litter beside other dark, still forms. Breathing my thanks to God, I offered the deepest thanksgiving of my life. I had spent the day staying alive, not fearing death . . . and I'd met the soldier's combat duty: I hadn't run away, and I hadn't broken down emotionally. Discipline, training, and God's grace prevailed.

> *Oh, God,*
> *Thou art a hiding place for me,*
> *thou preservest me from trouble;*
> *thou dost encompass me in deliverance.*

Comforted by the Psalmist's lines and enveloped by weariness, I fell asleep.

Patient and Replacement

France and England

January 21–May 10, 1945

Suddenly, I was floating. About 0235, medics lifted my litter, carried me out from under the open-sided aid-station tent, and slid the litter onto a rack in an ambulance, beside three other wounded GIs. When I asked the medic where we were going, he threw a blanket over me and said, "The evacuation hospital at Thionville." Before I could speak to the other wounded, my exhaustion and the warmth inside the ambulance lulled me back to sleep.

At Thionville, doctors were conducting triage in the spacious foyer of the *hotel de ville,* or city hall, which had been converted into an evacuation hospital. A doctor, accompanied by a male corpsman and nurse, was inspecting the wounds of GIs lying on stretchers on the foyer floor.

The doctor came over to me and asked, "How're you doing, soldier?"

When I told him I felt light-headed and wet all along my left side, he threw back the blanket, uncovering a long puddle of blood extending from my shoulder down my left side to my foot. The doctor ordered the corpsman to administer plasma where I lay. As the medic was preparing, the scene before my eyes slowly faded to black.

I awoke in a cavernous ballroom, surrounded by other wounded being tended by doctors, nurses, and orderlies. We were lying head to foot on our canvas cots, about three feet apart, which left enough space between us for medics to tend our needs.

My most urgent need was to empty my bladder. An orderly brought a urinal and left it with me, but try as I might I couldn't urinate. Another orderly, who discovered my predicament, brought a catheter and kidney-shaped basin. Explaining what he was going to do, he apologized as he slowly inserted the rubber tube in my urethra, trying to avoid hurting me. He asked if I had drunk water after taking the sulfa tablets; I explained how mine was frozen in the canteen and that I had to eat snow. He said snow didn't produce enough liquid to keep the drug from crystallizing in my bladder. That insufficiency and my failure to relieve myself for such a long time traumatized me. It took two more catherizations before I performed on my own. The procedure provided relief but left me extremely raw. About this time, they gave me an antitetanus shot.

I couldn't recall the trip in the ambulance to Thionville, so I didn't know how long I had bled. The doctors decided that the clot, which froze around the nearly severed artery in my left wrist, defrosted in the heated ambulance, and I bled slowly on the trip to the hospital. They guessed that if it had taken longer to reach Thionville, I might have died from the loss of blood.

Near daybreak, on January 21, the surgeons operated, removing only the larger pieces of shrapnel from my legs and concentrating on repairing my wrist. They cut my new OD turtleneck sweater off, to operate on my arm, nearly breaking my heart, because my new sweater was the only personal belonging I had, besides dog tags.

The surgeon said he would use a local anesthetic on my wrist, so I asked permission to watch the operation. Although he discouraged me, he reluctantly agreed.

The surgical nurse immobilized my left arm by strapping it to a board about six inches wide. After deadening my wrist, the surgeon carefully lifted out three oddly shaped chunks of metal. The largest fragment, lying beneath the skin like an extra-wide watchband, was about two inches square and an eighth of an inch thick. The large flat "band" prevented the other two triangular-shaped pieces from cutting all the way through my wrist. I watched the bloody work until I grew so faint I had to turn away.

When I couldn't see what the surgeon was doing, he described incising the surface of my inner wrist to expose the severed artery, trimming its ragged ends, and "anastomosing" the vessel, by suturing the artery's ends together over a tube made of a recently-developed soluble substance.

"It's a temporary stint," the surgeon said, "allowing the blood to flow while the stitches heal. In time, it'll be absorbed in the bloodstream."

The operation shortened the artery slightly. When the nurse removed the board beneath my left arm, it involuntarily bent at the elbow, curling my hand into a fist, with my thumb bent across my fingers. Attempting to extend my arm was so painful I couldn't do it, but the surgeon insisted that physical therapy, in the States or England, would return my arm and hand to normal. Meanwhile, my arm was bent at the elbow against my side.

Next, the surgeon removed only the easily accessible pieces of shrapnel from my legs and packed the wounds with thick gauze pads soaked in petroleum jelly. He said the operations on my legs would be performed later. Although I still had difficulty urinating, I was achieving some voluntary control. My feet—red, swollen, and aching—felt frostbitten but weren't damaged, and I didn't have trench foot. But after the anesthetic wore off, the thumb and heel of the palm of my left hand remained numb.

For the first time since escaping Orscholz, I was sufficiently clearheaded to hope the surgeons would find my wounds severe enough to transfer me from the Communications Zone (Com Z), behind the front, back to the Zone of the Interior (ZI) in the States. That seemed more likely, in my mind at least, listening to doctors speculating that the odds, after stepping on a land mine, were one in ten thousand of escaping alive without permanently crippling injuries. Following the surgeon's temporary patchwork, a nurse said I'd leave on a hospital train the next morning.

Medical orderlies carried me onto the hospital train the next day, January 22. Although I searched for familiar faces from Company B, because I knew so many were hit at Orscholz, I didn't recognize the soldiers near me. I expected to see at least one of the GIs wounded beside me in the minefield, but apparently their injuries weren't serious.

Nor do I recall conversing with any of the soldiers or nurses in the railway car. Being without old buddies wasn't troubling me yet or making me anxious about being alone, but I was sorry to be parted from those I'd known and liked since basic training. I was completely separated from the Ninety-fourth Division for the first time in eleven months.

The hospital carriage had double-decker bunks on each side of an aisle down its center, and the upper bunks, like the one I was lying on, were a little higher than chest level from the floor, allowing the medics easy access to the wounded. In the windowless hospital car, there was nothing to see or do, so I slept most of the time. My low-grade fever from infected wounds lulled me into a persistent drowsiness, and I remember only activity around patients who were restless and moaning much of the time.

Despite my wooziness on the overnight trip, one memory is indelible. When the train stopped somewhere en route, I heard the treble voices of women at the far end of the car, chatting and laughing. As they made their way down the aisle, I realized they were Red Cross workers handing out cigarettes and candy bars, asking for the names and hometowns of patients.

A GI near them asked, "Who are you angels, and where are you from?"

The woman in the lead said, brightly, in a familiar dialect, "Judy Dortch from Scott, Arkansas."

Excited to hear her name and hometown, right outside my own, I raised up on my elbow, shouting, "I'm from Little Rock!"

The short brunette walked back toward me, smiling broadly, showing as much delight as I over meeting someone from home. Besides my name, I told her I went to East Side Junior High with her sister, Virginia, and with Alfred Craig, whose plantation was next to the Dortches' in Scott. Virginia and Alfred also were at Little Rock Senior High.

As Judy and I talked, her companion reached us. I couldn't believe my eyes when I saw that the beautiful blonde standing beside us was Madeline Carroll, the famous English movie actress I'd seen in Hollywood movies throughout the '30s and early '40s. When Judy introduced her, Miss Carroll smiled and grasped my hand in her soft, warm fingers, wishing me, in her crisp English accent, a quick recovery. She gave me an extra pack of cigarettes before the two resumed visiting men in the rest of the car.

The encounter was exciting enough to fully awaken me. After six months without social contact with women, I met a world-famous movie actress and a hometown girl on the same evening. Musing about Madeline Carroll, I recalled her movies, including *Bahama Passage,* which Tumpy and I saw after we started dating in 1942. Thoughts like that occupied my feverish mind, off and on, for the rest of the night.

The hospital train arrived in Paris early the next morning. American doctors and nurses came on board to check our wounds before leaving us in the hands of German POWs. The prisoners carried us off the train on litters to a French civilian hospital that had become the American First General Hospital. The stoical prisoners, walking through the unlighted, empty corridors, never spoke to each other or acknowledged me the entire way to the room. Alone with them in the dark halls, their hobnailed boots clattering on the tile floors, I mulled the irony of being carried to my hospital bed in Paris by unguarded German POWs after German soldiers on the Siegfried Line, only forty-eight hours before, fired every kind of firearm trying to kill me.

The prisoners gently placed me on an empty bed in a room with three other wounded GIs. One patient turned out to be a pleasant young man who, like me, was in college before being drafted. The other two soldiers were memorable in contrasting ways. Directly across from me, a self-described "native Confederate from North Carolina" proved garrulous, profane, and mean-spirited, describing his heroic combat adventures, particularly in street fighting in Saarbrücken, where he'd been hit. He was the first true example of a "rodomontade" I'd ever met. The other patient, in a corner bed on my side of the room, never spoke. Though he was still and quiet as death, the nurses and ward boys tended him as if he were living.

Lying in the cool, high-ceilinged hospital room, feeling better, I contemplated what happened at Orscholz, realizing that I came much closer to killing someone accidentally, as a teenager, than I did purposely as a combat rifleman. In the '30s, on Arch Street Pike, my friends and I put glass insulators, discarded by Arkansas Power and Light, on the tips of tall reeds in a field beside the highway, and fired at them with our .22 rifles. We weren't aware the trajectory of our bullets crossed U.S. Highway 65, the road to Pine Bluff.

In Paris, the doctors again examined the deep holes and shrapnel under my knees, as well as the gaping slice out of the calf muscle of my right leg. But after cleansing the wounds, surgeons didn't close them; they only applied more Vaseline-soaked gauze pads. They decided my injuries weren't severe enough to return to the States; they were shipping me to England for operations and recuperation. I learned later that anyone expected to recover inside six months was held in the European Theater of Operations (ETO) rather than sent to the States. I didn't brood about their decision and my disappointment, for I happily assumed my wounds would keep me out of combat for good. After another night at the Army's First General Hospital, I was joyfully sailing back to merry old England.

Stolid German POWs returned the next morning and carried our litters to a hospital train. At Cherbourg, more German prisoners loaded us on the British hospital ship *Duke of Gloucester* for the short crossing to Southampton. In late January 1945, the English Channel still held potential for a submarine attack, even against a white hospital ship, clearly marked with red crosses. The German army was fighting fiercely and showed no clear sign of their imminent surrender. Fortunately, I was so feverish that I slept without a thought of the ship being torpedoed.

Late that afternoon, just before we docked, a British nurse waked me and offered a cup of hot tea, which she poured from a gigantic white enamel pitcher into an oversize white enamel cup. Even though the tea had cream in it (my preference is iced tea with lemon), it was the best I had ever tasted.

In Southampton, more German POWs carried us down the ship's narrow gangplank, holding our litters precariously high above their heads, on the way to hospital cars sitting at the wharf side. After a lengthy train trip, through Salisbury and Exeter, we reached Newton Abbot about 2200 and were transferred by ambulances to the 112th General Hospital out in the Devonshire countryside.

Although the night was severely cold, doctors, nurses, and orderlies, in heavy coats and hats, met us outside the hospital entrance to assign us to particular wards, depending upon our injuries. After triage, they wheeled me on a gurney to a canvas holding tent located next to a cinder block building, marked "Surgical Ward S-3."

The beds in the crowded, unheated tent were practically touching each other and filled with wounded men, all sleeping soundly, their faces hidden by mounds of blankets that were covered by tan canvas tarpaulins. The duty nurse and the orderly lifted me onto one of the beds, and she injected me with a sedative. I fell as fast asleep as my concealed companions already were.

Early the next morning, before I was fully awake, a ward boy rolled me on a gurney to an operating room, where a surgical team was already waiting. Even though I was too drowsy to understand, a doctor explained the operation before administering the general anesthesia, sodium pentothal. The anesthetist asked me to count backwards, beginning with ten. I may have reached eight before falling asleep.

The next day, I met the very young surgeon, Dr. Ralph Norton, whose hair stuck up on the sides of his head like Dagwood Bumstead's in the comics. I learned that he and the surgical nurses took advantage of sodium pentothal's truth-telling effects, asking me a lot of personal questions as he operated on my legs. He and his nurse said that while I was "out," I related stories and jokes and did vocal impersonations, but they wouldn't tell me if I had revealed anything more personal under the truth drug. Their cordial behavior while dressing my wounds each day implied I had said nothing embarrassing or disgraceful.

A thin strip of skin and muscle, about four inches long, was torn from the calf of my right leg by the exploding mine. Dr. Norton used stainless steel wires to hold the raw surfaces together, and attached ordinary coat buttons at their ends to prevent their tearing through the muscle. This unusual repair was supposed to close the wound and promote healing without skin grafts from other parts of my body. The surgeon also removed four pieces of shrapnel that had torn away the surrounding muscle behind my left knee and cut into the sheath of the tendon.

The doctor applied a partial plaster of paris cast to keep my left knee from bending during the healing process. He did nothing further to my left wrist because the successful repair at Thionville was healing rapidly. But parts of my left hand remained as numb as they were after I was first hit. The doctor tested regularly, pressing the point of a pin into the pad of my thumb and palm to check my sensory nerve responses. The sensation was thick and dull, like a foot that's gone to sleep.

After the operation, I was returned to Ward S-3, where nurses placed a wire cage over my body that reached from my shoulders to my feet. The frame kept the top sheet and blanket from touching me and allowed the nurses and orderlies easy access to check and dress my wounds. Even so, when they remade my bed, replacing the bottom sheet was awkward and pained almost as much as changing my bandages.

I was delirious from a high fever for two days and nights. According to Lieutenant Edwina Foss, one of the nurses in charge of Ward S-3, the surgeons on the Continent underestimated the severity of my infection when they left shrapnel pieces embedded in my legs. The lengthy operation in England compounded the infection, requiring the most powerful medicine then available to subdue it.

Fortunately, penicillin was practical by that time. For five days and nights, the nurses injected thirty thousand units of penicillin into some part of my body every three hours. The shots had to be given that frequently because the antibiotic, suspended in a saline solution, was absorbed too rapidly. Scientists hadn't yet found a proper medium to maintain for longer periods a constant level of penicillin in the bloodstream.

During that week, the nurses had difficulty finding new places on my body to inject the shots. The orderlies were monitoring my temperature hourly, while keeping an input-output chart of the water consumed and urine expelled by me. For two days, I sweated so profusely that the staff had to change my pajamas and linens repeatedly.

It was puzzling that so many pieces of shrapnel could pierce and lodge in my body without injuring me more severely. I asked Dr. Norton how nine large pieces of shrapnel could enter my wrist and legs with such great force without striking a single bone. He explained that shrapnel fragments tend to follow the line of least resistance, that the pieces that penetrated my legs moved parallel to the bone until emerging or stopping when their force was spent. He also speculated that the explosive charges in the mines were partially frozen and less powerful.

When my infection subsided and my temperature returned to normal, I learned my new address: Hospital Plant 4103, Ward S-3, APO 649, c/o Postmaster, New York, N.Y.

I wrote my parents on the last day of January, giving my new address and describing the day at Orscholz. The letter was first held up by an Army examiner, who wrote at the top of the envelope: "Rewrite. Mention only that which concerns yourself—not the company or anyone else. J. Rodriguez, 1st Lt." Yet the letter was never returned to me; it was forwarded to my parents, perhaps because the war was going so well by then.

Back home, my folks didn't learn of my injury until the morning of February 6. More than two weeks after I was hit, the telegram arrived:

REGRET TO INFORM YOU YOUR SON PRIVATE FIRST CLASS ALLIE C HARRISON WAS SLIGHTLY WOUNDED IN ACTION TWENTY ONE JANUARY IN GERMANY . . . MAIL ADDRESS FOLLOWS DIRECT FROM HOSPITAL WITH DETAILS.

J A ULIO THE ADJUTANT GENERAL.

The Army's message proved wrong on two counts: the incorrect date of when I was wounded and the failure of the hospital to forward details of my injury.

Although I knew my inability to walk was the result of more than a "slight wound," I was thankful, for my parents' sake, that the Army had not said I was *seriously* wounded. I learned later that particular term indicated a loss of limbs, or other extremely disabling injuries, like stomach wounds. If a soldier arrived at an aid station on his own two legs, he was "slightly" wounded. Frightened and in tears, Mother called Tumpy to give her the bad news, but Tumpy reassured Mom by pointing out the War Department's use of *slightly.*

As I was recovering, I became better acquainted with the other patients, nurses, and orderlies, and learned the ward's routines. As a rule, two female nurses and two ward boys were on duty at any time during the day. But at night, with no emergencies or new arrivals, only a nurse and ward boy stayed in the office at one end of the ward.

The hospital kitchen prepared three hot meals a day for all patients. A black man from the kitchen staff pushed a mobile steam table into the center of the ward and, assisted by ward boys and nurses, served trays to the bedridden. The tall, lean New Yorker, offering happy talk and jokes, spoke and carried himself with great dignity. Friendly and direct, if he didn't approve our food choices, he chastised patients, individually or collectively.

One day, too many plates were returned with carrots on them. Our "nutritionist" frowned as he glanced around the ward, growling in his resonant baritone, "Now, gentlemen, we *will* eat our carrots. If you don't eat them at noon, you will eat your carrots at supper. Gentlemen, rest assured, they *shall return*!"

Vowing like MacArthur and calling us "gentlemen," he left everyone in the ward laughing, not only at his playful vow of coercion but at his crisply articulated Shakespearean tone. However, he did return with carrots, until all of us ate a few to placate him.

One of the friendly, white ward "boys," on the day shift, was from New Hampshire. T/5 Mason—short, stocky, and in his thirties—had a high-pitched, nasal twang that inspired a lot of kidding, in and out of his hearing. His maternal manner and cheerful disposition inspired patients before us to call him "Mother Mason," an appellation we adopted without condescension.

He was especially attentive during my feverish crisis, and continued the attention by bringing copies of *Stars and Stripes*, books, and magazines, because I may have done more reading than others. Before I left the hospital, Mason and two fellows who arrived the same night I did—Americo Di Marcantonio and Thomas J. McCue—and I had our picture taken together.

My brother, James Franklin (called "Buster" by our family), went to England a year before me. He was serving in the Eighth Air Force, in the Forty-Third Troop Carrier Squadron of the 315th Troop Carrier Group. His outfit was based in the fen country of East Anglia, but he never told us which of the nineteen troop-carrier fields in England he was stationed at. When Mother learned my hospital address, she sent it to Buster.

The night nurse came to tell me that she had talked on the phone to Private Jimmy Harrison, who said he was coming to visit me in a few days. Since I hadn't heard from my brother for more than a year, I was surprised he knew my whereabouts.

Two days later, Buster arrived at midmorning. The story he told of getting leave to visit me typified my brother's approach if someone tried to prevent his doing what he wanted. Buster asked his squadron's executive officer for permission to visit his brother at the 112th General

Hospital, which was some distance from his air base. But with no official confirmation of my presence in England, other than our mother's letter, the officer wouldn't grant him time off. Buster waited a few days before requesting a twenty-four-hour pass, which his first sergeant granted without any questions.

My brother concealed his real objective by leaving the field without luggage, carrying only a comb and safety razor in his uniform pockets. After his overnight train trip through London to Newton Abbot, he shaved, without soap, at the railway station, and took a bus to the hospital. At my beside, he warned that he could stay only a few hours, because he had traveled too many miles beyond his base on a twenty-four-hour pass.

I had last seen my brother nearly two years before. Although I was happy he visited me, the time and distance we had spent apart and his natural reticence made it awkward. While I was growing up, Buster had little to say to me. Now, surrounded by other patients, he volunteered even less. The thirteen-year difference in our ages made him more like an uncle, and my adulthood, combat experience, and medical condition didn't alter the emotional distance between us.

I answered his questions about combat, and he related something about his life in the troop carrier squadron. His squadron transported paratroopers for the Market Square attack on Arnhem, and he described the event without revealing his emotions. He was a crew member on a C-47, or Dakota, that dropped British and American troops over Holland on September 17, 1944. Even before the planes left the ground in England, a few troopers accidentally detonated the plastic explosives they carried and were killed. Later over Arnhem, Buster watched parachutists floating down to inevitable injury, capture, or death, as his plane banked to return to England.

Our talk at the hospital, brief as it was, came nearer to a real conversation with my brother than any we had had in the previous twenty years. He left in the afternoon, and I wouldn't see him again overseas, although I remained three months longer at the hospital and the replacement depot before being sent back to the Continent.

There were several everyday pleasures at the hospital; foremost among them were being out of combat, living inside a warm, dry place, and having three hot meals a day. Two special privileges were daily baths and back rubs. Ambulatory patients were free to walk to the shower room at the end of the ward for a hot bath anytime they wanted. But the bedridden waited each morning for an orderly or nurse to bring basins of hot water and washcloths to give them baths, or let them do it themselves, depending upon their conditions. Later in the day, nurses gave back rubs to prevent bed sores on those confined to their beds. For two months, Lieutenant Foss, the dainty blonde nurse, applied alcohol and massage to my back with her small, strong hands.

Another daily ward ritual was doctors' rounds at midmorning, after we had breakfast and our baths. Examining and dressing wounds continued until nearly noon, especially after a new batch of casualties arrived. The doctor's small medical retinue crowded around each patient's bed to hear his diagnoses and study the surgical repairs.

Following lunch, the rituals for those of us confined to bed were naps, reading, or playing cards. The walking-wounded could roam freely around the hospital's whole premises, inside or out, in good or bad weather, because the halls and covered walkways connected all the different wards and offices.

At midafternoon, the ward staff served tea or coffee, along with cookies, what the British call "biscuits." The biscuit packets held four buttery, crumbly Scotch shortbreads, which almost everyone relished, or four thin, hard arrowroot cookies, which few ate. We received more arrowroots than shortbreads, and stored them in the drawer of our nightstands for ammunition in cookie battles after lights-out. Nurses and orderlies thought our behavior "crummy," in every sense, cleaning up after us the next morning.

In the afternoon and evening, we listened to the Armed Forces Network (AFN), when ward staff played the radio. We especially enjoyed Major Glenn Miller's Air Force Band and British Broadcasting Company (BBC) news, heralded by deep peals of the chimes of Big Ben, the clock in the tower of the Houses of Parliament in London.

As my health improved, restoring my energy and spirits, I began doing parodies of Franklin D. Roosevelt's fireside chats after lights-out. The atmosphere changed in the ward when the staff turned off the lights and retired to the front office. Although the nurse in charge was only a few yards away, darkness stirred more talk and levity among patients; the same spirit of raucous remarks and tricks that sprang up in cabins after lights-out when Boy Scouts spent weeks at Camp Quapaw in the summers.

In my brief fireside chats, I described what happened in the ward during the day that was worthy of satiric comment. My vocal pitch placement wasn't FDR's, but ward mates liked my impression because I caught the president's rhythms and phraseology. Citing familiar events and persons in the ward, in the manner of the president, made some GIs laugh and beg for more, while others were happily lulled to sleep. I always included a reference to the president's little Scottish terrier, Fala, or to his wife, Eleanor. One chat began: "My friends, prior to D-Day, Mr. Churchill and I worked out an intricate plan whereby we could keep Eleanor out of the lines of fire on D-Day."

I combined this improvised stuff with routines from my high school and college repertoire, including the lead tenor of the Ink Spots ("If I didn't care more than words can say, would my every prayer begin and end the same old way?"). Sometimes the distinctive personalities of ward mates were also material for my impressions.

One night, Lieutenant Betty Copeland, the nurse on duty, listened to my Fireside Chat without my knowing, and a few days later invited me to deliver one for the medical staff at their regular Saturday night dance. Dr. Norton assigned a wheelchair to me until my leg wounds healed, so Copeland had a ward boy push me to the hall. I performed a naive parody of Army medical life, concocted from observations of doctors, nurses, patients, and procedures in Ward S-3.

I circulated through the entire hospital in my wheelchair, meeting patients in all the wards, except the one for VD, which pals called the "clap shack." Soon after I got a wheelchair, hospital supply issued me a set of new uniforms. Until then, I'd been wearing pajamas, a robe, and cloth house slippers. My new wardrobe included underwear, socks, cotton fatigues, a combat jacket, and a wool dress uniform.

Surprisingly, my blood-stained combat boots, with my name on an attached tag, were returned to me. The boots followed me from the front lines in Germany to Paris and then to England, although no other part of my combat uniform or equipment had. How or why the boots were not separated from me at the different hospital stops I couldn't imagine.

My mobility in the wheelchair, after two full months in bed, made me eligible for some parts of regular GI duty. My assignment to KP at the hospital differed from my previous experience. Instead of peeling potatoes, washing pans in the kitchen, or serving trays in the dining room, the cook sent me to the officer's lounge to make ice cream in an electric freezer. He furnished a box filled with ingredients, instructions, and the necessary measuring and mixing utensils, and sent me off alone.

I always envied officers their ice cream because it was rarely on the enlisted menu. My preparation of maple-flavored ice cream, a favorite of mine, must have been satisfactory to the mess officer, for the cook reassigned me to ice-cream detail three more times. Given permission to eat as much as I wanted, I sampled ice cream until it was no longer one of my cravings.

The wound in my wrist finally healed sufficiently for me to have physical therapy with Lieutenant Redwine, a dark-skinned, brunette technician of American Indian ancestry. The slender, shapely therapist's sense of humor and great smile made me eager for her guidance. With Redwine's help, I was trying to free the fingers of my left hand from a clench and to straighten my left arm, which had bent at the elbow after the artery was repaired. The scar tissue in my wrist and my reluctance to hurt myself complicated the process. Until I overcame my fear of pain and exercised strenuously enough to stretch the artery, I wouldn't have full use of my hand and arm.

Daily therapy consisted of carrying and squeezing a rubber ball, and unfurling my fingers by pressing them on a tabletop, slowly increasing their flexibility. By adding weight to a barbell in my hand and elevating my elbow, I gradually raised my arm above my waist and extended it farther out from my shoulder. Although leg therapy was delayed until the open wounds healed, I walked before I could use my left arm and hand because my legs hadn't been frozen in position. By exercising my legs with weights, I quickly gained strength and flexibility.

One day during therapy a loud cracking sound from my left arm startled the lieutenant and me. She had me stop exercising and wouldn't allow me to continue, even though I felt no pain. After examining my wrist, she decided that when I fully extended and straightened my elbow, for the first time, scar tissue broke, making the loud snap. Even though no swelling resulted, Dr. Norton examined my arm and recommended continuing physical therapy. He complimented my personal discipline and cooperation, convincing me that diligence has its rewards; only three months after stepping on a German land mine, I was walking again.

Inexplicably, the medical staff's whole effort was to heal my physical wounds only. No one checked my psychological state, a lapse that didn't even occur to me at the hospital. Doctors didn't inquire about how I was wounded, or how I felt under fire at Orscholz, watching my comrades lying wounded and dying, or how the eight hours trying to escape affected me. Surely someone needed to know the effects on my mind and emotions, to determine whether I suffered a serious psychological trauma. A year or more would pass before the emotional residue of that day at Orscholz emerged. I expected no psychological problems and obviously no one else did either.

Soon after my success in physical therapy, the doctors allowed me an eight-hour pass. Another GI from Ward S-3, who had also recovered enough for outside recreation, joined me on the bus to Newton Abbot, the largest town near the hospital. Without any plans, we gravitated to the nearest movie theater and attended a matinee, which we probably would have done on a Saturday afternoon at home.

Only a handful of people were downstairs in the small theater, but heavy clouds of cigarette smoke, hovering between us and the screen, showed the balcony was filled with patrons. The feature film was forgettable, but I recall the Gaumount British News, the first British newsreel I had seen. The narrator, with his clipped speech and fruity voice, described scenes exclusively of victorious British campaigns, announcing that "the brave Tommies pushed farther into Germany, led by the valiant Monty."

We left before the feature ended to get something to drink before going back to the hospital. At the English tea room across from the theater we had cups of tea and cakes. The little gray-haired ladies presiding over the small place had covered the tiny, round tables with linen cloths and placed at their centers slender vases filled with spring blossoms. The other soldier and I felt out of place and awkward handling a tea strainer, loose tea leaves, and china cups, under the eyes of the Englishwomen at the other tables. Besides, the cakes weren't sweet and the tea was too weak.

A few days later, I returned alone to Newton Abbot in the evening and attended another movie at the theater, where I observed, for the first time, certain British movie house conventions. A community-sing filled the intermission between the features. An older man led the singing, playing at the keyboard of a mammoth, garishly lighted pipe organ at the center of the orchestra pit. At the end of the evening, we stood to sing "God Save the King."

On my third trip to Newton Abbot, I met a teenage girl ahead of me in the movie line. Her lovely name was Heather MacMillan, and we sat next to each other in the theater, talked a bit, and joined the community sing. Although reticent, she agreed to meet me at the same theater at the same time the following night.

We met as planned, but our mutual shyness made the date awkward. I didn't know what to talk about and neither did she. She was too young to go to a pub after the show, and the more appropriate places, like ice cream parlors or tea shops, were closed, so I walked her to her home in a working-class neighborhood. When her mother opened the door and saw her daughter standing on the doorstep with an American soldier, she yelled as if her child had done something wrong. Heather waved goodbye from behind her irate mother, who slammed the door on what many British considered an "overpaid, oversexed, and over here" American!

Soon bored with trips to Newton Abbot, I rode farther down the road to Torquay, pronounced "tar-kee" by the British. The seaside resort is warmed by the Gulf Stream, has palm trees, and is known as the "British Riviera."

On our first night in town, the Hole in the Wall was recommended to my buddies and me. The downtown pub at the top of a hill at the end of a narrow street was reputedly the hangout of Sir Francis Drake and his crew of sailors. The tiny sixteenth-century building had narrow Tudor latticework windows and a ceiling low enough for short men standing flat-footed to touch. Its military habitués, for good luck, had already covered the low ceiling with pound notes, dollar bills, and calling cards.

Although, under wartime conditions, the publican, or owner, received only a small allotment of spirits daily, he served Americans an equal share of his genuine pale ale. Though served at room temperature, it was our favorite English beverage. Natives encouraged us to venture across the main road to a small open-air stand at the top of the boat ramp on the quay for fish and chips. The owner served piping hot chunks of fish and potatoes, copiously sprinkled with salt and squirts of malt vinegar, in large cones shaped from old newspapers. Fish and chips on the Torquay ramp surpassed any I have ever had.

Torquay became our regular stomping ground. When my buddies and I had passes, we rode through Newton Abbot to Torquay, where we always found something interesting to do. Our chief pleasures were drinking ale and eating fish and chips, but with enough drinks under our belts and opportune meetings with English girls, we attended dances at the Pavilion at the end of the pier on Torquay Bay. The ballroom was filled every night with Englishwomen of all ages eager to dance with British and American soldiers and listen to swing music played by an English orchestra.

Another venue that attracted us on the waterfront was the Princess Theater, featuring English touring companies performing British plays. I enjoyed especially watching the theater's musicians rising from the orchestra pit on an elevator platform. The orchestra reached stage level while playing the overture or intermission music, only to sink out of sight as the curtain rose or fell on the play. The dramas were usually murder mysteries or drawing room comedies, and watching them taught me how to act and direct English comedy in the same light, speedy way.

If plays or dances didn't capture us, we toured the open but blacked-out shops lining the wide sidewalk on one side of the quay at the center of the downtown. Near the end of my stay at the hospital, we found a fortune-teller's booth among the shops, and I paid the middle-aged woman to read my fortune from my palm and playing cards. She predicted I'd do important work in the Army before going back to America, where "You'll live the lives of many men."

I interpreted that to mean a successful career for me as an actor. More than likely, she extracted my acting ambitions by obliquely asking my buddies questions while reading their cards. Perhaps, without realizing it, I had also obtusely revealed my theatrical dreams.

After a physical exam the first week of April, doctors decided I had recovered sufficiently for reassignment, even though I didn't have complete feeling and use of my left hand. Several other GIs were granted furloughs at the same time, and I teamed up with Sergeant Henry Marugo from the Bronx and Michael Pulaski, a young GI from Chicago, to go to London. The talkative Marugo was short and wiry, and his fine, curly black hair had already receded high on his pale forehead. But Pulaski was a good-looking blond, with aquiline features and a plentiful head of hair. I hadn't met them at the hospital, but we traveled together anyway because of shared circumstances and congeniality. If I hadn't visited London with them, I would have gone with other new acquaintances who were transients like me. That was the

Army way. After our one-week furloughs, we were to report to Whittington Barracks at Lichfield, in Staffordshire, for redeployment.

We left Newton Abbot in the late evening of April 12, 1945. On board the train, we found an unoccupied compartment, which seated six, so we had room enough to lie down and sleep on the way to London. Flipping a coin for bedding places, Marugo and I won the two seats; Pulaski settled for a hammocklike luggage net suspended above one of the seats. We were all comfortable, though, because the bench seats had no dividers and the luggage nets were the full width of the compartment.

A little after midnight, the sliding door of our compartment clattered open. The elderly train conductor stuck his head in, "The BBC has just announced over the wireless that your President Roosevelt has died."

Standing in the door, speaking very emotionally, the conductor offered his condolences, expressing admiration and affection for Roosevelt equal to that he held for Winston Churchill. Roosevelt's passing saddened and shocked us too; we didn't know about his poor health, and he was the only president we'd had in our lifetime. But combat left us with such an acceptance of death that we fell back to sleep in the time it took the conductor to close the compartment door.

Later, passing through the bombed-out city of Coventry, the old fellow waked us again, urging us to lift the compartment shades and see the ruins of the cathedral near the tracks. The train slowly wended through lots of railroad switches, past the black silhouette of the shattered cathedral, the worst destruction I had seen since Normandy.

We arrived before daybreak at Charing Cross Station in London, and took advantage of the service booths, for military personnel, on the platform beside the tracks. While a gnarled little Cockney steam-pressed our uniforms, we stood in shorts and undershirts behind the breeze-blown curtain of a chilly closet off the ironing room. Then, in our sharply creased uniforms, we sat on the high throne in the shoe-shine booth for a spit polish, whipped up by another Cockney, brushing and snapping our shoes until they shone like mirrors. Afterwards, we had coffee and doughnuts at the Red Cross booth before wandering into the dark streets, without knowing how to find Rainbow Corner, the largest American military service center in London. We wanted to book rooms there for our stay, but we had to wait until daybreak when there was light enough for us to locate Piccadilly Circus and find the Corner open.

In the blackout, without knowing what we passed, we walked through Trafalgar Square, past the National Gallery, meandering blindly but serendipitously into Saint Martin's Lane in the theater district. Under a theater marquee, struggling to read the playbills in the dim but growing light, we discovered it was the New Theatre, the wartime home of the Old Vic Company. Billboards advertised the stars Laurence Olivier and Ralph Richardson, appearing in *Peer Gynt, Arms and the Man,* and *Richard III.*

I couldn't believe that audiences had gathered in the close confines of theaters for live productions during Blitz air raids and buzz-bomb attacks, which ended only the month before, while we were in the hospital. I hadn't known that the brave and spirited English civilians demanded that theaters reopen after they were closed when hostilities first began in September 1939.

At daybreak, we walked back through Trafalgar Square, down Pall Mall to Lower Regent Street, and across the Piccadilly Circus to the corner of Shaftsbury Avenue and Rainbow Corner, which, to our relief, was already open. Soldiers outside said the service club for enlisted ranks never closed, that the key was thrown away when its doors first opened.

Even shortly after sunrise, the information desk was surrounded by soldiers with different requests. When we asked to book rooms there for the next five days, the clerk let us know that Rainbow Corner didn't have rooms, only a list of several hundred GI billets around the city. The middle-aged British woman gave us cards for the Milestone Club, formerly a private club for English gentlemen before the members adopted the motto "Nothing is too good for our boys" and converted it to lodgings for transient American soldiers.

Following the desk clerk's directions, we caught a red double-decker bus at a stop on Piccadilly Circus. Cold as it was in early April, we decided to sit on the upper deck. From the top of the steps, we saw two young women in pale blue American Red Cross uniforms seated among the English civilians. The women smiled and said, "hello," as we came down the aisle, so Marugo and Pulaski sat in the seat behind them, leaning forward to introduce themselves and me. The older brunette, Patty Kelly, was from Boston, and her blonde companion, Ruth Opp, was from Ohio.

When we asked for suggestions about something to do while in London, the women said they had arrived only a few weeks earlier and were exploring the city themselves. They invited us to join them on an afternoon trip to Hampton Court Palace. We agreed to meet after lunch, at 1330, at the nearest bus stop on Kensington.

Shortly after the bus passed Albert Hall, the Prince Albert Memorial, and part of Hyde Park, we got off and found the Milestone Club between DeVere Gardens and Victoria Road, within sight of the Dial Walk in Kensington Gardens. At the hotel, an elderly male desk clerk put us all in the same room on the first floor. Stumbling around looking for the room, another GI told us that, in American terms, it was on the second floor. From the window of our room, which faced Kensington Road, we could see in the distance the grounds and gardens surrounding Kensington Palace. We chose cots, stowed duffels, and went down to the basement dining room, which smelled of boiled vegetables.

For the first time since any of us came to England, we were away from American military quarters and food, and had to sample English lodgings and cooking. Lunch at the Milestone wasn't promising. Besides sliced bread or rolls, our choices were several boiled vegetables that were not seasoned in any way. I guessed the butter shortage and use of grease for making explosives partially explained why English cooks boiled everything, but I couldn't imagine why they didn't use herbs and spices for seasoning.

After lunch, we joined Patty and Ruth at the agreed-upon bus stop.

Even though the sun wasn't out, we again sat on the open top deck for the cool, drizzly, ten-mile drive to Hampton Court. Hardly anyone was on the bus, and the small number of passengers was matched by the few attendants at Hampton Court. Few visitors, military or civilian, were touring the palace that dark afternoon.

We conducted our own tour of the unlighted palace by referring to the free brochures, which identified the functions of the various rooms open to the public, describing their prewar furnishings. Since all accessories had been removed for safekeeping, the illustrations provided our only information. The brochure clarified the architectural arrangements in the rooms, such as the careful placement of doors and the angles of mirrors in Henry VIII's apartments, which allowed the king to see visitors at a distance before they reached his chamber. As soldiers, we were impressed by the elaborate display of Henry's weapons hanging on the reception room walls.

A large hole in the center of the roof of the main banquet hall puzzled us. The palace's poor state of repair prevented our knowing whether the hole was purpose-built, to vent smoke from fires on the open hearth at the center of the room below, or the result of an aerial bomb during the Blitz. Our brochure was no help because it was printed before the war.

But another puzzle at Hampton Court was purpose-built and three-dimensional. A maze of hedges provided the most fun we had at the palace, wandering like laboratory mice inside its green labyrinth of leafy walls, searching for the exit. By the time we rambled around aimlessly, laughing our way through and out of the maze, the cloudy day had faded to night. We rode back to London inside the partially blacked-out bus, along dark streets of outlying suburbs, to Kensington. Before parting, we found a neighborhood pub near the Milestone and said farewell to Patty and Ruth over drinks.

At the Milestone, we encountered one more English austerity. The next morning, eager to bathe, we learned that common bathrooms in English hotels are shared by guests, who book a specific time for their use. I looked forward to a hot shower, but the medium-size, high-ceilinged closet across the hall from our room had only a bath tub, large enough to hold two adults at one time. The room had no shower stall or shower head over the tub, nor did it have a commode (the British "lavatory"). The only other accessory was a giant-size, waist-high sink on legs, beside a floor-to-ceiling sash window with a frosted-pane. The frigid air in the room, which had no central heat or space heater, cooled the water before it was sufficiently deep for a bath. Bathing outdoors in France was good preparation for the Milestone.

On our second day, Henry, Mike, and I, sufficiently acclimated to the cold London air, visited in Hyde Park the Speaker's Corner, the Serpentine, and the statue of Sir James Barrie's Peter Pan. We climbed the steps to the platform to read the various inscriptions on the Prince Albert Monument, which honors Queen Victoria's consort and overlooks the mammoth, red-brick Albert Hall across the street.

Marugo stopped at a tobacconist's and bought black cigars, which he thrust upon Pulaski and me. We just stuck them in our mouths without lighting them, and mimed Groucho Marx. Marugo insisted on our being men enough to smoke the stogies instead of playing games. I was willing to clench the cigar between my teeth and strut around the parks for the machismo effect, if that proved my manhood, but I wasn't foolish enough to light up. For I found even English cigarettes, such as Players and Woodbines, were too strong and bitter. Marugo was disappointed in me and the "park rangers," or prostitutes, who failed to approach us in broad daylight in Hyde Park.

Looking like small-time gangsters, with cigar stubs protruding from our mouths, we walked three abreast through Green Park. A roving street photographer on a tree-shaded lane snapped a picture of us in that pose. He stopped us, performed his instant photo-development process, and showed us our comic images immediately. Approving our jaunty looks, we bought prints. Alas, I looked at mine the next morning and found only our faint, ghostly images lingered. The photographer's chemistry hadn't set them permanently; our pictures and money were gone forever.

Talking with other GIs at Rainbow Corner and in pubs, we heard tales about the bizarre parade around Piccadilly Circus every night, how numerous ladies of the night, professional and amateur, worked the central precincts of London. We couldn't imagine their numbers until we went there. Barely visible in the subdued light and shadows of a semiblackout, a procession of women—young and middle aged, pretty and ugly, military and civilian—moved slowly and constantly, seeking contact with the procession of sailors, soldiers, and airmen of all the Allies drawn to the roundabout.

London bobbies, supervising the parade along the broad sidewalks, wouldn't allow either men or women to stop and stand still. If anyone hesitated, or halted for any reason, the bobbies spoke politely to the service men and civilian women: "Keep moving along there like a good chap," and "No standing about now, love." Their aim was to prevent business from developing, by keeping everyone on the move around the Circus. Although the Piccadilly commandos, carrying their tiny torches (flashlights), couldn't dawdle on the Circus, they used the recessed doorways on nearby streets, performing "wall jobs" (standing up).

My only face-to-face encounter with a commercial damsel did not occur at night but at midday, near Piccadilly. Separated from Henry and Mike, I stepped inside the entry of a building on Regent Street to look at British souvenir jewelry in a shop window. A few moments later, a young woman, wearing a beige tam and trench coat, stepped into the recess beside me. Smiling broadly, without speaking, she opened her coat, revealing her totally naked body underneath. The brief peek surprised me so much that I couldn't speak, and when I didn't, she jauntily walked away. When I described to Marugo and Pulaski what the girl had done and how she looked, they expressed their regret about choosing to play pool and pinball!

We went to the Rialto Cinema on the Strand, between Aldwych and Trafalgar Square. The English musical comedy featured Vera Lynn, Britain's favorite young singer-actress during the war, singing "When the Lights Go on Again All Over the World" and "A Nightingale Sang in Berkeley Square." Her rich, liquid vocal quality was perfectly suited to the sentimental war songs of longing, love, and hope, which she made popular. The other favorite British singer-comedienne we often heard over the BBC was middle-aged Gracie Field, whose raucous soprano suited the music hall songs she was famous for.

On our way to catch a bus back to the Milestone, we were blocked by the outer fringes of a quiet crowd at Trafalgar Square. Londoners were holding a commemorative service for President Roosevelt, and on a platform some distance away from us, Winston Churchill was speaking. We arrived just as Churchill finished his remarks, and he rode away standing in the back of an open car, passing near enough for us to get a close-up view of his rosy, cherubic face.

Our last night in London, wandering down Kensington High Street, we encountered a happy group of young Londoners. After leaving a pub, eager not to waste our last hours, we stopped at the Town Hall, across from Derry Street, because the noise coming from the building and the crowd of young people hanging around its wide front doors suggested a happy place for a good time. We asked kids at the door what was happening inside, and they said it was a dance for Irish young people.

The kids were the friendliest persons we'd met in London. They invited us to join the dance, but the rapid tempo of the music convinced me I couldn't handle the dancing. Marugo insisted, anyway, on going into the ballroom, where a few teenagers persuaded us to join the group, singing words that described the steps we were taking as we danced the Lambeth Walk. The ensemble dance was as popular with the British as the Big Apple, which I had learned at junior high tea dances at the Woman's City Club in Little Rock, in the mid-1930s. We also attempted a dance the natives referred to as the "Palais glide." Although the kids had to show us every step, they overlooked our faults and found us funny. We danced until we were exhausted.

Our seven-day leave ended on April 20; it had been much too short. Scheduled to report at Whittington Barracks the following day, we were passing through Birmingham on the way to Lichfield. Before the train reached the big city, Marugo persuaded Pulaski and me to lay over there for an extra day before reporting. Doing that without official permission would be a first for me. But Marugo convinced us that the confusion at Lichfield, of so many GIs reporting after leaves, would keep MPs from noticing or caring we were a day late.

The stockade at the Tenth Replacement Depot, called "Stalag Lichfield" by GIs, was notorious for brutality. I didn't want to risk violating Article of War 107, for a prison sentence there and loss of pay. My acquiescence to a layover was my responsibility, and I'd pay for it too, because conscience and anxiety tempered any fun I might have.

The Birmingham station teemed with activities of all sorts, for the yard was a major railhead for British Railways, a disbursal center for the British-American military and an industrial axis for the British Isles. We struggled through crowds of soldiers to find the tiny Red Cross office, on the second floor of the railway station, to arrange places to stay overnight. When the Red Cross worker finally tore herself away from a GI trying to get emergency leave to the States, she sent us to transient barracks, situated on a height above the city, overlooking the sooty railway station and smoky town center. We climbed a steep walk, left our kits in lockers, and strolled back down to find a place for lunch.

Marugo caught sight of a garish storefront, its red paint peeling. He insisted on stopping there simply because he had never eaten at a Turkish cafe. The cafe's musty interior was darkened by a blue cloth canopy, covered with stars, overhead. A waiter, wearing a rumpled black jacket and a dingy white shirt with stained cuffs and collar, met us at the door. But his appearance didn't deter Marugo. We ordered, from a blotched menu, coffee and a Turkish dish of unknown ingredients. We could hardly see our food in the gloom, and its texture and odd flavor stanched our appetites. Attempting to make the best of a bad deal, we drank our coffee, only to learn that if the coffee is Turkish you should not stir. I'd heard of "Turkish delights," but this wasn't one of them.

Leaving the murky cafe, wandering down the smoky, misty streets with no plans in mind, we looked for something to *do* downtown. On a coal-blackened street near the railway station, we found ourselves under a theater marquee advertising a matinee performance of *The Trial of Mary Dugan.* In front of the box office of the Birmingham Repertory Theatre, just before curtain time, I persuaded Henry and Mike to see the play with me. The box-office lady convinced us to pay for tea and biscuits, which were to be served at intermission. We didn't know whether we'd like the refreshments, but we needed something to eat and drink to make up for the Turkish cafe.

The audience inside the theater was mostly women of various ages, along with a few much older men. A middle-aged lady usher, wearing a maid's black uniform, showed us to our seats in the orchestra section. Without knowing it, we had probably bought the best seats in the house. After we found our places, the houselights dimmed, and the curtain rose on a cast of actors whose faces were familiar to me from British movies shown in the States.

At intermission, the female ushers, having added white aprons and caps to their black uniforms, carried trays stacked with china cups and saucers down the aisles to each row. From our left, trays were passed to those who had reserved tea, and almost everyone in the theatre had. After the tray of cups and saucers came another, bearing a pot of tea, a bowl of sugar, and a pitcher of cream. Handling a cup and saucer, pouring tea, and adding cream and sugar demanded uncommon agility for us thick-fingered amateur tea drinkers. But with help from our neighbor ladies, we managed. Formal and polite, the hum of quiet conversation, unbroken even by laughter, made the tea seem endless. We finished sooner than our neighbors and waited restlessly for it to end. The ritual of gingerly passing trays, with china, slowly from one end of the rows to the other, until all were collected, seemed as long as the tea drinking.

The matinee lasted until 1700, and it was dark when we left the theater. We were hungry and thirsty again, but our thirsts dominated. We went inside the first pub we saw. I don't recall any food that evening, only one pale ale after another, and the ales in my empty stomach made me woozy. Nor do I remember when three young women joined us, but I'm sure Marugo asked them. They accepted the free drinks and what they must have considered the prospect of later monetary rewards from GIs.

At the witching hour of 2230, the publican cried, "Time, gentlemen, please," warning everyone that the pub was about to close. Marugo left with one of the girls, saying he'd see us later.

Pulaski and I took the other two girls out and wandered the dark streets. While Mike alternately hugged and nuzzled both of them, I pondered how to get rid of them. A short distance from the pub, we came upon a taxi stand, and one girl asked me to take her home. I would willingly pay the fare to lose her so I could go back to the barracks to sleep. But Mike insisted on my coming back to the taxi stand, and I agreed.

The girl in the cab must have thought I was a "john," but I had no sexual interest. I was a slightly drunk southern boy offering a lone girl the courtesy of a ride home in the blackout. The trip was shorter than I expected. We had gone only a few blocks when the cab pulled up in front of a house bursting with loud music and voices piercing its dark doors and windows. For a few minutes, the girl chatted away, I suppose waiting for my proposition, until the cabby snapped, "This is it, Yank!" Before I could get out to open the door, the girl kissed me on the cheek, leaped from the cab, and disappeared into the darkness. She vanished so quickly that I didn't see whether she entered the noisy house I had assumed was her home.

On a longer, roundabout trip back to the taxi stand, I realized I'd been taken for more than one kind of ride. Being led to the taxi stand by the girls, the smooth mechanics of the cabbie's pickup and drop, and the unreasonable fare, all convinced me it was a scheme used on drunken servicemen. As the cab pulled up, Pulaski and his girl, in a heated embrace, were leaning against the wall of a building. The cabbie repeated his outrageous fare to me, but I didn't argue. I just paid it to end the unhappy episode.

At first, Mike and the girl were so entwined in each other's arms that they didn't see me arrive. Mike, now bent on a more serious objective, had forgotten he asked me to return. But coming up for air, he saw me and sprang a second surprise, by asking me to join him walking the girl back home. I said okay because she claimed it was a short distance. But as we rambled for half an hour, through deserted downtown streets, I realized they had more than an innocent walk home in mind. Their frequent stops and long embraces convinced me they were looking for a suitable place to have sex.

Mike asked me to wait at the corner of an alleyway, and they disappeared down it. Mike came back to the alley's entrance and asked me to keep a watch for bobbies or passersby. Thus, I stood a silent sentry, the ale's buzz worn away, mulling over Mike's ulterior motive for asking me to come back. Feeling like a pimp, I still helped my companion.

My assignment didn't last long. Mike returned, without the girl, hurriedly saying, "Let's go." As we retraced our route to town center and up the hill to the barracks, he related the details of his sexual conquest. The retelling was ten times the length of the act itself. At the barracks, we fell on our cots in our uniforms. I was asleep instantly. I don't know when Marugo came back.

Early the next morning, cold sober and extremely worried about overstaying my leave, I was anxious to board the train to the replacement depot at Lichfield as soon as possible. Despite my impatience, Mike and I waited until Marugo woke, so we could report together, naively assuming there would be safety in numbers. We departed Birmingham at midmorning for the seventeen-mile ride.

At the railway station in Lichfield, armed military police manned a large booth for checking the credentials of GIs returning from leaves. Joining the end of a long line, we inched forward slowly. During the wait, I decided to admit what I'd done if MPs questioned me about being late. Once that decision was made, our line seemed to move with unexpected swiftness.

I aggressively thrust my pass across the counter, trying to cover my fear, and the burly MP sergeant looked at it casually, before shoving it back just as vigorously. He didn't refer to my being late. Marugo was right! The MPs didn't care, and I could stop trembling inside. If only I had known about the "day of grace," which allowed soldiers until midnight of the day following the last day of a furlough before they were counted AWOL.

Although Marugo, Pulaski, and I stood one after the other in the line, the MP sent us to different places to bunk for the night. We parted permanently in a blink of an eye.

My bunk that first night at Whittington Barracks was in a barnlike room, similar to a holding tank for prisoners. New arrivals, just back from furloughs, shared the honeycomb of double-stacked board bunks that crowded the dimly lit room. We were a scruffy lot of drunks, Army tramps (by military standards), and recovering wounded. Because the bunks were so low, one waist high and the other practically at floor level, almost everyone tried to find one on top. A few more belligerent GIs made it clear they were willing to fight for a top bunk, but I slipped into one without confronting anyone.

The nauseating odors and disturbing sounds in the room engulfed us. The single blanket on top of my bunk's straw-stuffed, canvas mattress smelled of old sweat and the stench of trench foot. And the fumes of liquor and vomit radiated from some soldiers asleep in nearby bunks. Repulsive sounds came from all parts of the cavernlike room: somebody breaking wind, snoring resonating in every corner, sudden shouts ringing out from soldiers disturbed by bad dreams, and mumbling by those who couldn't sleep. The cacophonies dragged on through the night. After midnight, a new arrival, claiming a bunk next to mine, assumed my feet were the source of the sour smells and cursed me to his bunk mate. I pretended not to hear. All of us added to our temporary dorm's miasma.

The next morning I was transferred to clean quarters, which had well-spaced metal bunk beds, equipped with clean blankets and fully-stuffed palliasses.

While I stayed in the dormitory, on the main base at Whittington Barracks, the Army issued me new uniforms and the standard equipment needed in reassignment, outfitting me with everything but a weapon. The 112th General Hospital had provided fatigues and one dress uniform, but at Lichfield the depot issued a canteen, mess gear, cartridge belt, canvas pack, and so forth. The second pair of shoes they gave me were British-made brogans, which had hobnail soles that clattered sharply on the pavement, reminiscent of the tin cans I smashed around my shoes to clank as I walked on the sidewalk when I was a kid.

Just to escape the monotony of waiting to be shipped out, I volunteered for KP—one of the few times I had done that in the Army and the only time I enjoyed working in both the kitchen and chow line. Ladling food on trays, I watched for Marugo and Pulaski, but they didn't show up. I never found them or met anyone who knew them.

I looked forward to my next assignment, but my orders didn't send me to another town or camp. Instead, I moved to the outskirts of Lichfield, to stay in a housing complex formerly occupied, before the war, by craftsmen in light industries. The mock-Tudor cottage had a kitchen, dining room, and living room on the ground level, and two bedrooms and a toilet upstairs. There was no bathroom with tub or shower, only a small toilet with a sink and commode. For bathing, the British army had built a large community toilet and bathhouse at the rear of the row of cottages. They had removed all the civilian furnishings and replaced them with bunk beds in all rooms except the kitchen.

From our cottage, I looked out the front window, across a curving cobbled street separating the subdivision from the fields and woods of the Staffordshire countryside. After our roll call each day, I walked alone along its many trails, exercising and strengthening my legs, freshening my spirits, and steadying my nerves.

I was only a name on a roster, in a kind of military limbo. No one knew or cared who I was, or what I did, as long as I reported for roll calls at reveille and retreat. I was a soldier in transit, responsible to no officers or duty, receiving no mail from family or friends, depending on no buddies and conceiving no image of my future in Europe.

This reprieve in the English Midlands was unlike any period in my life before or since. Living among the greening trees and blooming flowers, I contemplated the "happy accidents" of my life. In the hush, I pondered why I had been spared at Orscholz when so many of my companions were lost. I didn't know what happened to my platoon or my company that day. Company B may have been wiped out, every man wounded, killed, or taken prisoner. A new company would be organized with men drawn from other units in the 301st and from replacement depots. Why my life—in God's hands that day as it is every day—was spared remains part of the great mystery of His grace. I didn't earn or deserve life any more than my dead comrades.

My only immediate anxiety was the nature of my next assignment. The Army never told a soldier their plans until they sent him to his next station. Most soldiers asked, after reading war news in *Stars and Stripes* and listening to the American Forces Network, "What's going to happen to me now that the war is winding down?"

Our questions were about to be answered. One morning, after checking the roll at the cottages, the sergeant told us, as if the announcement wasn't important, "Pack your duffel bags and get ready for an afternoon departure."

As we broke ranks, one soldier asked, "Where are we going, Sergeant?"

And he snorted, "How the hell would I know, soldier?"

The new orders came without warning, and the suddenness of our departure worried some soldiers in the cottages, especially those who had fully recovered from their wounds and were in good physical shape. They had hoped to stay at the replacement depot longer, to escape reassignment to combat units, because they knew the end of the war in Europe seemed nearer. I sympathized with them. I would have felt the same way if I hadn't known the extent and seriousness of my own wounds would keep me from returning to combat, under any but the most unusual circumstances.

With our duffels packed, we emptied the cottages and boarded buses to the station, departing Lichfield on a troop train late that afternoon. After sitting up overnight in a chair car, I boarded a ship at Southampton to cross the English Channel for the third time, only under much less hazardous conditions. By then, the fighting in Europe had shifted farther east on the Continent, the Allies controlled the Channel, and the Germans were desperately defending their homeland against the Russians from the east and Great Britain and the United States from the west.

Our ship sailed for Le Havre in the early afternoon, completing the short crossing without any threat from the weather or the Germans. We disembarked on a still badly damaged pier, fell into ranks with our heavy duffel bags, and marched up the extremely steep road leading out of the deep harbor basin. Our laborious climb up the hill, in wool uniforms, carrying all our belongings, under a brilliant, late-April sun, left us sweating and exhausted. The straps of my duffel chafed my shoulders, even though I regularly shifted the bag from one side to the other.

Whoever ordered men only recently recovered from serious wounds to carry their luggage up a hill was cruel. Most of us had been physically inactive in the hospital, and a few, like me, were still recovering. The men who dropped out on the way up the hill were harassed by an impatient, unsympathetic NCO, urging them to keep going. Why hadn't they loaded us on trucks on the pier? Would it have been too difficult for trucks to negotiate the hill, or did a Com-Z commando arbitrarily give us a little workout. We seldom knew the motive for chickenshit, but we recognized it. When the last replacement dragged to the top, we boarded trucks to a "repple depple," somewhere inland.

Thus I commenced moving from one replacement camp to another, without any apparent reason or purpose. The moves all had one thing in common: they were temporary tent camps located on the grounds of large châteaus. With each new order, I expected to be assigned to a new outfit, only to be trucked to another camp. Without my knowing it, every move was carrying me closer to Paris.

Sleeping quarters were similar at the camps. The few officers in transit slept inside the château, while the larger contingent of enlisted men slept in tents on its grounds. At one camp, the canvas tents were small, pyramidal types, holding eight to ten men apiece; but at the other two, we slept in circus-size tents, large enough to accommodate thirty or forty men, side by side, on canvas cots. Toilet and bath facilities were always in separate, purpose-built bathhouses.

At the first camp, French officials from a nearby village invited us to join them in celebrating one of their holidays. The gala included a late afternoon parade down the short main street, followed, after dark, by a fireworks display. For the occasion, the prefect elders and officers in the police and fire brigades wore enormous metallic-silver helmets-of-office, shaped like those worn by Roman centurians.

Hospitality by villagers toward American soldiers that night was universal and apparently sincere, for citizens standing in front of their homes and along the main street handed out bottles of wine and tavern keepers offered free glasses of wine when we sat to rest a while. Because Frenchmen hadn't been so hospitable to us before, their night of camaraderie and entertainment was totally unexpected.

But, without intending us harm, their liquid gifts made us pay a price. Too late, we discovered the wine hadn't been aged sufficiently. Diarrhea struck me right away, but for others it came later. Our differences in timing were fortunate because our camp latrine wasn't large enough to accommodate everyone at the same time. Public toilets in villages, other than *pissoirs,* were almost nonexistent. My cramps were so severe that I needed more physical support than a hole with foot marks on each side; I had to get back to camp right away for a proper place.

Stomach cramps had overcome the majority by the time they returned to camp. As they straggled in, I already felt better. From my tent, I could see the latrine at the center of the intersection of the camp's two main streets. The canvas wall flaps were raised to improve air circulation, revealing the occupants sitting side by side, facing out, on a large doughnut-shaped commode seat. As quickly as one member of this grand-circle of fifteen or twenty celebrants departed, he was replaced by another.

At the second replacement camp, headquarters was in an old château that resembled an English manor house. It was surrounded by a variety of outbuildings that included a separate ballroom and storage sheds, the latter holding primitive farm machines. The pyramidal tents we lived in were scattered across a level stretch of ground near the barns. Since they weren't laid out in a grid pattern, there were no streets, only the paths worn by the regular flow of foot traffic. A standard, wood and canvas field latrine and bathhouse made up for the primitive conditions of the small camp.

Two odd but unrelated incidents occurred during my brief stay there. For the first time since leaving the United States, I had to submit to a short-arm exam. But this one had new features added. Instead of passing one at a time in front of an examiner, we lined up side by side in small groups, in the dimly lit ballroom, with nothing on, not even our raincoats. A committee of officers and NCOs, behind a long table, had us squat on our haunches to face them, then rise and turn our backs, before bending over at the waist to spread the cheeks of our buttocks. Although their requests were unusual, no one protested. As good soldiers, used to displaying our parts when told to, we complied. But not without a scornful reluctance and an exchange of questioning looks. The reason for the procedure, health or otherwise, was a mystery. I'm not sure what venereal diseases or anatomical fancies the committee wished to detect.

The other odd event followed shortly after in the same ballroom. The special service officer invited young girls from nearby villages to be our guests and dancing partners. When the girls arrived, under the chaperonage of their mothers or other older women, they sat like Spanish wards and duennas in a single row against one wall, waiting for invitations to dance. Only a few girls, and none of the older women, understood English. At first, language appeared to be an obstacle, but this proved fortunate when the band's master of ceremonies, a would-be comic, performed his routine. His rapid patter was a series of sexual quips and dirty jokes.

"I want to go to the South Pacific to meet Oriental girls," he said, leering, "to see whether their Oriental 'tracks' run up and down or slant sideways."

At the next replacement camp, sex was more blatantly available. The local prostitutes, young and old, hung about at the edges of the camp, behind the trees or in the high grass. The women came to the camp because soldiers were not allowed, even on the weekend, to venture into the nearest village several miles away. Perhaps the officers in charge, who restricted us to the base, failed to imagine the possibility of peripatetic prostitutes. Possibly, the brass considered the village too small for all the men to visit at one time, or believed they were protecting us from VD.

Since the women weren't allowed on the campground, they couldn't offer direct invitations to GIs without being seen by the MPs. To advertise, they sent little French boys and girls from tent to tent in the camp, repeating a simple message in pidgin English: "Suckee, fuckee, one buckee." The children may have understood the nature of what they were saying in a language foreign to them, but their innocent faces belied the intent of their words. Prospective clients asked for directions before taking a stroll.

According to fellows who indulged, the women washed their privates before the act and used some kind of mouthwash afterwards. To me, these men seemed desperate and immodest; the incidence of VD in Europe was exceedingly high, and the women performed fellatio and intercourse in view of other men waiting their turn. Of my several camps in France, this one was the most open about such activities. Sex may have been equally available at the other places, but it was quieter and more secret.

On May 7, I was staying in a tent outside a third château. After supper, I had my picture taken by a transient French photographer before strolling the grounds with another soldier, who slept on the cot next to mine. We were walking far beyond the tents when a voice from a loudspeaker attached to a nearby tree demanded our attention. Stopping beside the wide canal that crossed the estate, we turned back to face the château, where the voice originated.

I paid close attention because most announcements came at the beginning of the day, and the announcer's usually monotonous voice had an excited tone that evening. A long, pregnant pause followed, as if the speaker waited until soldiers who were talking and smoking with their buddies, inside and outside the tents, fell silent.

The camp was quiet with expectation before the public-address voice declared, "The mission of the Allied Forces was fulfilled at 0241, local time, May 7, when the Act of Military Surrender was signed at Reims. The formal end of hostilities by all forces will be on May 8 at one minute past 11 P.M. Central European time." Officially, war had ended in Europe; all active operations were ceasing the next day.

Ironically, only silence settled like a pall over the camp. My companion and I, without a word to each other, faced the canal again. We watched the sunset glistening on the canal's still waters, shining like gold in the tears in our eyes. We strolled silently along the bank, neither of us speaking.

It was not easy to accept the simple truth: the war in Europe was over, ended, *fini,* kaput!

Words could never express our exhilaration and relief, but the combat veterans did not shout or celebrate that night or the next day. Those wounded in action, whom I knew were waiting for reassignment to combat outfits, seemed the quietest. Their strange silence and my own emotions are unforgettable. Remembering all my comrades of the 301st who were left behind in the bloody, snow-covered field outside Orscholz, I lay on my cot weeping quietly.

Once again, as in the Great War, all was "quiet on the Western Front," and I hadn't died on the eve of the Armistice, as Carl Baumer had in Remarque's novel. I would soon be taking "the road back" home.

Though still gripped by unexplained anxieties, even without the prospect of combat, I was an untethered balloon that had dropped its ballast—free to fly again!

Clerk-Typist

Versailles, France

May 12–June 8, 1945

After V-E Day, I may have felt light as air, but I was still on the ground with the troops. A group of us, sitting in the uncovered bed of a two-and-a-half-ton truck, were on our way to an unknown destination. We didn't go far. About thirty-five miles down the road, the truck turned onto the broadest boulevard I had ever seen. Looking across the cab's roof, I saw ahead a tall iron fence and gates in front of a sprawling palace that resembled photos of the palace at Versailles I'd seen in movies and books.

What a piece of luck to be passing a famous historical site on our way to Paris, which we had arbitrarily decided was our final destination. Our truck bore straight toward the gates, as if we were going to park on the cobblestone expanse out front and tour the palace. But at the wide intersection of the cross street in front of the palace, our truck turned sharply right and passed through a small gate into the courtyard of a building directly across from the palace.

The familiar strains of Glenn Miller's music engulfed us inside the broad courtyard. A band in Army uniforms was playing on a platform beside a long, stone building. In front of them, at a microphone, was a short, brunet soldier singing "Serenade in Blue" to a scattered crowd of American soldiers, standing and sitting around the courtyard. But some GIs, hurrying across the cobblestones and disappearing through the many doors leading off the courtyard, paid no attention to the band and singer. By the time our truck stopped, we were sure it was

Glenn Miller's American Band of the Allied Expeditionary Force and that the young singer was Johnny Desmond.

A master sergeant nonchalantly strolled over to where we unloaded. One of our group asked, "Hey, Sarge, what outfit's this?"

"SHAEF," the sergeant replied casually.

I couldn't believe I was at Eisenhower's Supreme Headquarters of the Allied Expeditionary Forces. And I wasn't. By that time, his forward HQs was in Reims.

The sergeant asked, "You guys from a replacement depot?" We nodded affirmatively.

"Grab your bags and follow me."

As he led us through the high wooden gate of an archway in the big building facing us, one southern boy exclaimed, "I'm so-o-o happy to be near Pair-EE! I'm gonna see the EYE-FULL tower that my daddy told me about."

Inside a smaller courtyard, the sergeant said, "You guys'll get assignments in a few days. Meantime, bed down upstairs in the barracks. Over there through that door."

The sergeant's nonchalant attitude pervaded all of SHAEF, especially in the manners of GIs who had been serving in the top command for a long time. By adopting their lackadaisical informality, I almost relaxed myself into trouble.

Our group crossed to the door the sergeant pointed out and climbed steep, narrow stairs to a large second-floor room filled from wall to wall with canvas cots, most of them already claimed and neatly made up or with someone sitting or lying on them.

When I asked a soldier which beds were free, he said, "If it's empty, take your pick, Mac!" Luckily, I saw a bed in a far corner, while others searched in the next room.

After making my bed, I roamed through the building to find the toilet. The main toilet and shower room was on the ground floor, near the front entrance; another, equipped for showers only, was at the back. The front room had regular shower heads, duckboards on the floor, and a bench against one wall to sit on to dry your feet and put on your shoes. The back shower was an empty room with a network of perforated one-inch pipes suspended about seven feet above a raw concrete floor, which had a single drain at its center. In the days ahead, most guys bathed in the front showers, but I preferred the primitive back one, which was seldom used.

Back upstairs, I found a kid lying on a cot next to mine. The first thing he proudly let me know, without my asking, was that he was from Nutley, New Jersey, as if naming his hometown explained every important thing about him. A recent arrival from the States, eighteen-year-old Jerome Levin had been waiting at a replacement depot when the war ended, and he had been sent to Versailles only two days before.

From that moment on, Jerome eagerly sought to tell me all about SHAEF, his family, and his hometown. Talking incessantly, he began following me wherever I went. Jerome's insecurity, as a recent draftee, led me to treat him politely, though others rudely rejected him. I think he looked upon me as a big brother. My first day in his company revealed why the cot next to him was empty. During the week that followed, Jerome proved such a leech that I finally asked him straight out to leave me alone. My awkward confrontation made him pout, briefly, before resuming his talking.

I moved out of the room and found an empty cot next to Howard Spiegel, another Jewish boy, from the Bronx, who, like Jerome, hadn't fought in combat. I never suspected that Howy would become my roommate for the rest of my time in Europe. About my height and equally slender, with black hair and olive skin, he was an optimistic, smiling, big-city operator, who right away got a kick out of laughing at my naive Arkansas ways and expressions.

Our friendship developed as we roamed the Versailles palace and gardens. The building we were bunking in had been the *Grandes Ecuries,* where horses were stabled and grooms billeted before the French Revolution. And the *Petite Ecuries,* parallel with it, across the wide boulevard that led up to the Palace, was its match. Both buildings had been royal stables before the modern French army converted them to barracks for artillery and engineering troops.

The extensive palace grounds and buildings had remained beautiful, despite the many signs of neglect during the German occupation, like broken pedestals, empty fountains, murky ponds, and stained exterior stone. We strolled inside the palace through the many bare rooms, including the Hall of Mirrors, probably the most famous treaty site of World War I, where Clemenceau, Lloyd George, and President Woodrow Wilson held diplomatic conferences. We cavorted outside on the playground in front of Marie Antoinette's Le Petit Trianon, a simulated rustic playhouse for the French court before the Revolution, which I recalled seeing a facsimile of in David O. Selznich's movie *Marie Antoinette.*

The palace interiors were mostly bare; the French had removed the furnishings, paintings, and draperies from the apartments and stored them during the war. What couldn't be taken away—fireplaces, ornate friezes, and decorative wall panelings—had been encased in plaster for their protection. The barrenness of most rooms contrasted sharply with the sumptuously decorated sanctuary and altar of King Louis XIV's Chapel. Maybe the chapel had been restored by the Army for the wedding of Eisenhower's valet in December 1944. Howy and I visited the chapel on a Sunday, when a Protestant Army chaplain was conducting Christian services, to satisfy his curiosity.

Another weekend, as we walked along the edge of the high terraces of the palace grounds, I saw a theater marquee on the opposite side of the street at the foot of the wall. Howy and I located the building on the narrow lane, its doors open. No one was around, so we went inside.

The house was very narrow for a theater, about fifty feet wide by a hundred feet deep. The gallery seats on the ground floor, along the two side walls, faced across the bench seats in the pit. The stage platform was five or six feet above the floor and at the end of the auditorium opposite the theater entrance. Thin, black-pipe railings separated the sections of seats in the galleries from the pit. I didn't know enough theater history to recognize the historical arrangement, for in seventeenth-century French theater, indoor tennis courts were often converted to playhouses, because French actors preferred its playing space. I never went back to see if the theater was still in operation.

Our tours of other famous buildings around Versailles helped acquaint us with several parts of the city, more particularly the bars, cafes, and ice cream parlors near the palace. Our favorite sidewalk café, across from the *hotel de ville,* was a delightful place to sit. Under its canopy on sunny weekends we ate soft Italian ice cream while observing the rowdy mix of Frenchwomen and American soldiers passing by. From a seat there, I first saw a Dubonnet sign painted on the side of a building, not knowing what it represented. Being told Dubonnet is an aperitif still didn't help. So many of the scenes in Versailles and Paris helped me understand more clearly the romantic allusions I'd been singing about in "I'll Be Seeing You"—a small café with a park across the way, a children's carousel, a chestnut tree, and a wishing well, all were now familiar images.

Howy and I didn't learn for more than a week what our assignments would be at Versailles. No one ordered us directly to attend any reveille or retreat formations, so we didn't. And even though we wondered about our duties at SHAEF, we didn't ponder or discuss the question or seek an answer from anyone else. Our freedom was too much fun, doing what we wanted to do, when we wanted to do it. But by chance, my infantry training reasserted itself; I read a notice ordering enlisted men, under penalty of punishment, to stand formation after breakfast the next morning.

Howy and I turned out early for the formation that was held in a small inner courtyard. The first sergeant called the large group to attention before giving us a royal reaming out for not reading the bulletin boards and failing to stand formations. Howy and I were relieved to find so many others were guilty of not turning out or seeking their assignments. Why did it take so long for those in charge to note how few new men were reporting for duty? Maybe the frequent turnover of NCOs in charge kept them from noticing until some conscientious

NCO discovered our derelictions. Whatever the case, the sergeant ordered us to check the bulletin board when dismissed, warning us to read daily notices from then on.

Howy and I were to report to a Sergeant Alex Kocherga in a room in the barracks nearest the courtyard. We took off on the double and were greeted at the door by a handsome man in his mid-twenties, muscular and well over six feet tall. The sergeant had a room of his own, one of the benefits of rank, while we shared our big common room with dozens of others.

When we identified ourselves, he said, "Where in hell have you been? You were supposed to report days ago." Our claim of waiting for someone to give us orders made him laugh.

"You've been reported AWOL for a week. I'll fix the records if you two goof-offs report to the Political Division tomorrow morning at 0800." He described the location of a small hotel on a side street near the Petite Trianon. Howy and I, now relieved to be in a unit, had no idea what our duties would be.

The next morning, we found the old hotel that Kocherga described and reported to the Political Division of the U.S. Group Control Council (U.S. Group CC). A stocky, blond technical sergeant, Eric Schmidt, greeted us good-naturedly, gently chewed us out, and took us to different hotel rooms, introducing us to the NCOs, officers, and civilians in them. To our surprise, the majority of those we met were male civilians; and to our greater surprise, the organization was essentially an agency of the U.S. State Department. I soon learned that our office followed diplomatic and consular patterns, not those of the Army. After my eleven-month stint in the infantry, I recognized the special good fortune of an assignment to the Political Division, which in peacetime would have been the U.S. Embassy to Germany. But now Germany, as a defeated enemy, had no government, no diplomatic recognition, and no embassy.

Sergeant Schmidt explained that the Political Division and eleven other sections, which were parallel with German ministries that governed before the war, made up the U.S. Group CC, which eventually would govern the zone of Germany that American troops occupied. The other divisions were military; naval; air; transport; economic; finance; reparations, deliveries, and restitution; internal affairs and communication; legal; prisoners of war and displaced persons; and manpower.

In April, before hostilities in Europe ended, the Joint Chiefs of Staff appointed General Lucius D. Clay deputy commander of military government for the American Occupation Zone when Germany surrendered. General Clay, even before joining Eisenhower in Reims, won Ike's approval of a plan to remove the occupation government of Germany from the Army's control as soon as possible and place it in civilian hands under the State Department. Ambassador Robert Daniel Murphy, the foreign service, and State Department officers in the Political Division would be Clay's major advisers and functionaries during and after the transfer of this responsibility. The Political Division office was at Versailles until Generals Eisenhower and Clay moved their headquarters from Reims into Germany.

The other members of the Political Division were military attachés from the Army, Air Force, and Navy, and a small complement of enlisted Army NCOs who supported them and the State Department. At the time Howy and I joined, the division had only recently moved from Shrivenham, on the border of Berkshire and Wiltshire in western England, in early spring 1945, and was only partially staffed. The entire U.S. Group CC complement of 250 officers and 400 GIs had been in training in England for about a year.

Most of the State Department officers and their military assistants were in offices at the nondescript hotel on a small side street where Howy and I reported, but Ambassador Murphy and his personal staff had offices, some distance away, at the elegant Trianon Palace Hotel.

The few times I saw Robert Daniel Murphy in person I was impressed by his height. In his fifties, and well over six feet tall, he held his lanky, raw-boned body quite erect. His rather large head and expressive face were distinguished by a prominent nose, full mouth, and smiling eyes. Despite his Irish name, he certainly didn't look to me as if he had Hibernian ancestors.

At the Political Division, the State Department officers told us that the German surrender came before the Allies were expecting it. Many objectives and plans had been in the works since August 1944, when the nucleus of the staff for U.S. Group CC was formed, but procedures for implementing the military government of Germany still had not been fully determined and totally organized. In May, SHAEF was still in a planning stage; the Army, with the counsel of the State Department, had to find ways to put military government in place in Germany, to handle hundreds of thousands of displaced persons (DPs) and German POWs scattered across the Continent, and to cope with the already restive Russians.

After V-E Day, with the end of the war in the Pacific still uncertain, the U.S. public surprised our Army commanders by demanding an immediate demobilization of the soldiers in Europe. When the hue and cry of "bring the boys home" first appeared in European editions of the *New York Herald Tribune* and the *Stars and Stripes,* an anonymous War Department spokesman responded to the demand by announcing plans to release 200,000 to 250,000 men a month. But General Marshall quickly denied this news release, stating instead that the Army was sending combat units directly from Europe to the Pacific. The hubbub among the troops didn't affect us in Group CC.

Howy and I reported for work on time every morning, even though we had no specific duties. We typed letters, ran errands, moved furniture, and enjoyed long lunch breaks. Then, as other enlisted men slowly joined us, we were given more specific job assignments. I was cleared to handle top-secret Army and State Department documents and to destroy confidential trash. That meant collecting papers from office wastebaskets at the end of each day and burning them in the basement furnace.

After settling at the Political Division and being assigned a desk and typewriter, I regularly practiced typing, trying to regain strength and flexibility in my left wrist, which pained me to move and was sensitive to touch around the site of the old wound. Mentally, I still felt, too, the terror and pain of that day at Orscholz, and I used my typing exercises to compose bits of verse that somehow helped release some of my anguish over losing so many of my friends and comrades.

Shortly after joining the Political Division, Howy and I were bused to a supply depot in Paris to be fitted and issued an "Eisenhower jacket." They were given that name because when the general became the supreme commander in London, he was impressed so much by the waist-length jackets worn by British officers and enlisted men that he ordered the quartermaster to design a similar short jacket for Americans. But wartime material shortages made the general distribution of the short jackets impractical, and they were reserved for officers only until after V-E Day. In Paris, we exchanged our old hip-length, peaked-lapel service coats for the ETO Class-A "walking out" jacket.

Once I proved proficient at typing, running errands, and burning top-secret trash, Sergeant Schmidt assigned me to organize and label the personal belongings of State Department officers for shipment to our next station. Civilian officers were in a quasi-military status, with assimilated military ranks matching their civilian positions, so the Army assumed responsibility for their luggage and transportation.

The job of organizing luggage had more responsibility and interest than anything I'd done since leaving the infantry. All pieces had to be marked with owners' names, ranks, and serial numbers. I first compiled a list of the military and civilian personnel, plus their assimilated ranks, and cut individual stencils for each of them on a special machine. Afterwards, with stencils and yellow paint, I marked all the luggage.

Because I had to visit the lodgings of all military officers and civilian staff in and around Versailles, Saint-Cloud, and Paris, Sergeant Schmidt assigned a driver and vehicle to me for the excursions. My driver, Leo, was short and overweight, and treated the vehicles checked out to us as if they were race cars. Shades of Bradberry in old Company B! We rode in a jeep or sedan, depending upon which vehicle was available at the motor pool. When the ambassador's private secretary furnished me a map and addresses, I expected to learn only the geography of the French towns and city. What I really found out about was the sex lives of the military and civilian officers.

Our first afternoon in Saint-Cloud, Leo and I surprised an Army officer in bed with one of the maids who tended housekeeping at the military billet. While he was dressing and collecting his luggage for stenciling, the maids flirted with Leo and me. They were available for dalliance, and Leo was eager. But I pointed out that we had a dozen sets of luggage to stencil in that place alone, as well as calls to make elsewhere before going back to the motor pool. If Leo hadn't taken my advice, I'm not sure what I could have done. Before we left, the officer, caught in the sack with a maid, asked me not to say anything to anybody about the episode. Since I wasn't acquainted with him or his position in the division, I don't know who I would have told or why.

Another day, we drove to Paris to stencil luggage for officers living in apartments in the inner city. Since Leo and I were unfamiliar with Paris streets, we went to the American Embassy, on the Place de la Concorde; it was an exciting spot to look up the broad expanse of the Champs Elysees and see the Arc de Triomphe. We wanted to confirm the foreign officers' addresses and have someone at the embassy mark the locations on our map.

When we arrived around noon, an officer invited us to have lunch with the understaff in the basement dining room, beside the kitchen. Since military personnel had been discouraged from eating in French restaurants while civilian food shortages continued, we readily accepted. I was surprised by the number of flirtatious French and American girls at the embassy and by the wine and beer being served as a regular part of an otherwise simple meal.

On our rounds, we met the personal servants of several different foreign service officers. The most suggestive relationship was that of a diplomat, who had served in the Middle East before the war and had an Arab man as valet and house servant, rumored to be his lover. The handsome, graceful Arab greeted us at the front door and led us to the diplomat's bedroom. After stenciling the officer's bags, I asked the way to the valet's room so that I could mark his bags as well. He pointed to the single bed next to the diplomat's, confirming, in my mind anyway, that the rumor about their relationship was true.

But the valet surprised me by saying his own luggage was at another address, to which he would guide us. It was a white stucco house with a mansard roof in a residential neighborhood. A handsome woman greeted the valet, embracing and kissing him in a very sensuous way, as if Leo and I weren't present. The Arab explained to her in French why we had come, and led me upstairs to his and the woman's bedroom.

After I finished stenciling his bags, I asked if I could use the toilet off the bedroom. In it I saw what I was sure was a bidet, a fixture I'd read about in French novels but couldn't visualize. A first for me! Another first was meeting a bisexual man, an orientation that I didn't know existed. I had learned, after only one day in Paris, about two more aspects of the sophisticated European world.

Several days later, our stencil tour led us into the countryside to a mansion where a number of State Department officers lodged together. As we approached on the long, circular drive, I saw a window drape pulled aside, held briefly, and then closed. It was a relief to know someone would be there, since it was a long drive and we'd been told, before leaving Versailles, that a soldier was always on hand. But when I rang the bell, no one answered. All my ringing and pounding on the heavy wooden door didn't rouse anyone, so I walked around to the other doors, knocking and waiting futilely. We got back into the jeep and started driving away. Looking back, in frustration, I saw a face peering out the partially open front door.

Leo circled back. I leaped from the jeep as a half-dressed GI, with bare feet, stepped out the door, frowning and folding his arms across his naked chest.

"What d'ya guys want?"

Disregarding his surly manner, I pulled the stencils, paint can, and brush from the back of the jeep to remind him of why we had come.

Without apologizing, he led me inside the foyer, where a slight sound and flutter of movement on the landing above caused me to look up. Poised at the top of the stairs was a nude girl, pausing for only a second, to see who entered, before hurrying across the landing out of sight. I turned to face the soldier, raising my eyebrows. He grinned sheepishly, shrugging his naked shoulders, before leading me upstairs to the luggage. While stenciling bags in several rooms, I didn't see or hear any other activity or anyone else in the house. Apparently, the soldier spent part of his time, as the lone concierge of an officers' billet, in an amorous relationship with the maid.

Driving in the countryside around Paris, we saw many examples of French architecture. The luxurious houses, where our officers lived, displayed furnishings from many historical periods as well as paintings and sculptures by famous artists of France and other countries. Although two or more State Department officers occupied each plush house, Army NCOs, living on the property, supervised the residences.

My days in Versailles also introduced me to many Gallic attitudes, manners, and ways. One was the French predilection for some kind of celebration almost every third day, closing shops and parading in the streets—two days of work, then a holiday.

French currency was another item that occupied public attention practically once every week. Problems about their currency first arose, even before D-Day, when General Charles de Gaulle refused to accept the scrip notes printed and distributed by the United States to all Allied troops before the invasion. The troubles were continuing, for small, black Citroen sound trucks patrolled the streets every few days in May 1945, their loud speakers blaring "'allo, 'allo, 'allo," before the drivers proclaimed their latest lengthy explanation of General de Gaulle's new policy on money exchange. When I asked John Berry, one of our foreign service officers, what the problem was, he said the French were withdrawing certain notes from circulation in an effort to catch black marketeers and collaborators, who had acquired illegal profits during the German occupation.

I learned more about the Gauls, too, by having a beer and getting my hair cut. A French beer was weak in alcoholic content, had a faded amber color, and was small in volume. It was bottled in clear, untinted glass containers, which had white porcelain caps with red rubber seals permanently attached to their necks. My less delicate buddies claimed French beer looked and tasted like "piss," and refused to drink it.

That reminds me of the first pissoir, or open-air urinal, I saw in Versailles. It may have seemed more spectacular than the ones in smaller towns because of the crowds of pedestrians passing on the streets as the facility was being used. Approaching a public square, I saw two men's heads, side by side, facing outward, on top of a wall. It was comic to watch the two heads moving away in opposite directions only to emerge from the two exits with whole bodies attached.

Another time in Paris, I went to a toilet at a restaurant, and while I was standing at a urinal, an old woman attendant walked in, without knocking, to clean the fixtures. I hurried to finish, but she went about her chore as if I didn't exist.

When I had my hair cut, the French barber, who badly needed a haircut himself, used only a comb and scissors, and applied no clipper, razor, cream, tonic, or talcum.

Many Frenchmen seemed to resent the American presence. Occasionally, a group of us rode the train to Paris, a twelve-mile trip that took less than fifteen minutes. We usually stood all the way because French civilians filled every seat, staring at us unpleasantly, as we tried to keep our balance in the aisles of the unsteady coach.

Some French showed their negative attitudes when Women's Army Corps (WAC) Sergeant Sophie Tarzinski, a Political Division driver, and I accompanied Sergeant Percy Montague, one of our translators, on a visit to his relatives in a Paris neighborhood. Henry courteously invited us inside to meet his aunt and cousins, but after their friendly reception, Sophie and I waited outside in the car.

Maybe we and our Army sedan flaunted the fact that Henry's relatives had an American GI who favored them with food and tobacco. Whatever the reason, their Parisian neighbors stared at us from windows and walked past without acknowledging us, even though we waved and spoke to them. It was as if we were rude intruders. Few of the French we encountered daily were as pleasant as Pierre-Claude Leglise, the FFI officer I met outside Lorient. Most of them were cold and distant instead, and I couldn't fathom what they wanted or expected of Americans. Rescuing the French from Germany in two wars certainly hadn't endeared us.

My closest friends and I, many former infantrymen, explored Paris mostly on foot, even though several of us had suffered leg wounds. We often walked through the heart of Paris along the Champs Elysees, stopping at the Arc de Triomphe, viewing and reviewing the many famous landmarks, like Notre Dame, the Eiffel Tower, the Paris Opera, and the Church de Madeleine, that we had heard about all our lives. We wandered Montmartre, and climbed to the white majesty of the Sacré Coeur on its hilltop overlooking Paris.

On our walks, we found the Parisian women's colorful styles and inventiveness in clothing impressive. Responding to the austerities of the German occupation, the middle-class Frenchwomen made dresses, skirts, blouses, hats, scarves, and shoes from every sort of fabric, wearing them with panache, on foot or on bicycles. Paris also reeked with perfumes and colognes, whiffs of which came from any passing woman and some men. Although the scents were pleasing outdoors, they were almost nauseating in crowds. Now and then, going to entertainments in other sections of Paris on the Metro (subway), the mix of perfume and human perspiration almost suffocated me.

Searching for a bottle of Chanel No. 5 perfume as a gift for Tumpy, I found that whatever else the French lost during the war, the entrepreneurs didn't lose their knack for making a profit. When I told a friend I wanted to buy Chanel for Tumpy, he suggested it was cheaper at the factory. I followed his directions to a poorly maintained, white-frame building on an out-of-the-way street, only to find the factory closed on the weekend. Weary and disappointed, I walked back to the fashion center, searching until I found a shop that had Chanel perfume.

The chic female clerk emphasized, in broken English, that she had "only a few bottles." The price for less than an ounce was twenty American dollars, a sum far greater than its face value on French money markets. It was tough to pay, too, because I had already sent most of my money home that month.

We sometimes went to theaters in the evening. At the Folies Bergere, the nude models in the spectacular tableaux appeared, at first, to be bathed in pale blue light. But their splendidly erect nipples suggested their color and rigidity were responses to the frigid air in the theater. My own goose bumps were more of a reaction to the damp cold of the rainy spring that year than to their naked blandishments. In one act, when the French audience stomped on the floor, I assumed they were trying to warm their cold feet. But Montague said they were responding negatively to the performance.

In Paris, I also saw a popular Broadway comedy, *Kiss and Tell*, performed by an American civilian cast on tour for the United Service Organization. The play, later a popular Hollywood film, was presented in a suburban theater. I recall that particular night and theater because the signs posted at the back of the parquet circle were in German, *Rauchen Verboten* (Smoking Forbidden). How odd, more than eight months after Paris's liberation, for the defeated enemy's signs still to be posted on the walls.

At work, I didn't stencil luggage every day because I had other duties. My driver, Leo, also had days with different assignments. One of my duties, a few weeks before leaving Versailles, was to substitute for an NCO on furlough, who usually worked in Ambassador Murphy's main office.

When Eric assigned me temporarily to the Trianon Palace Hotel, he added, "Be careful about Mr. Swift. He's . . . you know . . . If he invites you back to his place, don't go."

With that muzzy advice, I went to the hotel reluctantly but filled with curiosity. Sure enough, as I was collecting top-secret trash from the ambassador's offices at the end of my first day, a burly man in an olive-drab civilian officer's uniform entered. Smiling broadly and lifting his bushy eyebrows, he said, "I'm Henry Swift. I don't believe we've met."

I introduced myself and turned to leave with the trash, but the officer asked, "How would you like a ride back to your barracks after we close the office?"

I accepted because it was dark, the barracks were several blocks away, and I would get to supper faster. Besides, there was no harm riding with Mr. Swift. After all, he couldn't do anything to me if I didn't let him. I burned the trash in the basement furnace and took the wastebaskets back to the offices.

Going downstairs to his car, the officer asked about my hometown and my combat experience. He continued along that line driving to the stables.

When he stopped, he said, "I like you, Cleveland. Why don't you come on to my place for a drink? I'll bring you back later." I explained that I had to get to the mess hall for supper before it closed.

"If you come over, I'll have my houseboy prepare us a bite to eat."

Thanking him for the invitation, I added a lie about Howy and me going to a movie. He smiled without saying anything, and I got out of the car. I had just weathered a man's overture, and, as I knew I could, escaped politely. Naturally, Howy was waiting to find out what Swift had said to me. I told him at supper, and, though he wasn't gay, Howy seemed to think it might be an advantage to accept a ride if one were ever offered to him.

On May 12, the Army's redeployment operations began throughout the ETO. SHAEF's forward headquarters, under Generals Eisenhower and Clay, transferred from Reims, France, to Frankfurt am Main, Germany, on May 26, 1945. Although U.S. Group CC was under the command of European Theater of Operations, USA (ETOUSA) rather than SHAEF, the Political Division, as diplomatic advisors to General Eisenhower moved too. SHAEF would soon dissolve, and the

American Army, under a new name, would aim to help our former enemy recover.

Within a week, the Political Division received orders to move by air transport to Frankfurt am Main. Sergeant Schmidt said our new headquarters would be a temporary station for U.S. Group CC until we moved to Berlin, after the American, British, French, and Russians had occupied their official zones throughout Germany and their four separate sectors of Berlin.

The American Zone of Germany, we were told, would consist of the old German states of Greater Hesse, Baden-Württemberg, and Bavaria. Also under American control, besides our sector of Berlin, would be an enclave on the northwestern edge of the British Zone, containing the ports of Bremen and Bremerhaven.

On my first airplane flight, we would be flying over parts of France and Germany that I had covered by truck, train, and foot with the Ninety-fourth Infantry Division.

Mail Clerk-Draftsman

Frankfurt am Main, Germany

June 8–July 6, 1945

Our big move to Frankfurt am Main started the morning of June 9, 1945. With a truck and driver assigned to me, I made the rounds of State Department billets in a thick mist, collecting luggage for our flight. The heavily overcast morning turned into a rainy day, adding to my anxiety about flying for the first time. I hoped the flight would be canceled and changed to a sunny day. But shortly after noon, on the tarmac at bleak Orly Field just outside Paris, we loaded the luggage on a C-47 and took off in a steady, driving rain.

A State Department officer on board who hadn't been to Frankfurt asked crewmen where GIs and foreign service officers could be housed and work in a city reputed to be totally bombed out. As we looked down at the desolate French and German countrysides from our low-flying plane, his question seemed a serious one.

Scrunching down in my bucket seat, I watched the scenes passing below through the narrow panes, the raindrops streaking down them like tears on a cheek. The plane flew at an extremely low altitude (I suppose because of the weather) giving us close-up views of the deep craters in the fields, the broken shells of buildings, and the abandoned military equipment—all the scars of old combat skirmishes extending from beyond Paris to the German border. Nearing Germany, a steady succession of foxholes in staggered lines traced the progress of past combat engagements.

The C-47's metal bucket seats were narrow, hard, and cold. But something outside my window was more discomforting. A few rivets near the plane's fuselage were rising from the surface of the wing. Though the old plane's mighty vibrations seemed likely to make them come out, I watched in stunned silence. Finally, when I was almost moved to tell a crew member, the rivets, which had extended far enough to fall out, slowly started working back into the wing. Relieved not to have embarrassed myself by revealing my alarm, I watched the rivets return to their proper positions before they started to emerge again. I forgot about them after that.

The unexpected play of the rivets in the wing left me eager to land. None too soon for me, we flew in over the appalling devastation of Frankfurt am Main. Although the areas around the airfield were in ruins, the tarmac landing strip was level and clear for our landing. In light rain, our plane taxied safely down the runway and parked alongside several other C-47s already lined up beside each other.

Climbing out of the plane, I saw Harry Hopkins standing under the broad wing of the airplane next to ours. The thin figure and gaunt face of President Roosevelt's former special assistant were familiar to me from newspaper pictures and newsreels. He and several civilians and military officers were talking; and when I pointed him out to my companions, they didn't know or care who the sickly-looking man was. But to me, it was exciting to see in person a national personality who had been so important in President Roosevelt's administrations throughout the Depression and the war. A few days later, the *Stars and Stripes* confirmed that Harry Hopkins had been persuaded by President Truman to come out of retirement to confer with Stalin on the United States' behalf before the Potsdam Conference. Mr. Hopkins, returning from Moscow, was the first of the famous visitors, in politics and entertainment, I would see or meet in Group CC.

Drivers in jeeps and army sedans were waiting at the airport to take the military officers and State Department officials to their quarters. As usual, the enlisted men boarded the familiar canvas-covered truck for transport to our new headquarters. We drove through Frankfurt's outskirts, along streets still only partially cleared of rubble from the bombings. Seeing demolished blocks in all directions, where almost every house on both sides of the street was rubble, I feared that our new office might be in a partially ruined building.

The trip from the airport took about thirty minutes, before the truck pulled up in front of an ivy-covered brick building that, in the fading light of a rainy afternoon, appeared unscarred. Our driver said we were outside the administration building of the I. G. Farben Chemical Works, a plant in Hoechst, a major suburb of Frankfurt. We would discover several days later that the building's excellent condition contrasted with the nearby dye works, which had been blown apart by British and American troops. We paused long enough for the driver to pick up a roster listing our billets.

On the trip from the office complex to our quarters, we traveled along narrow, winding cobbled streets to the opposite side of ancient Hoechst, which in modern times had become a company town, with housing designed for Farben employees, based upon their rank in the organization. The arrangement was ideal for billeting soldiers. But our truck pulled up at the front gate of what appeared to be a military citadel, a multistoried, red-brick building, surrounding a cobblestone drill yard, which occupied a square city block. The three-storied barracks suggested the Army was returning us to a more rigidly military style of life.

Happily, I was wrong! Howy and I were assigned to a German officer's second-floor, two-bedroom apartment at the main entrance to the complex. Our apartment mates, who occupied the second bedroom, were two D-Day Invasion survivors.

The next morning, Howy and I woke up to the shouts and hubbub of soldiers assembling in the drill yard below our bedroom window. After shaving and dressing, we boarded the Army bus that stopped at the street corner just outside our apartment. The German driver said, "The bus is going to the I. G. Farben building," pronouncing the letters *I* and *G* as "EE-GAY."

At the ivy-covered, blood-red-brick headquarters building, we found a great hurly-burly in progress, for General Zhukov, commander of the Russian occupation forces, was visiting General Eisenhower. Everyone involved with protocol and honor guards was busy and excited. We had breakfast in the commodious cafeteria before reporting to the Political Division offices, which occupied the entire ground floor of another wing of the main building. All the officers, military and State Department, were in moderate-size offices on either side of a long central hallway.

I noticed, too, that there were more female staff members in sight than we had in Versailles. In fact, the U.S. Group CC had undergone rapid growth in May and June, and by the time we moved to Hoescht, there were more than two thousand officers and civilians and four thousand enlisted men in the overall organization.

Most of the enlisted staff had separate desks in three large community rooms. But my new assignment, as departmental mail clerk and draftsman, required that my desk, file cabinet, and drafting table be in a smaller, narrow office, along with two other enlisted men. My new duties probably were assigned because of my experience as a clerk at the U.S. Engineers District Office and in Company B. Besides handling mail, I assisted John J. Muccio, an efficiency expert who had recently been sent from Washington to improve organizational functions of Political Affairs in U.S. Group CC.

Sorting and distributing mail took a small part of each day, so most of my time was devoted to typing and preparing organizational charts for Mr. Muccio. As his assistant and mail clerk, I served all the Army enlisted and officer personnel, foreign service diplomats, and members of their supporting staffs. These services led to party invitations and introductions to staff I might not otherwise have known socially. Some party hosts held influential positions, and my acquaintance with them and success in fulfilling lesser assignments must surely have helped me advance.

In fact, the traffic in and out of my office was so heavy, ruffling my charts and papers, that I had to post a sign, "Please close the door! One draft was enough!"

Headquarters for the United States Forces European Theater (USFET) opened in Frankfurt am Main on July 1, 1945, absorbing the missions and replacing the deactivated ETOUSA, which had been the purely American channel of command for administration and supplies for all American forces in Europe. On July 14, 1945, SHAEF was dissolved, as planned, when it accomplished its last Allied mission. General Eisenhower, who until then had commanded both SHAEF and ETOUSA, now assumed command of USFET and all American occupation matters and forces. His deputies were General Walter Bedell Smith, for military matters, and General Lucius D. Clay, the military governor of Germany, for military government. Ambassador Robert Murphy remained the political adviser to both Eisenhower and Clay. General Eisenhower chose this occasion to visit London before taking leave in the United States.

I saw General Clay shortly after our arrival in Frankfurt. Physically slight, he had a long torso and short legs, and his face was distinguished by deep-set, black eyes and a thin, hawklike nose under straight brown hair. The general's neat uniform and stiff, taciturn manner were strong contrasts with the rumpled, relaxed ambassador, at least on the day I first saw him. The cigarette in the general's hand was reputedly a regular feature, as he was a heavy smoker.

In Frankfurt, I met an enlisted newcomer in the transportation section of our office who was to become my best friend. Unlike so many other soldiers in the Political Division who came and went quickly, we both stayed. Our friendship had its beginning one night in the lobby of the Red Cross Club in downtown Hoechst. I was sitting beside a young Red Cross worker at a piano; she was accompanying our singing "I've Got You Under My Skin" and "That Old Feeling."

Not knowing anyone else was near us, we heard another voice join ours. I turned and saw a soldier behind us with the face—heavy brows and a crooked nose—as well as the broad-shouldered muscularity, of a prizefighter. But tough as his features were, he was relaxed and direct, as if we'd all known each other for years. His reddish brown hair had slightly receded, and his complexion was pale. His frequent expression was a happy, mischievous smile. Francis Anthony Rotondo, from Plainfield, New Jersey, preferred to be called Frank, but almost everyone used his nickname, Rote. An infantryman, he was wounded fighting for the Seventy-eighth Infantry Division.

A few days after we met, Rote came to my office with some material he wanted typed. He was submitting it to a servicemen's newspaper that was being organized by the military government. After I read his clever comments about enlisted mens' activities, correcting a few errors and some ambiguities, he graciously accepted my suggestions and asked me to be his partner writing the column. He hedged a bit by saying he'd have to persuade the editor to give us both a chance. He must have made a good case, because the editor decided to let us write regularly for the *Grooper,* the weekly newspaper for the U.S. Group CC.

We were billed in its first issue in Frankfurt as "Rotondo and Harrison," and our column was titled "Small Talk." In subsequent issues, our byline remained the same, but our column was rechristened "Completely Confused," to reflect what appeared to be disorder in the occupation, and we addressed gossip, jokes, and criticisms specifically to personnel of the U.S. Group CC, including WACS, Army doctors and nurses, Red Cross staff, and civilian employees of the State Department.

Rote and I became inseparable companions after work but seldom saw each other during the workday, because he was in transportation. We shared our interests with mutual friends at lunch and dinner in the cafeteria and at the Red Cross Club, where we often chatted with the two young women in charge. On weekends, along with other enlisted men, we played sandlot baseball in the park across the street from Howy's and my apartment. In our off-duty hours, together and separately, Rote and I collected news items, humorous stories, and critical commentary for the column. I believe working in separate units during the day sustained the energy of our collaboration and friendship.

We roamed Hoechst, or Alstadt (old town), becoming familiar with its environs. Although Allied bombs had demolished more than half of the city of Frankfurt, the Farben plant's administration building escaped. Only the chemical dye plant, a manufacturing section, was heavily damaged by air strikes and explosives planted by Allied infantry and engineers. Perhaps the excellent condition of the two Farben buildings in Frankfurt and Hoescht explained their being chosen by Eisenhower for the permanent site of USFET headquarters and a temporary stop for U.S. Group CC in Germany.

One Sunday afternoon, Rote and I explored the Farben complex, including the areas inside the dye plant that were marked off-limits. We asked the MPs for permission, justifying our request with the excuse of a newspaper story and our press passes. They assured us there was no danger from explosives or structural damage in the plant. Picking our way through the interior of the chemical and dye works, it was clear that its manufacturing capabilities had been totally destroyed.

But the handsome administration building had been completely spared. Except for a few signs of random damage by attacking troops, the interior, exterior, and office furnishings were undamaged. The entrance hall was an atrium done in a geometrical and utilitarian style, which would influence later German architecture. The ceramic floor of the main entrance hall was covered in a colored mosaic design inlay and was among the building's chief artistic features. The five stories of functional work spaces must have had a positive aesthetic effect on workers.

On the attic-like fifth floor, we found an enormous inventory of office supplies, scattered helter-skelter across the floor. Picking our way through the litter, we guessed the supply of paper, folders, pens, pencils, and paper clips would satisfy the Political Division's needs for a year.

The village of Hoechst, like the Farben building, showed few signs of combat damage. Its narrow cobblestone streets meandered through the heart of the largely untouched medieval village, until the streets widened into asphalt avenues in the outlying subdivisions of houses, apartments, and parks. The barracks behind the apartment house where Howy and I lived were the main sign of a German military presence. Directly across the street from our apartment was a section of the *Stadtwald* (city forest), a spacious public park that had acres of groves, gardens, and athletic fields, connected by a network of paths. Stone bridges spanned its streams; and pastoral sculptures and fountains decorated the grassy banks of the ponds, which were filled with water lily blossoms.

Civilian services in the village, for Americans, were extremely limited. Soldiers could purchase film, have it developed, and have studio portraits made at a German photography shop. For some reason, the photographic prints were always sepia colored. Other German services and goods were forbidden to soldiers, including the products of the only bakery, which displayed in its window each day one or two loaves of black bread, which looked petrified and dusty. The single grocery store we saw had few items to display or sell, even if their sale had been legitimate.

These restrictions were minor parts of a broader Army nonfraternization policy. Soldiers were forbidden to associate with Germans on any social basis and were required to carry firearms at all times. From the beginning of the occupation, the fraternization policy appeared largely unenforceable, with either officers or enlisted men. While American soldiers officially observed nonfraternization with Germans in large groups, they violated the policy in informal relations, particularly with women.

Requiring us to carry weapons in public was imposed, I guess, out of fear that the Germans, as conquered enemies, might prove rebellious. Officers wore side arms, and enlisted men carried carbines, following a policy that was largely frowned upon by combat soldiers, most of whom wanted to lay down their weapons permanently. While it was easy to fraternize with Germans inconspicuously, soldiers not bearing firearms were more obvious. Neither of the official arms-and-the-man policies caused major complaints; they were simply disregarded and soon abandoned.

The Army was screening all adult German men and women, if they wanted to be employed by American forces, for their connections with the Nazi Party. Thirty-three automatic arrest categories existed that were related to memberships in one of the large or small Nazi organizations, of which there were many.

As a means of weeding out former Nazis seeking government positions, the Army imposed upon adult Germans a *Fragebogen,* a six-page, 130-item questionnaire about their past activities, particularly political ones, which had to be completed. At the beginning of the occupation, the Germans were used exclusively as manual laborers at American facilities. But the German civilian workforce—secretaries, supervisors, translators, mechanics, barbers, cooks, waitresses and waiters—grew so rapidly at military installations that socialization with them developed naturally and easily.

The social scene among Allied soldiers and representatives of other Western countries seemed frantic, as though everyone was trying to make up for the party time lost during the war. Many in Hoechst met nightly at a small cabaret theater that the Army had requisitioned and turned into a night club for enlisted personnel. The cabaret was probably the most popular hangout in Hoechst, partly because it sold wine and beer, since hard liquor was not generally available to enlisted personnel.

On the cabaret's ground level was a dance floor, a small curtained stage, and a bar. The permanent theater seating had been removed for the dance floor, and ringed by tables and chairs. Theater seats on the balcony overlooking the dance floor had also been replaced with tables and chairs, which were filled nightly by GIs, WACS, Red Cross, and civilian clerical workers. On weekends, live bands and soldier artists performed variety acts. Rote and I visited frequently to catch the acts and latest stories.

The well-planned, fully outfitted Farben cafeteria must have inspired the Army cooks because they planned special menus for evening meals that exceeded the standard rations we'd grown accustomed to. The most memorable meal was a complete Italian banquet, including antipasto, freshly baked French bread, and a choice of lasagna or spaghetti with meat sauce, with unlimited red wine to drink. For Army cooks to serve an alcoholic drink was extraordinary but proved not to be a onetime thing. Later, the cooks prepared German and Polish meals, accompanied by cold draft beer. As long as we stayed in Hoescht, the mess hall offered such treats, but I don't recall a similar pattern after moving to Berlin. Perhaps the experimental Army cooks in the ETO were assigned to the mess at ETOUSA in Frankfurt or were shipped home early.

While beer and wine were regular features of enlisted soldier's nightly entertainment, hard liquor was available to us in the Political Division. The State Department officers had monthly liquor allotments and invited enlisted men to share it. Yet I recall few cases of excessive drinking at our parties, which may be surprising, considering the easy availability of liquor. Some units of the Army, in addition, were selling wine and champagne they had requisitioned from German vintners, at twenty-five cents for a magnum of pink and thirty-five cents for the white sparkling. Even so, really drunken episodes were unusual in U.S. Group CC.

One involved me, though I only heard about most of it. Colonel Young, the Air Force attaché, gave a party for friends and a few enlisted men, including Howy, Rote, and me. At his elegant apartment, the gray-haired colonel shed his usual formality, welcoming us as equals. After introducing the guests we didn't already know, he offered us drinks, recommending a "Rockefeller Special," which he said was a mix of gin and rye whiskey. I didn't know anything about its potency, but the colonel warned us not to drink the Specials too fast. Lured by its deceptive smoothness, I drank my first cocktail too quickly.

I was well into a second drink when the first one hit me. Sensing difficulty seeing the opposite side of the room, I assumed the blurry atmosphere was tobacco smoke. More troubling, though, my eyes wouldn't focus clearly on persons across the room either, as if the dark figures were viewed through an opaque filter. Crossing toward a fuzzy figure I thought I recognized, the floor tilted, and I slowly sank to my knees. I had not felt so helpless since Orscholz.

Rote and Howy hurried across the room to lift me up and hold me. Assuming cold air would sober me, they led me outside, and we walked around the block two or three times. But neither my eyesight nor rubbery legs recovered, so they decided to take me back to our apartment and put me to bed. Walking miles along the cold, windy streets, without overcoats, I remained blind and happy, pleading only that I wanted to go to sleep. Rote and Howy put me under the covers in my uniform and went back to the party. I slept so soundly, I didn't know when Howy came home to bed.

After my Saturday night debauch, I awoke on a bright Sunday morning without a headache or any bad feelings. The regular drinkers, who knew about my escapade, found my quick recovery inexplicable. By rights, according to them, I should have had a terrible hangover—headache, sick stomach, and dizziness.

"Perhaps, my quick recovery is testimony to the rewards of clean living," I said.

But I didn't kid myself. At least I learned a practical lesson about mixed drinks: be cautious about alcoholic drinks, and always consume one very slowly.

The other drunken-soldier episode didn't end so happily. I was not a participant, even though Rote and I were involved at its beginning. Nat Frohlic, a recent addition to the Political Division, hardly knew anyone in or out of our offices. So Rote suggested introducing the short, blond, twenty-year-old to people on our regular rounds.

Customarily, Rote and I didn't drink at all the places we visited, but our new acquaintance had done so. We were aware only that he had a drink at the cabaret with us, at our next-to-last stop, but was sober and talked clearly. Later, at a beer parlor, Frohlic met a fellow from his old combat outfit who insisted that he stay and talk. He waved us off, saying he'd see us at the office the next day. Rote and I, happy that he had found an old acquaintance, left without thinking he was drunk.

When Frohlic didn't report for duty the next morning, I assumed he was ill or on an errand and would come in later. Often soldiers didn't show up on time, since formal attendance checks were rare, and officers in charge didn't seem to mind some slight change, as long as soldiers completed their office duties on time. That night, after supper, Rote and I went by Frohlic's apartment to see where he had been all day. He didn't answer our knock, so we guessed he hadn't come back from his meal.

The next day making my mail rounds, I discovered Frohlic still hadn't reported for duty. I told Sergeant Schmidt, who sent me directly to Frohlic's billet to check on him. The soldier who shared the apartment with him said he hadn't seen him for two days. I reported that to the sergeant, who accepted the message silently.

The following day, Schmidt received a phone call from a medic at the Frankfurt Army Hospital about a patient named Nat Frohlic who claimed to be in the Political Division. He had been found by MPs, lying unconscious on a sidewalk in the outskirts of Frankfurt, covered in his own vomit and in need of medical treatment. At the hospital, the nurses cleaning him up found he had a high fever and severe pain in his lower right side. A blood test, showing an extremely high white corpuscle count, confirmed acute appendicitis, and doctors operated on him within the hour.

When Rote and I visited at the hospital, Frohlic was out of danger, and his health was improving. But as a result of his drunkenness and failure to report for duty, MPs had placed him under arrest. He told us that he had no memory of what happened after we left him at the beer parlor talking to his friend. For two more weeks, Frohlic remained at the hospital. He never rejoined us because he was charged with being AWOL. Under Article of War 103, he had to make up the time he lost.

As the weeks passed, Howy and I realized how fortunate we were with our two apartment mates. The D-Day veterans in the front bedroom were always quiet when we were at the apartment and didn't hog the bathroom. Their constant presence in their room or the front parlor surprised us; it was almost as if they had no duties. Both fellows told us how they were wounded on D-Day before reaching the shore. Tom was in a tank that was hit and sank moments after it rolled off a Landing Craft/Tank (LCT). He nearly drowned when his lungs filled with sea water, as he struggled to escape from the tank. Carl, the infantryman, was cut down by machine gun fire wading ashore, and had lain in the surf for a long time before a corpsman pulled him to safety. Both men were thin and sallow during our stay, and I wondered why the doctors in Normandy hadn't sent them to the States rather than returning them to duty on the Continent after hospitalization in England.

Our apartment had a living room, combination kitchen-dining room, two bedrooms, and one bath. Howy and I had the bright bedroom on the back corner, our windows overlooking the barrack's courtyard and the street that led to town center. The bathroom adjacent to our room had a tub but no shower. Our bedroom was furnished with a double bed, a large armoire, a chiffonier, a dresser, and a bench. The monster bed had a deep mattress and large pillows, with lots of blankets and quilts. Howy and I moved about easily in the room, if we didn't try to do the same thing at the same time.

A large framed photograph of a middle-aged German officer, dressed in full military regalia, hung in a conspicuous spot on the living room wall just outside our bedroom. Another photograph of the same man in a World War I uniform, with an Iron Cross at his neck and peaked dress helmet on his head, hung on the wall opposite. We thought the apartment may have been his, or some family member's, like the plump Fräulein who cleaned the apartment and washed our bedclothes each week. But rosy-cheeked Anna denied, through gesture and broken English, that the officer in the photograph was related to her.

Anna tended all the housekeeping chores for two weeks before an older woman, with steel-gray hair and eyes, appeared. She walked through our apartment with such hauteur and care, appraising the furnishings and rooms, that I concluded she was the owner. When I asked her in English if the place belonged to her, she responded, "Sprechen sie Deutsche?" I had to use pantomime, backing up my English and my sparse collection of German words, to communicate with her. The apartment was hers, and the officer in the photographs was her husband, who at one time was the barracks commander. Frau Curtius, without emotion, said she had not heard from the colonel since he was sent into combat and now assumed her husband was dead.

In subsequent weeks, the Frau cleaned the house herself. I never understood why she sent the girl in the first place, unless she feared American soldiers and used the girl to prove it was safe. Whatever her reasons, Frau Curtius showed different attitudes toward Howy and me. Even though Howy treated her with respect, she was coldly proper with him, probably recognizing he was Jewish. I'm sure that accounted for her calling me "der besser Junge" (the better boy) within Howy's earshot.

Although Howy ignored the older woman, he paid warm attention to robust, dimpled Anna. He became "ein Freund don Anna." Like so many other American soldiers, he pursued German women from the beginning, nonchalantly, successfully violating the nonfraternization rule. He also flouted the Army's policy by *not* carrying his carbine on his and Anna's dates. Maybe growing up in the Bronx exposed him to greater dangers than being unarmed among the defeated Germans. My own childhood, in a family of hunters in Arkansas, had shaped my outlook, and carrying weapons didn't seem out of order. After all, even though hostilities had ended a few months before, we were greatly outnumbered by the civilian and military enemies we lived among. I sympathized with Howy, though. A carbine slung over his shoulder was awkward when trying "to make time," even with a coy but willing Fräulein.

Although I didn't feel superior, or reveal a negative opinion, about soldiers dating Germans, I associated with Red Cross and State Department women, who had joined us by this time, because I could converse with them in English about common interests. Dating at service clubs and movies weren't like the furtive encounters in the city woods that I heard about daily. Soldiers had too much freedom, too few duties, and too little self-restraint. In the atmosphere of Germany, soldiers felt their anonymity—separated from the normal controls of home, school, and church—freed them to behave any way they chose.

Many spent their time pursuing German women. And the starving German Fräuleins and Fraus, many of them unmarried or widowed, sought affairs with soldiers for security and food. Back in the States, those of us who were single would have been dating for the first time as adults, learning good manners and how to treat women properly. But on the Continent, young Americans with normal urges let few social or moral restrictions govern their behavior.

A common male attitude toward some of the foreign females was shown when Polish women from a nearby displaced persons unit were treated to a meal at the Farben Cafeteria on June 22, when the nonfraternization order for displaced persons was withdrawn by USFET. Headquarters had arranged for soldiers to dance with the women after eating. During the meal, the Polish women sat on the opposite side of the center aisle from us. Men at my table traded remarks about the women's plain faces, sturdy figures, and ill-fitting dresses, and some soldiers made crude sexual remarks across the aisle to them. A few men nearest them made sexual gestures, leaving no doubt that they had little respect for the women.

At the end of the meal, the women and many soldiers went out to a brick patio behind the dining room where a German band was playing polkas. Only a few soldiers stepped forward to dance with the women, and most of the women were forced to dance with each other. I was reluctant because I didn't know how to dance a polka; maybe that was true of others as well. But some men rejected them because of their plainness; the same men, alone with them in the dark, would have found them suitable for sex. It was embarrassing to see our own attitudes and watch the women dancing with each other. Visits by displaced groups were not, to my knowledge, repeated at the Farben building in Frankfurt.

My office duties at Hoechst soon became routine. With more free time, I became better acquainted with the growing number of foreign service officers joining us, as we prepared for our imminent move to Berlin.

Our efficiency expert, and my civilian supervisor, John J. Muccio, was a formal, withdrawn person, never once removing his professional mask with me. By 1952, he would be the American ambassador to South Korea when North Korea attacked the South.

Muccio's opposite in age and personality, John Berry, a junior State Department officer, grew up in a small Arkansas town. In 1979, he was ambassador to Iran when the Shah was overthrown.

Fred and Jo Mann of the State Department had been staff members at the embassy in Tokyo when the Japanese attacked Pearl Harbor. They remained interned in Japan until diplomats worked out an exchange at sea for foreign service officers of both countries.

My direct civilian supervisor, Dorothea Lampe, had worked alongside her diplomat husband at the American Embassy in Berlin in the mid-1930s during Hitler's rise.

The majority of the State Department officers were men, assisted by a growing number of mostly female clerks and secretaries. As the staff doubled, the need for stenographic assistance increased. Some of the women joining our office were veterans of earlier foreign assignments, but many were recent recruits who had just finished their orientation and training in the United States. Although they represented a wide range of ages, most were single and bent on a little adventure. I wouldn't become well acquainted with any of them until we moved to Berlin.

The enlisted men assigned to the Political Division changed constantly. Several NCOs, who were skilled interpreters in French, German, and Russian, received commissions because they assisted at high-level diplomatic and military conferences. Sergeants Alex Kocherga and Robert Barrat, whose parents were White Russians, spoke Russian fluently and were commissioned second lieutenants right away. But Percy Montague, also a skilled linguist, whose parents were French, chose to remain in his enlisted rank. The only German translator inexplicably denied a commission was Sergeant Eric Schmidt.

Of enlisted men in the Political Division at Frankfurt, many came but few remained. One was transferred out because he was undependable and inefficient. Another, a Chinese American soldier named Lee, worked beside me in the mail office for several weeks before being given a one-week leave to visit relatives in Paris. Whether he had family there or not, Lee disappeared in Pigalle (a place in Montmartre, filled with nightclubs, dance halls, and less respectable commercial ventures) and overstayed his leave. When he was charged with being AWOL, Lee deserted, never to be seen or heard from again. The fat chauffeur, Leo, who drove me around in France, succumbed to a Fräulein's sexual invitation and became infected with gonorrhea. Under Article of War 103, he lost time and his pay for having VD, and just disappeared.

But slowly the chain of undisciplined, unproductive, and unhappy enlisted men was broken, and a permanent, productive, and congenial group formed in the Political Division. Besides my closest buddies, Howy Spiegel and Frank Rotondo, my pals were Christy Vasile, Zach Mitchum, Joe Baumgartner, Charles Leshak, and John Browne, and the peculiarities of each became conspicuous in our close, daily contact.

Christy Vasile (vah-*silly*), an Albanian American from Newark, New Jersey, was a driver in the division. He was the first person I'd met who suffered migraine headaches. When aches and distorted vision struck him, Christy disappeared into his bedroom, locked the doors, put blankets over the windows, and stayed in bed until the symptoms passed. As a rule, he remained incommunicado for two days, without eating or drinking. If Howy or I tried to bring food and drink or offer sympathy, he yelled angry refusals through his bedroom door. Without headaches, Chris was warm, energetic, and easygoing.

Zach Mitchum was a New Yorker from Manhattan. Rather cool and sophisticated in manner, he was a tall, good-looking brunet who smoked too much and ate too little. I believe Zach was involved at one time with an older German woman, or at least he suggested he was. He showed us photos of her doing chores in the nude in her apartment. One pictured her at the kitchen stove, wearing only an apron, revealing her bare buttocks and the profile of one breast, as she glanced back over her shoulder.

Joe Baumgartner, also from New York, was short, chubby, and homely. Joe devoted his thoughts and activities to sports, even though he was not a particularly coordinated and skillful athlete himself. His chief athleticism was as a walking, talking encyclopedia of major league baseball statistics. A fanatic, he could not talk about any subject, including women, without dragging in baseball.

Baumgartner's baseball buddy Charles Leshak was from Pottsville, Pennsylvania, and shared the same enthusiasm for the sport. Charles's reedy voice and gentle manner and his sincere effort to look after us led our group to call him Mother. An extremely boyish, bashful guy around women, he never attended the parties given by State Department secretaries, perhaps in disapproval of the liquor served.

Only one enlisted man in the Political Division held himself a bit aloof. John Browne ("with the final *e*," he was fond of saying) was from New Bedford, Massachusetts. Brownie, whose father owned a drugstore chain, appeared a bit older and better educated than the rest of us. He looked like a "square," with his large round lenses in thick tortoiseshell frames and his Army garrison cap set squarely on his head. A bit standoffish, he treated me as if I were a teenager, especially after I started dating Louise Byrnes, of whom he was very fond.

After hearing many rumors about when we would move out of Frankfurt, orders finally came through for the first contingents of Group CC to move to Berlin. We were forced to remain in Hoescht until the

Russians granted American, British, and French troops access to their separate sectors of Berlin, where the Allies would organize the quadrapartite government under the Allied Control Council. Ambassador Murphy and his personal staff were the first group to leave. The overall movement of thirty thousand American combat troops began July 1, 1945. The rest of Group CC joined them by the middle of the month when the Allied Kommandatura would be formally instituted to govern Berlin.

Approaching our departure date for Berlin, July 6, we assumed we would be flying, as we had from Paris to Frankfurt. Instead, we were ordered to pack our belongings in duffel bags to be shipped by train. A day later, a new order added that we should carry part of our stuff in a smaller kit to accompany us in automobiles.

After all my earlier trips in the open beds of two-and-a-half-ton trucks, I hadn't expected to travel in private cars. Still the vehicles used by the State Department had to move to the motor pool in Berlin, and this was a good way to transport personnel as well. The drawbacks were the distance and possible dangers traveling through a strip of Germany where American troops had been withdrawn to satisfy the boundaries set in the Yalta Agreement. Although the Russians had not yet fully occupied the territory, the route across their zone would have to be driven without armed protection.

To complicate reaching Berlin, the Russians had allowed American troops only two air corridors, a single railway line through Magdeburg and one autobahn through Helmstedt. This was the least direct autobahn of the three available, and clinched the Army's official decision to use the soldiers in the Political Division as escorts for female workers. That was the only reason enlisted men were fortunate enough to ride in cars.

Since the end of overall hostilities, the Russians were attempting to control the entry of all Allied troops to their zone of Germany and to their sector of Berlin. The Russian zone surrounded the capital, and, to limit access, the Russians required most of us to use land transport. On July 4, the first units of U.S. forces finally entered the American sector of Berlin, and other American troops withdrew into the U.S. zone.

The reports by the Office of Strategic Services (OSS), received in the Political Division message center, expressed concern about the safety of American women entering and crossing the Russian zone. One OSS report, logged shortly after I joined the message center, described a bestial rampage by Mongolian troops in Berlin, in which they raided houses, killing and raping civilians. The Russian forces who had captured the metropolis and held it for the first forty-eight hours were well disciplined. But those following them were uncontrolled, inflamed by liquor and an outspoken Soviet policy that encouraged Russian soldiers to punish Germans. This one OSS report was sufficient to confirm the need for armed escorts, as we crossed Germany to enter Berlin.

Message Center Chief

Berlin, Germany

July 10, 1945–January 7, 1946

On July 10, I was out of bed before daylight and in the cafeteria at sunrise, ready to leave for Berlin. After breakfast, we picked up K rations and thermos jugs of hot coffee to take on the one-day trip. Those being transported in our caravan were mostly junior officers and female clerks. I was accompanying two women from the message center—Lenore Bobbitt and Esther "Dusty" Rhodes—riding between them in the back seat of a black Mercedes. The car, commandeered from our enemy, reminded me of German sedans in movies about foreign correspondents and Nazis. Another enlisted man, Hershel Page, was riding up front with the driver.

Our wait at the motor pool was so long we assumed the senior State Department and military officers had to be accommodated in vehicles before us. We watched almost all the other cars depart before a driver showed up. If he worked in the Political Division, I had never seen him before. Maybe they recruited drivers from other divisions, because so many cars were heading to Berlin on the same day. Our lanky driver, named Orville, looked hung over and badly in need of a haircut and shave. He glanced at us in the backseat and growled, "Let's go," as if we, not he, held up our departure.

Our gloom on the heavily overcast day deepened driving through the eastern sector of Frankfurt, along streets barely cleared of the rubble now piled high along the curbs. I first saw part of the city's ruins close up a few days after our arrival on a short trip into Frankfurt with Sophie Tarzinski. In the downtown business district there were no streetcars, electric lines, water, gas, or telephone service. In the midst of the brick-and-stone wilderness, standing untouched at the edge of Grueneburg Park, was SHAEF's forward headquarters, the main I. G. Farben Industries building, a high-rise that miraculously escaped the bombs. Now, a month later, driving through other areas of the city on our way to the autobahn, I saw, down almost every ravaged street, how totally devastated the rest of the city was.

Beyond the city limits, traffic on the side roads and autobahn was surprisingly light, perhaps because we were driving through the outskirts, circumventing most villages and towns. American soldiers in military vehicles passed, honking and waving at our convoy like old friends. The Germans on foot near the roads ignored us. Sometimes our convoy passed very close to farmhouses, as we detoured across farmers' cultivated fields, and whole German families looked down or turned their faces away from us. If I were in their shoes, probably I would purposely refuse to acknowledge a dusty caravan of conquerors too.

Many German farmers had cleaned up their fields during the two months since the war's end and were planting crops. Other areas of the countryside were desolate, scarred by shell craters, collapsed or partially destroyed buildings, and the mounds of German soldiers' graves. We bumped and swerved from bad to good roads, sometimes circling spans of twisted or fallen highway bridges and taking detours across shallow streams. The bridges that were still standing had shell-pocked abutments, broken and twisted metal railings, and potholes in their decks. The fields, on either side of the autobahn, harbored the hulks of burnt-out trucks and tanks marked by the blistered paint of American, British, or German insignias.

Despite this contrast of carnage and cultivation through the car's dusty windows, there were long, undamaged stretches of well-paved highway on the autobahn. Its four lanes, divided by a median, had been built to allow the rapid deployment of troops and military matériel in all directions across the country. Later, in the 1950s, President

Eisenhower's memories of the German autobahn, along with General Clay's advice, inspired him to jump-start the economy by proposing the completion of the federal interstate highway system, already authorized by Congress.

Farther down the road, we began smelling the stale odor of alcohol in the car. At first, no one acknowledged the fumes; I'm sure everyone thought the others were sober, especially the man driving us. He certainly drove safely enough in the early morning along the paved autobahn. But eventually, Lenore, Dusty, and I agreed the fumes came from Orville, the effluviums of his last night out on the town in Frankfurt.

At our first rest stop, when everyone else drank hot coffee from thermos jugs, Orville pulled a bottle of vodka from his pocket and sipped from it.

Lenore and Dusty saw him tilt the bottle and quietly asked me to speak to him. So I approached "on behalf of the women," because I didn't want him to think I was interfering by asking him point-blank not to drink.

He laughed, pooh-poohing the women's concern, saying, "All I want is a little pick-me-up now and then. It'll help me get past this hangover."

When I told the women, they said, "Well, at least we have it out in the open."

On the autobahn, Orville handled the car more cavalierly. As Dusty and Lenore were busily conversing across me, I saw Hershel up front talking animatedly to the driver, apparently trying to convince him of something. At the next stop, when Orville went to relieve himself, I asked Hershel what he'd been discussing with him.

He said, "Nothing in particular. I was just trying to keep him from going to sleep."

The women heard this remark and begged me to ask an officer in the car following ours to speak to Orville. Before I got the officer's attention, Orville motioned us into the car and took off at breakneck speed. He made us the lead car and thought that position put him in charge of the caravan. He talked more about the bad road in a surly manner, and his erratic driving suggested he'd taken another drink.

As Orville's driving worsened, so did the condition of the autobahn, giving way to shallow potholes and a corrugated surface; in some places whole sections of the highway were almost completely torn up. Forced to detour hundreds of yards, or even miles, on unpaved side roads and across fields, we no longer ate dust from the cars ahead. But our driver steered against the road ruts, breaching their sides, changing speeds, and bottoming out in deeper holes.

As the lurching car threw us up against each other and into the sedan's walls, we shouted, "Slow down!" But the driver was a bronco rider, laughing and yelling, "Wahoo!"

The women pleaded with me to make Orville stop the car, but I suggested, "Tell *him,* don't whisper to me."

Finally, persistent honking from the cars behind us caught Orville's attention, and, cursing, he braked in a cloud of dust. Tumbling out, Lenore and Dusty demanded I tell an officer. I hesitated because Orville had a .45 automatic strapped on his hip and was in a nasty temper. I didn't want him to think I was a snitch. An angry drunk with a sidearm is formidable, even though I had my carbine. Besides, it was our lunch break; I figured he'd be more reasonable after eating something.

The other soldier and I pulled the loose-limbed driver aside to get him to eat and distract him. We found, in his condition, he wasn't thinking about a pistol or anything else. The women finally complained to the nearest officer, who led Orville away, beyond our hearing. When the officer came back alone, he said our driver had been relieved and that either Hershel or I would have to drive. I didn't know how to drive, and Hershel protested he didn't want to. Flabbergasted, the officer became our chauffeur the rest of the way to Berlin, with Orville a sleeping passenger in another car.

The contretemps over Orville's drinking diverted our attention half the way to Berlin, but we didn't miss the beauty of the cultivated fields in the countryside and the disarray of damaged towns and villages.

The farther east we traveled, the more sharply aware we were that by avoiding the centers of small towns and bypassing larger cities, we were quickly covering the distance to our destination.

Daylight was important to the convoy because of our less direct route to Berlin. We reached Magdeburg on the autobahn and began the final leg of our trip. The route covered between sunrise and sunset of one day was a diagonal line from southwestern to northeastern Germany—Frankfurt am Main to Magdeburg to Berlin.

While traveling in the American zone, we probably passed through the environs of Fulda, Herself, Bebia, Eisenach, and Gotha. At Erfurt, we entered territory first captured by Allied troops that was being yielded to the USSR for political reasons. Inside the Russian zone, our journey took us through or near Weimar, Weissenfels, Brandenburg, Potsdam, and Charlottenburg. I was too unread at twenty to recognize the historical significance of Gotha, Weimar, and Potsdam.

Although military activities were subdued inside the American zone and the territory our troops were relinquishing to Russia, the Soviet zone was extremely active, at Magdeburg and beyond, especially as we neared Berlin. On the way to the American sector, armed and green-capped Soviet guards stood at fifty-yard intervals on opposite sides of the road. They were well dressed and apparently well disciplined, contrasting sharply with OSS descriptions of the Mongolians who pillaged and raped Berlin. We guessed the good-looking troops were handpicked for the Potsdam Conference, which was scheduled to begin soon.

When our convoy reached an entry to the American sector of Berlin, Russian guards again stopped us and checked the occupants in each car. Happily, the Soviet officer in charge spoke fluent English and handled our credentials expeditiously. We passed Wannsee, in the southwestern sector of Berlin, long after dark; driving down wide, empty streets until we drew up to a brightly lighted suburban housing project behind a high, wire fence. There were no signs of destruction in the complex.

How fortunate we would be if these semidetached apartments were our living quarters. Most American soldiers in the occupation forces probably would be living in tents, Quonset huts, and barracks. The number of soldiers in U.S. Group CC was infinitesimal compared to the other thirty thousand troops in Berlin. Most of the Americans who arrived before us were in the Second Armored Division, which would be replaced in the middle of July by the Eighty-second Airborne. They were there to maintain order and protect our American contingent.

The first American Army detachment that entered our sector of Berlin had difficulty locating undamaged buildings for occupancy. Intact ones whose interiors hadn't been partially or completely damaged by American and British bombings and Soviet artillery attacks were few in number. Even the walls of Ambassador Murphy's quarters had been riddled with rifle and pistol bullet holes by Russian soldiers. But the State Department officers and civilian staff were staying in the best houses that could be commandeered in the American sector.

The officer driving us stopped at the front gate of the wire fence in front of the semidetached apartments to let Hershel and me out, before he took the women to their quarters in another part of the American sector. An armed guard at the gate checked several lists before he found our names and the numbers of our billets.

Relieved to have arrived safely, I was even happier that the apartments inside the compound, on both sides of the street, were undamaged. The buildings were landmark architecture, designed by a group of famous architects, chief among them Walter Gropius. Onkel Toms Hutte, where we were quartered, was named after an old local inn. It was commissioned and built in the 1920s to provide middle-class housing with comfortable rooms, gardens, electric lights, and hot water systems.

Hershel reached his apartment first, and I found mine farther down the street. Howy greeted me at the front door and led me upstairs, laughingly calling attention to the irony of a Jew from the Bronx and an Arkansas "hillbilly" living in an apartment formerly occupied by a member of the *Schutzstaffel* (SS), the Nazi elite guard.

We shared our apartment as we had in Frankfurt, only this time with pals. Howy reached Berlin before me and chose for us the smaller bedroom in the rear of the apartment; it had twin beds and two windows overlooking a quiet garden. Rotondo and Mother Leshak, our housemates, were in the front bedroom.

Our compact apartment provided space enough for four guys who rarely hung around the house. The living room, dining room, kitchen, and walk-in pantry were on the ground floor. To the left of the front door was a large closet. At the top of the stairs, off an L-shaped landing, was a small, skylit artist's studio, and our bedroom to its right. The other bedroom and the bath were across the landing.

Both bedrooms had rectangular, porcelain-tile stoves, tall enough to reach to within two feet of the ceiling. Near the base of the stoves were shallow recesses behind wrought-iron doors, in which charcoal or coal briquettes were burned. In theory, the coals heated the stove's bricks and tiles, which then radiated warmth into the room. Actually, the stoves gave off so little heat that you had to press whatever part of your body you wanted to warm directly to the stove's surface.

Howy chose the bed under the window that overlooked the garden, and mine was against the inner wall, on the opposite side of the stove. I was especially grateful for that location one morning later in the winter, when he awoke covered in snow, which had blown through the window we customarily left open.

Another novel feature of our apartment was the geyser in the bathroom. A geyser, instead of drawing hot water from the reservoir of a tank, heated the water flowing into the tub through a coil of copper pipe over a gas jet. Opening the spigot to increase the flow of water also increased the flow of natural gas to the flame of the jet under the coil, raising the temperature of the water passing through the pipe. Our adjustments of the flow produced temperatures that were either too hot or too cold, with no comfortable gradations in between. Yelps or deep intakes of breath characterized everyone's baths. Ironically, the British invented the geyser the Germans fancied.

The U.S. Army added their special touch to the Teutonic taste of our apartment's dark woodwork, furniture, and wall paper. Secured to the top of the large newel post at the foot of the stairs was a topless cigar box filled with piles of condoms. Chaplains and doctors, knowing they couldn't ban sex, believed they could protect our health, if not our morality, by making rubbers easily available. The more useful purpose for them at our apartment was cutting the sheath off the thick rim at the open end for rubber bands to hold our trouser bottoms when we bloused them over our boots.

My first morning in the German capitol, I found that the American sector was six boroughs in the southwestern part of the city: Zehlendorf, Steglitz, Templehof, Schoenberg, Kreuzburg, and Neukoelln. Group CC headquarters was in Zehlendorf.

I wanted to explore the Political Division offices before beginning my duties as message center chief, so after breakfast Howy and I hurried to Onkel Toms Hutte, the subway station nearest our apartment, to catch a ride on the *unterbahn.* The most distinctive features of the station were a movie house on one side of the subway platform and empty Nestle chocolate candy bar dispensers on walls outside its lobby.

We joined other American soldiers on the subway, but most of the passengers were German civilians, who looked at us in different ways. Many smiled openly and friendlily, others cast their eyes down in frowns, and some simply stared at us, expressionless. To escape their stares and the rank odors of old sweat and ersatz tobacco, Howy and I stood at the back of the car smoking. As we puffed on our cigarettes, the Germans stared at us with the intensity of hungry leopards gazing at a freshly killed gazelle. Cigarettes, especially American-made ones, whether package perfect or partially-consumed butts, had become Germany's chief currency at war's end.

Howy said, "Watch what happens when I throw this butt away."

As we stepped off the car, he reduced the cigarette to a smoldering nub and tossed it toward a gutter. Several boys and men scrambled for the butt, violently intent on reaching it first, to stuff it into the little tin cans they held. Howy, poised to become a habitué of the black market, said that German men, women, and children scouted for cigarette butts and collected them. They later field-stripped them, sifting the ashes from the unburned tobacco and rolling the good tobacco into fresh cigarette papers, for buying or trading on the black market.

Headquarters of the U.S. Military Government in Berlin was on Kronprinzenalle, a wide, busy avenue. Group CC, including the Political Division, was in the sprawling German Air Defense Command Building. When we arrived, they told us it was Hermann Göring's headquarters as commander of the German Luftwaffe, but later we discovered that the Reichsluftfahrt-Ministry, like most of the other major Nazi government buildings in Berlin, was on Wilhelmstrasse.

The architecture of the Air Defense Command Building was not the neo-Grecian phase of romantic classicism characterizing so many historic Berlin buildings; nor was it in the operatic mode of the projected Nazi monuments designed by Hitler's architect Albert Speer. The complex of three buildings was purely functional in design. The central building, housing the Political Division and General Clay, was four stories tall, its four wings enclosing an open garden. The multitude of windows admitted maximum light on both sides of each floor, an advantage during the almost sunless fall and winter months of 1945.

The gray stone building, stained by weather and smoke from battles, was screened from the street by a high stone wall. Between the wall and the sidewalk, tall pines grew at irregular intervals, and small sentry boxes were on both sides of the iron gates at the entrance. A guard checked our credentials before allowing us to cross up the cobblestone drive encircling the courtyard and leading to porte cocheres, which framed entries to the two wings of the central building.

Howy led me into the wide, marble-floored lobby, where a window two stories high faced the garden. Standing at the foot of the stairs, I imagined the porcine Reichs-marshall entering dramatically and ascending the stairs. The arc of wide steps swung past the high window to the second floor, where I reported to the first office off the wing's central corridor. The building, having survived years of air raids, was singularly plain inside, and nothing had been done to relieve its austerity. A long hall, with State Department offices on both sides, led to Ambassador Murphy's and General Clay's adjoining offices.

Sergeant Schmidt told me I had been promoted to corporal, even though my position as message center chief really warranted the rank of master sergeant. He cautioned me not to expect anything more; I had to advance through staff and technical sergeancies to attain it. A real stroke of luck would be needed because so many high-ranking NCOs were transferred into Group CC at war's end. Like transferring from ASTP to the Ninety-fourth Division, the likelihood of promotion was slight. At least, my pay was raised to sixty-six dollars, which made it possible to buy a twenty-five-dollar war bond each month and still have spending money.

Eric added that Colonel J. C. McCawley, commandant of troops in Berlin, had issued Rote and me, as members of the *Grooper* staff, official Army correspondents credentials.

The two-room suite of the message center was halfway down the hall. Dorothea Lampe and I shared the outer room, with our desks facing each other, her back to the windows and mine to the office entrance. The arrangement screened me from the distractions of traffic in and out of the office and allowed me to talk directly to Mrs. Lampe about classifying and routing documents. The other, larger room in the suite housed file cabinets for documents and desks for the file clerks.

The women in the file room were from different states, unmarried, and in their mid-20s to mid-30s. Lenore Bobbitt from Iowa and Dusty Rhodes from Utah, my companions on the way to Berlin, had worked in the State Department before the war began and later transferred to London. The two younger women, Louise Byrnes, from Baltimore, Maryland, and Anna Mary Gring, from Lancaster, Pennsylvania, had recently joined the State Department and volunteered for Europe.

During the first week in Berlin, I located officers I knew and met the new people on the ambassador's expanding staff. Knowing every officer's specialty was essential because I read all documents (except coded ones), summarized their contents, logged their subjects, and directed them to an appropriate officer.

The regularity of my office routine was soon set. I reported to the message center at 0730 and remained until 1700, or later, depending upon the urgency of processing and routing the documents we received. When I completed logging, I often joined the women in the file room, talking and kidding while helping them file. Our daily sessions helped us get better acquainted as coworkers and friends.

In my mind's eye, I still see tall, slender Lenore Bobbitt—her back rigidly straight whether sitting or standing, her prim facial expression, and her oval face's aquiline nose and small, shapely mouth. But Lenore's restrained appearance camouflaged her love of fun and parties. The same was true of her pal, Esther Rhodes, who was shorter but just as slender. Dusty had reddish-brown hair, a prominent nose, and deep set, laughing eyes. As informal in manner as her nickname, she claimed she left Utah "to escape from a Mormon harem." Both women were easier to talk to at work than the younger clerks who were less sure and more restrained.

Anna Mary and Louise were about the same height, but Anna Mary had a softly curved figure that matched her round face. Louise was angular and lean. Anna Mary was peaches and cream, her natural blonde hair parted on the side and curled at the ends. Louise was a plainer, younger Katherine Hepburn, her long oval face freckled like a redhead's, her large, green eyes framed by reddish brown hair, curling just above her shoulders.

For the office, all the women dressed in khaki skirts, shirts, and ties, similar to those of WACs. Off duty, they wore civilian dresses, skirts, blouses, and suits. We enjoyed hanging around together at their personal billets and service clubs.

Our boss, Mrs. Lampe, insisted on being called "Dodo" (dough-dough). Probably in her late forties, she had a son younger than me in a private school in the United States. Dodo was about five feet seven inches tall, with a full figure and a round, happy face. Although I cut up and joked a lot around the office, she never called me down. In fact, she entered into the tricks, pranks, or surprises we were playing on each other, in or out of the office. Until I joined the Political Division, I had never associated with anyone Dodo's age who accepted me as an equal, free of middle-aged attitudes, manners, and proscriptions. Not even officers and NCOs in Company B treated me that way.

As a senior State Department officer, Dodo was privy to more of what was going on in the upper echelons than anyone else among us. She confirmed, denied, or corrected our speculations about rumors and official matters, while letting us know the facts about the past and present lives and current relationships of other staff members.

On July 17, at Potsdam, the first postwar conference began among the Big Three—the United States, Great Britain, and the USSR—to complete plans for governing Germany. Four days later, President Truman and an entourage of U.S. congressmen and generals visited our headquarters. A special armed guard honored the president by raising the same American flag that was flying over the White House the day Pearl Harbor was attacked, and which later flew over U.S. Army headquarters in North Africa, Rome, and Paris after major victories. Truman spoke to Group CC staffs and to the Congressional dignitaries. Except for the less-public individual sightseeing tours taken by Truman, Churchill, and Stalin, we heard little about the Potsdam Conference held from July through August.

While the world leaders were conferring, the dazed Berliners were still roaming the city, trying to find or arrange some place to live if their own quarters had been destroyed or commandeered by the Army. Hundreds of DPs also wandered around the shattered city, seeking shelter, fuel, and food to sustain them.

The smell of the air had improved since U.S. Group CC's advance party had described how offensive it was in early June, when Ambassador Murphy and General Clay first visited. But we still caught the stench of death emanating from the flooded U-Bahn tunnels, where thousands of Berliners, who sought refuge from Russian artillery, had drowned. The German SS flooded the maze of tunnels by blowing up the safety bulkhead control chamber of the Landwehr Canal, after they discovered Soviet troops were entering and following them.

The shortages of electricity in the city prevented the U.S. Army engineers from providing street lighting, so travel on foot at night was extremely dangerous. We resumed carrying our carbines when we went out after dark.

Since the weather and temperatures remained comfortable enough for wool uniforms from late July into August, Howy and I walked to work or hitched rides on military trucks traveling the Berlinerstrasse. As we walked and thumbed rides, we saw many modes of transportation that German civilians devised for getting around Berlin—bicycles, baby buggies, handcarts, wagons, and four-wheeled Rube-Goldberg-like contraptions.

By July 11, the nonfraternization rule was relaxed to allow conversation with German adults in streets and public places, and I asked a German about the unusual sources of power used with their buses and trucks. They had large black cylinders on their right running boards, spouting smoke from burning wood, which made combustible gas for fuel. He said that it was common practice in Germany, even before the war, to convert the engines of larger vehicles to that system. When carrying large supplies of wood proved bunglesome, they switched to charcoal, which produced enough carbon monoxide in the stovelike generators to drive the motors.

Going to and from the office, exploring outside our daily route on weekends, I saw parts of the American sector where almost every building was destroyed, much like Frankfurt am Main. Sophie Tarzinski took Rote and me on a tour of central Berlin, where Allied bombings and Russian artillery had destroyed Wilhelmstrasse and left most buildings smoke-blackened ruins. Along the Unter den Linden, the U.S. Army engineers filled the huge craters in the boulevard, but they couldn't restore the blasted linden trees in the Tiergarten, or force the seared leaf buds to bloom again on the few trees standing near scattered foxholes.

More of an anomaly than the ruins around the Tiergarten was the monument the Soviets erected in the American sector in honor of their victorious troops. The Russians mounted a huge tank on a high, wooden platform, with plywood sheets concealing the supports of the base. They painted the whole mint-green, perhaps their attempt to make it appear to have the patina of aged bronze, like statues in Russia.

Farther down the avenue, at the gashed and chipped Brandenburg Gate, one of its cornices lay in the street, but all twelve of its massive Doric columns remained standing. The Reichstag building nearby—an architectural mixture of classical, Renaissance, and baroque styles—was an empty ruin. First set afire by the Nazis in 1933, it was totally incinerated by the Russians as the last site of Nazi resistance. The bronze eagles above the front entrances to the yellowish-brown Reich's Chancellery lay among the piles of smashed bricks from its fallen walls.

Many neighborhood streets, which Allied saturation bombings and Russian artillery bombardments had pounded, lay under piles of rubble from collapsed buildings. Even the daily efforts of Berlin's famous rubble women, the *Truemmerfrauen* (women who scavenged bricks), hadn't cleared most of the streets. The few signs indicating life lay beneath the rubble were thin coils of smoke rising from stove pipes that projected from basement walls, marking the presence of survivors, who clung to the remains of their homes—uninhabitable, windowless, roofless hulks.

Although many parts of Berlin lay destroyed, the metropolis hadn't suffered as badly as many others, for a third of the city was covered by dense woods. Trees, shrubs, and sculptures in public parks, only a block from the ruins, were not touched by bullets, bombs, and artillery shells. The parks and buildings more distant from the city's heart hadn't been seared, smashed, and broken. The mounds of dirt marking graves on level ground were crowned with wooden crosses at their heads and piles of wilted flowers at their feet. On the trail through a park between our apartment and the *Grooper* editorial offices, I passed coal-scuttle helmets resting atop posts at the graves of German soldiers.

So many undamaged buildings for entertainment remained that it appeared Russian artillery purposely avoided aiming at nightclubs, theaters, and opera houses. Purportedly, the Russian generals directing the attack against Berlin had a three-dimensional map with miniature buildings, bridges, railway stations, streets, canals, and airfields, which was their reference in choosing artillery targets. If such a map and strategy existed, it wasn't surprising that entertainment sites survived intact.

The Titania Palast, a large theater on Kurfurstendamm, was in excellent shape when I attended an American road company's production there in October. The theater in which the Berlin Staatsoper performed was also in good condition, except for the natural deterioration suffered during the war. The Club Femina on Kurfurstendamm wasn't seriously damaged either, for the multistoried nightclub was in full swing every night, featuring a different decor and style of entertainment on each floor for an international clientele.

In Berlin, our social relationships with our former enemies were changing. At Hoechst, we mostly met Germans, like Frau Curtius and Anna, who were housekeepers for their requisitioned apartments. The nonfraternization policy and the slow progress of the U.S. de-Nazification program kept most GIs at a distance from Hoechst's citizens, except for clandestine dating.

By the time the nonfraternization policy ended, a sufficient number of Germans had been cleared of Nazi complicity for the Army to organize an adequate civilian workforce. At first, those with good records were cooks, bakers, waiters, and dishwashers. But by December 1945, Germans worked in non-security-risk positions in units of the U.S. Group CC, operating telephone exchanges, driving trucks and cars, barbering, and serving as beauticians.

The attitudes and behavior of Germans employed by the Army naturally depended upon their individual characters and personalities. Many English-speaking Germans I had contact with behaved at one of two extremes, being either talkative and sycophantic or sullen and superior. The majority who spoke little English smiled a lot but were otherwise restrained in their body language and reluctant to deal candidly with GIs. They were open, though, seeking to satisfy their hunger and remain in our good graces.

When lunch was served every day at the outdoor kitchens, near the former Air Defense Building, large numbers of German adults and children gathered alongside our food lines and beside the garbage cans. In the early months of the occupation, they collected scraps from garbage cans because food of any kind among German civilians was in short supply. The faces of the adults watching us eat showed their resentment against conquerors who had so much food and against themselves as supplicants beside the victor's garbage cans.

Despite the negative attitudes of some Germans, GIs shared their food. We often took more than we could eat in order to put half the food into the containers Germans held out to us. The good will and generosity of GIs toward German children seemed boundless; many returned for seconds and carried the food directly to children. This ritual persisted until sufficient food supplies were distributed among the Germans. From our arrival, German children, as if they knew the American penchant for chewing gum, asked GIs, "Kau-gumme, bitte?"

Russian enlisted soldiers were restricted to their own sector by the Soviet Army. Although American soldiers seldom dealt directly with Russians, fire fights between them occasionally broke out. The disputes grew out of drinking too much alcohol, competing for the same women, or misunderstanding each other's language. When American and Russian soldiers were killed in clashes, the news, though not officially publicized by either government, passed by word of mouth among the troops.

The hovering Soviet presence was felt in our zone, without our encountering Russian soldiers face to face. The Russian zone surrounded Berlin. The American sector of Berlin, adjacent to the Russian sector, was 120 miles from the U.S. zone of Germany.

My closest German acquaintances in Berlin, recalling days of the city's capitulation, claimed the Russian combat troops who captured the capitol behaved in a civilized manner but that their replacements, Mongol troops from remote states of the Soviet Union, committed vengeful rapes and murders of men, women, and children. By the time American troops arrived, the Mongols had been replaced by occidental troops, better dressed with stricter discipline. Yet these new troops were difficult to deal with because Soviet policies reinforced language barriers and prevented Russian soldiers from going into other national sectors.

To deal with Russian restrictions, we made elaborate preparations to gain entry to their sector. We asked an American officer to sign a letter stating our visit's purpose and requesting entry. If they granted permission, after the anticipated delay, the Russians required a list of the persons visiting their sector, including ranks and serial numbers. (The United States placed no restrictions on Russians in the American sector, until our borders were closed to the USSR in December 1945.) We decorated our letters to impress officials at Russian checkpoints, using legal-size stationery, large type, gold and silver metallic seals, embossed stamps, sealing wax, and colored ribbons.

When Group CC flew from Versailles to Frankfurt in June, Germany had no civilian government, and the national zones, projected at Yalta, had not yet been officially occupied. They were in the hands of the armies who captured them. When hostilities ended, the several Allied armies and numberless displaced persons were in extraordinary disorder across the whole Continent. But evolving policies of the Allies had a few positive solutions for major civilian problems in Germany.

Near the end of July, with American help, Berlin theater artists gave signs of an emerging normalcy when they performed *The Taming of the Shrew* in Schoneberger City Park. The internal German civil government in the American zone was also beginning to take shape in the first weeks of August. And by the end of the month, the first official session of the Allied Control Council convened.

The Army calculated every individual soldier's Adjusted Service Rating (ASR), or point system for redeployment and discharge, by the middle of May, planning to send those with high points home in August. The points for service, announced shortly after European hostilities ended, allowed one point for each month of service and for each month overseas, five points each for battle stars and individual awards like the Purple Heart, and twelve points for each child under eighteen. Soldiers in all combat theaters with 85 points or more were eligible for discharge in the fall of 1945. My ASR was 46 in May, but General Marshall promised to lower the discharge points from 80 to 70 by October 1, and to 60 points by November 1, which encouraged me.

After the United States dropped the second atomic bomb, Japan surrendered on August 14. When hostilities in the Pacific ended, the soldiers in Europe sensed closure and so did the general public, which made stronger demands for soldiers to be sent home as soon as possible. Obviously, neither group was thinking of the need to govern the disorganized Germans and DPs and assist in Europe's recovery. Until the Pacific war ended, military government in Germany had the luxury of huge numbers of soldiers, which made civilianization, below the top levels of U.S. Group CC, unnecessary. But the rapid demobilization in September led General Clay to try to induce GIs, particularly commissioned officers, to convert to civilian status and remain in their positions in Germany.

Several members of the State Department, including Dodo Lampe and Mr. Swift, encouraged me to take a discharge in Germany and accept a position as a code clerk or diplomatic courier. Civil salaries were excellent, but the contract required me to remain in Europe for a minimum of another year. Since Tumpy and I planned to marry as soon as I was discharged, I asked if she wanted to join me by taking a clerical position in the State Department. But we weren't seriously tempted; she was reluctant to work in war-torn countries, and I was eager to go home.

My twenty-first birthday celebration on August 17 was quiet. Anna Mary Gring and Louise Byrnes invited Rote and me to their apartment for drinks and cake. Louise played the upright piano in their dining room, and they sang "Happy Birthday."

Rote and I continued our column, "Completely Confused," generally including nonsense and news items about Group CC that would interest other Americans—such as two brothers or a father and son assigned to Berlin at the same time, a WAC spending time on furlough with her relatives in Wales, or a Special Service librarian trying to find an empty building to set up a reading room. We congratulated the cooks who served good food regularly without receiving praise from the troops. We defended WACs from unwarranted male prejudices, in an effort to improve relations between men's and women's units in Berlin. We praised the troop commander who built a nightclub exclusively for enlisted personnel and the soldier-designer who decorated its interior.

In the beginning, we wrote almost nothing about the upper echelons and stayed out of trouble. But soon, officers preempted the rights of enlisted men, and German employees denied GIs their services, arousing our ire and the need to criticize them. First, a captain in U.S. Group CC attempted to arrange a large club exclusively for enlisted personnel, but certain general officers discovered the building as it neared completion and requisitioned it for officers only. Their presumptuous last-minute act, revealed to me by Evelyn Belton, who was in a play with me, inspired our response in the *Grooper*:

> Looks like the advertising of the Rendezvous Club in the Special Service Bulletin was a little too good. Anyway some people seemed impressed by it, so now the majestic 42-room mansion is a transient billet for general officers. Special Service, and Captain James Garaghan in particular, did all they could to swing the deal for GIs, but unfortunately didn't have enough weight to swing. So-o-o, our Rendezvous has moved to a lovely, yet none too big,

Doenitz Den. It is a swell place for 200 CCs, but it will hardly accommodate all 4,000 of us. Just grin and bear it . . . anymore of that and we won't give 'em their jobs back after this is all over.

The Associated Press repeated the item in the Monday, September 24, 1945, edition of the *Stars and Stripes,* and the European edition of the *New York Herald Tribune* picked it up the next day:

Generals Get the House, But Men Have Last Word

Berlin, Sept. 24 (A.P.)—The generals got the house but the soldiers had the last word.

A forty-two-room mansion, formerly owned by the Nazi Minister Funk on the green shore of Wannsee in suburban Berlin was all ready for a gala opening as "Rendezvous Club" of 4,000 enlisted men. Twenty-four hours before the opening it was requisitioned for the exclusive use of general officers and full colonels. A non-commissioned officer columnist in "The Grooper," weekly newspaper of the United States Group Control Council, commented: "Anymore of that and we won't give them their jobs back after this is all over."

Pointing out the tenuous status of officers, who might return to less authoritative positions in civilian life, didn't strike us as seditious. The item received such widespread attention, however, that the *Grooper* editor was reprimanded by General Clay's adjutant for letting such a critical item slip past his editorial eye. The adjutant warned that any other remarks of that sort would lead headquarters to censor our column.

In the weeks after, we filled the column with inconsequential foolishness. But eventually the negative behavior towards GIs we noticed in German cooks, waiters, drivers, and barbers provoked us. We naively assumed that our criticism of American officers was our only offense and that we could safely criticize Germans who gave small servings to GIs in mess halls, drove Army vehicles dangerously fast, ignored GI hitchhikers to pick up German civilians, and gave German workers priority over GIs in Army barbershops.

All of these items may seem small, but in the long run they will add to the discomfort of each of us. The mounting number of what we see as violations of our policy toward the Germans will, if they go unchecked, grow into something so big that our basic plan with regards to these people will topple and accomplish nothing. If our legislators would look into the low men on the totem pole as well as the high, they would find much lacking. Someone is failing. Perhaps the GI, or the higher-ups. More than likely a combination of us all. You might chalk this column up by saying, "Into each life some rain must fall."

Brother, we're wearing water wings.

General Clay's headquarters responded immediately, ending not only our column but our journalistic careers. Neither Rote nor I really cared. We stopped writing in November 1945, when Rote decided to devote full time to earning a promotion and visiting relatives in Naples, and I had enough points to go home in December.

From the end of August through November, I acted roles in the American Little Theater Company, sponsored by Army Special Services. Auditions for the first play, *Cradle Snatchers,* to be presented in late September, were held in a penthouse above Onkel Toms Hutte Cino. I failed to persuade Rotondo to attend auditions, but with the prospect of acting again, I really didn't need the reassurance of a companion.

A surprising number of men turned out for auditions, but as usual there were more women, younger and older WACs. No civilian men or women from Group CC showed up. The efforts of those auditioning to be friendly with each other while sizing up the competition were typical of play tryouts. I won the role of Jose Vallejo, a young osteopathy student, by proving to be the only one who could switch quickly between Brooklynese and a Spanish dialect. Rehearsals, which began the next evening, continued every night for the next three weeks. We were guided through the process of blocking by the experienced actors and the assistance of Reginald Pasch, an older professional German actor, who shaped our production.

Two cast members became my friends during rehearsals. West Point graduate Lieutenant Robert Pappas, a swarthy brunet from Chillicothe, Ohio, had been an artillery observer in combat. With a memory that made mental imprints he could read like a printed page, he learned his role in one reading. But he claimed these pictures weren't always permanent and sometimes produced negative results. His memory helped him pass exams at the Point, but on one occasion in combat, an enemy barrage shook him so badly that he couldn't recall necessary calculations for return fire.

My other friend was Sergeant Chester Elliott. About five feet eight inches tall, slight of build, with wavy blond hair, Chet had taught English and dramatics at the public high school in his hometown in Kansas before the war. On the OSS staff, with hush-hush duties, he never mentioned his work, colleagues, or office location.

At rehearsals, our German assistant, Reginald Pasch, helped me develop effective acting techniques. I was reluctant to listen until he revealed his theatrical experience in opera, operetta, plays, and motion pictures in Germany and the United States. He had worked under major directors—Max Reinhardt, Ernst Lubitsch, and William Dieterle—in several important German and Hollywood films. Forced to remain in Germany after he returned to make a movie, he continued his stage and opera career throughout the war.

Reggie insisted that most actors had little to do with Nazi officials, and faced the same deprivations of food, clothing, and fuel and the dangers of Allied bombing as ordinary citizens. He applied at the District Information Service Control Command unit, where all Germans in public communications—editors, publishers, musicians, and actors—would be approved for work only after being cleared of Nazi involvements.

Before he was interviewed, Reginald filled out a detailed questionnaire about his politics, education, employment, affiliations, and general social outlook. He proved to be a "white German," the category for those who never gave in to Naziism. He received a "Persil" certificate (alluding to a kind of German soap), a document that allowed him to work in a restricted profession. His talent, American connections, and sympathies for the Allies allowed him opportunities to sing traditional American songs at state dinners for U.S. generals, congressmen, and civilian officials. At one performance for heads of military government in Germany, Reginald met Lieutenant Phillip Byrnes, who hired him to coach actors at the little theater.

Byrnes had a hard time finding a rehearsal space that would be free every night and large enough for the set. To block the play's action, we needed space enough to arrange a room in proper scale. The lounge at the theater penthouse was too small for anything but reading rehearsals and the least damaged buildings, with rooms of the proper size, already housed military offices. The lieutenant used a science lecture hall, across the *unterbahn* tracks at the rear of the Air Defense Building, where we rehearsed beside an immovable lab table on one side of the shallow lecture platform.

In its initial run, *Cradle Snatchers* opened September 24, 1945, and played through the twenty-eighth. Byrnes had difficulty finding civilian clothes for men's costumes, and I still had no costume at the final dress rehearsal. Less than an hour before curtain time of the opening performance, the crew brought me a tuxedo, starched shirt, cummerbund, and bow tie. I had worn a tuxedo only once before, in my senior play, and I was not successful in tying the bow tie. None of the other actors could help me.

I shouted, "Can anyone tie this damned bow for me?"

Lieutenant Byrnes yelled from his office, "I have someone who can help."

Seeing the diminutive Marlene Dietrich, standing beside the lieutenant in his office, startled me. She was in a black lace gown, like one she wore in the film *Desire,* costarring Gary Cooper. Smiling, she held out both her arms to me, saying in her husky voice, "Sit on zuh edge of zuh desk and I'll do it for you."

I sat down, and she spread my knees so she could stand between them to reach my bow tie. When she stepped between my legs and looked into my eyes, I gulped like Mortimer Snerd.

She observed in her rich nasal English, "You tie it just as you vould tie a bow in your shoelace, but *I* have to do it backvards."

She tied the bow, adjusted it, patted the finished product, and leaned forward to kiss my cheek. Her kiss was so unexpected, I didn't know what to do except say "thank you." I walked back to the dressing room in a daze, amazed not only by her presence and kiss but also by how short and slender she was.

Miss Dietrich was visiting her sick mother, who still had a boutique on the Unter den Linden. To introduce our show, she presented her customary signature for GI audiences in the ETO. A spotlight focused on the front curtain, and she extended her bare leg through the curtain break into the circle of light. GIs recognized its owner instantly and broke into wild applause and yelling. Their uproar was her cue; she stepped through the curtain. Then, in the midst of catcalls, she praised our show, even though she knew nothing about us or the play.

An anonymous reviewer described the play in the next issue of the *Grooper* as "a smash performance . . . that drew rounds of applause and acclaim from all quarters, including that hard-to-please character himself—G.I. Joe of U.S. Group C.C."

> Originally scheduled for three showings, the play was so successful it was held over two more nights because of popular demand. Spontaneous crowds hailed each performance, and a Capt. Howell flew up from Paris to judge its worth for the All-Soldier show contest.
>
> Evelyn Belton and A. Cleveland Harrison had the two choice roles, and with the aid of Russel Medcraft and Norma Mitchell's racy (at times, downright naughty) lines, this pair ran off with top honors.
>
> Group C.C. will be looking forward to more stage efforts by the Little Theater.

The reviewer didn't know that Lieutenant Byrnes had chosen *Room Service* for our next production. I had read the play and was eager to try out; even though rehearsals were time-consuming and my overall schedule very busy, I wanted a role.

On October 1, 1945, under General Clay's orders, the United States Group Control Council became the Office of Military Government, United States (OMGUS), and the Political Division became the Office of Political Affairs. Unlike the other divisions, the Office of Political Affairs was placed under the immediate supervision of the commanding general.

Those of us in Political Affairs were the luckiest of the enlisted men working in higher headquarters. Most of the personnel in other OMGUS divisions had to cope with two systems of supervision. During the day, they were under the command of the various division officers where they worked; at night they were controlled by officers who had no professional assignment at OMGUS headquarters. So while enlisted men in military government positions were respected by their officers at work, they were often harassed by other officers who tried to grind them down with extra duties and no passes when they were off duty.

In Political Affairs, enlisted men worked regular hours at the office on weekdays, and sometimes until noon on Saturdays. Off duty, no other Army officers were over us to give additional orders. We merely kept our rooms clean and orderly, even though I don't recall a single inspection of any kind. Each of us washed his own underwear and socks, but our wool uniforms and cotton shirts were cleaned and pressed by an Army laundry, staffed by Germans.

Though we weren't aware of it, those of us in Political Affairs were really an exclusive group. Much of the work we performed required professional attitudes and skills even if our duties were routine. The diplomatic environment and work accomplished by the enlisted men required special personal qualities. The educational backgrounds of ASTPers made them good choices for assignments in U.S. Group CC, but I recall meeting very few in any military government division.

Some Army routines were the same as they were in the States. We had regular VD exams, monthly payroll lineups and signings, and a set schedule for meals in mess halls. But no close-order drills, reveille calls, retreat formations, or other military activities ordered our lives. Less military formality existed between enlisted men and officers, in and out of the office. At the plebeian levels of enlisted ranks, almost all military barriers between NCOs and lower ranks were lessened or ended altogether in their social relationships, leaving matters of rank and power in official situations only. While all of us welcomed the relaxation of military protocol, it produced a loss of certain constraints, like uniform hours sleeping in our own quarters, and led to major abuses. In the chaos that evolved, the commanders in Berlin took steps to protect our health.

We had no VD lectures, but short-arms remained a standard preliminary to the monthly payday. The VD inspection before pay made it possible to exclude those who were infected because they violated Army regulations by contracting VD. Our group was examined at an aid station in an apartment across the street. The clinic's official mark was a large red cross painted on its door. Its unofficial symbol was an erect penis carved by an anonymous sculptor from the branch of a tree limb beside the front walk.

The increasing numbers of soldiers cohabiting with German women raised the incidence of venereal diseases to epidemic proportions within all ranks, which led to VD lectures for the entire military command in Berlin. The compulsory lectures for enlisted personnel, en masse, were presented at Onkel Toms Hutte Cino.

The first lecture, in early October, was very much like those in the States. A young lieutenant spoke briefly, admonishing us not to have sex. But if we did, we should use condoms, urinate immediately after intercourse, and visit an aid station as soon as possible. After his remarks, they showed a standard black-and-white film, dramatizing the dangers of casual sex, demonstrating the application of a condom, and showing treatment at an aid station. The audience was inattentive.

Whether severe cold weather (the first snow was on November 11) increased sexual activity in Berlin would be impossible to say. The affairs between American men and German women and the increased rate of VD forced the chaplaincy and medical corps to schedule another VD lecture for the whole command. This time two far more impressive men in rank and appearance—a gruff medical doctor and a manly-looking chaplain, both bird colonels—greeted the male-female assembly.

The doctor, introducing his remarks, insisted that he and the chaplain understood how much warmer two bodies in one bed could be on a cold winter's night. Imagining our lecturers together in that circumstance, the audience roared in laughter. Puzzled by this response, the doctor insisted that setting our comfort aside, we had to understand how such behavior jeopardized our health and the aims of the military government. He pointed out, for soldiers personally and the Army generally, the disruption of military routine and the cost of time lost when not performing one's duty.

Following the doctor, the rough-hewn chaplain spoke of the moral consequences of sex outside marriage and of adultery for the married. Concluding, the chaplain shamed us for violating the trust of our loved ones back home. No film was shown after their speeches. Attention at the lectures was alert; after our dismissal, the responses seemed derisive or guilty.

Where sex was concerned, I liked women and wanted to be around them; I had as much energy and as many fantasies as the next GI. But the German women I met seemed to me not nearly as attractive as Americans. And my response to all women was tempered by what I learned at home, at church, and in the Boy Scouts, that sex outside marriage was against God's will and was immoral. I did not violate that conviction. Since I was engaged to marry Tumpy, my relationship with Louise Byrnes was warm but innocent.

While medics took care of our physical health, the public relations officers tried to shape our attitudes toward our former enemies and our allies. General Eisenhower and congressional officials had toured the concentration camps when they were freed in April, and signal corps cameramen filmed their tours. USFET command ordered that films made at Belsen, Buchenwald, and Auschwitz be shown to all military contingents to expose German guilt. The camps and victims pictured in the uncensored films proved the depravities practiced by Nazis in exterminating internal "enemies," principally Jews and dissenters, through starvation, torture, disease, and murder. Silence at the film's start was soon replaced by sniffing, nose blowing, and curses as scenes of emaciated survivors and piles of dead bodies flashed across the screen. I have never seen films of any kind, before or since, that literally made me hurt as those did.

The other films we saw focused on the Russian attack on Berlin. The Russian combat films were propaganda, but the powerful pictures were made by photographers who risked their lives in the midst of the action. In fact, credits at the beginning included a long list of cinematographers who moved ahead of the troops to film Soviet soldiers advancing under fire toward the German lines, many of whom died in the attack.

Film scenes showed barrages laid down by Russian artillery pieces of all sizes surrounding the city, waves of soldiers carrying automatic weapons charging across open fields, and the individuals and squads of infantrymen fighting building by building through the city. American combat films didn't match them because U.S. photographers weren't ordered to risk their lives unnecessarily as the Russians were. Those of us who had been in combat understood and respected what Russian combat photographers and soldiers had accomplished.

Almost daily, Group CC headquarters received and entertained famous and important civilian and military visitors. To enhance military receptions for guests, the Eighty-second Airborne Division formed an honor guard after replacing the Second Armored Division as the American sector's constabulary. Volunteers were selected on the basis of their individual records, overall appearance, specific height and weight, and skill in close-order drill and the manual of arms. The honor guards wore standard enlisted dress uniforms: an Eisenhower jacket, OD slacks bloused over the tops of their combat boots, all embellished with red neck scarves and shoulder lanyards, and white gloves, web belt, rifle straps, and lacquered helmet liners. Civilians witnessed a rifle drill in the courtyard, and military men conducted an inspection of arms.

In November, General George Patton, temporarily replacing Eisenhower as commander of USFET, visited Berlin. Many of us from

Political Affairs stood under a porte cochere at the front of headquarters to watch the Eighty-second honor guard's welcoming drill and Patton's inspection in the courtyard.

The general was shorter than I expected and looked like a dandy in pale pink whipcord riding breeches, a forest green Eisenhower jacket, and highly polished riding boots. His helmet liner, covered in many layers of lacquer, glistened like a star, and the two ivory-handled pistols on his hips gleamed. He strolled through the ranks, joshing with the men, before passing within arm's reach of us at the door, nodding pleasantly as he entered. To me, his pink, crinkled, tissue-paper skin was his most striking feature.

When Patton was relieved as the military governor of Bavaria in September, the story was that the general wanted to use more former members of the Nazi party in administrative jobs. Egged on by reporters at a press conference, he implied that ordinary Nazis joined their party in much the same way Republicans and Democrats did in the United States. When newspapers repeated Patton's remarks, General Eisenhower purportedly dressed him down and reassigned him to another position.

Most of our other famous visitors were civilian entertainment personalities. Two popular comedians, Bob Hope and Jack Benny, each gave shows for GIs, toured the ruins of Berlin, and came by our office to visit Clay, Murphy, and their staffs. I was surprised at how short both comics were and how fragile Jack Benny looked. Of all the guests, the happiest and friendliest were the Wagnerian tenor of the Metropolitan Opera, Lauritz Melchior, and his wife. Melchior's jolly face peeked into all the offices to say hello to enlisted personnel. Marlene Dietrich was permitted to visit her mother, who had fallen ill but was no worse off than many Berliners of her age. Others, however, didn't have a famous movie-star daughter who could use her position to gain entry to the highly restricted American sector of Berlin.

In my leisure time after work and on weekends, when I wasn't rehearsing a play or variety or radio show, I joined Rote and Howy at movies and at Club 48, which the Army built to make up for the Rendevouz Club fiasco. Before General Clay ended our column, we described his attendance at the club's opening:

> Just drapped [sic] into Club 48 opening night to see what I could see. Because there were no more seats at the tables, I had to sit on one of those very comfortable couches beside the decorative and warm fireplace. From there I could see what was going on all over the place, which is without doubt the nicest, most complete, and entertaining club I have encountered in the Army. Our frazzled old toboggan caps are off to Colonel McCawley and all the others responsible for Club 48.
>
> The many photographers roaming around shooting Generals and Privates alike on opening night missed all the really good shots. General Clay was inspecting a marble table top just across from me and one of the fellows offered him a gin. He declined but took a beer instead. There was the boss drinking with the office boys . . . the thing that makes the American Army the nearest to a democratic Army in the world. No sooner had the General put his glass down than one of our WACS asked him to dance and he graciously accepted. The photo boys missed both shots but not being ones to give up easily they spent a good hour trying to trace the WAC in order to get her picture. As far as I know they never did find her.

The club, built within a block of OMGUS headquarters on Kronprinzenalle, was accessible to all soldiers in the American sector. The original newspaper release describing plans for the club's construction started a contest for a suitable name. The winner was "Club 48," an allusion to all the forty-eight contiguous American states in 1945. Marble inlays in the shapes of the states were installed on the tabletops.

Colonel McCawley and his staff gradually added other places and forms of entertainment for enlisted personnel. Venues presenting some type of amusement and other forms of Army-sponsored entertainment, besides eating and drinking, opened throughout the American sector.

In autumn 1945, when American thoughts turned to football, Special Service organized games between teams of soldiers. At halftime, at a Saturday afternoon football game, one team of engineers introduced an Engineer's Homecoming Queen to the crowd. About the game, our only comment was "brief uprisings kept the game interesting, and, as one player declared after the game, 'I got combat fatigue.' "

The Information and Education (I&E) section provided more serious opportunities for leisure by distributing paperback books, many of them serious instead of diversionary fiction like those we got in combat. Directed by a trained, experienced librarian, Special Service opened a library with holdings in nonfiction and fiction, reference materials, and recent periodicals. Serious students could take courses taught in English by regular university faculty at the free or open University of Berlin.

The number of women in the occupation army in Berlin was greater than male GIs ever encountered in the States. This was true in other areas of Europe where Army units were stationed. Until WACs had filled administrative and clerical positions in almost every office in Europe after the war, men had few occasions to reveal the depth of their negative attitudes toward women in general and WACs in particular. Attempting to counter the male chauvinism we saw every day, Rote and I made some observations in our column. These remarks, written in November 1945, suggest we were, in some respects, ahead of our time in our respect for women:

> This week we're really going WACky to devote this entire epistle to the other half of this world and the Army . . . women.
>
> We have been in the Army for quite some time and during our stay we have heard many things about the social relationship between the WAC and the GI. There are some grave misunderstandings existing between the two which should be corrected immediately.
>
> We think the primary reason for such petty bickering is the fact that most GIs don't know any WACs. Once a fellow knows some of the girls, he can't help but like more of them and in the long run his entire attitude toward the fairer sex in uniform should change. The girls who are assigned to work with men go to bat with strikes against them as far as many GI's are concerned. This feeling isn't fair to the WAC or the GI.
>
> In many instances, we fellows still think that a woman's place is only in the home, but the war and the job that women did in it have proved such an

argument wrong. Women today are very versatile and have proved themselves fully capable of handling almost any job they are given the chance to perform.

During the war, the women in war factories did their jobs well, but the girls who stepped into uniform came just a little nearer the actual front line and the men fighting on it. Many of the WACs gave up good paying jobs to join the corps for a salary the same as ours. They could have worked in defense plants for huge salaries and the "gravy train" we always think of as the home front. Instead they chose the service in the hope that by relieving a man for active duty they could do their part in bringing the war to a speedy and successful conclusion.

Maybe you don't know of any case where a man was relieved for active duty by a WAC, but the records show that the WAC replacement sent many service club commandos over to join the ranks of the fox hole commandos.

The WACs have done their part, but while they have done it, they have had to put up with cat-calls, remarks and slanders which are entirely uncalled for and without basis of fact or reason. Until last winter, the doughboy didn't receive the praise he should have had long before, but as yet we know of few instances of WACs receiving the words of appreciation they deserve.

We can't change the GI and WAC attitude towards each other. All we can do is suggest that we make an effort to meet and try to understand each other and by doing so lose many of the false ideas which have cropped up between us.

As fumbling as our writing style was—and as naive as our defense of women was—we were clearly on the side of truth and equality, despite our use of "girls" and "the fairer sex." Sensing, I suspect, the inadequacy of our comments, we ended on a lighter note:

Since we are devoting this entire column to women, we'll let you in on a little story we heard a few days ago. Seems there were two American soldiers in Egypt who had been living on ever-delectable dehydrated beef, dehydrated milk, and dehydrated vegetables and butter. During their travels, they visited the Cairo Museum and saw their first mummy. "This is going too far," one piped.

"Now they're dehydrating women, too."

Howy never participated in theater or newspaper reporting when off duty. He devoted himself, along with many Germans, Russians, and

Americans, to making money on the black market at the Tiergarten. Howy wanted to make a fortune and have a new Cadillac waiting on the dock when he returned to New York.

Black market activities of different kinds took place all over Berlin, but the chief site was the Tiergarten. Barters, trades, and sales of jewelry, small art objects, and foodstuff went on among multinational operators, using Occupation Reichsmarks and American cigarettes as their principal mediums of exchange. The most sought-after objects, particularly by Russian soldiers of all ranks, were watches and clocks.

Even though I smoked, Howy wanted to buy my monthly cigarette allocation to add to his in trading on the black market. Perhaps my ignorance and lack of interest in the market suggested I was naive because he offered the same price I paid at the PX—a nickel a pack or fifty cents a carton. I laughed at him because a single carton was worth fifteen dollars in the U.S. rate of exchange and several hundred dollars in marks on the black market. Ordinary kitchen matches were used to make small change.

Many transactions were in Occupation Reichsmarks, printed from special plates made by the U.S. government. While the war was in progress, and our relations with the USSR more positive, the American government gave the Russians a set of plates, on the assumption that Russia would support the scrip they printed with rubles, as we did with dollars. The GI black-marketeers and gamblers, who accumulated marks from the Russians, had no banks in the U.S. zone to deposit their profits, so they sent the money home through postal orders. That way, Occupation Reichsmarks printed by the United States and the Soviets were exchanged for American dollars.

Eventually American officials recognized that the United States totally underwrote all Reichsmarks. On July 24, the Berlin district postal officer stopped selling postal money orders and war bonds. General Clay, effective at the end of the first week of August, limited the total amount a soldier could send each month by postal order to the States. The transmission by any individual of a sum in excess of his pay, plus

10 percent, was forbidden. Commanding officers verified and certified the transmittals.

Many GIs circumvented these restrictions by having close acquaintances send money orders to the profiteers' families. I sent one to Howy's parents before learning what was going on but later refused. I didn't want to encourage my friend in what the Army defined as racketeering. By November 10, further currency control was initiated, requiring that cash and bank deposits, the net amount of pay drawn in the preceding three months, and the amount of money sent from the ETO be listed in control books issued to each of us. None of these procedures involved me, but they kept Howy busy.

In the weeks between performances of *Cradle Snatchers* and *Room Service,* Christy Vasile invited Rote, Howy, and me to a performance at the Berlin Staatsoper, which was on the Russian side of the Brandenburg Gate. We never asked how Christy obtained the tickets. He took us in a State Department sedan, and one of our official-looking documents, typed on State Department stationery, helped us gain admission to their zone. Through the guarded gate, along almost deserted streets, we drove to an undistinguished, smoke-stained theater where the Staatsoper was performing. Christy claimed he had never seen or heard Tchaikovsky's *Eugene Onegin,* because it was seldom performed by the Metropolitan in New York.

Our arrival in an American Army sedan was conspicuous; other opera-goers, most of them German, came on foot. Inside the theater, we were the only Americans and the only enlisted men sitting in the center section of the orchestra, alongside Russian officers. The majority in the animated audience appeared to be Germans, dressed in their best clothes for the occasion. The balcony tiers above us were filled too, as were two levels of box seats on each side of the proscenium arch. The women in the boxes were more elaborately dressed than the rest of the crowd.

The theater interior was not battle damaged but had a rather seedy elegance, similar to the audience's. A few bulbs in chandeliers were not burning, seat covers were worn, and the gilded decor on the walls and balcony edges was faded and chipped. But after the curtain rose, the opera's radiance warmed the unheated house, subduing our awareness of the unwashed odors and overwhelming us with the music, despite our ignorance of plot and language. From the orchestra's first overture notes, the music stirred tears, and an ache persisted in my throat throughout.

At the operas performed by traveling companies at the Robinson Memorial Auditorium in Little Rock, I had never seen such beautiful costumes and stage settings. The enormous scenic dimensions and the coordination of actions and stage pictures were reminiscent of Busby Berkeley production numbers in 1930s movies. The flawless technical facilities of the three-dimensional settings and silence of scene changes almost diverted me from the nonrealistic opera conventions.

The curtain calls taken by principals after each scene were theatrically romantic. I had seen *LaBoheme* and *Rigoletto* performed by the Metropolitan Opera in Little Rock, and performers hadn't taken such frequent curtain calls. But at the Staatsoper, the singer in the title role came through the break in the grand drape at the end of each scene and bowed to the orchestra leader and audience before walking across the apron to bow deeply to a handsome woman in black in the upper box.

At intermission, we went out to smoke. In the austere lobby, uniformed attendants were selling cold sausages and ersatz coffee. None of us would risk eating the sausages or drinking coffee, even if we were hungry, because they may have been prepared in unsanitary conditions, or we might deprive Germans, whose rations were so small.

Shortly after *Cradle Snatchers* closed, Chet Elliott found a German woman photographer, Liselotte Winterstein, who made portraits of GIs for a reasonable price. Fräulein Winterstein was a studio photographer for the movie industry in Berlin, which was the largest, most powerful film center in Europe before the war. With her professional pretensions, she preferred her subjects meet her in individual sessions of an hour or more, but Chet persuaded her to work with us together. Eager to send pictures to our families, we arranged an evening appointment at her studio and, following her instructions, brought a variety of uniforms for different poses.

Fraulein Winterstein's Foto-Atelier was on the second floor above her flat, at 244 Kronprinzenalle, in the Zehlendorf district. She greeted us, in fluent English, as if we were friends paying a social visit. The short, middle-aged brunette had a deep olive complexion and dark eyes and was wearing slacks and a heavy sweater for warmth in her unheated studio.

The studio was a high-ceilinged loft, decorated in the mode of 1920s Mediterranean architecture, with rough stucco walls, indirect lighting in art-deco metal wall sconces, and ornate wrought-iron benches, chairs, and stools of different heights. The upholstered furnishings—a richly brocaded sofa, love seat, and high-backed armchair—were all props for photo sittings. Large still-cameras, on mobile tripods, were in the room, and a variety of small theatrical lighting instruments hung overhead from a grid.

She asked us to call her Lilo and said she wanted to know something about us personally, which helped her find a setting and approach for our portraits. As she interviewed Chet, Howy, and me, she guided us through her studio, showing the furnishings, equipment, and her laboratory and darkroom. In the lab, the walls were lined with unframed black-and-white portraits of German motion picture actors. We ducked the strips of negatives held by clothespins hanging from a grid of thin wires above our heads.

At the end of our tour, we sat on the cushioned furniture talking until Lilo decided who to photograph first. I sat for three poses in three different uniforms: in a khaki shirt and tie, sideways in a chair, with my legs over one arm and my back against the other; a full-front chest shot in my Eisenhower jacket, with ribbons; and sitting on a bench, a circle of light behind me, in an open-collared wool shirt.

Chet insisted on exchanging pictures with each other for keepsakes, especially his and mine. He wanted the artsy photo, with the halo of light. I sent all three poses to Tumpy and my folks.

Not long after our photography session, Chet invited me to attend a late-afternoon matinee of an American production, *Up in Central Park,* at the Titania Palast. We rode the *unterbahn,* but, since we didn't know the theater's location, we got off too soon. Arriving just before the curtain rose, we found our seats were on the front row, thanks to Chet's connections.

The musical had a nine-month run on Broadway before the company came to Europe to entertain soldiers. For the tour, the producers brought a full orchestra, a strong cast, and elaborate scenery. The large corps de ballet was surprising, as most traveling companies were smaller. The musical score was appealing, but I remember only one line from a duet sung by the romantic leads: "We'll be close as pages in a book, my love and I. So close we can share a single look, share every sigh."

During a dance number, Chet pointed to a tall, muscular, extremely graceful man in the chorus, and said, "You know what he is, don't you?"

I wasn't sure who he referred to until he described the dancer's costume and prominent lips and eyes. Not a soloist, he wasn't doing anything different from the other males in the line, only showing a little more grace in his movements.

"You know he's a homosexual, don't you?" Chet said.

"No. How do you know?" He didn't answer, and I said no more about it.

It was dark and raining lightly when we left the theater. Unfortunately, we hadn't brought our raincoats, and the rain began falling heavily. Signaling the passing American trucks and jeeps for a ride, our waving arms and extended thumbs finally caught the attention of a driver whose cab was already filled with two other soldiers. He stopped and motioned us into his uncovered truck bed, and we jumped aboard. By the time we reached Chet's apartment, we were shivering wet, and he invited me to dry off and have a cup of hot tea before going to my place at the other end of the compound.

Chet then suggested we take hot baths to keep from catching bad colds, and he gave me a pair of his shorts and a T-shirt to wear afterwards. We hung our wet uniforms on his tile stove to dry. After our baths, we sipped cups of tea, with him sitting on his bed and me in a chair tilted back against the side of the stove, where it was warmest.

Chet brought up the show and the young man he said was a homosexual, "At the theater, you asked how I knew about him. Well, I'm sure because I'm that way too."

He moved on the edge of the bed toward me. "How does that strike you?"

Without lowering my chair or moving away, I said, "I don't know, really. I knew some guys at high school and junior college who were supposed to be homosexual, but they never told me they were."

Chet asked, "Did they make a play for you?"

"Maybe so, but I didn't recognize it if they did."

Chet persisted, "How do you feel about men like us?"

"You're different, I guess. I don't feel your way, but I don't want to hurt anyone like you, the way some guys do."

By this time, a flush of blood had rushed to my face. In undershorts and T-shirt, I found the situation more difficult than at the office in Versailles with Mr. Swift. I wasn't cold any longer, just anxious and embarrassed, but I didn't want to offend Chet by grabbing my uniform and racing out of his apartment.

Apparently Chet took my lack of response as a sign to go further, telling me how much he was attracted to me at the first auditions and how he'd wanted to tell me his feelings for a long time. I was shocked when he told me he visited my apartment during the day, when Howy and I were absent, and lay in my bed, imagining us together. Although our apartment doors weren't locked, because we had no keys, I never imagined that anyone, other than my roommates, entered our apartment when I was away.

After confessing, Chet said he hoped we were still friends. I told him nothing had changed, put on my slightly damp uniform, and left.

Back at our apartment, Howy asked about the show and wanted to know where Chet got the tickets. I reviewed the story, musical score, and performers, without revealing what had happened afterwards. I never told anyone in Berlin.

After Chet's revelation, I dated Louise Byrnes every night I was free, in a defiant statement about my own sexual orientation, I guess. Although I didn't think about it at the time, maybe that was my unconscious reason. On a conscious level I enjoyed the company of Louise, who was physically attractive, well educated, musically talented, and entertaining. My chief competitor was a young lieutenant in Political Affairs who pursued her, using his rank to take her places and entertain her in ways I could not. But it was my good fortune that she preferred my company over that of the other men.

The second play of the American Little Theater of Berlin, *Room Service,* was a farcical hit on Broadway in 1937. I played the role of the young playwright, Leo Davis, and Rote joined other newcomers in the cast. After Rote saw how much fun I had in the first play, he read for the role of the producer's big-muscled, small-brained gofer, Faker Englund. Rote's high energy, New Jersey accent, and broken nose fit the role, but his comic sense and line readings clinched the part.

A Soldier Show Production Team from the 6817 Special Services Battalion guided our own Berlin crew preparing costumes, collecting props, and managing the stage. Sold-out performances of *Room Service* provoked wilder laughter in the soldier audience than I had ever experienced before, particularly from lines, movements, and gestures in which the crowd could find a double meaning.

Soon after *Room Service* closed, a Seventh Army Special Services tour played at Onkel Toms. An all-male parody of the opera *Carmen,* the company had its own small orchestra and chorus and a single set to back the action. They retained the main incidents in the libretto and rewrote the principal arias. A tall, thin soldier, with a large nose and long black wig, played Carmen, wearing a flaming red floor-length dress, in a spectacular performance. Without changing the pitch of his voice or using effeminate gestures, he made his songs and behavior considerably funnier.

In the middle of November, I learned that my total points in the Adjusted Service Rating made me eligible to return to the States in December. The total number of points required had dropped steadily since the original 85 or more required for discharge in early fall. My points were 28 for my months in service, 18 for overseas duty, 15 for three battle stars, and 5 for the Purple Heart, a total of 66. I wrote celebratory letters to Tumpy and my folks, saying I'd probably be home by Christmas.

About the time I learned I'd be going home, Lieutenant Byrnes told us the Little Theater was chosen to tour camps with *Cradle Snatchers* and *Room Service.* The "cigarette" camps in the vicinity of Le Havre—named Lucky Strike, Old Gold, Herbert Tareyton, and Twenty Grand—had thousands of soldiers waiting for ships back to the States. Although definite dates for the theater tour weren't set, I obviously couldn't be included if I went home in December. Many roles besides mine had to be recast, because the original actors had already left Berlin or were also sailing home soon.

An engraved invitation from the United States Political Adviser for Germany reached me in late November: "Mr. Robert Murphy requests the pleasure of the company of Corporal Allie Harrison at 19 Specht Strasse, Dahlem, Saturday, November 24, 1945. R.S.V.P. 76–1951. Buffet 8 P.M."

Military and diplomatic officials of the American, British, Russian, and French staffs of the Allied Kommandantura attended the reception and buffet that evening. The presence of enlisted men from Political Affairs may have been a ploy by Murphy to suggest that all ranks of the American Army contributed democratically to the success of military government. The ambassador introduced Howy, Rote, and me to diplomats and attachés of many countries, as if enlisted men were an ordinary part of such occasions in the United States. It was flattering to be invited to eat and drink with high-ranking foreign officials.

A team of Civilian Actress Technicians (CATS) came to Berlin in December to produce a variety show using our Little Theater group. Evelyn Russell directed the overall production, and Bette Larson directed musical numbers and accompanied them on the piano. *Take the Air* was produced as if it were a radio show, featuring comic skits and musical numbers, in which almost every cast member played several roles and sang solos. The show was popular with GI audiences and attracted so many talented soldiers to our troupe that another variety show, *Especially for You,* was organized for patients at the 101st General Hospital in Berlin. I was emcee for the show, which included vocalists, an accordionist, pianists, and the pièce de résistance, a man playing the mandolin, singing, whistling, and beating a tambourine between his knees in the same piece. Nurses and doctors who saw our performance asked us to come back to entertain at the intermission of a weekend dance for medical personnel.

The following week, many doctors, nurses, and medical technicians were drunk. Some sang along with vocalists or instrumentalists, and others laughed and talked loudly among themselves. The drunks heckled during my stand-up routine of one-liners and stories borrowed from professional comics in Army variety shows. I didn't know how to handle hecklers, so I just left the stage. Lieutenant Byrnes, agreeing there was no reason to entertain a bunch of unruly drunks, gathered the company, and we left.

A few days later, my scheduled departure from Berlin was delayed until later in the month or in January. No reason was offered for the cancellation, which was SOP. After my enthusiastic letters telling my folks and Tumpy I was coming home, I hesitated to write them the disappointing news.

My low spirits were raised when Mr. Swift, in the ambassador's office, threw a farewell party for three of us enlisted men in Political Affairs. He let us invite our best friends to the party at his residence.

I picked Rote, Howy, Christy Vasile, and Zach Mitchum. They kidded me about Mr. Swift wanting to seduce me before I left for the States. Although I wasn't threatened, I asked the guys not to leave me alone with him during the evening. At Swift's palatial residence, the Filipino houseboy laid out an elaborate spread of canapes and a great array of alcoholic beverages. Mr. Swift was his usual gregarious self, hospitable to all his guests, but especially solicitous with me.

He told me how impressed he was by my acting performances. He heard me sing in the variety shows, so near the end of the evening, he invited me to join him at the piano in the large drawing room to sing favorite songs. I went along, expecting at least one of my pals to follow, but they had all disappeared, and I was embarrassed to refuse or break away. After playing a song or two, Mr. Swift insisted on my sitting next to him on the bench. He moved closer, playing a romantic piece like "I've Got You Under My Skin."

To my relief, Rote and Howy appeared, saying, "Here you guys are! We wondered what you were up to." They stood behind us as we all sang.

On December 14, the Little Theater group, using the dance floor of Club 48 as a studio, recorded two thirty-minute radio scripts that were to be broadcast on the day before Christmas in the vicinity of New York City only. In a kind of swan song in the theater group, I played a comic devil, Lucifer Beelzebub, who took a Scrooge-like attitude toward Christmas and what the holiday represents.

A poem I wrote about the previous Christmas, during the Battle of the Bulge, which Rote showed to the *Grooper* editor, was published as an editorial in the Christmas edition of December 22. The poem may have expressed the sentiments and hopes of many Allies and Germans who fought before, during, and after the Bulge.

The year 1944, the 25th December.
Remember?
God be with us if you forget quickly—
You who starved, fought, and froze that day.
Christmas colors were the same:
Red and white,

Our blood on snow,
Shadowed by the green of German firs.
It was a prayerful Christmas.
Prayers not for gifts—
Our gifts were wrapped in steel shells.
Our Yuletide decorations—
Strings of scarlet machine gun tracers,
Stars of silver-flame phosphorus.
We prayed for ourselves that day
And in the interminable days that followed.
Our prayers, like those of all soldiers
clasping hands with death,
Were not in patriotic fervor for a nation.
We prayed to Christ, the greatest of all Gifts,
For our lives.

The year 1945, the 25th December.
Today.
Christmas in peace, Christmas again in
Germany.
A day still echoing prayers
From that day a year ago—
Unselfish now, not for ourselves alone.
Our Father,
Clasp our hands and lead us, Thy children.
Lead us to the light of world peace.
Let us bathe in it that we,
The followers and leaders,
May know the formula.
Give us strength to make Thy plan work.
Give us courage to walk head-up
Against the evil forces
Striving to envelop and destroy this world.
Give us wisdom to distinguish those
who would make peace a living force
From those who would use the peoples
of the world.
Greatest of all, give us faith to do Thy will.
Amen.

After a Christmas Eve party at Lenore Babbit's house, she, Zach, Dusty, Anna Mary, Louise, and I put on our heavy coats and walked through the snow to a nearby Lutheran Church to attend the midnight Christmas service. The church, lit by candles, had no heat of any kind, and the minister conducted the service in German. In the loft at the rear of the sanctuary, the organ and choir played and sang traditional Christmas songs, as each of us worshipped privately, in his or her own thoughts. I was thankful to be alive, to have recovered from my wounds, to have worked and played with persons I liked so much, and to be heading home.

I missed Rote and Zach. The foreign service officers, Fred and Jo Mann, checked out a weapons carrier from the motor pool and took the Catholic boys in Political Affairs to midnight mass. The mass was said by a bishop from Chicago who had chosen to be with the soldiers at Christmas.

The same group, this time including Rote and Zach, gathered again at Eleanor's and Dusty's house on New Year's Eve, this time to celebrate with drinks and camaraderie. For me, the party was a farewell not only to the old year but to Berlin and Europe as well. I would be leaving for a port of embarkation on January 7, 1946.

I made a last visit to the theater at Onkel Toms Hutte to say goodbye to Lieutenant Byrnes and the theater group. Reggie Pasch embraced me emotionally, handing me letters of introduction, written in German, to introduce me to his Hollywood friends and colleagues, William Dieterle and Ernst Lubitsch. He also gave me a large watercolor of a boat sailing on Wannsee Lake, done by a painter friend of his. Close to tears, he insisted no one in the company had treated him with such respect and kindness and that the theater group would never be the same without me. I thanked him for his friendship and professional advice.

Chet Elliott visited me at my apartment before I left, saying how much he would miss me, and tried to persuade me to join him in New York City to go on the professional stage. I told him my plans to marry and go to college first, and then consider a stage career after I finished. He promised to keep in touch, letting me know how his career in New York developed.

When I kissed the girls goodbye at the office, Louise, Anna Mary, and Dodo each gave me pictures to remember them by. After bidding farewell to all the State Department officers I had worked with, I closed the door on my last official Army assignment.

Returning Veteran

Little Rock, Arkansas

January 7–February 16, 1946

On the gray, frigid Monday afternoon of January 7, while I was packing to leave Berlin, Rote was preparing for a furlough with Howy, hitchhiking on Army vehicles to Switzerland. Rote helped me carry my duffel and smaller bag down to the truck. We chatted until the sergeant bellowed, "Saddle up, you're moving out!" Rote and I shook hands, urging the other to keep in touch by writing. He told me later that as I boarded the truck, he walked back into our billet with "a grenade-size lump" in his throat and watched me depart from his front window upstairs. Mother Leshak accompanied me to the train station.

Before leaving the apartment, I inserted Reginald Pasch's gift, the Wannsee Lake watercolor, in a cardboard tube for Howy to mail to me. Carrying the watercolor on the train and ship would be awkward, and I trusted Howy to send it because he'd remain in Berlin for a few more months before going home.

Threatening to snow, the cloudy afternoon was so severely cold that I wore my wool Army topcoat and gloves, even though I had usually avoided them in Berlin's clammy, intensely cold mist. But I was too excited about leaving for home for a heavy overcoat to hamper my movements. I didn't notice the stiffness.

My single duffel held everything I owned except my sleeping bag. I hadn't collected loot like so many soldiers. In the devastated cities I'd lived in, there were no souvenirs I wanted badly enough to carry home, especially foreign weapons, which many GIs were smuggling home against Army regulations. There were a few men on the train platform carrying a few pieces of luggage like me, but others were struggling with lots of bags and boxes of different sizes. They appeared to have goods enough to open curio shops back in the States.

We boarded the train's passenger coach without any idea of where we were going, only that we were heading west. For once, ignorance of my next destination didn't annoy me. All of us soldiers in our car appeared to have one thing in common, a sense of relief and happiness to be heading home, even though we didn't know how long it would take. Doris Day's hit song, which I had heard dozens of times a day over the American Forces Network, drifted into my mind: "Gonna take a sentimental journey, gonna set my heart at ease." The melody played by Les Brown's Band of Renown echoed in my head as the locomotive jerked the train to a start, and I waved goodbye through the frost-fogged window to Leshak.

The train chugged slowly through bleak ruins in parts of Berlin I'd never seen before, allowing a reflective farewell to the gray metropolis and the American zone, all totally surrounded by Russians. The sunless afternoon darkened as the train crawled through the forlorn outskirts into the countryside, and the scenes passing the car windows faded from sight.

Unable to watch anything more outside the window, I settled down in the cozy warmth of the car, talking about Berlin, the Army, and going home to the strangers in the seats opposite and beside me. Among the congenial fellows was Pat Smith, the son of the president of the American Container Company in New York City, who had been in Berlin for the same length of time I was. He recounted short stories he'd been writing and how much he wanted to be a playwright or novelist. I shared my theatrical ambitions with him, and we talked and smoked late into the night. The train plowed across and out of the Russian zone after we fell asleep, sitting up, thinking we'd wake at the port of embarkation.

In the British zone, the metronomic clacking on the track slowed down and waked us. The train stopped, probably at Goslar, and we heard shouts and a whistle. To our surprise and dismay, an NCO came into the coach and ordered us to grab all our luggage and get off. Standing in the dark beside the train, watching the vapor of our breath condensing in the frosty morning air, we asked each other, "What the hell is going on now?" We got the shocking answer: we were boarding boxcars for the trip through the British and American zones. The NCO in charge of our transfer said the standard-gauge tracks from Berlin had ended, and the train out of Goslar would be on narrow gauge. Although no one liked the change, we were so eager to reach our mysterious destination in the American zone that by Army standards we didn't bitch very much.

The old boxcars we climbed into were stripped. There were no heaters to warm us, no seats to sit on, no bunks to sleep in, and no toilet facilities. A thick bed of straw covering the floor was the only comfort. These travel facilities were no better than the ones we had during the fighting, except that now we had plenty of space to lie down and stretch out. This primitive transport, roomy as it was, was a lousy way to treat soldiers in a victorious Army who were heading home!

There was nothing we could do about the situation, so we didn't waste time complaining. Instead, half a dozen of us, seeking a way to bed down comfortably and warmly, pushed the unbroken bales of straw against the forward walls of the box car to cover the largest cracks and cushion our backs while we huddled side by side. We had all ridden boxcars before, but we still assumed that the front section of the car away from the doors was less drafty.

Even though we were strangers to each other, we lay close together in our overcoats as the train crossed toward western Germany. We still weren't warm enough. So we pulled our sleeping bags out and slipped into them, hoping we might hold enough body heat to make the trip to our next stop bearable.

We slept fitfully for the rest of a very long night before a dim sunrise pierced the cracks in the walls of our car. Lying around, half-in and half-out of our sleeping bags, we ate the K rations we'd been given the night before. To entertain ourselves the next day, we opened the boxcar doors and sat with our legs hanging out, watching what seemed like the entire countryside of the American zone of Germany.

After dark our train slowed, and we heard shouts up ahead alongside the cars that convinced us we'd reached our destination. Leaning out the open car door to check where we were and what was happening, I saw GIs and duffel bags tumbling from the boxcars in front of ours. A sergeant stopped beside our car and told us to grab our luggage and fall in beside the railroad tracks.

The locomotive had stopped beside a small railway station that had a few bare bulbs sparkling along its narrow platform. At the top of a high hill behind the station, I saw a few more strings of tiny lights. Waiting for someone to lead us away, I also made out in the dim moonlight that the twinkling lights at the top of the hill outlined the roof of a towering castle. To get to the castle's ramparts, we climbed up a narrow, steep path until we reached the heavy wooden doors at the front and gathered inside a high-ceilinged entryway.

Another sergeant greeted us and checked our names off his list. We followed him up a wide staircase that led to the several floors above. On the second landing, he stopped outside a room fifty feet square divided by several sections of low partitions. In the sections were canvas cots, most with men sleeping on them.

The sergeant said, "Take any empty bed you find and settle in for the night. If there are no vacant cots, try the next floor."

I found an empty cot against a wall below a high window. After only catnaps on the train for two days and nights, I slept soundly.

A clanging bell jarred us awake the next morning, and I followed men who seemed to know where they were going. They led me to a primitive washroom and latrine on our floor, just off the stairwell, where I washed and shaved with cold water, which was all there was. Then, with my mess kit in hand, I walked down to the basement. The long breakfast line stretched the full length of the wall next to the kitchen and mess hall.

While talking with GIs who had been at the castle for a few days,

I noticed that the wall we were leaning against had a row of cast-iron doors about as high as our chests off the floor, which extended all the way to the kitchen, where they were serving. Flipping the latch, I opened one of the doors and exposed a long, cylindrical oven, its deep grate about the length of an average man's height. My nearest mates said they'd been told these were furnaces to cremate political prisoners and euthanasia victims, before and during the war.

What an irony that our way station to a seaport turned out to be the castle at Hadamar, which had been an infamous asylum, jail, and slaughterhouse throughout the Nazi reign. In the early years of the Third Reich, the Nazis used the castle as a euthanasia center for persons of all ages who were allegedly feebleminded or insane, for the state didn't want to keep anyone alive who might corrupt pure Aryan genetics or fail to serve their purposes. At other times, the castle was a POW camp for officers and later a prison for POWs of any rank who escaped repeatedly. Near the war's end, the castle was once more an asylum for the insane. When the Nazi staff learned that an Allied army was advancing toward them, they turned the inmates loose in the countryside in freezing weather without proper clothing or caretakers. The staff doctors, nurses, and guards fled, escaping farther east into Germany.

Everyone I met at Hadamar was a stranger, even though many had served in Berlin at the same time I did. Soldiers, like me, being sent home separate from any organization had to be redeployed as members of a specific unit. The sergeant in charge called us individuals from Berlin "filler replacements" and assigned us to a tank destroyer (TD) battalion that had already gathered at Hadamar. The TD's regular members served together throughout the war and were going back to the States, where their unit would be disbanded and placed on the inactive list.

I spent a week killing time at Hadamar as a member of the tank destroyer battalion, which was more boring for me than for the regulars, who shared old times while playing cards or gambling. Neither pastime appealed to me, and writing letters home seemed redundant;

I assumed I would be back in Arkansas within a few weeks. It was too cold to explore the countryside comfortably, so I stayed inside reading Victory paperbacks, taking regular naps, and discussing plays and playwriting with Pat Smith.

After months of clerking in the message center and acting in theater productions, I was gripped by a kind of indolence at Hadamar. Although eager to leave and be on the way home, I sensed no urgency about getting there. But the day the sergeant announced that we were leaving the next morning for Bremerhaven to board a ship, I was relieved and eager to move again.

After breakfast, we packed our bags and walked down the steep path from the castle to the small train station. Expecting this leg of the trip to be as cold as the last, I wore long underwear, every wool item in my uniform, my old combat boots, and my overcoat. I carried my sleeping bag and duffel bag, which contained slacks, a pair of brogans, changes of underwear and socks, my raincoat, mess kit, and canteen cup. Walking down the hill, some fellows in the tank destroyer unit, like soldiers on the platform in Berlin, were loaded with souvenirs from the war. My mementos had no weight or awkward shapes because they were in my mind.

I suppose they had to transport us in boxcars because of the number of men the Army was sending to European ports at one time for shipment home. At least that's how I excused them for making me ride in another boxcar from Hadamar to Bremerhaven. The journey was considerably shorter than the one from Berlin, but we rode back into the British zone to reach the Bremen Enclave, which was U.S. territory.

At Bremerhaven, we received the disappointing news that we wouldn't be sailing right away but would be waiting for a ship. Our tank destroyer unit was joining the large contingent of men already on hand, bunking in a spacious barracks building near the docks. The well-furnished barracks and dock facilities had been a training station for German sailors, and the Allies had captured the naval complex intact, without attempting to destroy it.

The architectural arrangement of the barracks was unusual: a high-ceilinged lounge was set between adjoining dormitory barracks on each of its sides. Another oddity was the placement of windows in the walls of the bedrooms on both sides of the dormitory halls. Solid up to the height of a wainscot, the upper two-thirds of the walls were filled with glass panes, like those in window sashes, up to the ceiling. Although windows robbed the dorm rooms of privacy, the sleeping quarters were well lighted on overcast days.

Along with Pat Smith, I was assigned to one of the small bedrooms, which held three others, including Corporal Olson from Wisconsin and a master sergeant from New York City. Smith, Olson, and I were congenial, but the big, hairy master sergeant (whom I called Sergeant Grouch, in my mind) was garrulous, gruff, and profane. He monopolized everyone's time by telling incongruous stories about his fighting in the war or sailing in peacetime on Sheepshead Bay near his home in Flatbush. By an odd coincidence, Corporal Olson also owned a boat and sailed it on Lake Michigan. I suppose having that in common induced the NCOs liking for each other because their personalities were such opposites.

To escape their running conversation about boats and to enjoy the hot coffee, fresh doughnuts, and comfortable space in the lounge, Pat and I spent a lot of time on easy chairs and sofas talking about theater and books. But if an interesting conversation developed between GIs near us, we eavesdropped because Pat was trying to capture a sense of the rhythms of conversational speech for his playwriting, and he wrote what he heard in shorthand. Later he expanded his notes into dialogues and read the give-and-take to me, so we could study the characteristics of ordinary speech.

One night, we were so bored with the same routine that Smith, Olson, and I wandered over to the German naval training facilities at the edge of the pier. There, inside a multistoried building, the Germans had built mock-ups for training of the main parts of a ship's bridge, engine room, and gun emplacements. Like rambunctious boys, we played sailors, sliding down brass poles from one deck to another, ducking up and down the narrow companionways, and twirling the wheeled handles of the bulkhead doors, locking and unlocking them.

Before returning to the warm comfort of the barracks, we stood on the cold, windy deck of the fake bridge, enjoying the brisk salt air and watching the cresting waves of the North Sea, part of our watery pathway home.

On January 29, 1946, an icy wind was blowing off the heavy swells of the North Sea as we boarded a Liberty ship to cross the stormy North Atlantic. The vessel was obviously built for cargoes of inanimate materials, not men. Standing on the pier looking up at the *Aiken Victory,* I realized that, though larger than any of the three ships that previously carried me across the English Channel, she seemed much too small, compared to the *Queen Elizabeth,* to sail thousands of miles safely across the Atlantic during the winter storm season. The mighty passenger ship had carried us on a placid summer sea, with only the threat of the slower German submarines.

While standing on the pier watching the high North Sea swells surging strongly toward me, I sensed their virtual movement up to and over me. Others with the same sensation feared they would get seasick. Having never been sick at sea and unaware of the early symptoms, I didn't worry.

The usual group of Red Cross workers were gathered on opposite sides at the foot of the gangway handing out goodies as we boarded the ship. A surprise among them was Ruth Opp, who with Patty Kelly had accompanied Marugo, Pulaski, and me to Hampton Court outside London in April of the previous year. In our brief moment, Ruth claimed she remembered our tour and gave me extra cigarettes for old times' sake.

Our single file crossed the top deck of the ship to a hatchway and descended narrow steps down to the number three hold, a low-ceilinged compartment lighted primarily by red and white emergency lamps. The dark hold was crammed from one bulkhead to the other with tiers of small canvas hammocks, tightly suspended on pipe frames, one above the other, with only about two feet between them. The narrow vertical space separating the hammocks made sitting upright impossible.

After we chose our bunks, the sergeant came down and forced everyone to take motion sickness pills, threatening to keep us below decks before sailing if we didn't swallow them. I told the sergeant I really didn't need any medication because I hadn't been sick on previous trips at sea, but he insisted. With the pills down, I hurried out of the smelly dark hold into the fresh air on deck to watch the crews on the pier and deck weighing anchor and getting the ship under way.

The North Sea on our way to the Atlantic churned and roiled around the ship's hull, even before we reached the choppy English Channel. When I felt slightly queasy, I went forward on deck to stand in the freshening breeze, hoping I would recover while looking across the fore deck in the direction we were sailing. But seeing the leaden waves rolling up higher and feeling them slapping against the ship's prow, each oncoming wave furling higher than the one before, stirred up my stomach, and bile rose in my throat. The choppy seas and the ship's rocking motion as it plowed into the open waters overwhelmed my sight and balance, making me sick at my stomach.

By the time I entered the head (latrine) on the main deck, I was shivering with nausea and had to run to the nearest basin. Dozens of men had beaten me to the head and were vomiting in the urinals and commodes and on the floor. After some relief, I still felt so sick in the pit of my stomach that I was afraid to leave, so I remained standing beside a basin holding onto the metal wall rail as more sick men came in.

Soon the sounds of gagging and the odor of vomit were so overwhelming that I decided I would be better off going below to lie down and recuperate. When I let go of the rail, the ship suddenly rose and struck the water a hammer blow, knocking me totally off balance. Sprawling on my elbow and one knee, I skidded in slick vomit across the deck and slammed into the bulkhead. I decided I would never be physically clean again, only to discover that the ship's evaporators couldn't supply sufficient fresh water for normal needs, and the showers and washbasins ran seawater. The special soap supplied by the Navy wouldn't lather in salt water either.

From the late afternoon of the first day on the *Aiken Victory,* I lay in my bunk for four days while the ship rolled, dived, and wallowed in one Atlantic storm after another. I was afraid that if I stood up I would throw up. Fortunately, I never fouled my canvas nest but reached the head in time to subdue my dry convulsions. There was one good outcome from my *mal de mer*; I didn't want to smoke.

Olson bunked next to me and insisted from the beginning that I go to the galley each morning because he said my nausea would end sooner if I ate part of every meal. With Olson's encouragement, I weakly rolled off my hammock each morning and climbed the stairs for breakfast in the galley. But before I could reach the steam table, the aromas of food wafting from the kitchen set my stomach roiling again. When I wanted to run back to my bunk, Oley would push me and my tray in front of him farther down the line, putting food on it at every stop. But before we came to the end of the line, I pulled out of his grasp and hurried back to my bunk.

The ship's motion must have stimulated Olson's appetite; at any rate, I suspect he was eating both our meals. Still, he led me to the galley every day, and after I escaped to my bunk brought me hard-boiled eggs, encouraging me to peel and eat them to get well. Gradually, the eggs did stay down; I had recovered. One morning, I awoke with an appetite, eager to go to the galley even though the ship still bucked and rolled. Despite my eager willingness to die, I had survived *mal de mer.*

My challenge in the galley during boisterous weather was no longer physical health but manual dexterity—keeping my tray on the table, food on the tray, and a drink in my hand, all at the same time. The ship's deep rolls and shudders sent everything that wasn't held down skittering across or along the length of the tables onto the deck. In fact, keeping one's seat on the bench beside the table was chancy if the ship wallowed, reared up at a steep angle, and slapped the water coming down.

Fortunately, my nausea had disappeared because the violent waters in the North Atlantic didn't. Thunderstorms came in series, the winds making the seas rise so powerfully high that our ship, riding the peaks of mountainous waves, crashed into the precipitous troughs that formed under them, sending deep shudders and creaks from one end of the vessel to the other. The tumultuous ocean waters and the blinding sheets of slashing rain caused the ship's captain to order GIs to stay below off the deck during squalls. Crew members had strung hemp lines across the decks and held onto them while crossing between hatchways. Without the ropes, some crew members would surely have been carried overboard by the waves. At the end of one storm, the voice on the PA announced that if the ship had keeled over a few more degrees at the height of the gale, it would have capsized.

There was no formal recreation on the ship, but soon after the voyage began, a ship's newspaper *My Aiken Back* rolled off the mimeograph machines and was distributed to everyone on board. These news sheets appeared to be a common amenity aboard a military ship, for the *Queen Elizabeth* had one too. I think members of the regular crew must have organized and produced the paper with the assistance of the troops en route home. *My Aiken Back* had general information about shipboard routines that we were to observe, schedules of daily events, unusual stories about soldiers on board, announcements of shipboard entertainments, and risqué jokes.

After the sea quieted a bit, the crew showed moving pictures in one of the deepest, almost empty cargo holds of the ship. I went one night to see *The House on 92nd Street,* a suspense movie about wartime espionage. The projector was mounted on packing cases, and the screen was a sheet of canvas attached to a bulkhead. The audience members sat on top of the loaded crates and boxes of supplies that were scattered across the hold.

The most memorable movie was a short subject featuring Jack Benny and his troupe of Hollywood performers. The film had been shot on a tour of the China-Burma-India (CBI) theater of operations. King Farouk of Egypt entertained Benny and his troupe in Cairo with a company of buxom belly dancers. The soldier photographer captured not only the belly dancers but Benny's wide-eyed reactions to them. Our raunchy audience whooped and hollered at the muscular gyrations of the overweight ladies and at Benny's hand movements and facial expressions. We were loud enough to drown out the creaking and thundering of the ship's hull.

Not long after I recovered from seasickness, Sergeant Grouch put me on KP. I hauled supplies from frozen food lockers, rearranged foodstuffs in the wire-cage pantries, and emptied garbage over the ship's side after meals. In the first two duties, KPs had the privilege of eating as many ice cream bars as they wanted because the supply was insufficient for general distribution. My third duty offered no such reward, only an accidental penalty if it were not performed correctly. In discarding garbage, the cook's helper instructed me to check wind direction before tossing the bucket's contents over the ship's side. If it was mistakenly thrown into the wind, the slop plastered the garbage man and the deck.

After two rough weeks at sea, the *Aiken Victory* stood off the U.S. coast the night of February 12, 1946. We gathered on the cold deck to look at the brilliant lights of New York, silently sharing our awe not only of the luminous skyline but of being back home.

All of us stood silently, except Sergeant Grouch, who pointed ashore, repeating, "If I had a dinghy, I could row across Sheepshead Bay and be home in an hour."

We docked early the next morning and rode a train to Camp Kilmer, New Jersey. I was there a day or two before boarding a special Army car to Jefferson Barracks, Missouri, to be discharged.

The chair car I rode from New Jersey to Missouri had been converted to a sleeper for troops by adding rigid wooden bunks above the seats. I remember, as we traveled south, lying in the upper bunk at night, alternately sleeping and waking, listening to the clacking of the wheels on the rails, the clanging of crossing bells, and the rumble and swoosh of passing trains, and feeling the tug of times of the recent past pulling against thoughts of tomorrow.

The train trip took the better part of two days before arriving on the evening of February 16 at the Separation Center at Jefferson Barracks, Missouri. Although the train reached the center after 1700, we were assigned to a barracks and had a meal in the mess before reporting to a large hall.

The room was filled with clerks seated behind small tables with typewriters in front of them completing discharge forms for soldiers, who were instantly replaced by others from the crowded waiting lines. The loud clatter of typewriters and the gabble of voices filling the room made me wonder, as I took my seat, if the clerk would be able to hear my answers to his questions. My clerk-typist's weary manner and disinterested appearance led me to ask him what his status was. He had been recently drafted and confessed his torture in helping us get out while he still had his time in service to fulfill.

In answering the barrage of questions, I said that I had no wish to serve in the Army Reserve or to apply to the Veterans Administration for a disability pension, but I did want to continue my National Service Life Insurance. The clerk told me I could choose the military unit I had served in that I preferred to have on the face of my discharge certificate. I chose the infantry. Although I had enjoyed my duties and friends in military government for almost as long, serving with the men of Company B in the 301st Infantry Regiment was not only my most climactic wartime experience but the one of which I was proudest. After completing and signing the forms, it was so late that I went to the barracks for a good night's sleep in the upper bunk I was assigned. I fell asleep thinking of the next day.

Two memories remain of my last day in the Army at Jefferson Barracks, one personal and the other official. The next morning, February 17, the first drill was to turn in all of my Army clothing except the uniform I would wear home. After relinquishing my overcoat, cotton khakis, and other extras at the supply room, I kept my best pair of slacks, my favorite khaki shirt, the Eisenhower jacket, wool garrison cap, and barracks bag. Officially, the supply sergeant should have let us keep two khaki shirts, a pair of khaki trousers, both wool and cotton garrison caps, and the wool overcoat, but he seemed arbitrary and ill-tempered.

Back in the barracks, I put on the uniform and lay down to wait for the discharge ceremony. When the call came, I leaped from the edge of the top bunk to the floor without remembering that the barracks floor had been heavily oiled that morning. The hobnails on the soles of my brogans slipped on the oil, and I sprawled on the floor. My best slacks were so badly stained that I had to replace them.

The supply sergeant was impatient with my clumsiness and wouldn't allow me to search for the pants I had turned in less than an hour before. Instead, he thrust upon me a pair of brown slacks made from wool blanket material, which had no crease and wouldn't hold one. He insisted that was the best he could do. I appealed, reminding him that this was the only military uniform I had after my service and how much I wanted to look sharp going home. But he had no sympathy and wouldn't change his mind. Time ran out, and I had to run to reach the discharge ceremony promptly. After our two years apart, my parents would see me in a rumpled uniform.

The discharge ceremony was in a small auditorium that seated about two hundred men. The presiding officer congratulated us for service to our country and handed out discharge papers, mustering-out pay, and an honorable service lapel button, or "ruptured duck." We also received a printed letter from President Harry S Truman:

ALLIE C. HARRISON

To you who answered the call of your country and served in its Armed Forces to bring about the total defeat of the enemy, I extend the heartfelt thanks of a grateful Nation. As one of the Nation's finest, you undertook the most severe task one can be called upon to perform. Because you demonstrated the fortitude, resourcefulness and calm judgment necessary to carry out that task, we now look to you for leadership and example in further exalting our country in peace.

THE WHITE HOUSE
Harry S Truman

I took a train from Jefferson Barracks to Saint Louis and waited for another train in the gargantuan station, which must have had a hundred water closets or booths in the toilet. I boarded a Missouri Pacific train in the late afternoon.

We arrived at Union Station in Little Rock at midnight on February 17. The place was quieter than it was the time I was there when my group left for basic training at Fort Benning. Only a few servicemen had ridden in the chair car with me from Saint Louis, and none of them left the train, which was headed to Houston. With my duffel over my shoulder, I climbed the steep metal stairs to the huge platform high above the tracks.

Mother and Dad were waiting at the top of the steps. My mom hugged me so tight that she knocked her hat askew. Even at that late hour, she had to wear something on her head. Dad, standing as slender and erect as any soldier, smiled and shook my hand. They were the only ones to meet me because Tumpy, after graduating from the University of Arkansas, was working at Woodward and Lothrop's Department Store in Washington, D.C.

Dad drove us the short distance home in his old blue Chevy. He and Mother sat up front, and I scrounged up beside my duffel bag in the sample case area behind the seat, just as I had as a boy growing up.

Dad parked in the backyard at 322 Spring, and we entered the screened back porch, passing through the kitchen and dining room to the living room. I could have walked through those rooms blindfolded without stumbling over anything. Every piece of furniture was located precisely where it was when I left three years before. And the questions the folks were asking and observations they were making were the same. Perhaps the only real changes were in me—three years older chronologically and an untold number of years psychologically.

The soldier's life for me was at an end, and I could honestly claim, "I have fought the good fight, I have finished the race, I have kept the faith."

Afterword

College Student, Head of Family, and University Professor

1946–1991

My neglect of the letters I wrote during the war forced me to draw principally upon my memory in these recollections. My mother had saved my letters to her and my father, in chronological order, in the bottom drawer of her secretary. Tumpy kept hers, too, but after graduating from college in 1945 and moving to Washington, D.C., she left my letters in a small overnight case in the basement of the Pi Beta Phi Annex at Fayetteville. We forgot about both sets of letters for years, remembering them again when Mother died in 1981, leaving only a handful in her secretary drawer. Tumpy's collection had been thrown away by the new owner of the Pi Phi Annex.

Two months after my discharge, the Army sent a package to my parents' home. The small box contained fragments of personal items I had packed at Wehingen before the attack on Orscholz: an old leather wallet—empty except for an ID card—a pocket-size New Testament, a broken fountain pen, a leather wristband and the innards of a broken wristwatch, a letter from my mother, a Maltese cross medallion, and the bowl of a stemless pipe.

The hunter's knife, with spoon and fork attachments, which Dad's furniture dealer friend sent me, was missing, as were other valuable belongings I left behind. Wondering why the Army bothered to return such useless trivialities led me also to ponder the nature of GIs who would raid the personal belongings of soldiers who might be dead, wounded, captured, or missing in action.

Such losses were inconsequential. It was the farewells to soldier-friends that concerned me, for goodbyes in wartime are frequent and often final, which proved true with almost all my acquaintances and the friends described in these remembrances.

I have had contact with only two men who shared ASTP basic training at Fort Benning and pre-engineering at the University of Mississippi with me. Ernest Enochs, now retired and living in Houston, Texas, was a runner in Company A, 301st Infantry, and was taken prisoner at Orscholz on the day I was wounded.

My closest buddy from Arkansas, Adam B. Robinson, was discharged before I returned from Europe. He had become a forward observer with the 428th Armored Field Artillery Battalion, was in Hawaii and the Philippines until the war ended, and had lots of experiences but no fighting. Soon after getting home, I called him and he invited me to visit him in Pine Bluff. I accompanied my father, a hardware-appliance salesman, when he drove there to call on several of his accounts. Robbie had married Betty Fox and headed Ralph Robinson and Son, Funeral Service, which he owns to this day.

Except for a postcard from a former Ninety-fourth member, attempting to organize a division reunion in 1947, I lost touch with the men of Company B. I knew nothing of the outcome at Orscholz, or how it affected our company, until Captain Straub's letter appeared in the *94th Infantry Commemorative History, 1950–1989*. The letter, dated January 15, 1946, described his and Lieutenant Sundheimer's several escapes from German prison camps, reported the names of company members confirmed dead and named the men he had heard from after returning to the States.

The captain, Sundheimer, Palma, Boguski, and many others in Company B who were captured at Orscholz spent four months as

POWs before being freed. He knew my whereabouts and activities: "Harrison is in Berlin putting on some good shows."

Ironically, Captain Straub survived combat and imprisonment only to be killed in May 1947 in an accident in the heavy moving and rigging business in Michigan.

I met only one person from Company B face to face after the war. In the spring of 1948, walking across the Ohio State University campus in Columbus, I saw a young man coming toward me who looked familiar. It was George Holbrook, who led me and others through the minefield at Orscholz. He was one of the twenty-two thousand students at OSU. In our brief conversation, George was as cool and laconic as he was the night of our escape. Although I remained at OSU for another three years, I never saw him again.

Long after the war, I learned from a high school classmate that he had studied theater with Anthony Palma at the University of Southern California. When Palma joined the Ninety-fourth Division Association years later, his address appeared in the 301st Infantry's *Hoodlum News,* and I wrote him. He revealed in his reply that he assumed I died at Orscholz. Today, he is a playwright, living with his family in Granada Hills, California.

Locating Palma encouraged me to write Howard Davis, Morris Berry, Charles Schuette, and Joe Boguski. First to respond was Shirley Boguski, from South Plainfield, New Jersey, who married Joe in 1948. She described their son and daughter and Joe's career as a letter carrier for the U.S. Postal Service, before revealing he had committed suicide in 1977. Joe's taciturnity made him "hold everything in," so Mrs. Boguski had learned little after their marriage of his life in the Army or as a POW.

Of my other three comrades, one was lost, another dead, and one retired. My letter to Shootie, who shared the outpost with me in France, returned after being forwarded to another address, where someone added a new address, before the letter came back marked "Addressee Unknown—Return to Sender."

Howard Davis died of lung cancer in May 1988, after retiring from the Defense Construction Supply Center in Columbus, Ohio. His widow, Betty R. Davis, wrote, "When you were getting your degrees in 1949 and 1951, Howard lived at 57 East 8th Avenue which is in walking distance of Ohio State. If you had known this, you could have talked over old times."

After finding Morris Berry's address in the *Hoodlum News,* I inquired about company members whose whereabouts he may have known. Morris had worked in Indianapolis for forty years before retiring and moving to Seymour, Indiana, to take care of his mother. He claimed that only ten Company B enlisted men were left after Orscholz and that in rebuilding the company, they were offered NCO ratings, the battalion executive officer even hinting at commissions. Morris, after serving behind the front lines, wasn't confident that riflemen would trust him and declined the promotion.

Morris had remained in touch with Arthur Shocksnyder, who revealed how Sergeant Kelly was killed. Long after the Orscholz debacle, Shock and Kelly ran toward a barn to escape artillery fire; Shock made it safely inside, but Kelly was hit in the back of his head as he reached the barn door. For someone who seldom ran for cover in France, when the rest of us did, the circumstances of Kelly's death seemed to reinforce the superstition of "a bullet that has your number on it."

After Company B was all but wiped out at Orscholz, Shock took command of the Second Platoon; six weeks later, he received a battlefield commission as second lieutenant. He was recommended for the Silver Star before the war ended, without his knowledge, but didn't receive the award until the medal was bestowed at special ceremonies forty years later.

Howard Spiegel—my roommate in Versailles, Frankfurt, and Berlin—never wrote or sent Reginald Pasch's watercolor. I have never had any further contact with him. But Frank Rotondo, my "Completely Confused" partner, wrote soon after I returned to the States, describing his and Howy's furlough in Switzerland and saying that he was going to Fordham University. I didn't have Frank's address, so I asked the post office to forward my letter to his dormitory at Fordham, but it was returned, marked "Addressee Unknown."

Much later I learned Rote was discharged in June 1946 and attended Fordham for a year before quitting to take a job in newspaper advertising. Later, he joined his father in the liquor business that he now owns near Scotch Plains, New Jersey. By the strangest coincidence, Frank Rotondo and Joe Boguski, my closest friends at different times, were in the same high school graduating class in New Jersey.

Chet Elliott, from the Little Theater group in Berlin, kept in touch after he moved to New York City. He auditioned for Broadway plays and took theater classes, appearing regularly in a series of Public Library play productions. He won a major role and toured in Diane Barrymore's company of Maxwell Anderson's play *Joan of Lorraine.* Afterwards, Chet became the coordinator for civic opera productions in his hometown.

My separations from these men were no more planned than our accidental partnerships in our Army assignments. But like them, I made no serious effort to correspond after the war, once obstacles stood in the way. But time has not weakened my warm regard for my old comrades.

After I returned to the loving embrace of my mother and father, we became reacquainted as adults. I checked out familiar places and old friends while waiting for Tumpy's and my wedding. We were married by her paternal uncle, Reverend John Hoover, on June 22, 1946, in the Methodist Parsonage at Malvern, Arkansas. After our honeymoon, we lived in Little Rock, where I returned to college and adjusted to marriage and civilian life in the familiar environs of our hometown.

Under Public Law 346, I completed my sophomore year at the junior college while waiting to see if Harvard, New York University, or the Ohio State University would allow me to transfer. I was accepted by all, as an advanced undergraduate, but their letters warned that living conditions for married students were so crowded that I should delay registering until assured of a place to live. Tumpy was teaching freshman English at the junior college, and told Elizabeth Hardin, a colleague in speech, about our dilemma. Liz's aunt in Columbus knew a place we could rent. With that assurance, I enrolled at OSU.

Beset, in the meantime, by physical and psychological problems, I filed a claim with the Veteran's Administration, and physicians decided my "nervousness, and muscle injuries of the left forearm and hand, left thigh, left leg, and right leg" were permanent service-connected disabilities, which made me eligible for college education under Public Law 16. To qualify, though, I had to take a battery of exams to determine an appropriate educational objective for my intelligence and talents.

I wanted to teach theater, but the VA manuals listed no such objective. The VA counselors didn't know how to reconcile my personal objective with their official categories until I scored high on the Ohio State Psychological and the Cooperative English Examinations. They set my objective as "college professor—English," assuming that I could realize my aims in drama and speech by that means.

I received an Associate of Arts diploma (with honors) from Little Rock Junior College in June 1947, winning the G. J. Francis Memorial Award for scholarship, leadership, Christian ideals, and fellowship. At the Ohio State University, supported by Public Law 16 and a working wife, I completed the Bachelor of Science, cum laude (1949), and the Master of Arts (1951). My second M.A. in play directing was earned at the University of Arkansas (1958), followed by a Ph.D., with distinction, in drama and theatre (1967) at the University of Kansas.

Professionally, I taught English, speech, and theater courses at Ohio State, Little Rock Junior College, Little Rock University, University of Arkansas at Fayetteville, University of Kansas, and Auburn University in Alabama. Over those years, I supervised basic speech and basic fine arts programs and chaired speech and dramatic arts at Arkansas, before becoming head of the theater department at Auburn. In forty-two years, I directed more than a hundred full-length plays of all genres at universities, and acted roles in radio, stage, motion picture, and television productions.

Tumpy and I toured the West Country of England in the summer of 1978, driving through Torquay and Newton Abbot on our way to Salcombe. Newton Abbot and Torquay had grown so much that they bore only the slightest resemblance to the towns of 1945. We also drove to Erlestoke, where Company B had waited, in 1944, until the Ninety-fourth went to the Continent, and we discovered that the camp was now Her Majesty's Prison. As I was having my photo made, peering through the prison gate, a middle-aged man, who had been clipping hedges in front of his house, came across the road to ask if I'd been there during the war. I told him how brief my stay was, but he insisted on thanking me for being one of the generous GIs who camped there.

Returning to England for the fifth time, in June 1985, on our thirty-ninth wedding anniversary, Tumpy and I took a train from Exeter to Torquay to see places I had visited while a patient at the 112th General Hospital. It rained heavily as we toured the town. The Palace Theater, the green-turreted playhouse with a cupola, was closed. So we looked at the quay's boat ramp for the small canvas-roofed cart where I first ate fish and chips. The ramp was empty, fishy-smelling, and littered. Through the mist, I saw the Pavilion, the old dance hall, still standing across the quay at the pier's end.

Under umbrellas, we braved the traffic, crossing the crowded curve of the main street, to climb a steep hill to the Hole in the Wall, where buddies and I drank pale ale. We ordered pints and talked to the new owner, John Davis, who had restored the pub to display its original timbers and bar. He said many American veterans returned for old times' sake, attaching cards, dollar bills, or other personal mementos to the low ceiling.

We also visited Birmingham and stayed at the Midland Hotel across from the huge New Railway Station. The physical reconstruction of town center had changed even its topography. I couldn't locate where the Army barracks for transient soldiers had been, unless it was near what is now the Bull Ring Shopping Centre, on high ground near the railway station.

Exploring the station, we walked out a lower street-level entrance and faced the front of the old Birmingham Repertory Theatre, where Pulaski, Marugo, and I saw a play on our one-day layover. Its front doors were sealed, and bills posted on the front explained it was closed and no longer used, since the current repertory company is housed in a new plant.

In spite of the tornadoes and hurricanes I've lived through since World War II, my greatest travail thus far was at Orscholz, Germany, on January 20, 1945. Since that fateful day, I've read brief descriptions of that attack in the Ninety-fourth Division history, as well as oblique allusions to the Ninety-fourth in the Saar-Moselle Triangle in General Patton's *War As I Knew It.* He identifies our specific enemy at Orscholz in the casual statement, "94th Division ran into elements of the 11th Panzer Division . . . on this date [January 19th]."

Though Patton doesn't name the First Battalion of the 301st Infantry, he says he learned on January 23 that "one battalion of the 94th Division lost forty men killed and wounded and four hundred missing in action." He ordered General Walker to investigate the cause but does not reveal his conclusions. I'm convinced, as I was in January 1945, that the ambush and loss of Company B resulted from poor intelligence.

German General F. W. Von Mellinthin, in *Panzer Battles,* confirms our division's lack of solid military intelligence before the attack, reflecting that American Intelligence "knew remarkably little" about the "Orscholz Barrier" and that "attempts to force a gap were easily repulsed."

For years I wondered about the mysterious tank our group encountered the night we escaped from Orscholz. Robert Cassel, of the Ninety-fourth Division Association, believes it was a tank from the 748th Tank Battalion, which John Flanagan, Second Battalion Headquarters' operations officer had immobilized rather than leave it to the enemy as the battalion withdrew.

I rarely wept before I survived the day at Orscholz, but for weeks afterwards tears welled up in the midst of the smallest recollections so that for the longest time I did not talk about that day and my lost buddies. I subdued my emotions for years. Then, shortly before my retirement, I was forced to avoid certain subjects in class and didn't read aloud certain passages of dialogues in the plays I was teaching because they roused tears, an embarrassment for me and the class. Today, memories of old Army comrades, church services, songs, poems, and stories of human courage and kindness plumb my emotions, making me cry, no matter how much I attempt to restrain myself.

Perhaps a fitting close to this memoir are lines from a dedication I wrote for volume 2 of *The Commemorative History of the 94th Infantry Division*:

> *Now as shadows lengthen in the lives of those who survive,*
> *extending the distance between our youth and present age—*
> *as our numbers shrink and recent memories fade*
> *while those of the distant past freshen in our reveries—*
> *it is fitting to record more about those who served,*
> *revealing anew the stories emblazoned on our minds,*
> *which rouse our laughter from old camaraderies*
> *and stir our tears in the haunting sense of their loss.*

CORA J. BELDEN LIBRARY
3 2534 08125 3171

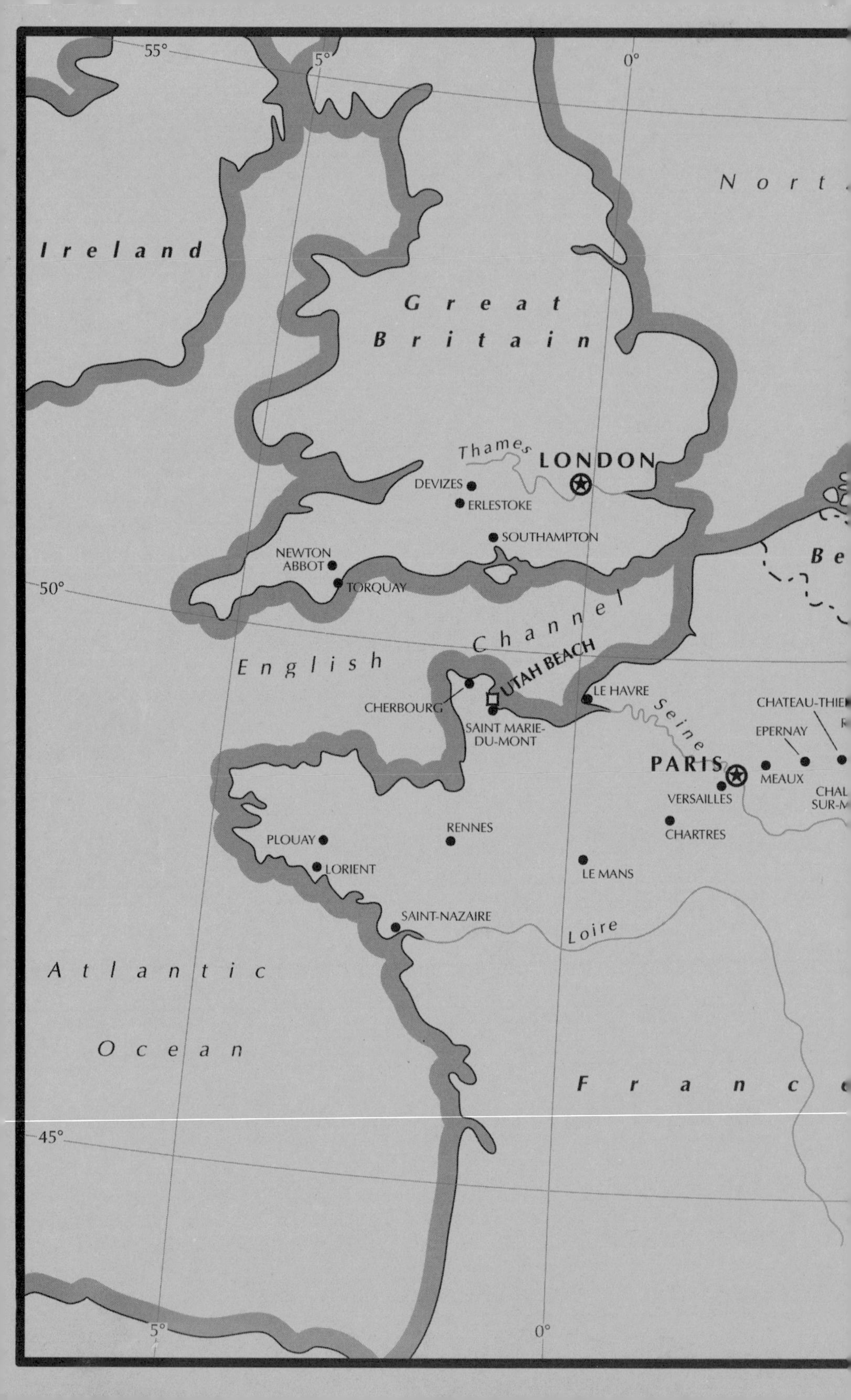
55°
5°
0°
Ireland
Great
Britain
Nort
Thames
LONDON
DEVIZES
ERLESTOKE
SOUTHAMPTON
NEWTON
ABBOT
TORQUAY
50°
Be
English Channel
UTAH BEACH
CHERBOURG
SAINT MARIE-
DU-MONT
LE HAVRE
Seine
CHATEAU-THIE
EPERNAY
PARIS
MEAUX
VERSAILLES
CHAL
SUR-M
CHARTRES
PLOUAY
RENNES
LORIENT
LE MANS
SAINT-NAZAIRE
Loire
Atlantic
Ocean
France
45°
5°
0°